Earth Muse

Earth Muse

Feminism, Nature, and Art

Carol Bigwood

Temple University Press
Philadelphia

Temple University Press, Philadelphia 19122
Copyright © 1993 by Temple University. All rights reserved
Published 1993
Printed in the United States of America

The paper used in this publication meets the minimum requirements of American
National Standard for Information Sciences—Permanence of Paper for Printed
Library Materials, ANSI Z39.48-1984 ∞

Library of Congress Cataloging-in-Publication Data
Bigwood, Carol, 1957–
    Earth muse: feminism, nature, and art / Carol Bigwood.
        p.   cm.
    Includes bibliographical references and index.
    ISBN 0-87722-986-4 (alk. paper).—ISBN 0-87722-987-2 (pbk.: alk. paper)
        1. Ontology.   2. Femininity (Philosophy)   3. Feminist theory.
    4. Ecofeminism.   5. Feminism and the arts.   I. Title.
    BD311.B494   1993
    111'.082—dc20   92-20270

To Leah and Blue

Contents

Illustrations   ix

Acknowledgments   xi

Introduction   I

Chapter One   **Is "Woman" Dead?   II**
Gender-Skepticism and a ''Philosophy in the
Feminine''   II
A Heideggerean Defense of Gender and
Genesis   **23**

Chapter Two   **Renaturalizing Gender (with the Help of
Merleau-Ponty)   39**

**Turning out of Despair: *The Seal* (The Miracle), 1924–36,
by Constantine Brancusi   61**

Chapter Three   **The Will to Power and the Feminine   75**
Can We Ascribe a Gender to Being?   **75**
Nature in Metaphysics   **82**
Zarathustra's ''Love'' of the Earth   **84**
The Phallocentrism of the Will to Power   **88**
Implications for a Feminist Ontology   **96**

Being Moved: *Mlle Pogany*, 1912–33, by Constantine Brancusi   105

Chapter Four   **Deconstructing the Culture/Nature Dichotomy:
Preparations   125**
Women and the Culture/Nature Dichotomy   **130**
Art (Techne) and Nature (Phusis) as Ways of
Bringing-forth   **136**
The Coming-to-be of an Entity from Techne and an
Entity from Phusis   **139**
The Challenging-out of the Will to Power   **145**

Chapter Five   **Mother Doesn't Matter   152**
Aristotle's Analysis of the Coming-to-be of a
"Man" from a "Man"   **155**
The Ontological Demise of Nature   **161**

Soft or Hard? Or? Or How to Philosophize with Breasts:
The Minoan Snake Goddess, 1600 B.C.   173

Chapter Six   **Toward and Backward: An Ecofeminist**
Revisioning of Human Be(com)ing   188
The Question of Tools   **188**
Respecting the Earth's Drawing Pull   **190**
Playing in the Gap Between Culture and Nature:
Moving into Nearness   **200**
Culture as a Cultivating   **207**

Chapter Seven   **The Being of Water in the Hydroelectric**
Plant   224
Unlocking Energy   **224**
Energy as the Transforming Form   **232**
The Storehouse of Energy   **236**
Distributing and Switching About   **243**

The Holding Sway: Cycladic Figurine, 2800–2300 B.C.   249

Chapter Eight   **Ecological Be(com)ing in the World-Earth**
Home   261
Whitewashing the Earth   **263**
Eco-*nomos*: Backward to Laws of Social
Gathering   **271**
Logos: The Laying-out that Gathers   **280**
Eco (home): Gathering-Round   **289**
Giving and Power   **297**

Notes   **305**
References   **343**
Index   **359**

Illustrations

Constantine Brancusi, *The Seal* (1924–36)

       front view   **61**

Constantine Brancusi, *Mlle Pogany I* (1912)

       front view   **105**
       side view   **106**

Constantine Brancusi, *Mlle Pogany III* (1933)

       front view   **122**
       side view   **123**

Minoan Snake Goddess statuette

       front view   **174**
       side view   **175**

Cycladic figurine from Amorgos   **249**

Clay "frying pan" from cemetery of Chalandianc, Syros   **250**

Acknowledgments

I would like to thank the Toronto Island Community for being an unusually neighborly neighborhood. Next, I would like to thank my mother for taking over for me during the last critical weeks of completing this book, and my father and my brothers and sister, Bob, Phillip, and Sally, for making fun of my writing every summer. I would like to thank Samuel Mallin, Claudio Duran, Evan Cameron, and Monica Langer for their help and encouragement in the early version of this book. I would also like to thank some of my friends for their conversation and compassion over the years while this book was being written: Andreas Andresen for building the wild home on Manitoulin, Michelle Murata, Carmen Circelli, John Harris, Kate and Ken Lywood, Chris Jackson, Laura Hamilton, Dierdre Cruickshank, Grahame Beakhurst, Peter Holt, Cindy Jones, Lynn Harpell, Martin von Mirbach, Beatty Popescu, Lani Maestro, Stephen Horne, Iain Robertson, Sheila McCusker, Irina Schestakowich, and Carol Pedit. Finally, I would like to thank Jane Cullen, the senior acquisitions editor, for her encouraging voice, and Deborah Stuart and Mary Wyer, for their careful editing work.

Earth Muse

Introduction

But.[1] But . . . having come from attempting to end this book, I find it harder to introduce it, to invite you across the threshhold with written words alone. But maybe a poem to you will help:

> " 'In Tobago they say, "The earth comes up to catch children
>   when they fall."
> "Well, that's different from what I've been thinking." she thought.
> She?: single mother, once and again,
> half-British, half-Italian, surname Bigwood sounds Indian.
> (Going to Canada from a damp basement and back alley
>   of Great Britain as a child, she wished she could be
>   an Indian in the forest.
> She didn't know about the reservations.)
> She?: me—ambiguous class:
> factory worker, student, assistant professor, welfare recipient.
> Color?: dirty white. "What do you hustle?" a friend of color asked.
> "Philosophy." I said.
> Me?: *she*—gender amphibian:
> bisexual, currently celibate with an arborescent orientation.
> "At the end of six years of writing this book and
> well, it should have been
> more brownish, more black,
> more lesbian,
> queerer in general,
> wilder, more and more wilder,
> more unconscious, more Paleolithic
> and a lot funnier.
> But, please, follow wherever your mood takes you.
> Not every sentence *is* as I would like it.
> And I forgot to talk about *art*.
> I?" ' she wrote"; they read.
> They?:

But for those who are rushed for time let me categorize this work as a cautious, ecofeminist, postmodern art-philosophy. I am interested in the phallocentrism of western Being, the privilege accorded to the phallus as a mark of presence (i.e., unity, teleology, linearity, self-identity), or, in other words, the morphological marks of the male body in some of our most important concepts. I attempt to think back to the beginnings of this uncanny erection, to disrupt and undermine relations of dominance, to find ways of opening up new spaces where differences can be. However, I do not so much aim to produce results as to engage in a process of reflecting back on the "toward" itself, on the ways in which writing, making, thinking, and doing take place.

But let me begin again in my younger "rabbinacal" voice from a few years back.[2] If I were pressed to locate the beating heart of this book, I would trace its pulse, not to a philosophical idea, but to the beautiful swelling of Constantine Brancusi's marble. There, in the gentle stony swells, I encountered what can be described simply as a radiant fullness and a gathering-round. The uncanny simplicity and beauty of the smooth rounding marble drew me close and gave me to thought. I was moved to think what I call feelingful thoughts, thoughts that resist coalescing in complete sentences. Touch: a swelling that both gives and holds. Gathering-round shelters. Holding-round: a healing joy, the bodily feeling of being, a still balance. These simple "thoughts" are embedded in the texture and turns of Brancusi's marbles and gleaming bronzes. They are tangible thoughts that are felt bodily, rather than thought reflectively, and that are still held somewhere in my womb and chest. They are not thoughts that can be analyzed and that develop into other thoughts, or thoughts that lay themselves out like a flat foundation or ground to be built upon. Instead they are quiet thoughts that tend to keep to themselves, resisting explanation despite their sensuous presence. These mysterious, self-secluding thoughts evoked by Brancusi's art gave life to this project many years ago. This philosophical work has been to attempt to turn round these well-rounded vague thoughts. (And even now as I read this old version of the Introduction in retrospect, after the completion of the book, it is still these thought fragments that hold the articulation.)

My turning round these fleshy thoughts has been guided by at least two central aspects of my experience. It was my in-depth involvement with Friedrich Nietzsche's philosophy as a naive graduate student that evoked for the first time in all my philosophical studies a feeling that being a woman made a difference to my actual thinking. I felt alienated by Nietzsche's description of Being, which I found biased in favor of a specifically male dynamic, and I began to suspect that if his metaphysics was gender biased, then perhaps the entire history of western philosophy was also (as some feminist philosophers I found out later have shown). I thought that maybe the phallocentrism of western metaphysics is not only a confluence of historical ontic relations that produced a gender-biased metaphysics but might somehow be the genderization of what Heidegger would call Being itself.

But, it is important to pause here with this big word *Being*, which is related to such necessary little words as *be* and *is* (but which itself as a totalizing concept is best crossed out in the manner of the later Heidegger and Derrida) and no doubt is best dropped altogether. What is Being? Being is not a being, not God, an absolute unconditional ground or a total presence, but is simply the living web within which all relations emerge. It is the constellation of art, science, politics, and religion within which a historical people dwells (Heidegger 1971c). In our everyday lives we are rarely struck by our inherence in existence as a whole, by the relation between our own individual being and all beings. If the wonder of sheer naked spatio-temporal existence should strike home, it is a significant personal experience. Nonetheless, although we do not often have an explicit consciousness of Being, we always already necessarily exist in relation to Being. We always, says Heidegger (1962), have a "pre-ontological," prereflective, and preconceptual understanding of our inherence in Being by virtue of our spatiotemporal embodied human be-ing. Metaphysics is the conceptual comprehension of our relations to Being that can be experienced in the immediateness of everyday cultural life.

If we turn to western metaphysics with a view to what I am with regrets calling the feminine, we find a consistent privileging of the masculine (I am aware that the use of these concepts is most problematical, but in turning to metaphysics we appear condemned to work with binary oppositions in order to subvert them). This phallocentrism stems from, among other things, the economic, political, and social power relations that allowed me to write philosophy and that permitted the masculinization of important cultural ideals, such as self, reason, and culture itself, and which have informed the structure of sexual difference and the deepest presuppositions or our lifeworld. What I find most thought-provoking is that western phallocentric ontologies are more than the way various philosophers have conceived of Being (i.e., as a transcendent principle, a first cause, an absolute spirit, a divine power, etc.) in different periods. Western metaphysics is a perspicacious revealing of the phallocentrism of western Being itself.

I am exploring the "woman problem," then, on an ontological level, with a view to re-visioning and re-conceptualizing important cultural notions in a way that lets in women's experience, which has been marginalized and devalued, and, moreover, woman's subjectivity.[3] Because I am focusing my study on western Being, I am limiting my claims to the suppression of *western* feminine. The coherent identity of the West that is presumed in the early pages of this book begins to crack, however, in later pages. In attempting to reconceptualize important notions like culture and nature, it is helpful to go back to the birth of western phallocentric Being in the Greeks. This feminist Heideggerean return to beginnings entails exposing the phallocentric nature of many western concepts that inform our lives, attempting to indicate possible pre-western ways of understanding and living that were left behind, and examining the complex ways particular qualities came to be associated with the feminine and the masculine, respectively. As I see it, an analysis of the exile of the "feminine" in metaphysics (and the related exploitation of the earth and oppression of non-western peoples) involves a postmodern attempt to disrupt the phallocentric unity, stability, and fullness of pure presence of western Being with a view to restoring the ruptures and irregularities, the movement, flux, and play of existence.[4] In this subversive way "we" might begin to feel new muses and cultivate new ways of being that let in difference as difference.[5]

The attempt to describe the peculiar erasure and subsequent disruptive possibilities of western femininity is not merely an abstract academic exercise in fundamental philosophy but implicates our localized personal and social ways of being. As Iris Marion Young (1990, 4) says, "Social relations, practices, and institutions are constituted by ideas, symbols, forms of consciousness. Ideas materially affect people's lives because they influence, motivate, and structure people's actions." An investigation of the metaphysical presuppositions at work in our cutlural ideals and attitudes, in our personal relations, and in localized modes of bodily being can contribute to the task of deep global change. Since this kind of deconstructive analysis that, for example, questions the very meaning of thinking and doing, tends to be theoretical and speculative and tends to be concerned, "not . . . with what we do or ought to do, but with what happens to us over and above our writing and doing" (Gadamer 1989a, xxviii), its political force nonetheless is diffuse.

> There is some new breed of insect that lives on the oil-saturated line on the beach. I don't know what it is. I wonder if anyone does. Looking at these unobtrusive bugs happily thriving in the quiet sun, I am overwhelmed by the magnitude of the problem. How can I understand and cope with these new neighbors that seem to be a product of both nature and technology? How can I name the conflicting multitudinous powers of growth and transformation at work here?

Another aspect of my being that guides my turning round the sensuous thoughts embedded in Brancusi's sculptural flesh is my deep love for "the bush," one would say in northern Ontario. Western philosophy undoubtedly shows a profound disrespect and distaste for the earth. I turned to Nietzsche with the hope of finding a philosophy that finally stayed close to earth and body but discovered, on deeper analysis, that his metaphysical overturning of the hierarchical supersensuous/sensuous dichotomy is not a liberation but a fulfillment of that oppositional ecodestructive dynamic. My love for the bush drew me early on in my studies to the philosophies of Martin Heidegger, whose later writings offer a self-critical understanding of our ecodestructive age, and of Maurice Merleau-Ponty, who attempts to resuscitate the body for philosophy. These works have already proven useful in deep ecology. In feminism, moreover, the promising use of existential-phenomenology (the philosophies of Heidegger, Merleau-Ponty, Edmund Husserl, and Jean-Paul Sartre) is well recognized. Existential-phenomenology's return to the world of lived experience, its critique of transcendental philosophy that presumed an external relation between consciousness and the world, and its focus on the situated freedom of human existence overlap with some feminists' critiques of traditional philosophy and their attempts to found a feminist philosophy.[6] Given, however, that those philosophies tend to use illustrations and metaphors drawn from the male world and to present a masculine point of view, it is necessary to critically transform them in a feminist appropriation of them.[7] Aspects of Merleau-Ponty's philosophy of the body, for example, need to be reconstructed in the light of women's experience. So, too, I find the early and middle Heidegger too embedded in phallocentric metaphysics to be useful for my purposes but find the concepts of the neglected later and more radical Heidegger (concealment, letting-be, releasement, and nearness) helpful as a way of feminizing so-called Being. I also make use of his analysis of Nietzsche, of *phusis,* (nature) and technology, and his method of returning to Greek thinking.

But. But I am obliged to pause again to say a few words about Heidegger's "political misadventure." It seems I have left this most difficult subject for the last day I have to rewrite this introduction before sending it to the same press that published the English translation of Victor Farías's work, *Heidegger and Nazism,* which unleashed a storm of controversy. Much has been written either defending or condemning Heidegger's association with the Nazi regime, and I wish neither to defend nor to condemn him here. On the one hand, once one separates the hard "evidence" of his involvement with Nazism from the contorted and well-recognized inaccurate "evidence" in Farías's book, the remaining evidence is, for the most part, circumstantial and open to interpretation. On the other hand, however, there are without a doubt certain indefensible disturbing facts, such as Heidegger's refusal to write explicit retractions about his identification with National Socialism. The important and disturbing question for anyone using Heidegger's philosophy is, Does his thought lend itself politically to an ideal form of National Socialism (which Hitler distorted)? It is most important to remember in this regard that Heidegger's writings have been taken up by influential French thinkers whose political bent is most definitely leftist: for example, Jean-Paul Sartre, Maurice Merleau-Ponty, Herbert Marcuse, Claude Lefort, and Michel Foucault. From my own study and use of Heidegger's thought, I am convinced that his other-responsive, earth-respecting philosophy does not favor a National Socialist politics.

The use of existential-phenomenology has been somewhat usurped by the new poststructuralism that has dominated French philosophy since the 1970s (Foucault, Derrida, Jacques Lacan, Jean-François Lyotard, Gilles Deleuze, Roland Barthes, and feminists Julia Kristeva, Luce Irigaray, Hélène Cixous, and Monique Wittig). In North American feminism, the exciting and daring analyses of Kristeva, Cixous, and Irigaray have met with a wave of sympathies and criticisms. Some feminists are using the work of Foucault and Derrida in particular to develop poststructuralist feminist critiques of foundationalist ideals and of tendencies within feminism itself toward essentialism.[8] My work is most indebted to the work of Irigaray and Cixous, for in a similar manner I am attempting both to expose the discourse of patriarchy to contradiction and difference and to find alternative models of subjectivity based on an openness to the other and the body. I am also sympathetic to and make use of Derrida and, to a lesser extend, Foucault. Although their work can provide valuable tools and analyses for feminism, and Derrida offers important radicalizations of key Heideggerean ideas, I find their neo-Niezschean underpinnings dangerous.[9]

This work has grown by means of both philosophy and art, and this combination has affected its content and its style. The question of method and style, of course, is central for many current feminist writers and scholars, because the methods of scholarly and scientific research have been shown to be biased in favor of a male perspective. Given that the language we use both shapes our conceptual frameworks and is shaped by them, some feminist philosophers are cautiously searching for new methods of discourse and analysis different from those of the Anglo-American analytic approach that characterizes much philosophy today. The methods of existential-phenomenology can be useful for feminists in this regard because this school of philosophy is not analytic in its approach but descriptive. It attempts to describe how things appear to us rather than attempting to analyze them from a supposedly objective standpoint. This phenomenological method emerged from a concern for the dominance of the pure sciences, whose description of existence is so distant from actual lived experience. My own attempt to search for a new method of writing is most evident in the personal exerpts that occasionally interrupt the narrative and in the ''art writings,'' which apply a descriptive, phenomenological approach to specific artworks. The presumption in these art writings is that art can speak to philosophy and help it out.[10] Art can help philosophy because art holds in place the very phenomena that philosophy attempts to describe. Making contact with the sensuous presence of the artwork allows one's thinking to bend to the noncognitive. By opening my thinking to sensuous contact, I have found that my thinking becomes strangely sensuous itself. I have felt that I can touch the artwork with my words in a way that is uncannily similar in its gentle care to the way I touch the artwork with my drawing lines on paper. (Sketches of the sculptures I write on accompany the art writings.) Thinking through art allows me to do philosophy in a way that lets in my body and desire, as long as I take care not to translate or explain away the art's sensuous presence. It lets me, for example, actively receive and hold ideas and follow indeterminate curves of thoughts, rather than aggressively grasping concepts *(begriff)* and penetrating problems with rational thought, as in traditional phallocentric modes of thinking. Art writing, then, for me, is a possible way of writing "with my body" and writing with "white ink," as Cixous (1975, 94) has called it in her attempt to describe *l'ecriture feminine*.[11] The art meditations, which are placed between the chapters that belong to a "proper" book, seem to hold in a sheltering way the deepest thought from which the chapters evolve and into which they recline. While the chapters lay out and gather thoughts surrounding philosophical, feminist, and ecological problems, these art essays are the ruptures and well-springs of thought.

But, let me now briefly lay out the logic of the chapters to follow. In the first two chapters, I defend the need to develop "philosophy in the feminine," as Margaret Whitford (1991) aptly calls it, in the face of a new and important strand of poststructuralist feminism that is skeptical about the very use of gender as a meaningful category to promote social change. I discuss how the current trend to "denaturalize" nature and the body perpetuates our modern alienation from nature and contributes to the cultural repression of nature. The body, I maintain, needs to be "renaturalized" so that its earthy significance is recognized. Through a critical use of Merleau-Ponty's phenomenology of the body and Heidegger's later thought, I develop a noncausal link between gender and the body and present the body as an indeterminate constancy that is culturally and historically contextualized on the one hand, yet part of our embodied giveness on the other.

In the next three chapters, I analyze Aristotle's and Nietzsche's philosophies (which can be understood as site markers for the beginning and completion of western metaphysics) and put into relief the phallocentrism of their metaphysics. Chapter Three is a description of the gendered dynamic of Nietzsche's metaphysics through an analysis of the character of Zarathustra and the Will to Power. In Chapters Four and Five, I clarify woman's inextricable entanglement in the culture/nature dichotomy and attempt to deconstruct this destructive cultural dualism as it appears within the context of Aristotle's metaphysical discussion of the birth of a human being. I maintain that the culture/nature opposition is not just one metaphysical dichotomy among others within which women are entangled but is a central dichotomy that underlies many modes of western existence and our white conception of being in the world. I trace this opposition between nature and culture back to the crucial Greek distinction between *phusis* (nature) and *techne* (art) and analyze that critical moment in Aristotle's discussion of birth in which *techne* overpowers *phusis* and the male principle, the female: the moment when the seed has to be "properly placed" by the male in the womb to do its work. My overall attempt in these chapters is to philosophically reconstruct the oppressive traditional association of the feminine with the body and earth in a way that allows for female experience, desire, and subjectivity.

In Chapter Six, I get into the swing of the work, as it were, and attempt to work positively toward an ecofeminist description of the natural-cultural situation of the human being by swaying backward in the writing process. By the time I get to this chapter, I begin to question more critically the way in which I am pursuing the "matter." Thus in this chapter, I engage more directly in a play of going to and fro between discursive horizons of what is understood and what is yet to be understood. Both this chapter and Chapter Eight are very free-wheeling and speculative. They attempt a "supple" kind of thinking—a thinking that searches for ways even though the ways are not laid out beforehand (Caputo 1987, 213). Like the *bricoleur* (a professional do-it-yourself person), I make do with things that were meant for other ends (Spivak in Derrida 1976, xix). Substantively, at the end of

Chapter Six, I suggest that a feminist philosophy involves an ecological consciousness, and, in the manner of Nancy Hartsock and Sara Ruddick (among others), that a cultivator and caretaker model of being human should replace the model of constructor, designer, and controller.

Chapter Seven is an investigation I undertook as a graduate student to describe the being of water in a hydroelectric plant. Although it is a separate analysis, it can be seen as continuing the discussion of *techne* and *phusis* of Chapters Four and Five and continues the musing of Chapter Six on the fluidity of nature and on the problem of domination.

The basic theme of Chapter Eight is our wider being in what I call the "world-earth-home." It works toward a postmodern ethic of place (with the help of Jim Cheney, Vandana Shiva, Trinh T. Minh-ha, Gayatri Spivak, and Teresa de Lauretis, among others) and simultaneously reflects back on the need for self-criticality. It attempts to create a caring place from which to openly encounter differences between cultures; races; the past, present, and future; and genders, and between the human and nonhuman. As an overall structure, the chapter etymologically explores the odd interesection of ecology and economy in eco (from the Greek *oikos* meaning home).

But maybe you would find it more interesting to start between the chapters, or look at the pictures?

Chapter One

Is "Woman" Dead?

"Could it be Possible?" thought Sarathustra, "This old witch in the forest has not yet heard that woman is dead?"

—freely adapted from Nietzsche (1954) 1978, 12

Gender-Skepticism and a "Philosophy in the Feminine"

Many feminists today rightly balk at the very idea of a "philosophy in the feminine" because it would appear to necessitate a reinforcement of traditional gender models and a privileging of specific female values, characteristics, and experience as an alternative to male-stream ontologies that have exiled the feminine. To simply and unproblematically affirm female values that have been devalued and marginalized in western phallocentric thought has come to be viewed by many feminist theorists as a theoretically disastrous move because of the dangers of conservatism, essentialism, and biologism and, in general, the danger of perpetuating hierarchical binary, gender relations. The feminist ontology that I am introducing here is, indeed, one that lets in female experience and perspectives and thus affirms to some degree something specifically female. The very cultivating of a philosophy of the feminine, as I see it, however, is, necessarily and most importantly, precisely a project of working out on a metaphysical level the deep problem of how certain qualities came to be associated with the feminine and others with the masculine and, moreover, working out what a historicized female specificity might look like.

The philosophy I am cultivating in this book takes as a key principle the stepping back from and reconceptualization of dualistic oppositions that dominate western thought, such as culture/nature, active/passive, mind/body, subject/object, and masculine/feminine. I particularly work to deconstruct the culture/nature dichotomy, which I understand to be stubbornly lodged in feminist discussions of crucial issues such as reproduction, gender difference, and essentialism and to be central to the constitution of western Being itself. Because I attempt to step back from and deconstruct dualistic thought, I do not valorize a universal feminine principle in opposition to a masculine principle that has guided western metaphysics. Nor do I suggest an ontology that simply perpetuates the present binary division of gender identities into male and female.[1] I understand female values and our experience of being female to be thoroughly historically and culturally contextualized and yet to possess important cultural and transformative possibilities.

Although I want to free up the binary heterosexual opposition of men and women, I agree with Whitford (1991, 83) that "the move from the masculine subject to the disseminated or multiple subject bypasses the possibilities of the position of woman as subject." In other words, the multiple can exclude woman just as the one or the same that helped structure the masculine/feminine dichotomy (see Whitford 1992, 82), unless particular attention is given to a positive feminine (rather than feminine as lack or negativity). The crux of the matter, as I see it, is to understand female specificity in a way that releases it from the culture/nature dichotomy. Female values are not natural, innate universal characteristics, but nor are they exclusively cultural constructions relative to particular cultures and historical periods and formed solely through social power relations. By understanding female specificity in what I will simply call for the present a natural-cultural way, I hope to ward off what I see as the key danger of some current feminist (especially poststructuralist) theory: that of dismissing nature as a cultural fiction and leaving culture as the only determining force in the constitution of our reality and the being of all things.[2] Female values and experience are, on the one hand, importantly formed by culture and history, as many feminists rightly point out. Yet, on the other hand, I maintain that what is feminine possesses a certain historical continuity that prevents it from being a purely relative notion. Moreover, because the body is a key player in this problem, it is necessary to work out a new natural-cultural notion of the body, one that goes beyond both the fixed, biological body and the poststructuralist culturally inscribed body. Thus I maintain that there is a certain continuity in the connection of gender to the body. In Chapter Two, I show how gender cannot be entirely purged from its grounding in the sexual body, even though gender is not, at the same time, determined by it. I claim that in attempting to understand the link between gender and the body, we need not be forced to resort to fixed, biological differences that dictate innate ahistorical differences. We must instead understand the body phenomenologically as a living body, which is culturally and historically contextualized, on the one hand, and a part of our embodied givenness, on the other. Let me now, however, discuss the current dilemma over the affirmation of anything female.

> I am writing seven months pregnant, bending over my large round belly to write at the desk, thinking about the connection between body and gender. He kicks and squirms, there amidst my thoughts. "He" because I saw on the ultrasound a protrudance between its legs, and that has certainly made a difference in the way I experience this pregnancy. Male stereotypes arise, alienating me from this alive and kicking creature carried deep inside. I combat them with resolutions about how this boy will be brought up differently. No throwing stones, no hockey, no . . . silly rules. Not even born and already fighting with the bind of gender division. Either pink or blue. I console myself: at least at first he will be a baby and I'll dress him in all colors.

An important task of feminism, especially in the 1970s, has been, on the one hand, exposing the male-gendered nature of history, culture, institutional and political power structures, and so-called human ideals and, on the other hand, discovering and reclaiming suppressed female history, values, and experience. There are many feminists who, in various different disciplines, continue this project. Of increasing concern to many feminist theories today, however, is the very use of gender as a category for criticizing western culture and its history of ideas and for valorizing specific female values. Susan Bordo (1990, 134) aptly calls this contemporary current in feminism, which has emerged in different forms and across different disciplines, "gender skepticism." Gender skepticism, as she puts it, holds that "any attempt to 'cut' reality and perspective along gender lines is methodologically flawed and essentializing." Bordo sees this view as dangerous to feminism mainly because it discredits and disables cultural critiques of hierarchical, dualistic power structures and thereby threatens feminism as a movement of cultural resistance and transformation.[3] Like Bordo, I am sympathetic to the concerns of this new trend in feminism, and I too see this new shift in focus as dangerous to the cultural transformative possibilities that feminism has to offer. In order for the important feminist political project to continue, it seems to me, there must be some affirmation of female specificity. This affirmation must be informed, however, by the valuable criticisms of particularly poststructuralist feminism, from which the most pointed critiques of past feminist theory and new developments in feminist theory have come. In the following pages, I lay out the difficulties of gender identity that encourage one to adopt a skeptical approach to gender, focusing on a general poststructuralist approach to gender. As the discussion progresses, I point out the dangers of the poststructuralist approach to gender and the body and sketch out directions and ways to reconceptualize "something female" and the body using the existential-phenomenology of Maurice Merleau-Ponty and the later Martin Heidegger.

Although gender skepticism is becoming more acute in feminist theory, fueled mainly by the work of poststructuralists like Michel Foucault and Jacques Derrida, criticisms of those who have attempted to reclaim traditional female values, are not new. Given that feminism is committed to a healthy self-critical approach in its attempt to change the social order, it is not surprising that in the 1980s feminists recognized the pitfalls of the tendency both to make a homogeneous patriarchy the scapegoat for their oppression and to present a feminine perspective as the alternative to male domination. The main difficulties with the general feminist project of exposing the gender bias of culture and history, and of articulating a female identity, are associated with essentialism. I understand essentialism in a broad sense to mean the use of any categories that tend toward universalizations and internal stability through insufficient attention to historical and/or cultural diversity. With regard to gender, essentialism is the attempt to identify men and women on the basis of supposedly transhistorical and/or cross-cultural characteristics. Essentialism often, but not always, involves some dependence on the notion of the body as a natural and thereby ahistorical, cross-cultural foundation from which gender arises. I turn now to some of the more specific criticisms that have arisen in feminism concerning the general feminist stance that became prominent from the late sixties to the mid-eighties.

A major difficulty in suggesting, for example, that there is a certain commonality in female experience that underlies the differences among

women is that it can unconsciously privilege a certain kind of female experience and exclude other kinds, depending on who is laying out the norms.
Given that most feminists tend to be white, heterosexual, middle-class
women, those who tend to be excluded and marginalized in accounts of female experience are women of color, lesbians, and working-class women.
Thus, the feminist project to let the voices of women be heard in history,
discourse, and culture is faced with an important question: Is it possible to
discover common grounds to female experience, and common stories in
their histories, in the face of such diversity?

There are many feminists who, to varying extents, believe that this is
possible. Canadian feminists in *Feminism from Pressure to Politics* (Miles
and Finn 1989), for example, advocate a transformative politics and an in-
tegrative approach to feminism that can encompass both the similar experiences of women and their differences. Diane Fuss (1989b, 75) suggests
that we need both a global politics that deals more theoretically with the
problems of women's oppression and a local politics that addresses the particulars of each woman's situation. It seems to me that, for theoretical and
political reasons, it is both helpful and necessary to use broad categories
like "female experience" and "feminine" and that these concepts can be
formulated and used in such a way as to be neither exclusionary nor fleshless, ahistorical concepts.

We do not need to deny commonality of experience in principle but we
need instead to become sensitive to marginalized women and to contextual-
ize our generalizations by making them as historically and culturally specific as is appropriate to the claims we are making.[4] The point of feminist
theory should never be to abstract a few universal, unchanging propositions concerning women that are emptied of all concrete particulars and
purged of all context but, rather, to form the woof that allows for a rich,
multicolored weave of female experience.[5] It is worthwhile, for example,
to explore and describe the broad lived lines of the female body, which
most women share to some extent regardless of their class, race, or sexual
orientation, while allowing for one's descriptions to be enriched by the
great range in the way women experience their bodies. What is important
is to avoid setting up one's general description as the fixed norm from
which other descriptions can only appear as deviations. One's generaliza-

tions must be indeterminate enough to adapt to concrete diversity and temporality.

> Since I decided to get pregnant, there is a growing awareness of the domestic institution that is waiting to envelop me. It was really my project from the start. I was the one who wanted to experience having another child. I planned it carefully. I will have it just after my Ph.D. No, I had better take this one-year, full-time position. Now's the time, interrupt your career now, before a tenure track comes up for grabs. Have it at the beginning of April, breastfeed for five months, and then teach again in September. Calculations and more calculations. Counting the days: O.K., lets' try today. Waiting. Yes, I think I'm pregnant. I feel full. There's new life. No, I'm not pregnant at all.
>
> It didn't happen as planned. The baby will be born in September. I gave up an extension of my contract. I couldn't see breastfeeding, teaching, and commuting two hundred miles or uprooting my family just for a year. So, I'll stay at home with the baby for this year—and write.

The problems of essentialism often become most acute and perspicacious in feminist issues concerning the sexual and reproductive capacities of the female body, for these issues are associated with the body upon which essentialism is often based. Because of this perspicacity, I discuss essentialism within this context.

Essentialism is a well-known problem in the writings of spiritual feminists, such as Mary Daly and Starhawk, and ecofeminists like Ariel Salleh, who appear to rely on and advocate a universal, ahistorical, feminine principle.[6] It is also a well-recognized and much debated problem in the writings of those whose theories, to different degrees and in different ways, appear to rest on biological grounds. For example, Luce Irigaray's evocation of female genitalia, Hélène Cixous's "feminine writing," Julia Kristeva's "prediscursive maternal body," Mary O'Brien's "reproductive consciousness," and Adrienne Rich's analysis of motherhood have all been criticized to varying extents for relying on ahistorical categories ultimately grounded in the female sexual and reproductive body. Recently, as I have mentioned, even the category of gender identity is claimed to be essentialist because of its ahistorical overtones. Thus, for example, although Carol Gilligan does not claim that the different voices she discovers are necessarily linked to gender, she is, nonetheless, criticized for her construction of an alternative, ahistorical, feminine model of moral development.[7] Not only ahistorical categories but also cross-cultural categories like mothering, sexuality, and reproduction are now being criticized as essentialist. Sara Ruddick's "maternal thinking," for example, is socially produced, yet she is criticized because she affirms some cross-cultural characteristics. Moreover, even though Nancy Chodorow's notion of motherhood, for example, is historically contextualized and one of her main points is to show how the exclusive role of mothering can create gender identities that perpetuate patriarchal power in the modern public world, she has been criticized as essentialist for relying on a cross-cultural notion of motherhood.[8] Feminists like Nancy Hartsock, Michelle Rosaldo, and Jean Bethke Elshtain, who rely on the notion of a separation between the public and the private spheres, are also criticized for their use of this cross-cultural category. In fact, any attempt to identify basic human practices or general human needs in order to form one's theories is seen to rely on cross-cultural and therefore essentialist categories.

When one looks at the long list of feminists accused of different kinds of essentialism, one fears that the recent move to purge the last vestiges of essentialism from feminism might be in danger of turning into a kind of gender theory inquisition whereby certain kinds of feminist theories are silenced as heretical. In order to prevent many productive strands of feminism from disappearing and future ones from appearing, it is important to find a way of reconciling the renewed attempt to purge feminism of essentialism with the established feminist project to reclaim female perspectives. As I have said, in order to do this we must be able to affirm female specificity without falling into biologism, ahistorical categories, and inflexible cross-cultural categories. We must be able to show that the use of the category "women" does not need to be predicated on an essential feminity that is ahistorical and ultimately determined by a fixed biological body.

Before getting into this involved theoretical reconceptualization of such notions as "feminine" and of the "body," however, we can at least safely affirm at the outset that on political grounds alone it is crucial both to affirm female values and to realize the extent to which they are culturally constructed. A practical and immediate concern in the face of gender skepticism is that if female specificity is denied, then the wind will be knocked out of the sails of the feminist political project of social resistance and transformation.

It would seem essential for feminism to continue to develop a specific feminist ontology, epistemology, and politics grounded in female ways of being in order to criticize the tradition and develop alternative views that challenge the current social order. Retaining the genderized notions of "female," "women," and "feminine" is necessary given the phallocentrism of our present way of being in the world. Because our structures of being are oriented around men, our culture has tended to define women in terms of men. What this means on a concrete level, for instance, is that even though women have made a lot of important progress in achieving social equality, they are still only permitted to participate in the culture more or less to the extent that they take up its ready-made phallocentric structures, living and working according to them. Women can join in the making of culture as long as they accept its man-made methodologies and institutions and the misogynist philosophical foundation upon which they are based. To be truly liberated, however, women must be defined in terms of themselves, although that is so difficult to accomplish given their social construction and the differences among women themselves. Women as a whole need to find and develop ways of living in the world that are appropriate to their unique bodily being, and women must no longer be forced to live within specifically male-oriented institutions that often favor male modes of embodiment. Surely it often makes important differences in the constitution of any woman's social experience that she has a female body. Having a female body does not only have to do with genitals and reproductive capacities; it also has to do with one's susceptibility to different kinds of disease (breast and ovarian cancer, for example) and with ways of moving, holding oneself, and generally living the body.

Moreover, even though many women choose not to have children, any deep changes in the social order must, nonetheless, take into account the fact that it is women who bear babies. Concrete changes, such as more financially accessible quality daycare and radical readjustments in normative gender identities, can only occur with simultaneous changes in the philosophical and ideological presuppositions of the western world, which provides the conceptual framework for economic, political, social, and gender power relations and helps define our very being. Gender openness in our philosophical conceptualizations would encourage radical restructuring of social institutions in unforseeable ways. It is only by reserving a conceptual place for feminine specificity (even though the feminine as such *is* not), that we can understand the deep dynamic of phallocentric binary oppositions and find alternatives to break down the oppositional relations that have historically developed between the masculine and the feminine (as nonmasculine) and between other categories such as culture and nature, mind and body, and public and private. We need to expose the phallocentrism of metaphysics and to open spaces for feminine, cultural, and nonhuman differences, not only so that women, for instance, would not be so oppressed by sexist ideologies and practices, but so that we may all live healthier lives by respecting our bodies and remaining close to the young and the old, to our food, and to the earth and all living things.

Affirming female specificity can, at the very least, then, on one hand, be viewed as a temporary political strategy. As Jill Vickers (1982, 55) says, "Female experience reveals a praxis which can be used as an interim guide." It is, however, on the other hand, also politically important to explore how far supposedly female ways of being have been culturally constructed. For if normative female ways of life are taken at face value, the patriarchal oppression of women is being unwittingly reinforced. Without adopting an attitude of caution in advocating female reproductive ways of being, for example, one tends to romanticize and idealize reproductive values, perpetuating pronatalism and stereotypical gender identities such as the self-sacrificing woman in the service of her husband and family. One also encourages the internalization of these stereotypical ideals, which have served to keep women economically, psychologically and socially suppressed.[9]

In advocating, for example, female reproductive ways of being, it is politically important that one realizes how the culture has worked to form them and how these very ways of being are oppressing women. Values associated with reproduction have been influenced, for example, by various forms of cultural sexual divisions of labor where traditional women's work (domestic housework and childcare) is devalued in comparison with men's wage work. We must explore not only how female reproduction has and is keeping women oppressed and marginalized but how female experience and values themselves have been informed by a masculine culture.[10]

We cannot, in any case, simply valorize female perspectives and ways of life without understanding how the culture has worked to form them and how these perspectives and ways of life have oppressed women. It is, in fact, because of this very cultural, rather than biological, formation and marginalization of, female reproductive practices that one can even hope for a future society where the oppressive sexual division of labor would dissolve. The transformed "female" perspectives could be socially taken up rather than assumed to be the result of one's sex, perhaps, for example, by parents sharing equally in home and childcare or through some kind of radical reorganization of the public and the private realms. It is only because nurturing attitudes, empathy, receptivity, and so forth can be learned and discovered in other ways than through female bodily experience and because they are historically and culturally informed that gynocentric feminists perceive them in the first place as having the potential to transform the social order.

> I dread being economically dependent. It's a privilege to be able to experience motherhood and not have to work a double shift and outside the home like so many women. But not to earn my own money! So demeaning, restricting. Shall we negotiate a weekly wage for my domestic labor? We will still wash our own clothes, of course.

We should, then, continue the political program of feminizing culture before giving up on female specificity altogether. We have not yet understood what, for instance, female reproductive practices and, more generally, body and nature would be like if freed from the patriarchal devaluation of women's work. There is no doubt that reproductive practices, values, and experiences would be radically different if freed from, for instance, the present capitalist public/private dichotomy that forces women to choose between having a child and having a career (or attempting the difficult but often necessary task of juggling both at once) and that keeps women who have children economically and psychologically dependent on their husbands or, as single parents, socially and economically disadvantaged. However, by too quickly denying reproductive values altogether and by understanding gender exclusively as a result of the cultural context, feminism risks enacting the final fulfillment of this specifically phallocentric culture with its traditional exclusion and denigration of female perspectives and ways of being. In other words, if women were to relinquish their unique reproductive and sexual capacities as of no consequence in the formation of a new social order, they would risk assimilating themselves to a man's world rather than attempting to transform it.[11]

It would be, then, politically paralyzing to claim that the old order of female difference has been overturned in favor of a new gender skepticism that on theoretical grounds disapproves of ahistorical, cross-cultural categories like "female," "feminine," and "woman." "Woman" is not dead but is, rather, under close investigation. Such questioning and criticism of such well-worn concepts, as I see it, can be most healthy and strengthening. It gives those feminists who advocate the revolutionary potential of sexual difference some puzzles to work out that can only help clarify their project. It is puzzling, for example, what aspects of a reproductive value such as nurturance should be kept as beneficial for social transformation and what aspects should be thrown out as oppressive. What, moreover, is left of a characteristic such as nurturance to affirm as specifically female if we do not know the extent to which it has been culturally informed? Indeed, one would expect that in a new nonsexist society a traditional characteristic such as nurturance would be so thoroughly reworked, it would bear little resemblance to its past culturally genderized form.

Many have recognized that a key piece in the puzzle of gender is the body. It is important to keep in mind that the body has been either ignored or devalued in western thought, and that this somatophobia, as Elizabeth Spelman (1988, 126–30) calls it, is related to the oppression of women and peoples of color and to the exploitation of the earth.[12] It is important that feminist philosophies do not follow somatophobic suit. A feminist onology, for example, should attempt to describe how ontological traits of our openness to Being manifest themselves in distinct ontic ways of our bodily being, in the ways, for example, that we touch, taste, smell, hear, and see things; how we move and feel; and the ways that we care for others.[13]

In affirming women as women, we must also affirm to some extent a link between the female body and woman's ways of being, between the sexual body and gender. If we do not somewhere in our argument recognize and carefully begin to understand this link, then theoretically the position of gender specificity is left without a leg to stand on. One could always comfortably refer to past and present characteristics of woman's values and experience, but it would be unproductive to bring the concept of woman forward when envisioning a future society (as, indeed, Monique Wittig [1978] argues), even as a provisional term, because it prejudices the new ground with a fixed gender. As I see it, then, one must go further than claiming that the advocation of female specificity is a temporary, politically expedient move, for such a stance rests on shaky theoretical ground. One would be claiming that we should make social and political gains for women but that the group for whom we are fighting will dissolve once the gains are made and, indeed, was but a cultural fiction in the first place.[14]

We cannot ignore the fact that the more feminists have dug into the concept of women, the more they have found only more cultural construction and no true ground to stand on. I am suggesting, however, that we must dig deeper yet and that we will find a ground for sexual difference in the body, but a ground and a body that is not fixed and is unlike anything we expected. Once the body is affirmed as a source of gender, of course, one enters a mine field of problems associated with essentialism and biological determinism. In the next chapter, I attempt to find my way around these explosive problems. First, however, I argue for a notion of ground that is neither the firm foundation of metaphysics criticized by Derrida (and before Derrida by Heidegger) nor the nihilistic groundless ground that is currently in vogue because of the poststructuralist critique. This discussion of ground and the associated notions of identity, subject, origin, and essence will help us come to terms with the body and will help orient readers within the region of a feminist ontology. It is important to begin with a discussion of the notion of ground because the criticism that one should not hold any ''givens'' or natural grounds has helped fuel the feminist debate on sexual difference.

A Heideggerean Defense
of Gender and Genesis

> Certainly we can translate *genesis* as origination *(ent-stehen);* but we
> must think this originating [as going forth *(das Ent-gehen):*] as a move-
> ment which lets every emerging being [go forth from *(ent-gehen)*]
> concealment and [come forth here *(hervor-gehen)*] into unconcealment.
>
> —Heidegger 1975, 30

My discussion and criticisms of the new feminist poststructuralist denial
of gender identity and my exploration of a nondeterminative ground will
focus on Judith Butler's recent book *Gender Trouble* as an important representative of a developed feminist poststructuralist stance. Using the tools
of poststructuralism, Butler offers a sustained critique of gender norms
and the marginalization of lesbians and gays. She argues that both gender
and the sexual body have no natural genesis but are thoroughly culturally
constructed. Gender, she says, is the effect of phallocentric institutions,
practices, and discourses that have enforced internally coherent gender
identities within a rigid hierarchical, hetrosexual framework. The task, as
she sees it, is to decenter such defining institutions, which enforce a binary
gender division, and to affirm a gender fluidity and proliferation that finally
deposes the gender norms of "man" and "woman."

Although Butler's Foucauldian exposure of the forces at work in the creation of heterosexuality is helpful and useful for clarifying lesbian and gay
gender identity, I find the notion of a gender fluidity unacceptable. Seriously applying the poststructuralist critique to gender identity as Butler
shows us leads one to affirm that gender categories are solely cultural arti-
fices divorced from the body (which is itself seen as a cultural construction), and to advocate that our present binary gender framework
should be replaced by multiple gender identities whose totality is not fixed
but permanently deferred. What is most disturbing to me about this view is
that culture is privileged over nature. Indeed, nature and the body disap-
pear altogether. Although I agree that theoretically gender identity is essentially incomplete and must open to future changes, I do not think that
gender can be entirely disconnected from the body or that the body and na-

ture can be dismissed as a cultural artifice. There is certainly a need to reconceptualize gender, but it is crucial, as I see it, that this occur in a way that is respectful of the body and of the indeterminate and open-textured givens of our natural-cultural situation. We certainly need to rework the hierarchical binary gender division so that one gender does not dominate another and so that a heterosexual orientation is not enforced as the norm. But we cannot entirely throw out gender structures that take their direction from the body (as, indeed, do even lesbian and gay genders) in favor of gender formations that are solely the product of our cultural wills.

Generally I argue that the poststructuralist position concerning gender is dangerous because it is relativist, nihilist, and ecodestructive, and I present a new way of reconceptualizing gender (in this chapter) and the body (in the next). While I agree with the poststructuralists that notions like ground, truth, origin, nature, the body, and gender identity are not fixed, stable signifiers, I maintain that these notions possess, nonetheless, a certain constancy and continuity that prevents them from being merely relative. Origin, meaning, and truth are not endlessly deferred, as Derrida would like us to believe, but are what we can provisionally call indeterminant constancies (which are constancies, nonetheless). I show how we can reconceptualize gender identity in a way that is neither fixed nor relative and, moreover, how we can reconceptualize origin as an earthy ground that is neither a fixed foundation nor an endlessly deferred difference.

One of Butler's primary claims for denaturalizing gender is based on the Derridean critique that there is no unified subject that can be represented. She criticizes the feminist assumption that the term *woman* denotes a stable, coherent, common identity. Feminism has represented women as a stable subject at least in part because in order to represent oneself in politics and law, one needs a stable subject. It has also, moreover, pointed to the universal structure of patriarchy as a singular oppressor and stable subject. Butler rightly points out that there is little agreement about what constitutes the category of women among feminists because of the complex way it intersects with one's race, class, culture, and age. Given the poststructuralist critique of foundations and the problems of essentialism, feminists, says Butler, should no longer feel the need to assert a female specificity, to construct a stable subject, woman, and a singular oppressor, the patriarchy. Instead the political goal should be to get rid of these stable gender categories and construct variable gender identities, paying attention to concrete cultural and historical contexts.

Butler's gender argument clearly relies on the general Derridean post-structuralist critique of foundations. In order to expose the deeper philosophical implications and presuppositions of her argument, it is necessary to unravel the philosophical basis of her argument. In Derrida's view of language, the relation between signifiers and signifieds, and between signs and meanings, is unstable. Signifiers and signifieds are continually breaking apart and rejoining in new combinations. Meanings are never fully present in any one sign but are dispersed in a network of signifiers. One can never, moreover, arrive at a final signified meaning which is not a signifier in itself that refers beyond itself. Meaning, then, cannot be found in either an origin or an end because it is always haunted by the traces of other meanings that are absent. For Derrida, there is no meaning to be discovered behind a sign, beneath a text. The search for meaning is an endless game of deferring, a play of traces.

Using this theory of language, Derrida directs his critique at the western metaphysical tradition, which has depended on foundations, first principles, or grounds upon which to build hierarchies of meanings. First principles or grounds, Derrida notes, are commonly defined by what they exclude. This dynamic sets up binary oppositions between two fixed concepts in which one concept, validated by the presupposed ground, is the superior term, and the other concept is the inferior. Derrida deconstructs such conceptual oppositions by showing how the subordinate term subverts and is even determinative of the dominant term.

Although Derrida's deconstructive techniques are most effective and helpful in undermining the foundationalism of metaphysics, there is a certain respect for nature, for flesh and blood existence missing in his writings. Moreover, at times Derrida seems to be suggesting that we simply abandon the language of metaphysics and take up his thought of *différance*, which he claims does not operate within the horizon of metaphysics. However, because metaphysics is not just a thought system constructed by philosophers but describes the broad living lines or ways of being that still hold sway in this epoch, we can at best only marginally step back from metaphysics, from these sedimented attitudes, concepts, ideals, and ways of being that broadly guide our cultural, and our most intimate, lives.

Derrida's alternative to the foundationalism of metaphysics, moreover, is ultimately a nihilistic, endless play of deferred, text-generated meaning. Abandoning the metaphysical search for fixed grounds, we are left with the bleak prospect of constituting relative meanings and truths and playfully tracking down textual traces that merely make continual referrals to other traces. I might add, although I will not argue it here, that despite Derrida's attempt to subvert hierarchical oppositions, he privileges textual signs over the living word, and, despite his attempt to leave metaphysics, he maintains a neo-Nietzschean nihilism, which remains bound to metaphysics.[15]

It is important to point out, however, that Derrida cannot be *simply* dismissed as a nihilist, for there are, as it were, many Derridas (and many Heideggers). The reading of Derrida I am giving here is of a Nietzschean Dionysian textual master gleefully pushing a conservative Heidegger back into the grips of a metaphysics of presence. I am in agreement with John Caputo's excellent analysis of Derrida and Heidegger in his *Radical Hermeneutics* (1987) where he shows that a more humble (though still laughing) Derrida and the later radicalized Heidegger can be brought into a productive, life-affirming complicity in such important notions as truth, *Ereignis*, difference, and play. So, too, there is an indeterminacy (and ambiguity) to Nietzsche's nihilism. I would like to affirm free play, becoming, innocence, chance, and nature along with Nietzsche while rejecting the Nietzschean self-and-other destructive will to nothing.

In any case, we surely do not need to choose between a metaphysics that presumes fixed, certain grounds and stable, authoritative truths, and a nihilism that denies all grounds, meanings, truths, origins, and living presence, affirming only the clever cultural-textual play of perpetual deferment.[16] There must be a way of thinking beyond stable grounds of metaphysics without falling into a many-faceted mirror-play of dispersed and deferred meaning. From a feminist standpoint, if we engage in this form of Derridean play, we will be encouraged to denaturalize gender, disconnecting it from the body, privileging culture over nature, and advocating relativistic, socially constructed gender pluralities. We must find a new way of thinking about grounds (and this includes thinking about our bodies, subjectivities and identities, and about origins, presence, and truth), which have become central to feminist issues such as female specificity, essentialism, and gender identity.

To find a way of thinking about grounds that is not entrapped in either traditional metaphysics or a poststructuralist nihilistic dance, it is most helpful to turn to Heidegger's later consideration of ground, for Derrida's thought of *différance* operates within the space that Heidegger had earlier cleared. Not paying sufficient heed to Heidegger's critique of Nietzsche, as well as Heidegger's notions of *a-letheia* and *Ereignis,* Derrida pushes hermeneutics to the edges of relativism and nihilism. Heidegger's own pathway of thinking remains life and earth affirming even though he is, indeed, guilty at times of romanticizing an ethnocentrical German earth, and of a nostalgia for a native land and language of Being.

Heidegger (1977c, 115–54) criticizes metaphysical thinking as a "representational thinking" which gives grounds. Metaphysical thinking represents what-is in terms of its ground in order to account for it as something grounded, or secured and known. From the very beginnings of philosophy, Being has appeared as the ground, *arche* (principle), and *aition* (cause) from which beings as such can be known and can be at the disposal of reason. Thus, in the metaphysical tradition, Being has variously grounded beings, for example, as the ontic causation of the real (Aristotle), as the transcendental making possible of the objectivity of objects (Kant), as the dialectical mediation of the movement of Absolute Spirit (G.W.F. Hegel), and, with Nietzsche (who, Heidegger convincingly argues, completes the metaphysical tradition), as the Will to Power positing values.

One of the most significant dangers of metaphysical thinking is its way of representing beings. The peculiar representational nature of metaphysical thinking becomes prominent with modern, post-Cartesian thought, particularly with Leibniz.[17] To represent is to set a being before oneself in such a way that one can account for and be certain of that being. By means of the ground, interpreted now as ratio, what-is comes to stand in such a way that it is certified as an object for a representing subject. The ground guarantees that the object is firmly placed and secured as a calculable object for representational thought. The disturbing point of all this is that the ground determines what is allowed to pass for something that truly is. According to Leibniz's principle that "Nothing is without ground," something *is* in its being only to the extent that it can be set up by the human subject as a fixed, grounded object at the subject's disposal. What-is in the modern age thus becomes solely what can be represented, what can be referred back to the power of self-consciousness. Representational thinking assumes that the rational human subject is the stable, relational center of what-is. This anthropocentrism and rationalism of representational thinking holds sway in our modern technological age. Our human being, says Heidegger (1974b, 1977e), is everywhere challenged to devote itself to the planning and calculating of all beings, which, moreover, can appear only within the horizon of what is calculable.

The task of philosophy, according to Heidegger (1977d), is to dislodge the calculating subject from its controlling, representational position and its self-certain securing of objects, which it achieves by means of a ground that gives sufficient accounts. In the place of calculative thought, which constructs ideas on firm validating grounds and is focused on the securing and manipulation of what-is (understood as a standing reserve of energy at the disposal of a subject), he advocates a "meditative thinking" that springs away from metaphysical foundations, away from thinking that is fixated solely on what-is, and springs into an abyss.

This abyss, however, is neither an empty nothingness nor a perpetual deferment of meaning suggested by the Derridean *différance.* Instead, the abyss to which a thinking beyond metaphysical grounds leaps is variously called by Heidegger the "ontological difference," the "event of appropriation" *(Ereignis),* the "Open," and the "belonging-together" of beings and Being. Crucial to the notion of abyss is the fact that Being has been interpreted as the ground in which all beings are grounded. Metaphysics, then, has concerned itself with the ground, with Being only in order to account for beings. Being itself, however, in the metaphysical tradition has been forgotten, for it cannot be reduced to that which is present; it cannot be reduced to beings. To think meditatively on the ground itself, then, requires a leap away from all grounds into an abyss because the ground, Being, is itself without ground. It is enigmatically the groundless ground that grounds beings.

"Meditative thinking" in contrast to the "calculative thinking" of meta-

physics is not concerned with fixing the meaning, truth or "givens" of beings, but with thinking on the giving or granting of Being. It is a musing on
the simple "that it is" of beings, on wonderous reasonless emergence itself. This naked "it gives" of existence has been forgotten in metaphysics,
for it itself remains without fixed ground, cause, or reason and, moreover,
without truth, if by truth we mean the certainty of knowledge (Heidegger
1974b, 213).

If we attempt to think on the enigma of Being, it becomes apparent that
Being cannot be directly thought upon because it is not present like a being
and has no ground upon which we can gain a sure footing. Being withdraws as it reveals beings. It lets beings appear, grants difference, while
concealing itself, holding itself back from that which is present. This crucial withdrawing of Being which occurs in one enigmatic movement of
genesis with the emerging of beings Heidegger calls "presencing."[18] Presencing, for Heidegger, is not the property of presence in present objects but
is a verb that denotes genesis as difference. It is a movement that simultaneously emerges, granting the unconcealing of beings, and holds itself
back, concealing itself. Presencing vibrates, shimmers, because it is a presencing that is always simultaneously absencing. This absencing is not the
emptiness of nihilistic deferment, however, but a fullness like that of the
dark holding of the inner recesses of a jug.[19]

The presencing of any being, then, involves its enigmatic relation to Being. What should be kept in mind (and body) is that Being, as presencing,
is not identical to its whatness or mere presentness. The Being of a being is
not its essence in the traditional metaphysical sense (i.e., its abstract universality or unchanging ground) but is the self-concealing, groundless
ground of a being. What this all amounts to for our purposes is that, first,
fundamental to the presencing of a being is its historicality and, second,
that a being in its presencing can never be fully represented as a stable subject or identity.

Returning now to the problem of asserting stable gender identities, it becomes possible to affirm the presencing of women without installing a
fixed, ahistorical, cross-cultural notion of woman. In the face of essentialism, we can affirm the concept of the feminine as a notion that has a lasting
presence of some sort but that is not an atemporal unchanging essence.

Moreover, in the face of poststructuralism, we can affirm the notion of the feminine as a historical concept, and thus open to future change, yet not entirely abandon it to the cultural play of political, institutional, and social powers.[20] But let us explore this new notion of the presencing of women in more detail.

The typical problem with essences (which is a way of grounding a being), understood in a traditional metaphysical sense, is that they hold the truth, substance, and whatness of beings in a way that tends to separate beings from their particular, temporal, ever-changing embodiment.[21] Central to this new notion of presencing, however, is a dynamic historicity. The emergence, giving, or granting of beings is thoroughly historical. The presencing of a being includes not so much what it is but the way that it comes to appear from out of the concealed into the unconcealed. Presencing is the way a being historically pursues its course. The presencing of a woman, and of women in general or the feminine then, does not imply a fully fixed, atemporal meaning. Rather, these concepts derive their meaning from the changing historical, political, social, ideological, and, moreover, fleshy presencing of women in what I call the world-earth-home.

I use the terms *world-earth-home* and *being in the world-earth-home* because the term *being-in-the-world*, familiar to existentialists and taken from Heidegger's *Being and Time*, is biased in favor of a male perspective on our being. Our being here is not merely a being in the world. *World* for Heidegger, seems to connote specifically a man's world and his public institutions, thereby tending to neglect the domestic realm, and connotes a human world in opposition to the earth. The term *earth* reminds us that we are here with other animals and on an earth that gives rise to a myriad of life that has been increasingly marginalized by our human world and, worse yet, thoughtlessly used up by it. The term *home*, moreover, reminds us that we are here as human beings not primarily to participate within the perhaps misnamed public world, but to dwell humanly, in other words, to be at home, whether we are in our offices, in the woods, or in our own dwellings.

The feminine, which I understand to be noncausally and indeterminately connected to the presencing of actual women, is, then, a fluid constancy that always remains open to further determinations but has a historical and existential continuity. Furthermore, since the presencing of women can never be represented by fixed homogeneous ideals or concepts, the feminine must ultimately remain a question full of enigma and controversy. This is not only because the presencing of women is always historically changing in a broad way, as I have discussed, but also because any being in its presencing can never be fully represented. It is not only that a being in its presencing has future hidden potentials, but that as merely *existing* it is steeped in mystery. A being in its Being is never fully present all at once for complete rational penetration but vibrates and shimmers, for in its existence it is continually self-concealing even as it emerges out of concealment into unconcealment. The feminine, then, is not a representation of women fully transparent to self-consciousness but always remains immersed in its latency and mysterious life.

It would seem, moreover, that the presencing of women must in particular remain an open question because historically the presencing of women has appeared more as a peculiar kind of absencing. In the binary oppositions of metaphysics, the category of the feminine has been invariably associated with the subordiante terms, and thus it has derived its meaning in a secondary way from the dominant terms.[22] The ontological significance of this particular historical absencing of the feminine will be discussed in later pages.

It would be a mistake, however, to assert that the gender category of women has been man-made and can now be abolished by women in favor of a new gender plurality or simply reconstructed in our own terms. Given that presencing always involves more than cultural determinants, we can see that the presencing of women is not a matter of man as subject accounting for a woman as object by supplying an underlying fixed ground or identity. It is also not the result of a poststructuralist subject's cultural play of meaning, where the subject, though dispersed in institutional and social power centers, is nonetheless a cultural authoritative synthesis that grounds all meaning. Like metaphysics, this poststructuralist description of how gender (and meaning) is constituted disregards the nonhuman and reifies an anthropocentric (although multiple) subject.

It is, indeed, hard for us in this age in which the subjectivism of the human being has reached its height, and in which we have assumed the technological command of the earth and all beings, not to presume that our destiny (including that of gender) is fully within our control. Given that we order and constitute everything from the perspective of our self-certain subjectivity and with our progressively powerful technology, it is hard to allow for the presencing of anything but ourselves and our own products.

> As I write, a cicada calls from a pine tree behind me, numerous crickets creak in the grass, a bee buzzes over a white clover, flies whine here and there, a car in the distance goes down the highway. There is a slight breeze. The leaves of a birch and some low bushes beside me rustle, waver, tremble. Patches of sunlight on the solid, grey granite boulders. Flecks of mica. A crow caws suddenly, clear and distinct. Another car down the highway. The sky, simply a pale blue.

We must not assume that our destiny and the destiny of the earth are totally within our control. Although human beings, indeed, actively participate in the unfolding of Being and help shape it, we cannot take the broad lines of existence fully into our cultural hands and bend them as we will. This is not because history is predetermined or, in the case of gender, that our biology is our destiny, but that the way life articulates itself has as much to do with the response of other beings, with the currents of the earthly and skyey environment, and with temporal contingencies as it does with our subjectivist cultural wills.

It is important to recognize, then, the ontological significance of the contemporary "gender trouble," as Butler aptly names it. A crucial way of opening up to that which has been deemed other to our self-consciousnesses is by recalling the unobtrusive, groundless ground of our Being. The hierarchical binary gender division and the silence inherent in the feminine's historical presencing are not only the result of various conflicting cultural discourses of power but are the result of Being; that is, the historical play of cultural *and* natural articulations. By thinking on gender in ways that deliberately step back from western metaphysical thinking that has been flesh and earth loathing, we might help turn Being from its present eco-destructive and phallocentric historical presencing.

We can affirm sexual difference without having to fix that difference and the constitution of the terms of the difference. The fact that the terms masculine and feminine are not always coherent, that they cannot comprehensively include all variables, does not deter a thoughtful use of these notions, as long as we are attempting to thinking meditatively or in a way that attempts to step back from the foundationalist, calculative thinking of metaphysics. We cannot affirm a stable ground that certifies and secures an object for human representation and rational penetration. However, the alternative is not to leap into a nihilistic endless game of *différance* where dispersal and the lack of relationship are given the last word and nature as nontextual is banished altogether. On the contrary, we need to affirm a groundless ground that gathers beings, not into a stale unity, but into relational differences.

This ground, which is without a why and upon which everything rests, is like the unobtrusive ground upon which we dwell. Our earthy ground is what lies in the lived depths: the dark depths of the sea, the blue clear depths of the sky, the fertile bottom of the valley, the unknown depth of the horizon, and the bottom of the heart. This ground is always there for every being as a supporting presence taken for granted. Everything rests and endures, comes to be and passes away upon and within this unfathomable ground. This "upsurgence of the healing [*des Heilens*]" (Heidegger 1977d, 237) cannot be represented as an object for representational thought.[23] Our existential, historical, finite existence is not grounded in transcendent truths that rise above time, as we used to think at least since the beginnings of western metaphysics, but is given within this self-concealing, supportive presence.

> This morning, I adjusted the white plastic table I've been using to write on so it was more or less level on the grass and yet would still remain in the shade by the afternoon. The lawn up here inclines toward the lake, which I can see through the tops of the spruces. I have found the best place to park the table is behind a birch tree, just at the edge of the steep slope toward the lake, although the ground here is so uneven. I put my cup of coffee on the table and went to get my laptop and notes. When I returned, the table was on its side, my coffee spilt all over. I didn't bother going all the way down the hill to my parents' cottage to get another cup (since it is so hard to come back up again with my pregnant belly) but set right to work.

A particular kind of ground that Derrida criticizes and that some post-structuralist feminists take up in the context of gender is the notion of origin (see, for example, Derrida 1976, p. 1). Butler, for example, criticizes the feminist search for both the origins of patriarchy and a prepatriarchal, originating presence of the feminine.[24] Now, one can easily agree that there is no need to search for *the* single cause of sexism. It does not seem to me, however, that feminists who propose that a cause of women's oppression lies, for instance, in the sexual division of labor, in child-rearing practices, or language are making strong monocausal claims. In any case, it would not seriously hurt their theories by making room for other causes of phallocentrism. Their investigations, however, should not be rejected on the grounds that any search for causes and origins is theoretically flawed. Surely there is still a pressing need to explore the origins of the gendered hierarchical power structures that inform our daily lives.

It is helpful to make a distinction between cause and origin. An important problem with Butler's particular analysis is that she conflates the notion of origin with that of cause. A cause is, indeed, a kind of origin, but an origin need not be a cause. A cause is a scientific, mechanistic term that is in a necessary and external relation to an effect. Origin, on the other hand, as I argue in later pages, is a springing up, which need not imply any deterministic effect, and, for a radicalized Heidegger, is itself a kind of effect.

Again, it is helpful to look into the philosophical debate in the background of this poststructuralist feminist argument (which again involves Derrida and Heidegger). My analysis can be fairly brief, since an origin is but a variation of the notion of ground, which we have already discussed at length. Derrida supplants the metaphysical notion of a stable, unified origin with his notion of *différance* (see, for example, Derrida 1982). As we have discussed, *différance* is text-generated and is always differing/deferring, divided from itself. In the Derridean search for origins we discover only traces making continual referrals to other traces. A sign is not a homogeneous unit, bridging an origin or referent and an end or meaning, but is haunted by the trace of another sign that is absent. Thus, *différance* is not ultimately a genesis but a perpetual play of traces.

As I have already mentioned, Heidegger's critique of metaphysics opened the space for Derrida's own thought of *différance*. Heidegger criticizes the metaphysical notion of origin as a first cause or unified beginning and develops his notion of origin as difference. This difference, however, unlike Derrida's *différance,* gathers rather than disperses what is differentiating itself.

In *Identity and Difference*, Heidegger attempts to step back from the traditional way of thinking about identity in Western metaphysics by showing how identity depends on difference, on the relation between. The common formula of identity, A is equal to A, conceals what the principle means: that every A is itself the same. For something to be the same, one term is enough. The unity implied in the identity is not one of equality between two identical terms but of sameness within the same term. Sameness, however, implies a gathering into a unity that is not the stale emptiness of that which is without relation and persists in monotonous equality (Heidegger 1974a, 25). It is a belonging-together in which the belonging is stressed. Belonging-together is not a mere coordination of two in order to produce their unity. It is not a matter of assigning them in a unifying center of an authorative synthesis or togetherness. What is important to realize is that the principle of identity tells us how every being *is*: it is the same with itself, has unity with itself. By paying attention to the *is* that binds A with itself, room is made for the all-important difference whereby that which *is* first receives its determinations. This original difference, which names how every being is the same with itself, is the ontological difference, or the relation between Being and beings. The more radical Heidegger attempts to go beyond even this formulation of Being because it relies on a traditional dualism, and think on that which lets Being happen, naming this *Ereignis*, and the open.

In "The Origin of a Work of Art," a much-cited article from his middle period, Heidegger understands origin as a creative strife between world and earth, where earth and world attain the "simplicity of intimacy" through their relationship that both unifies and differentiates them. In his later writing, however, Heidegger moves away from this thought of difference as a strife between two terms (even though the terms are not stable unities as in metaphysical thinking but are constituted by their relation of difference). Instead, he speaks simply of the "Open" (which had already appeared in "The Origin of the Work of Art"), "Openness," and in his later works, *Ereignis, Es gibt,* "the rounding dance" of the fourfold of earth, sky, mortals, and immortals. The Open is the same as that primordial enigma we have discussed which lets entities appear even as it withdraws, and which remains unthought in philosophy. In order for something to be illuminated as what is present, the originating presencing of the Open is needed. This concept, as John Caputo (1987, 99) points out, is related to the notion of horizon in Heidegger's *Being and Time.* The horizon is the look or sight in terms of which we make objectivity possible. Horizonality is the circle of the look and implies the notion of Dasein's projective understanding. But as the teacher in Heidegger's "Conversations on a Country Path" (1966, 64) points out: "What is evident of the horizon, then, is but the side facing us of an openness which surrounds us." The horizon or field of vision is a perspectival view of the open and does not originate within us but is instead cogiven by the open. Thus, Heidegger rejects his earlier notion of horizonality (from Husserl) in favor of the Open, which is understood as that which lets horizon be. The Open is, as it were, "a prior invasion of Being" (Caputo 1987, 99). It is not a stable presence or ground, however, for in the free space of the opening, what is absent also presences.[25]

A way of understanding the simultaneous withdrawal and appearance involved in the notion of the Open, which is in some sense an origin, is to introduce Heidegger's crucial thinking on *aletheia,* which is commonly translated as "truth."[26] We must not, however, understand the concept *aletheia* to mean mere correctness or a fixed, objective truth. Truths as we know them are the effects of *aletheia.* To retain a sense of the Greek meaning for truth, says Heidegger, it is better to translate the term *a-letheia* more literally as "un-concealment." Unconcealment is neither a matter of a publicly observable objective truth nor a private subjective truth, but a revealing of Being. It is the historical coming into the unconcealedness of appearance from out of concealment *(lethe). Aletheia* is not truth in the sense of the correspondence of knowledge with beings, but rather first grants the possibility of such evidence and certainty. *Aletheia* is the ongoing various process of give and take by which beings emerge in different epochs. It is the historicity of truth events, an endless flux and transciency.[27]

What I want to emphasize here because it is central to my thinking in this book is the aspect of concealment intrinsic to *aletheia*. A crucial difference between *aletheia* and our usual notion of truth is the *lethe* in *aletheia*. This self-concealing aspect belongs to unconcealment, says Heidegger (1972a, 71), "not as a shadow to light but rather as the heart of *aletheia*." Conceal- ment, then, is not to be understood as the negative of unconcealment but is a positive source of unconcealment. Mystery, darkness, chaos, absence, ambiguity, the play of chance all belong to concealment. Nature, too, with its unrelenting rhythms of growth and decay speaks of concealment. Inso- far as anything exists, it exists as unconcealed, and that is what we see when we look at present beings. But the way beings appear or are revealed is open to ambiguity, change, error, and further determinations because of their historical context and simply because of the incarnate nature of being.

These usually ignored, because they are unruly, aspects of our existence are included in the Greek word *aletheia*. Heidegger is not suggesting, how- ever, that the Greeks had a special hotline to concealment through their word *aletheia* and is thereby engaging in a nostalgia for a native land of Being, for Heidegger admits that the *lethe* of *aletheia* remained unthought by the Greeks themselves (1972d, 70). As Caputo (1987, 182) points out, *aletheia* "is no more Greek than *différance* is, merely French." *Aletheia* is not the final master name of Being that has been forgotten in metaphysical thought and that poetic thinking can recover. If *aletheia* is the "unname" that points to that from which all of the metaphysical master names (the names that pretend to have mastered beings) issue, then the Greeks cannot lay claim to this un-name as their master name either. As Caputo (1987, 183) goes on to explain, "they never said *a-letheia*, never hyphenated it, never made it an unword, never wrote it the way Heidegger, our meta- hermeneutical Heidegger, tried to write it."

Although Derrida will read with Heidegger against Heidegger, all too often in his criticisms of Heidegger's metaphysics of presence, Derrida neglects to emphasize this crucial aspect of concealment involved in pres- encing. In a like manner, he neglects the concealment involved in Heideg- ger's notion of origin. Whereas for Derrida, origin is a trace of an absent origin, for Heidegger, origin is an event of simultaneous emergence and withdrawal. Heidegger, it is true, attempts to go back to the concealed origins of the metaphysical tradition in traces left within Greek philosophy. Because of this return, Derrida accuses Heidegger of attempting to lead us back to a rehabilitation of immediacy, of original simplicity. What Derrida overlooks, however, is that Heidegger's return to Greek beginnings is not for the pure, original presencing of western Being, since such origins are concealed: "The beginning of Western thought is not the same as its origin. The beginning is, rather, the veil that conceals the origin—indeed an unavoidable veil. . . . The origin keeps itself concealed in the beginning" (1972e, 152).[28]

Origin as *ursprung* is not a firm foundation or virginal a priori. Origin is a birth, literally a springing up *(ur-sprung)* that swells, gathers, asks for interinvolvement. There are beginnings, births that do not necessarily and mechanically lead to certain effects but that grow. Such phusical (from the Greek *phusis*, commonly translated "nature") beginnings do not rest secure on unshakable origins or grounds but indeterminately interinvolve with other currents and confluences of earthy existence along the way. Birth is a beginning whose origins are mysteriously concealed, darkly as in the womb, and deeply, always, in the stark open pulse of existence. Moreover, play, whether it be the play of gender configurations or the play of concealment and unconcealment, becomes a meaningless nihilistic flux without the diastole and systole of origins and ends, uncertain and ambiguous as they may be, for it is this inspiration and expiriation that gives play its rhythm and field.

Chapter Two

Renaturalizing Gender
(with the Help of Merleau-Ponty)

> My body metamorphoses into pregnancy. Are these my breasts? I start
> wearing a bra, put away my jeans. I look at medical drawings of pro-
> gesterone and estrogen levels. I feel nauseous a lot of the time, delicate:
> ill. A bad start.

The poststructuralist attempt to denaturalize gender centrally involves a
redefinition of the body. That gender has been naturalized means that the
binary structure of "man" and "woman" has been conventionally understood as fixed and innate, as a natural outcome of the unalterable, biological determinants of the sexual body. In this view, the basic binary division
of gender rests on the firm foundation of the natural body. Some poststructuralist feminists maintain, on the contrary, that both gender and the body
are purely the products of conventional cultural forms of meaning, practice, and representation and are wrongly used to found various epistemological and ontological claims. They understand the body as completely
culturally inscribed, as having no natural (which for them means ahistorical and cross-cultural and thereby fixed) determinants.

Although our concepts of the body and of sexual difference do not simply reflect the natural world, I do not believe they are purely cultural arti-
fices. In this technological age, the illusion prevails that everything is a
product of cultural powers. As Arne Naess and many others have pointed
out, however, it is vital to the ecological health of our planet that we recognize that our human existence is not only intervolved in cultural fields of
forces but is a part of an interconnected web of relations with the nonhuman. In the context of feminist gender theory, stepping back from our ecologically destructive, anthropocentric worldview means that the feminist
reconceptualization of gender ought to be envisioned in a way that is ecologically sound, that pays respect to the earth, and that takes into account
the silent, carnal wisdom of our bodies. We must free gender as much as
possible from the external and internal ideologies that have enforced a heterosexual, hierarchical binary gender division. But to divorce gender from

the body is to further alienate ourselves from our terrestrial situation and to entrench ourselves (with a new poststructuralist twist) yet deeper in the nature/culture dichotomy.

In the following pages, I argue that our human bodily being takes place within a natural/cultural situation and thus is neither the result of biological determinants nor purely culturally constructed. With the help of Maurice Merleau-Ponty's phenomenology of the body, I present a paradigm of the body as an indeterminate constancy. I focus in particular on Merleau-Ponty's attempt to recover a noncultural, nonlinguistic body that accompanies and is intertwined with our cultural existence and thereby argue for what I have called the body's fleshy presencing in the world-earth-home.

The well-known problem of advocating that gender is rooted in the body is that such a rooting predetermines on biological grounds the nature and roles of the sexes. It is claimed that women, because of their biological reproductive function, naturally belong in the home, having babies and taking care of children. The circumstances of female oppression, according to such accounts, are biological and thus unalterable. Biology is used to perpetuate hierarchical power relations between the sexes that keep women dependent, suppressed, and excluded from culture. Aristotle and Sigmund Freud, for example, argued that women by nature are inferior to men.

Feminists have countered such sexist accounts of the female body by arguing that gender is a product of early childhood socialization, psychological development, gender identity formation, and cultural ideology. Gender identities and roles vary in different cultures and historical periods. Moreover, biological accounts of the sexual difference, feminists convincingly argue, are not objective and gender neutral but are often invested with gender, class, cultural, and racial biases.

If gender can be freed from, rather than grounded in, the body, it has the advantage of being open to radical change. Some earlier feminists, for instance, who believe gender is separate from the body, advocated androgyny as a solution to the hierarchical binary division of gender. They envisioned an androgynous society where gender would be up to individual conscious choice and tendencies, where being human would be stressed and sexual difference would be comparatively of little significance.[1]

The new poststructuralist attempt to denaturalize the body is directed more in response to feminists' own attempts to resuscitate traditionally degraded feminine characteristics, reproductive capacities, and roles. They object, on theoretical grounds, to the use of concepts such as nature, the body, and origin as foundations for perpetuating ahistorical, cross-cultural categories such as men and women, mothering, and reproduction, which they claim are essentialist, and for enforcing a heterosexual binary gender division that marginalizes bisexuals and homosexuals. It is not an androgynous society that is advocated but a proliferation of gender identities.[2] Gender, moreover, is not viewed as simply a matter of individual choice but is understood as a complex matter of cultural signifying practices. To discuss the poststructuralist understanding of gender and its relation to the body, I again use Judith Butler's book *Gender Trouble* because it is a strong representative of this strand of poststructuralist feminism.[3]

Butler uses the poststructuralist critique of foundations to help purge gender from its connections with the body and any natural determinations. Just as there can be no recourse to an original or genuine femininity in a prehistorical past or a femininity outside the phallocentric order, so there can be no recourse to a pure body before or outside its cultural context. The sexed body is not the firm foundation upon which gender is formed. Butler agrees with Wittig that sex is not an "immediate given" belonging to the natural order but a "mythic construction." Sex is a mark that can be erased by taking up practices that undermine cultural constructions (p. 25–27; 119–28). Butler's goal is to proliferate gender configuration, destabilize substantive identities, and thereby deprive the "naturalizing narratives of compulsory heterosexuality of their central protagonists: 'man' and 'woman' " (p. 146).

Butler critically takes up Michel Foucault's terminology and analysis of the body (with the occasional use of Merleau-Pontian terminology) to explain how gender identity, and, moreover, the body itself, is culturally constructed. Gender, she says, is a corporeal style, a performative, contingent construction of meaning. It is a play of signifying practices inscribed on the surface of bodies and within a cultural field of gender hierarchy and compulsory heterosexuality. Gender identities are created through a stylized repetition of acts, bodily gestures, and desires that produce the il-

lusory effect of an internal stable core and give the appearance of a naturalistic configuration of sexual bodies (p. 136). "Man" and "woman," then,
are not only false gendered stabilities but are cultural constructions that
conceal their artificial origins and masquerade as natural configurations of
sexual bodies (pp. 139, 140).

In this view, the body is still related to gender, not as its ground or origin, but as a surface upon which the cultural play of significations takes
place. The body, says Butler, is not a "being" but a "variable boundary,"
"a surface whose permeability is politically regulated and established,"
for instance, through prohibitions (pp. 33, 139). It is shaped by political
forces with strategic interest in keeping the body bounded and constituted
by sexual markers that impose an artificial unity on an otherwise discontinuous set of attributes (pp. 129, 139).

> Is this really my belly? I am so fat, enormous. Constant adjustment to my
> body-image. They look at me in my bikini with my protruding bare belly.
> I can't carry myself with my usual athleticism. I become self-conscious
> by the surprised gaze of others. No longer nice to look at. Knocked-up,
> taken, unappealing. In the eyes of others, before being a person, I am first
> and foremost pregnant. I refuse to be embarrassed; I am still my own
> body—but I try to be discreet so as not to appear too bold. Well, this
> is what I wanted: to experience pregnancy again.

Butler does not make the mistake of claiming that the body is a natural
surface or a passive medium for cultural inscription, thereby falling into a
nature/culture dichotomy.[4] She is helpfully critical of the hierarchical
binary relation between culture and nature where culture freely imposes
meaning on nature rendering it Other (p. 37). Using Foucault's analysis of
the body, Butler maintains that the body is not an abiding *natural* ground
but is always already a "*cultural* sign" (p. 71; emphasis added). It is not a
ready surface awaiting signification but a set of boundaries, individual and
social, politically signified and maintained (p. 33). The naturalness of sex
and the body is illusory and thoroughly culturally produced. Gender is not
to culture as the sexed body is to nature. Instead, both the body and gender
are thoroughly culturally constructed (p. 37).

Although Butler takes up Foucault's analysis of the body as the inscribed surface of events upon which culture leaves its marks, she is critical of what she sees as vestiges of foundationalism and the nature/culture dichotomy in his own theory. For Foucault, the body is not sexed prior to its determination within a discourse and in the context of power relations. Sex is an artificial concept that has become invested with an idea of a natural or essential sex. However, Foucault, she claims, appears to nonetheless maintain a natural body prior to signification, inscription, and form. The body is a medium, a blank page upon which history writes. In this historical process of signification, the body is destroyed and transvalued into a sublimated domain of values. If the creation of values, which is the historical mode of signification, requires the destruction of the body for Foucault, then, says Butler, "there must be a body prior to that inscription, stable, and self-identical, subject to that sacrificial destruction" (p. 130). Foucault, moreover, she claims, subscribes to a prediscursive multiplicity of bodily forces that can break through the surface of the body to disrupt the regulatory practices of culture imposed on the body.[5] She argues, on the contrary, that even this weak form of the natural body, which Foucault's theory appears to rely on, is itself a production of a given historical discourse, an effect of culture rather than its cause. The culturally constructed body must be liberated, she says, not to its natural past or its original pleasures but to an open future of cultural possibilities (p. 93).

What body can this be that is but a cultural surface, inscribed by cultural significations, and masquerading as natural?[6] What meaning is left to gender (from the Greek *genos* meaning "origin") once it is separated from living, fleshy bodies and set adrift in a sea of cultural significations, discursive practices, and power configurations? It seems to me that in her zeal to advocate a gender fluidity, Butler goes too far in her denaturalization of the body. Her Foucauldian attempt to avoid metaphysical foundationalism (which, indeed, with regard to the problem of gender, can only eventually lead to biological determinism and essentialism) leaves us with a disembodied body and a free-floating gender artifice in a limitless sea of cultural meaning production.[7]

What is most disturbing and dangerous in her poststructuralist analysis is its complete abandonment of nature and support of purely cultural determinants in the construction of gender. Nature, for Butler, it is true, has been shown properly to be no longer the direct opposite of culture, but it has lost any independent, nonanthropocentric status to become merely the product of human action. Nature is thereby reduced to a cultural idea, the body to a signifying cultural surface, and our incarnate, natural-cultural situation to purely cultural discursive practices and configurations of power. A body and nature formed solely by social and political significations, discourses and inscriptions are cultural products, disemboweled of their full existential content. The poststructuralist body, it is true, is historically and culturally contextualized and thereby achieves some of our experienced significances. However, the poststructuralist body is contextualized only as a place marker in a linguistic system of signifiers. It is so fluid it can take on almost limitless embodiments. It has no real terrestrial weight.

> Going into my ninth month now: feeling heavy, out of breath, emptying my bladder every hour, sweating under my pendulous breasts. This weight. It is not a weight that I willfully bear with muscular strength like a pack on my back. It is a weight that I live with, that has slowly entered into every aspect of my bodily being. Heavy like stone. If this were a permanent female state . . . ! To unwillingly bear a pregnancy like this in the center of one's being would be one of the worst forms of torture. Far better to push a boulder uphill like Sisyphus.

If we reduce the body as a whole to a purely cultural phenomenon and gender to a free-floating artifice, then we perpetuate the deep modern alienation of our human being from nature.[8] We reinforce the current anthropocentric and, moreover, the androcentric worldview that sees everything only in the light of humans' cultural use.[9] Such alienation and anthropocentrism cripple our sentience to the extent that we are able to contact only ourselves and our own products. By ignoring the earthy importance of our bodies and our interconnection with the nonhuman earth we join in the contemporary drive to transform and reduce the earth as a whole into a "standing-reserve" of energy resources at our disposal.[10]

It is vitally important to dissolve the nature/culture dichotomy because it both perpetuates our ecodestructive way of being and enforces the domination of women. But the way to deconstruct the nature/culture dichotomy is not to make everything cultural. Nor does making gender solely a product of cultural determinants militate against an oppressive heterosexuality. As Teresa de Lauretis (1986, 12) says, "For merely to say that sexual difference is 'cultural' allows no greater understanding of female subjectivity, and of women's actual and real differences, than to believe it to be 'natural.' And this is so since all accepted definitions of cultural, social, and subjective processes start from the same assumption: that sexual difference is the difference from man, the difference of woman from man—man being the measure, standard or term of reference for legitimated discourse."

At least part of the solution lies in redefining our human being in the way the deep ecology movement has suggested, that is, to understand ourselves not as human beings in control of the environment but as a part of a relational total field of the human and nonhuman.[11] Butler is right to argue that there is no pure body or untouched nature that can be found and isolated prior to culture, but she makes no attempt to reconceptualize the body and nature in a nonfoundationalist way that still allows, nonetheless, for their own noncultural presencing. Her response to the myth of a purely natural state prior to culture is merely to posit a pure culture that is always already there. This pure cultural state prior to nature, it seems to me, is also a myth and a theoretical construct. I cannot agree that our human existence is "only a taking up of the tools where they lie" (Butler 1990, 145). For the health of our human being and the earth as a whole, we must work to understand that human existence consists not only of a responsiveness to a cultural world but a responsiveness and response-ability to the nonhuman world. As I argue in later pages, our human being takes place within a *natural*-cultural relational field.

The task as I see it is to reconceptualize the body and nature in a way that avoids both the foundationalism of traditional metaphysics and its denigration of the body and nature. It is necessary to affirm the body and our connectedness to the earth in new terms if we are to rediscover our mortal belonging to the earth, not as cultural constructers removed from, and in control of, the earth, but as thinking sentient beings open to the earth.

On our path toward this "renaturalization" of the body and gender we should not forget that the body and nature in western metaphysics have traditionally been put in opposition to mind, spirit, and reason and, moreover, that the feminine has been identified with the body, and the masculine with mind, spirit, and reason.[12] In Platonic thought, the body is that which drags the immortal soul down to earth, and nature is that imperfect sensuous realm of coming-to-be and passing-away. For Descartes, the rational mind or intellect is radically separate from the corporeal body which, with its emotions, imagination, and sensuousness, intrudes upon the mind's efforts to secure clear and distinct ideas.[13] In metaphysics, women have traditionally been identified with the body, immanence, nature, and passive matter and have been viewed as being intellectually and essentially inferior to men.

While postmodernism is most critical of metaphysical foundationalism, it has overlooked its own alliance with traditional metaphysics in its similar privileging of culture over nature and the body. The postmodernist disembodied body unwittingly reinforces the same phallocentric metaphysical structures that have contributed to the domination of women and nature.[14] While we should applaud postmodernist criticisms of foundationalism, any attempt to reconceptualize the body ought to be concerned not only with the implict gender hierarchy but with the ecodestructiveness that the oppositional dichotomy between body/mind and nature/culture has traditionally encouraged and is presently reinforcing.

A sign of poststructuralist disregard of nature is the very language some poststructuralists use. Their talk of cultural inscriptions, plays of significations, signifiers and signifieds, deferring/differing, referring, referent—in short, their semiotic terminology and textual metaphors—is alienated from embodied existence. The fleshless abstractness of their terminology and the nihilistic playfulness of deconstruction display an intellectual intoxication.[15] Feminist discourse, it has been argued, should, on the contrary, attempt to disrupt such fleshless terminology and ground language in experience.[16] When poststructuralists make epistemological and ontological claims about our being, moreover, they generally place too much weight on language as a constituting force and on cognitive meaning (for example, Jacques Derrida's emphasis on the textual) and thereby disallows any true being to the nonlinguistic.

The notion of inscription and signification, moreover, might well rest on a model of domination and is not gender neutral. Part of Butler's (1990) objection to the image of a passive, natural body that awaits signification is her recognition of its sexist associations with the feminine awaiting inscription for the incision of the masculine signifier and thereby entrance into language and culture (p. 147). By replacing the natural body and the material page with an already cultural body and culturally constituted page, as Butler advocates, I do not see how we thereby succeed in deflating the male stylus. It seems to me we have instead joined the process of inscription, the pricking of the stylus, and have affirmed Derrida's (1977) claim that women have no essence.

We should be wary, similarily, of a theory like Foucault's where our lifeworld is constituted solely by configurations of power and conflict (although his description of the dynamic of power is most important and helpful for understanding contemporary Being).[17] His notion of power that involves domination and resistance is Friedrich Nietzsche's, whose metaphysics, I show in detail in Chapter Three, is invested with hierarchical gender biases. Indeed, it seems to me that the major reason why poststructuralism in general, despite its best intentions, reifies phallocentric metaphysics' privileging of culture over nature and the body is that French poststructuralism is essentially a neo-Nietzschean movement. Although Nietzsche's overturning of philosophical dualisms at first glance appears to resuscitate the body and the earth, his philosophy, as Heidegger has shown enacts the final and complete abandonment of the body and the earth. Rather than join in a postmodern abandonment of nature and the body and thereby contribute to the ecodestructive attitudes that dominate our world-earth-home, we should try to develop a nonfoundationalist account of nature and the body that allows for their fluidity and yet gives weight to their nonlinguistic silent presencing. In order to reconceptualize the body and nature, let me clarify in more detail the notions of nature and the body that poststructuralists find objectionable. (I will, however, deal with the problem of nature here only in a brief, provisional way since following chapters are involved with this larger task.)

The common conception of nature to which many poststructuralist feminists like Butler object, and that some other feminists rely on in their search for an original or genuine femininity, is that of a precultural ground that is fixed and unchangeable. They evoke nature as a pure original state that lies beneath our cultural selves or that once existed in a prepatriarchal historical period.[18] Butler asserts, to the contrary, that nature is not precultural but is an effect of culture and that the natural is a cultural idea, a production of a given historical discourse. Both of these positions, however, are too extreme.

If we look at the history of metaphysics, it is undeniable that our conceptions of nature have changed through the centuries. It is most significant, for example, that for the Greeks, nature as phusis was precisely that which was changeable and fluid, and it was culture or techne that evoked the eternal. In stark contrast to this early Greek conception, nature, within postmodernist feminist discourse, is understood as fixed and eternal, and it is culture that offers flexibility and change.[19] Clearly, this peculiar overturning of the relation between culture and nature is worth investigating.[20] Given the historicality of the notion of nature, however, does not mean that we must assume the presencing of nature to be purely a cultural phenomenon. On the contrary, our ontic understanding of nature has deeper ontological underpinnings that include natural and cultural determinants. We can, in fact, examine our changing historical conceptions of nature in order to better understand our present drive toward denaturalization (as I do in later chapters).

Let us now, however, turn to our discussion of the body. The prevalent conception of the body is a scientific, biological one. The body as a biological entity refers to the physical body as an external object of analysis that can be measured. From a scientific point of view, the body is defined by certain fixed anatomical features as well as by a certain genetic and hormonal makeup unique to its sex. According to the biological view, the differences between the sexes have to do with physical attributes, hormones, genes, and reproductive functioning for continuing the species.[21] A reconceptualization of the body would involve going beyond this fixed, scientifically measured body to an experiential body that included personal and social experiences that are outside biology's sphere of analysis.

How can this independent, kicking little demon inside become a sweet, vulnerable, needy newborn once out? The kicking and moving tires me out. I brace myself, try to adjust to active matter. All around, a thankless task. I have been infiltrated. My walk has changed, the way I sit, stand,

> eat, sleep, the way I breathe, the way I make love. I can't sit up straight
> at my desk for long anymore. I have to lean back on the chair to write
> over my belly, legs apart, giving my belly as much room as possible. *My
> belly?* All of a sudden it seems my belly has become too big too fast for
> me to adjust to it as mine.

Maurice Merleau-Ponty's philosophy of the body, which owes much to
Edmund Husserl's phenomenological work, offers a fresh paradigm of the
body which is lacking in feminist discussions.[22] A serious problem with the
scientific account of the body is that science distances the body, admitting
only phenomena that can be mathematized and objectified, and thereby ignores the body as it is lived by each of us. In response to the limitations of
the scientific method, the phenomenological method, as I mentioned in the
introduction, entails describing phenomena as they appear to us and are
lived by us in our experiences rather than as they objectively appear from
above and at a distance. It attempts to describe the world-earth-home that
is already there before theoretical reflection in order to reachieve for philosophy a direct and primitive contact with the world that goes on underneath our everyday attitudes.

Since feminism needs a model of the body that is not biologically fixed,
I believe Merleau-Ponty's work can lead us to some methodological and
philosophical grounding for the feminist task of describing an incarnate,
genderized body. His phenomenology of the body is far more developed
than any other and thus provides a solid beginning from which to critically
develop a feminist philosophy of the body.[23] This feminist reappropriation
of his work, however, must rework many of his notions since the neutral
human body he attempts to describe is often prejudiced in favor of the male
body.[24] Let me, then, outline a few of his main positions, for they will
demonstrate how helpful his phenomenology of the body can be for clarifying some of the difficulties involved in the present feminist debate on gender and the body that I have outlined above.

Working within a dialectical framework, Merleau-Ponty hopes to show
up the limitations of both the empiricists' denigration of the body as a passive receptor of sense data and the idealists' desregard of the body in favor
of consciousness (which the idealists claim is the truly active performer in

the constitution of phenomena). The body, he says, is a sentience that is born together with a certain existential environment. It does not just passively receive sense data but has a unique sensitivity to its environs. It genuinely experiences rather than merely records phenomena as empiricists claim, and it does this through an openness that is fundamental to its sentience. The body is actively and continually in touch with its surroundings. It is directed outside itself, inextricably entangled in existence.

In order to understand the active participation of our bodies in the constitution of our world-earth-home, let us take an example of sensuous contact such as that of looking deeply at the sky. If I fully attend to the sky, gazing up into its blue, my body gradually adopts a certain bodily attitude in response to the spacious blue. My eyes and my whole body slowly yield, relax, and enter into a sensuous rhythm of existence that is already there and that is peculiar to the sky in its blue depths. In its contact, my body adopts a ''certain living pulsation'' of the sky itself that is not its own but that it lives through and that also lives through it and becomes my body's being of the moment (pp. 214–15). My living situation becomes one of blue. I can feel the blue profundity and become immersed in it because of a bodily openness that lets the sky pulse through me and, in the same trembling stroke, lets my sensing breathe life into the blue sky. Existence realizes itself in the body because of this incarnate communion with its surroundings. I am not a passive spectator of the sky; I commune with it, or, rather, a coition takes place where the sky and myself are only abstract moments of a single incarnate communication. This bodily-skyly sensibility that tremulously runs through me and that is neither passively received nor actively willed and constituted makes me realize an ''anonymous self'' that has ''already'' sided with, and is already open to, nature and my surroundings (p. 216).

This body that is sensitive and in deep communion with its environment is not the biological object body that science describes but is the ''living body'' or the ''phenomenological body.''[25] It is not a separate physical entity in a world external to it but is of the same stuff as its environs. Nor is it in the world like an object in a container but is with the world-earth-home, oriented toward it and directed toward certain tasks as part of it. The phenomenological body is not fixed but continually emerges anew out of an ever-changing weave of relations to earth and sky, things, tasks, and other bodies. The living world, moreover, is not understood as a collection of determinate objects or as a material objective reality merely external to the body. The world-earth-home is the ever-present horizon latent in all our experiences. It is a unified field of relations present to the body as its familiar situation (p. 92).

Keeping in mind the participation of the body in the incarnate constitution of sensory experience, and this communion of body and its environs, will help ward off our inclinations to give empiricist interpretations of the body. But we have yet to deal more directly with idealist objections. An idealist would object that the intellect is the active subject of sensation here and not the body. The idealist interpretation of sensation holds that sensation takes place in the mind and the mind interprets and orders sensible matter. For Merleau-Ponty, by contrast, living bodily sensation has to be experienced and not merely thought about. It takes place within a particular situation of tasks and relations, of which the body-subject is the locus.

We are not pure minds (or pure bodies), then, but sentient beings drawn out by our tasks and relations. The crucial point Merleau-Ponty wants to make here about the idealist claims is that this sympathetic relation of our sentient body with the sensible world-earth-home is primarily a precognitive one.[26] Our minds at this level need not confer significance on phenomena. Such dominance by the mind reduces living bodily sensation to sensation that is merely thought about. My seeing the sky, for instance, becomes my thinking I see the sky. Experience shows, on the contrary, that as living bodies we are sensibly attuned to, and harmonize with, our surroundings through a "latent knowledge" that is present before any effort of our cognition (p. 20). It is not our intellectual judging that makes sentience possible but this silent, noncognitive, intimate bonding of our body with the world-earth-home. As living bodies, we are not in full cognitive possession of determinate, sensed objects but are irretrievably immersed in an ever-changing and indeterminate context of relations. We find ourselves in a field constantly filled with fleeting plays of colors, noises, and tactile feelings that nonetheless usually emerge as meaningful by means of a communication with our surroundings that is more ancient than thought (p. 254).

Given this description of the body's sympathetic relation to its surroundings, bodily *sentience* emerges as a third term and resolves the metaphysical dualism between passive matter and active spirit and between self-conscious subject and object-world. Although the body is nonrational and nonlinguistic in its communications, it nevertheless has a significance and way of ordering or *logos* of its own. As I have already argued, it is important to maintain this nonlinguistic, noncognitive *sens* or bodily meaning that some poststructuralist feminist theory neglects in its affirmation of only cultural meanings. The poststructuralist's culturally inscribed body is disembodied and lacks terrestrial weight and locatedness because, like both empiricist and idealist accounts of the body, it has left out this aspect of the body's incarnate situation.

To understand in more detail what Merleau-Ponty means by the noncognitive or nonlinguistic order of the body the poststructuralist account of the body has overlooked, let us discuss an important perceptual capacity of our bodies, namely, our ability to see things as unified. Our perceptual field is composed of unified things and spaced between things. Merleau-Ponty says that the parts of a thing are not bound together by a merely external association acquired through experience (p. 15). To see is not to experience a host of impressions accompanied by memories capable of clenching them (p. 22). Nor does a thing appear as unified because we judge it to be so according to adequate signs in the visual field (p. 35). The unity of a thing is arrived at, not by a cognitive operation of association or judgment, but by a noncognitive apprehension of immanent meanings in the sensible field.

Let us take another of his examples (p. 17). I am walking toward a ship that has run aground on a beach and is now merging into the sand. For a moment, I do not perceive the resemblances or proximities that finally come together to form a unified upper part of the ship. How is it that the figure emerges as unified from the background of sand and trees? Merleau-Ponty helpfully describes the experience by noting that at that moment when the landscape was on the point of altering, there was something imminent in the tension of the visual field. An order was about to spring upon me as a reply to questions merely latent in the landscape. Tensions run like lines of force across our visual field and breathe a secret and magic life in it for perception by exerting here and there forces of distortion, contraction, and expansion (pp. 48–49). Relationships that I first perceived start breaking apart, and new ones form, motivated by an immanent significance in the perceptual field.

Our sentient body is attuned to this life "which steals across the visual field and binds its parts together" (p. 35). It creates at a stroke the noncognitive meanings that unite clusters of relations. Or rather, it both discovers the meanings that they have and sees to it that they have meaning (p. 36). In other words, perception actively apprehends meanings inherent in sensible signs of the visual field. It does not cognitively constitute cognitive meanings but takes up perceptual meanings that are already there, latent in the background. It does this through a silent communication, a questioning that finds its echo in the perceptual horizon.

Our perceptual body is guided in its synthesis by motives in the environment. Motives are not, however, objective causes of perception because a motive is never entirely articulate and determinate, and thus perception is free to be creative in its taking up of incarnate meanings. Motives present only a practical significance that asks for bodily recognition. They are expressed as part of an open situation that asks for a certain kind of resolution (p. 71). It is always indeterminate whether the phenomenal meanings that motives hold out are released and find their echo in the body. Our phenomenological bodies, then, are not biological, fixed entities geared into and determined by a biological world but are fluid movements toward a world wherein they find indeterminate supports.

The signs offered to perception, moreover, are not separable from their significance, even theoretically, for Merleau-Ponty (p. 38). The incarnate sign does not refer to its signified but is filled with its significance (p. 161). The immanent meanings or significances inherent in the signs of the visual field are not cognitive or linguistic. We must, Merleau-Ponty points out, give *meaning* a new meaning if we are to understand these noncognitive capacities of the body that have already sided with its perceptual surroundings (pp. 146–47). We can go a long way in understanding this new meaning simply by noting that, in French, *meaning* is *sens,* which means "sense," "significance," and "direction," for the meaning of *meaning* is thereby broadened to include nonlinguistic and noncognitive meanings.

Latent sensory meanings are not discrete and closed but open and indeterminate tensions that guide our perception, give it direction, and that to be phenomenally meaning-ful must be taken up by perception.

Perception, for its part, is not in possession of fully determinate objects but is a logic lived through that cannot account for itself (p. 49). Its syntheses are always partial and of limited power, dependent on their being blended with things. When I suddenly see that there is a ship in the sand, my eyes anchor themselves on the boat, and the surroundings recede into the background. My eyes inhabit the boat, synthesizing it as a unified thing. But the boat does not thereby become a completed object, translucent to consciousness (p. 71). An object purports to be the same for everybody, valid in all times and places, and to be there in itself arrayed before consciousness. A perceived thing, however, always remains indeterminate and incomplete. Such significances remain somewhat confused; such meanings, somewhat opaque.

A thing can appear, display itself, only because of other hidden aspects of itself. A necessary aspect of our incarnate bodily situation, then, is that there is always a horizon of other things and sides of the thing that are not sensed, a background that nonetheless persists as a nonsensory presence. I sense this hidden, spatial side of things even though this sensing is not physiological. Bodily perception, moreover, is incomplete not only because it is spatially spread beyond its present focus but because it is temporal and must be untiringly reiterated in us. Our living present is always torn between a past that it takes up and a future that it projects. There is always being beyond what I sense at this moment because my incarnate existence takes place within the indeterminate horizons of space and time. This indeterminacy and ambiguity of our incarnate natural-cultural situation is crucial for understanding and reconceptualizing the nature of our body. If our existence is always indeterminate insofar as it is the process whereby the hitherto meaningless takes on meaning and, moreover, is ambiguous because the primary sensory meanings that are reached through our coexistence always have several meanings, then there can be no inflexible bodily structures that could once and for all determine our sexuality. We can never posit a single completed and explicit totality such as the binary gender division of male and female because the world-earth-home is an open and indefinite multiplicity of relationships that are of reciprocal implication and that our bodies ambiguously join (p. 71). However, even though our bodies are not fixed foundations, it does not mean that our bodies are merely cultural constructions or that gender can be entirely purged from the body. Our body is our medium for having a cultural world, indeed, for having any world at all (p. 146). It is not a fixed given untouched by the dominant representational system, but its anchorage in the world nonetheless consists of an interconnected web of relations with the human and the nonhuman, the cultural and the natural.

The poststructuralist account of the body leaves out this anonymous noncognitive cleaving of our bodies to others and things, to the general incarnate structure of the world. This nonpersonal perceptual existence that underlies and intertwines with our personal cultural lives Merleau-Ponty indeed calls a "natural" body. It runs through us, independently of us, providing the possibility of phenomenal presence (p. 165). Every perception takes place in this atmosphere of generality and is presented to us anonymously. Just as we are thrown into our mortal situation where we find ourselves already born and still alive, so are we thrown open into incarnate situations, modalities of existence already destined for a fleshy world. Just as birth and death are nonpersonal horizons, so is there a nonpersonal body, systems of anonymous functions, blind adherences to beings that I am not the cause of and for which I am not responsible (p. 216). I am connatural, with the world through no effort on my part (p. 217). This connatural body that continually finds its way into the core of our personal lives enunciates our communications to others and things. It is not, however, a firm foundation or origin in the sense of a fixed metaphysical ground that certifies but is a ground in the sense of a groundless ground, which I discussed in the previous chapter, and of an indeterminate constancy, as I have explained in this one. This ground can be easily repressed, ignored, or forgotten.

The connatural body is neither empirically nor logically prior to the cultural body but is existentially a codeterminant of the body and thus can be at least distinguished abstractly from cultural determinants. There can be no doubt that we are in communication with an inexhaustible sensory world that we do not possess and that takes place anterior to ourselves.

However, this nonpersonal self cannot be separated from its intermingling existence in things and in our personal life. This natural self cannot be separated from our cultural self except in an artificial, abstract way. It is an implication of a certain manner we all have of existing in our incarnate situation and of being involved with a field of presence that has indeterminate spatiotemporal horizons. Our connatural body is an indeterminate constancy, not an a priori closed to historical change and cultural variation but an a priori that continually opens us to them.

This fresh model of the body helps us realize, then, that we exist simultaneously in cultural and natural ways that are inextricably tangled.[27] We are always already situated in an intersubjective (and thereby already cultural), spatiotemporal, fleshy (and thereby already natural) world before we creatively adopt a personal position in it. Moreover, nothing determines us from the outside or inside, precisely because we are from the start outside ourselves, thrown open to our surroundings in a semideterminate but constant coition with things. There is, in the final analysis, only this incarnate communication, this natural-cultural momentum of existence, this "unmotivated upsurge of being" of which the body and the environment are only abstract moments (p. xiv).

We are never just a factual thing and never a bare transcendent consciousness. The world-earth-home, moreoever, is both already constituted and yet never completely constituted (p. 453). There are no immediate givens in perception because phenomena can be phenomenal only to the extent that they are internally taken up by us, melded with the body, and lived. Our human body with its habits weaves things into a human environment and into an infinite number of possible environments, eluding the simplicity of a merely physical bodily life. For example, we give new significances to motor actions in rituals and dancing. Yet, this occurs not because of purely cultural practices but because we are fleshly involved in a certain momentum of existence that is the general horizon of all horizons for our manner of being and interconnects us with all beings.[28] There is not a single human cultural configuration or form of behavior that does not owe something to natural existence, that is not bound up with the rest of the intersensory environs and lodged in the mysteries of other beings (p. 189).

Nature, then, and our natural bodies are not fixed biological totalities.

The natural body that Merleau-Ponty speaks of is an indeterminate movement toward the world-earth-home wherein it finds its support. It is a lived body that coexists with its environment, magnetizing existence and inducing a direction in it. We do not need to denaturalize gender, then, if we understand nature as an indeterminate yet intimate characteristic of our incarnate situation. Gender is not caused by a fixed anatomical and biological functionalist structure of our sexual bodies. Yet it is motivated by ambiguous, natural-cultural structures of the body, and thus we must affirm a certain continuity in the connection of gender to the body. Our human manners of existing maintain a fidelity to a certain enduring bodiliness that coheres from culture to culture without ever being identical, and yet our human existence is not an innate human essence or structure guaranteed at birth but must be constantly reforged.

It is important to realize, for example, that the body's organization though not fixed is far from being completely contingent and arbitrary. It is not that the body's experienced structure depends only on what we decide to make significant or that we can manipulate and construct it as we want. The sexual body's phenomenal organization is seen as arbitrary only if we take an abstract biological view of the body, regarding its parts as isolatable fragments of matter and ignoring their living function. On the contrary, the parts of the body, understood as phenomenological, are repeatedly integrated into a functional totality, into a distinctive way of patterning our surroundings (p. 170). Human functions are integrated into an intersensory and motor syntheses in such a way that our bodily composition maintains an indeterminate and fluid constancy. Thus, for Merleau-Ponty, everything in the human body is both a necessity and a contingency. The body's form and function are neither contingent attributes nor fixed possessions because human existence is the transformation of contingency into necessity and the dissolution of the latter into the former (p. 170). Existence has no fortuitous attributes since whatever is, is always taken up and integrated in it. It has no necessary attributes since it is that indeterminate process whereby hitherto latent meanings become phenomenally meaningful.

Our present binary gender structure is a result of the way we have taken up the indeterminate significances latent in our fleshy being and no doubt under the pressures of our traditions and institutions. It is conceivable that we could take up the ambiguous confluences of meanings latent in our sexual bodies in such a way that a gender fluidity resulted such as Butler, for example, advocates. However, such a radical reconceptualization (aided by reproductive technology) is unlikely since it would involve a denial of broad ways of our bodily being. It is an important feminist task to reconceptualize sexual difference in such a way that relations of opposition and domination within the difference are increasingly dissolved and, moreover, that this gender division no longer be used to enforce a compulsory heterosexuality. But the advocation of a gender fluidity appears to me to be a subjectivist attempt to change our general manner of existing. I have argued in company with Merleau-Ponty that nature is a codetermining force in the constitution of our bodies. A specific phenomenology of the female body must recognize and begin with this earthy significance of the body that is so quickly repressed in our ecodestructive world. The female body has its own indeterminate natural structures that noncausally motivate female ways of being in the world-earth-home. An obvious example of the non-cognitive connatural body that is often part of the female incarnate situation is what I will call the mothering body.

The female experience of pregnancy, childbirth, and breastfeeding perspicaciously shows up a female bodily wisdom and fleshy openness that intertwines with a mother's personal and cultural life. In pregnancy, a woman actively and continually responds to the fresh phusical upsurge that independently runs through her body with a life of its own. She creatively takes up the profound changes of her body, constantly readjusting her body image and weaving subtle relations to a phusical pulse that has emerged from elsewhere. Motivated by her new mothering body, she makes dramatic changes in her cultural, social, and personal life. For example, a western middle-class woman might educate herself on the details of pregnancy, childcare, and breastfeeding; make adjustments in her career and home to accommodate the newborn; change her eating and sleeping habits; wear different clothes; and make new friends with other mothers. Although a woman has much flexibility in taking up the pressing but indeterminate directives given by her mothering body, she is not like a subject in control of a growing object inside her. It becomes especially clear in pregnancy that, as Merleau-Ponty argues, the metaphysical dichotomous categories of subject and object, and self and other, fail to describe our incarnate situation, for the subject is blurred and diffused in pregnancy. A woman is inhabited by a growing sentience that is not truly other to herself.[29]

Repressing her mothering body (which is encouraged in our culture) and attempting to revert back to her familiar self, she may experience the lack of control over her rapidly changing body and the ever-more demanding growth within as frightening. At such times, however, there is a need to recall the wisdom of the mothering body that has already sided with, and is already sensitively attuned to, a phusical current entwining her flesh with that of the unborn before any of her efforts.[30] It is especially in labor that a mother needs to trust the intelligence of her connatural body. It would be difficult to find another experience where the body is so dramatically gripped by what Merleau-Ponty calls a "certain living pulsation" that is not the body's own but that it lives through and that also lives through it. The laboring mother is advised to relax as fully as possible into the natural rhythms of the contractions, thereby allowing her body to do its own profound work in preparation for the birth. It is not, however, that the laboring mother merely "lets nature take its course," for her manner of giving birth is codetermined, for example, by her individual strength and attitude, the medical institution or midwife, and her labor coaches.

> I went into labor about 3 A.M. The contractions came on immediately, hard and strong. On our fours, I breathed through each one, determined to ride out the waves of pain. Unfortunately, his head was stuck in the wrong position for birth. Timeless, dark, fleshy pain. I was no longer giving birth but losing life. The epidural saved me, after which I fiercely pushed him wrong way out, his heart stopping with every contraction.

Breastfeeding is a more visible continuation of the connatural existence of the mothering body that takes place anterior to herself. Mother and newborn together learn how to adjust to this new phusical expression. The gush of sweet milk from soft, warm flesh undifferentiated from its own is always on the horizon of the newborn's every-expanding world-earth-home. Mother's body is the constant, pleasurable flesh that helps cushion and establish the new little being in a social and cultural environment.[31]

We are living in a historical period in which, through technological advances in our information, transportation, and production systems, the cultural world has become small and accessible, and nature has shrunk to a mere standing reserve of energy, or resources awaiting human disposal. In our modern everyday lives, our sentience is attuned to things only sufficiently attentively to discover in them their familiar cultural presence but not to disclose the nonhuman element that is an essential part of the thing's presencing (Merleau-Ponty 1962, 322). Sometimes, such as when we linger in a forest or over a work of art, we glimpse this bare "that it is" of a thing, this aspect of the thing that holds itself aloof from us, transcending our experience of it (Heidegger 1971c, 65). At such times we may be struck by wonder at this upsurge of existence beyond our control. It seems to me that in our feminist attempts to change the prevailing social system by reconceptualizing sexual difference we would do well to keep trying to reflect on the wonder of our bodily situation.

> Born September 6, 1990, in unbearable pain. My heart goes out to those unknown women who died in childbirth. He suddenly appeared and is here in full presence, fully preoccupying me with his needy existence. Two weeks old and still, in a peaceful moment, I look at him in wonder, blissfully suckling my breast. *How* did this little wonder come to be?

Turning out of Despair
The Seal (The Miracle), 1924–36, by Constantine Brancusi

The Seal is immediately recognizable as a representation of seal because at first glance we see it merely through its outline. Only when we see the off-centered broad bulging of the body from which the neck rises and which the lower body stabilizes do we begin to appreciate its miraculous balance. The main gesture of *The Seal* is the slight bend of its turning toward us. If our eyes follow its delicate, strong outline, this bend is most noticeable in the thickest part of the marble back, and it is here that our vision is held. Our eye rests on this swelling, for it is surprisingly thick and has an inner intensity that emanates out and confuses our vision's common attempts to schematize its shape. As we linger here, stroking the stone with our eyes, we encounter a changing chiasm of slight nuances in its outline that disrupts our cognitive habit of judging shape and size and releases us into the simplicity of its radiating beauty.

The beauty of *The Seal* gives itself most obviously in this swelling that joins the rising of the neck and the reclining of the lower body. The swelling is not a balancing of two

movements that tend in opposite directions but, rather, emerges as a thick fullness in which, moreover, the reclining back unusually obtrudes and endures. To
see so clearly such reclining back or earthward pull is surprising in this age that
is geared toward transcendence of the earthy. The broad bulk of the lower
body is not as articulate as the narrowing neck and head. It mutely, sensuously
reclines, remaining undisturbed by the reaching-out gesture of the neck. For the
slight gesture of the head toward contact does not strain or reach beyond
the earthy weight of the lower body but participates in the overall balance of
the stone. Because of this overall balance, we are able to see *The Seal*'s thick
body resting, enduring, reclining in fullness.

The reclining back obtrudes in the full swelling not only through the meeting
of the rising neck and reclining body but also through the tension of what might
be called the inner and outer spatial horizons of *The Seal* or, to put it more
simply, *The Seal*'s inner intensity. The rounding marble shows fullness to be a
lingering in depth and holds this intensity enstoned for us to contact. When we
linger with the work's own lingering in depth, we begin to see the inner intensity of the broad, turning body and feel its radiant beauty. The marble dwells
thickly in its density, glowing a soft white. Its inner intensity is not a straining to
contain or limit an energy. It is not a pressure like that contained by a balloon,
where the artificial pressure of air is forced to press against a resistant surface foreign to it. The inner intensity is, rather, the restraint of a bountiful giving
whose radiance we see emanating from the white marble in response to light
and space, here, at the broad, slow swell. The radiance is a soft, gushing glow;
the restraint, a sheltering holding of the giving. The pure white marble of the
underbelly clearly shows the soft vulnerability of this giving-saturated-with-
restraint. This restrainful giving is like the full rounding of a mother's soft
breast, swelling painfully with its holding and, drawn out by a baby's needy cry,
already spilling white milk.

This soft vulnerability and responsiveness is lacking in our common understanding of fullness, which is taken from the scientific model of internal
pressure. We understand fullness as a storing of energy (using this model, a
mother's breast is reduced to a storage container that supplies food energy),
and giving as an unlocking of energy. Thus, we moderns understand the mysterious inner intensity of *The Seal* (its simultaneous dense holding of itself to itself and extending out, thereby making space and radiating light) at first as an

unlocking of invisible or dark, earthy energies and releasement of them into visibility and light. If we linger and make contact with the radiant fullness of *The Seal,* however, we are struck by this new sense of vulnerable holding, this simple openness to touch.

The Seal is not only open to touch but, moreover, to be touched. The fullness is thick and fleshy, like a sea creature's blubber, healthy and round, like that of a baby plump with sheltering care and the promise of its future. *The Seal's* thick rounding invites us to hug and enfold it, just as a seal is enfolded by warm ocean currents. Its seeming exposure out of water moves us to provide a certain protection and, through touching, to give a certain thickness to its milieu. *The Seal's* neck, moreover, vulnerably comes forward and begs for touch. Its neck and body appear to be leaning over to the point of falling onto one. When we stand close to it, it appears to want to lean on us, and we cannot help but want to offer it support. (This is especially evident in *The Seal* of 1943, which does not have a wedge at the bottom.)

The Seal has a certain soft fleshiness that invites a fleshy touching. It has the muscular fluidity of a seal's flesh. Yet it is not the resemblance to a seal's flesh that invites our touch but rather the marbled flesh, for the marble is fully present as marble and has not disappeared in the representational form of a seal.

The Seal is enfleshed stone. It is not that the stone-matter has been shaped into the representational form of a seal which, thereby, informs the matter, or even that the stone's otherness has become infused with human spirit. When we see Brancusi's marble vibrating throughout under our sentient gaze, we sense how his work comes to full appearance through his carving strokes and polishing caress and not, as we might have first thought in seeing the seemingly abstract, rationalized form, through conceptual idea.

But isn't the stroke or caress, though perhaps gentle, ultimately an imposition of form? Brancusi was, above all, a carver. He used clay and plaster mainly to study or sketch out his subjects before carving. For Brancusi, direct carving is a making of pathways with the hand. The hand cannot impose a form on the stone as it can with clay but must heed the stone's density and grain. It does not, moreover, merely travel over the stone in such a way that it willfully makes its own pathways; nor, on the contrary, is the hand guided solely by the marble's textures and grain, which would result in a merely well-crafted thing. Rather, it is through the contact of the sentient hand and the sensible stone

that the pathways emerge. Brancusi's movements in accordance with the originating order (arche) of his bodily being (his cultural, emotional, and spatial
being-moved) and with the originating order of the particular stone (its phusical
lines of growth) brought forth this artwork. His forms emerge as the enstone-
ment of his being-moved in touch with the stone's being-moved.

Brancusi's laborious polishing of his works is also a kind of making of pathways. This touching care slowly brings the stone's darker depths to emerge and
gleam. When we look at *The Seal,* we see the dark veins coming forth to the
surface and other veins that are deeper down. The marble is a chiasm of textures and of lights and darks. It is seething with light and movement. The stone's
movement is neither a chaotic nor a homogeneous coming forth from the deep
but an emergence along certain lines and in different intensities. The marble
here is shown to be not inert matter but a fluid stone that has participated in
and aligned itself with Brancusi's own being-moved.

Our own looking at the marble is more tactile than our usual seeing. We are
aware of our seeing as a visual stroking. Indeed, this piece, like so many of his
stone works (especially *Sculpture for the Blind*) calls for a silent, even blind
touching of the cold, smooth stone. In mutely feeling the earthy depths of the
veined marble, our very seeing is more like a groping in the thick dark than a
clear cognitive seeing of forms.

The Seal is so much about fleshy contact. In the enfleshed stone, we find
touch enstoned. The emerging depths of the stone hold up and let us encounter
the depth of mortal touching, for in touching the hard stone's depth, we are
thrown back upon ourselves and touch our touching of the impenetrable closed
deep. Our eye does not merely travel along the surface of the stone but sinks
into the density of the marble through its dark veins. The marble veins lead
us to confront the impenetrability of the stone's inner sanctity. We rest with
the emergent depths.

The Seal is a gathering, a close holding of the deep. With Giacometti, depth
is felt as a distance between mortals, as the withdrawal of touch, and as a
kind of threshold of contingency. He shows mortality as the deep in mortal
relating. With Brancusi, the self-secluding of the deep, sensed in the density
of the polished marble, also brings us to reflect on mortality. However, with
Brancusi, by contrast, mortality is celebrated as the source of our fleshy birth.
Depth is not a fearful limit that cuts off, but an origin from whence our fleshy

being springs, an origin in which we are rooted yet cannot make transparent. Our fleshy eyes embed themselves in the enfleshed stone. Embedded in the impenetrable stone, we confront the limitations of our soft flesh. This is not a frustration, however, but a joy. For the flesh of our eyes, which so fully and sensitively nestle into the darker depths of the radiant white stone, en-joys the stone. They evoke the joy of the rounding, singing stone and vibrate with the beauteous welling up.

When we walk around *The Seal,* it does not stay still like a central, fixed point but bends, twists, and changes remarkably. Its front rears up to face us and then turns away, and we slide down its back, captured by its full, round middle. We stay here with the jointure. We rest our eyes on its massive fatness and thickness. This swelling is a joining between the stretching up and out of the neck and the lying down of its body, between a skyey gesture and an earthward pull. The jointure holds both movements together. In this holding, the lying down is no mere stagnant passivity, and the stretching out is no attempt to escape the pull of the earth. The sheltering swell, rather, shows both movements as belonging together and interdependent.

The swelling joining rests in its holding. We can understand this jointure as the originating order (arche) of these two fundamental movements that belong together. The drawing forth, or turning toward, and the withdrawing that comprise *The Seal's* bodily composure are not held together by external force. Rather, the holding together itself already gives the relation of these two movements. The movements grow out of their belonging together that is the gathering swell or jointure. They draw out the twofold nature of the jointure. These two movements can be characterized in a Heideggerean way as the coming-toward into unconcealment and the withdrawing into concealment, which describes the most primordial ontological jointure that is Being itself. The jointure is not a welding together of two movements foreign to each other. It is misleading to think of it even as a rift (as Heidegger called it in "Origin of a Work of Art") or line that unites two halves. In *The Seal* we cannot make such a clear line that demarcates where the two movements join, yet we sense the gathering ordering of the movements. It is a spatial ordering that gives the two movements over to their compelling attracting *(phile)* and orients them within their own place *(topos),* in other words, within their belonging to a space.

The stretching forth and lying back are in proportion to one another and in their joining gave *The Seal*'s balanced bodily composure. *The Seal* both gestures forward and lies back in magnificent, gently beauty. ("Beauty *is* absolute balance," says Brancusi [in Giedion-Welcker 1959, 28].) There is not a point of balance in *The Seal* that gives an objectively equal prominence to the stretching forth and lying back. The balance here is not the equalization of opposing weights. Its balance lies somewhere inside its fullness, there, where it swells and slightly bends. The balance, especially of *The Seal* of 1943, is gentle and quite precarious. *The Seal* rests ever so slightly on its front chest. Its tail is tilted slightly up off the pedestal. Once we notice this lack of base, the marble seems to tilt even more precariously, to the point of nearly falling over. It barely maintains its own independent uprightness. The contingency of its balance is so evident that we feel its balance has just been achieved and may be temporary. We would expect that to stabilize its balance, making it a more permanent state, it would have to learn back more to where most of its weight is. Yet, on the contrary, it leans forward and is on the verge of toppling over, held only by the downward pull of the heavy bulk of its body.

In thinking on *The Seal*'s gathering ordering that gives balance, I am not involved merely in an interesting spatial balance of this particular form, but I am, rather, sensing a different nature of balance, of ordering, and of a system than that which I normally encounter in my everyday life. *The Seal*'s sensuous presencing speaks of an ordering or a system that need not be a force organization of unrelated parts but is a bringing together through certain lines of contact like an ecosystem. Such a relational weave allows for a continuance, an enduring of relation, or a holding together. (Our word "system" comes from the Greek *sunistema,* which literally means a standing [stema] together [sun].) An appropriate balance between parts is not, then, an objective measure of one against another but arises from a close inhabiting together.

We can also learn from thinking on balance with *The Seal* that an appropriate balanced ordering would let in contingency and not work to secure itself against what appears to be disorder in this relation of opposition. *The Seal*'s balance is so beautiful precisely because it is laced with contingency. It is not comfortably self-sustained reaching forward securely from a firm foundation, but wavers. Its leaning forward jeopardizes its grounding. Its earthy grounding is not being used as a stable foundation upon which to build. This phenomenon leads us to question our common conception of the earth as a secure, flat plane upon which we build. *The Seal*'s precarious balance shows its ground as moving, as changing, not as secured, inert matter. This ground is not the permanent, unshifting foundation upon which we build high-rises or philosophical systems but is a ground returned to its original ground: the shifting, uneven earth.

The rising and reclining movements of *The Seal* do not come out in a straight, uniform way from the jointure. There is a slight tilting or turning. *The Seal*'s body bulges to one side, and the neck tilts slightly in its rising. It is through these two broad, slow swellings of the body and neck that a most beautiful tilting or turn is held. There are many nuances that occur as we walk around *The Seal*. These bends, changes, or nuances are not superficial but come forth from deep within the stone. Nor are they highly evident, which would make them formal design features. Rather, they just barely emerge. The single, broad turn that is *The Seal* itself is one such nuance, but one that is all encompassing and most elusive.

Since we will think on this turn in more detail, it might be helpful first to describe how it occurs visually. If we walk in front of *The Seal* from left to right, we first see the pure whiteness of the marble of the left underside. We sense both the vulnerability and the weightiness of this gravity-bound, white, fleshy side. The movement of its soft, heaving weight is earthward. Then, as our eyes travel up the neck, the neck appears to twist ever so slightly to the right. As we move more to the right, we begin to see the right side of the neck and its great thickness. Now the weight is lifted up to become a tremendous swelling, welling out from the left side and resting slightly forward. *The Seal* now turns to look toward the left, and we remain facing its swelling side. As we move from left to right, it appears to totter out of balance, but when we rest our eyes on the thick bend, the joint where the balance of the turning is held, *The Seal* remains poised throughout its turn.

The slight turn that is articulated and held in stone here is more subtle than any movement that could be imagined. The miraculous subtlety lies in its sensuous gentleness and softness. This enstoned nonhuman turn brings wonder. *The Seal*'s turn is not really a gesture (the turn of the neck alone could be characterized as such) but might be more deeply understood as a wholehearted turn in one's being in the world-earth-home.

Moreover, by lingering with this sensous, wondrous turn, we could attempt to think on the nature of turning itself and muse on a possible epochal turn of Being. Being needs to turn out if its present nihilistic, life-destructive mode into a new mode that would involve, among other things, a new respect for, and responding to, nonhuman meaning, for the meaninglessness that confronts the nihilist is a result of an extreme subjectivism that recognizes only human meanings.

A turn is a specific kind of change. We tend to think of turning as a change of direction that can be plotted or represented on a graph. The turn that we sense in *The Seal,* however, helps to overcome these scientific prejudices. The turn here is neither a turning toward nor a turning back. It is not a mere change in direction but a change that occurs throughout the radiant stone. The turn only occurs either when we move around the work or it turns around on its base. This turn is not a two-dimensional curve but a bend that is multidimensional, moving up and down *The Seal*'s back and around its sides. To turn into the new is not to willfully change directions but to be released into an all-encompassing direction.

When we turn *The Seal* around on its base, we see its bending unfold from the jointure, the swelling of its belly. We do not sense a backbone, though it holds itself upright in its turning round. There is only rounding flesh open all around and a concentrated gathering-protecting of its turning round. *The Seal,* as though in water, playfully turns round and round enjoying its milieu on all sides. It joyfully dwells. It moves with pure joy, even though here *The Seal*'s currents are not those of the sea but the worldly waves of museum goers who saunter back and forth to artworks here and there.

Turning, we learn from *The Seal,* is not so much a turning *out* from one place into another but more like a turning *round,* an alteration that occurs through dwelling in one place. Likewise, it is misleading to think of Being's turn as an entering of a new utopian age, leaving old orders behind. Being's turn is perhaps more like dwelling more deeply than journeying somewhere else. Change is not ordained from above by God's will, nor from below by human willpower but happens through swelling contact, through inhabiting or living responsively. Through dwelling, a belonging-space (in Greek, *topos*) occurs, and place becomes a sheltering location or home.

The turning swell of *The Seal* tilts ever so slightly toward the earth. Its heavy, enstoned flesh settles lopsidedly earthward. Perhaps to dwell deeply is to be drawn aside to the earth. Our bodily dwelling is a swelling of relation all around, not in the sense of a geometrical sphere, but in the sense of a turning or tilting that both gives and shelters.

Most of us do not "dwell." We do not turn round in our belonging to human space and time and stay or hold our earth-home. Rather than a gathering-round, our relational movement would seem to be one of advancing upon *(fordern)* whatever we encounter. We rarely sense our belonging to the soil, to the vigorous growth of spring plants, to the rattle of dried leaves in the winter wind, to the lightening and darkening of the sky, to the babbling of infants and complaints of childhood, to the call of the white-throated sparrow. We are too busy with our lives to simply rest with another, to touch the intimacy of our morality. In this human restlessness and homelessness, other beings and entities find it difficult to find a belonging space for their nonhuman presencing.

If an appropriate dwelling of our bodily being in the world-earth-home helps bring about the turning of Being as a whole, then Being's turning rests to some extent in the relational movements of humans. However, it should not be forgotten that dwelling is essentially an openness all around and not a willful human action. *The Seal* may help us think further on this moving to be open, for the reaching forward of *The Seal*'s neck speaks of an appropriate going forward or action.

Brancusi tells us that the upward movement of *The Seal*'s neck can be seen as that of a young woman who, after a period of inner despair, turned to face the world once more. It might at first appear strange that we can think about human action through a movement that is supposedly a seal's movement. However, *The Seal*'s movement does not only express the essential movement of a seal but evokes us in our own seal-like movement. Because humans have a unique openness and a capacity flexibly to attune themselves to nonhuman others, they have broad resemblances to all other earthly creatures. We can thus see in *The Seal*'s yearning neck a resemblance to our own yearning and gesturing.

The Seal's upstretched neck comes forward to greet us, reaching out. It is a gesture in that it is a bodily articulation that has meaning for others. *The Seal* is limbless and faceless and can gesture only with its neck. The broad movement of the neck, thus, speaks with a radical simplicity. This simple movement, moreover, articulates its whole body. The gesture is not made carelessly or with only one part of the body but occurs through a moving of its entire bulk toward the new orientation. Its lower body adjusts to the reaching out of the neck and remains continuous with it. We cannot really find where the movement of the neck begins, for it appears to have emerged right out of its tail. As we have said at the outset, *The Seal*'s reaching out is not a willful action because it does not attempt to transcend earthy weight and, in fact, allows the reclining back of the earth to obtrude. *The Seal*'s going forward is a simultaneous reaching back into its inner depths, and these movements arise according to its swell, its jointure. Its going forward does not lose touch, then, with the enduring rest of the body.

   The Seal's gesture is open and friendly. It is not a soaring straight up but a leaning forward toward the world and most particularly toward others. Its face is just at the right height for contact with another face. From the front, *The Seal* flatly faces us. Its face, in fact, is sheer flat. It is reminiscent of another Brancusi sculpture, the bronze *Little Bird,* in which, when we face it, we find our own self reflected clearly on its highly polished, flat surface. The flatness of *The Seal*'s face surprises us, for we look to its face for eyes and mouth, but it is blind and voiceless. It touches the world with a startling primordial simplicity such as we might find in the simplest life form or in the newly born. The flatness of its face, so unlike the swelling rounding of its body, suggests a being up against a hard world that grinds down sensitive features. Despite its being mute and blind, *The Seal* invites us to contact it. It gestures toward us and butts up against our face. We want to press our face to its oval simplicity and touch its vulnerable facing the world.

   When we greet it with our face, we feel our own vulnerability in the intimate introduction. Its face closely outlines ours, almost too closely for comfort. Its facing the hard, complex world is joined, in this face-to-face encounter, to our facing its simple fullness, and together we form a kind of arch or bridge. We become aware of the contrast between the swelling fullness of its body and our own stiff stance, upright and closed in. Its full facing contrasts sharply with our suspicious, tentative facing; its simplicity, with our complexity. In comparison with *The Seal,* our bodies are so unfleshy and are overly articulated with heavy styles and a surplus of sedimented overt gestures. Our bodily being in the world lacks the fluid movement of *The Seal,* which moves from the swelling jointure of contact. Our affective movements are not determined by an inner intensity, integration, and equanimity but are motivated by willful desire and external stimulants that are infused with cultural standards. Such external measures, which suppress the body's own measure, are very evident in this gallery space where all but the most confined bodily movements are eyed suspiciously and are acknowledged as sophisticated signs of certain comportments. Our bodies do not reach out with the natural simplicity of the mute, face-to-face touching of *The Seal* but are held up for and against others in cold preservation.

We also become aware, in facing *The Seal,* of our own face. Expression is most complex in the face, for it is where our emotional disposition gathers. This most important public surface of our social being in the world, however, is also the most stylized and built up, not only by makeup, but by cultural, ready-made expressions (produced to a large extent nowadays by the advertising industry) that we habitually wear to suit the occasion. How would it be if social action were rooted in a whole bodily comportment, instead of being structured according to principles of power? If, in other words, dwelling through touch were the originating order of our community? In encountering *The Seal* face-to-face, I feel a need to turn my body away from the present systems that pull me and attempt to recover its integral balance.

The Seal's gesturing forward that remains continuous with its lying back and that faces the world with such simplicity teaches us of the need to stay close to the earth and body. However, when we look at the moving forward and up-ward of the neck as such and see that it does, indeed, embody, as Brancusi suggests, the sense of a woman's turning out from under the heavy weight of despair toward life, this yearning forward appears to contradict our previous intuitions of how *The Seal* lets the reclining back of the earth obtrude. The moving forward of the neck is so remarkable because the neck yearns up and forward despite its heavy weight. Doesn't one bring oneself out of despair by overcoming a negative, self-destructive pull down toward death, and isn't this pulling of oneself up the victory of the will to live? In other words, isn't the yearning forward of *The Seal* evidence of a kind of willpower, and its bulky weight indicative of a burden to be transcended? If this is so, then its turn can-not indicate the epochal turning out of Will to Power, for obviously the turn out of Will to Power cannot occur through a willful overcoming. If *The Seal* has, indeed, told us about an existential turn into a more whole bodily inhabiting, it must sensuously articulate a movement that, though forward and upward is nonetheless not willful and away from the earth. What confuses us in our thinking is precisely the prejudice that the only way to turn out of a destructive state such as that of despair is to overcome it through sheer willpower, which is a main characteristic of active spirit, and that what is overcome is a kind of earthiness (i.e., passivity, darkness, weight, and irrationality).

By returning to *The Seal*'s wonderfully protruding neck and thinking out this problem through it, we might release ourselves somewhat from the tenacious metaphysical dichotomy of spirit/nature and, moreover, offer a way of human building that is not a willing, for we in this age commonly understand willpower as the backbone of human building or action. Human doing, for us, fundamentally involves having a will (purpose, determination, or conscious intention) and though we share with all life forms a will to live, we understand human creativity to be the highest expression of the will.

To begin with, *The Seal,* as we have said, does not appear to have a backbone that holds it upright or even limbs to help support its weight. Rather, it finds its balance through its thick flesh. Its upward gesture is soft, gentle, and full because it is so continuous with its rounding body. An effort of the will, by contrast, would show a more forceful uprightness and thrusting out. *The Seal,* moreover, does not stretch forward from a firm foundation. Its broad, swelling body is lifted up at its tail and leans forward precariously, as we have said. The will, by contrast, must always move forward from a stable reserve of power. Perhaps the most significant difference, however, is that *The Seal* reaches *blindly* forward, amorphously seeking a responsive touch, as a newborn searches for its mother's nipple with the side-to-side movements of its head, or the way one might prod searchingly for one's lover's fleshy opening. This blind reaching of *The Seal* is also reminiscent of the *Little Bird's* blind reaching out from its bulging body for food. The thrusting out of the will, by contrast, must have an aim clearly in view in order to be purposeful and determined (essential characteristics of the will).

The Seal gathers itself toward contact. It is an inherent attraction toward others, toward touch, that seems to draw it out. Pulling oneself out of despair is more like this being drawn out by the need for contact, a need that reaches into the intimate depths of one's being, rather than being a matter of independent willpower. In willing, one already has the power inside oneself standing by, ready to serve the will, and the will is motivated or drawn out only in order to overcome an opposing force. *The Seal,* however, is drawn out by being drawn outside itself, seeking fleshy contact. Its fleshy face, which bespeaks of its whole body, is blindly and vulnerably seeking others. *The Seal's* turning toward others shows its deep need, a need that saturates its flesh. Flesh, which for Merleau-Ponty names Being, is saturated by the need for touch, for contact. Humans, whose fleshy being is more far reaching than any entity, have a particular need to touch and be touched. To dwell humanly, we must live in and through touch.

The Seal comes forward, begging to be touched. Its reaching is motivated by need, not willpower. Of course, we moderns understand need as a negative state of want, a lack that necessitates an overcoming and thus, in fact, as merely the accompaniment of the will. Need is understood as a kind of appetite or desire that demands fulfillment which is provided through willpower. Thus, we say that a baby finds its mother's breast through a biological will (instinct) to grow stronger, and lovers' intercoursing is merely a fulfillment of the sexual will or sex drive. In economic terms, the consumer's need creates market demand, which is then fulfilled by the producer's supply. *The Seal,* however, silently speaks of a needfulness that is not a lack. Its reaching forward is not an attempt to aggressively fulfill its need to be touched (How can touch be forced?). Its reaching forward holds up needfulness as a being open all around, as a vulnerable seeing, a gentle questioning. Such needfulness is not eradicated through touch but, on the contrary, is deepened by it.

Our touching of *The Seal's* vulnerable prodding bears on our own vulnerability. The search for immortality and stable ground that marks the Platonic-Christian tradition would seem to be a description of the western attempt to escape our deepest vulnerabilities. We attempt to secure ourselves against the changes of earth and sky, to direct our will toward independent, eternal fulfillment, and thereby to ignore the independent presence of historical emergent nature.

Our mortality gives us a unique vulnerability, a deep openness, a grav-ity. Need draws us to this human depth. *The Seal's* yearning is, indeed, a kind of laboring under great weight, as we first surmised. However, it does not strain against its earthward pull but moves with it. There is, moreover, a simple joy in its efforts that can be seen especially in its holding of itself in turning around.

Similarly to bear, to endure our own openness in the face of passing-away requires a holding of ourselves open, a cradling or sheltering of ourselves. Appropriately sheltering our human openness to death and birth is a kind of laborious joy, a giving. Recognizing our need to keep in touch with our mortality, we mortals truly build.

Chapter Three

The Will to Power and the Feminine

> Power must be analyzed as something which circulates, or rather as something which only functions in the form of a chain. It is never localized here or there, never in anybody's hands, never appropriated as a commodity or piece of wealth. Power is employed and exercised through a net-like organization. And not only do individuals circulate between its threads; they are always in the position of simultaneously undergoing and exercising this power. They are not only its inert or consenting target; they are always also the elements of its articulation.
>
> —Foucault 1980, 98

This chapter enters into the region of feminist ontology by offering a reading of Nietzsche's Will to Power as a phallocentric driving force that excludes the feminine. However I do not want to imprison all of Nietzsche in such a closure. His texts are not unambiguous. It may be that given Nietzsche's commitment to the destabilization of truth, he does not even believe in the will to power, as John Caputo (1987, 118) claims. Certainly Heidegger, whose reading of Nietzsche I am following here, can be faulted for marginalizing Nietzsche's affirmation of free play, for never seeming to hear the laughter of Zarathustra that unsettles any coherent interpretation (Caputo 1987, 291). The texts of Nietzsche and Heidegger slip out of place, burst out of their "metaphysical malic moulds" (Caputo 1987).

Because I understand the Will to Power, following Heidegger, as a possible fulfillment of western metaphysics and thereby a possible final manifestation of western Being, putting into relief the phallocentric movements of the Will to Power implicates western Being as a whole. If, moreover, western Being is phallocentric, then the exile of the feminine from western Being suggests that the feminine possesses an ontological significance for our age. Before we delve into these feminist matters, we need some background.

Can We Ascribe a Gender to Being?

One can only agree in passing that it is impossible exhaustively to represent what woman might be, given that a certain economy of represen-

tation . . . functions through a tribute to woman that is never paid or
even assessed. The whole problematic of Being has been elaborated
thanks to that loan. It is thus, in all exactitude, unrealizable to *describe
the being* of woman.

—Irigaray 1985b, 21

Only if Being itself were somehow genderized could the feminine (or the
masculine) have an ontological significance or, in other words, have a significance for the being of all living things and not be limited to the sphere
of human sexual relations.[1] Now one cannot, of course, ascribe a gender to
Being itself in a permanent sense since Being itself is always historically
contextualized. However, I suggest that, like Irigaray, Cixous, de Beauvoir, and many others, western Being could be characterized through the
notion of gender because the way it has historically shown itself in western
metaphysics reveals a consistent privileging of traditional masculine characteristics. We will see that, in fact, gender can be most perspicacious in
revealing the deep metaphysical currents of present western Being.

It is most important for readers to understand that, although I am in some
ways working toward a feminist ontology as an alternative to traditional,
male-stream ontologies that have exiled the feminine, I am not blindly
privileging traditional feminine characteristics and experience and de-
nouncing those of the traditional male. (Moreover, nor do I necessarily
associate the structure of feminine and masculine with women and men,
respectively.) I am instead letting in what has been omitted and devalued
in traditional thought as a preliminary step in working toward a nonsexist
ontology (which, as I suggest in later pages, may be a non-ontology). I am,
then, working within the boundaries of the traditional dual-gender structure
but, only in order to disrupt the hierarchical, antagonistic relation of this
sexual dynamic by giving a positive sense to that which has been regarded
as negative and diffusing the opposition between the terms. The broad
ontological movements of what I provisionally call coming-to-be and
passing-away, or rising and reclining, and which I describe as basic to the
concepts of masculine and feminine, respectively, in metaphysics, are not
meant to be fixed gender characteristics. They are instead indeterminate,
open-ended ontological structures that have developed within literary, phil-

osophical, and mythic discourse in a certain hierarchical fashion. One would expect that they could be adapted to a fresh relation and, indeed, that they might be so transformed through new relations that they themselves no longer serve as productive concepts to broadly characterize the nature of western Being. Certainly the association of each ontological movement with the masculine and feminine respectively is historical rather than essential. It is also important to emphasize that, in my view, the process of developing (i.e., going toward) a feminist ontology is backward looking, whereby the way in which particular qualities have been associated with the masculine in metaphysics and others have clustered around the feminine is put into relief. What is thereby revealed will, I hope, give indications and hints for a way toward a nongendered ontology. Like Cixous and Irigaray, I believe it is most important first to locate a space for feminine presencing by disrupting gender dualism and dualism associated with it, rather than moving immediately to a postmodern gender multiplicity. The gender multiplicity advocated by many risks repeating the same dualisms within which we are entrapped, unless it is accompanied by an explicit effort to make space for difference, and thereby break the heterosexual domination of gender that has developed through a singularity and sameness (i.e., masculine and nonmasculine).

To understand how western Being itself might be gender biased, we must discuss to some extent the nature of Being. (The following investigation is limited to the nature of specifically western Being, which, however, is currently overpowering most world cultures.) The question of Being is not merely an academic question confined to the sphere of metaphysics but is a question that raises itself in a variety of ways in those moments when we are struck by the sheer wonder of merely *being*. Such questioning of Being may be a fundamental characteristic of our human being (Heidegger 1962). This questioning might be phrased, "Why is there something rather than nothing?" "What *is* that?" or simply, "What's happening?" These questions appear to be ultimately unanswerable because they lead us to think on the enigma of Being itself. On one hand, Being seems to be the most general and the most abstract of all concepts and thus devoid of all particular content and meaning. Yet, on the other hand, the question of Being seems to be completely obvious and the fullest of concepts, since everything is involved in Being or, to some extent, *is*. All things would seem to be bound by the fact that they *are,* and thus the world-earth-home is not a mere totality of parts but is in some sense a gathered indeterminate whole.

My work makes use of Martin Heidegger's philosophy of history.[2] According to Heidegger's story, western history is a movement of Being that shows its implicit structure and dynamic most clearly in and as western metaphysics. For Heidegger, western Being was first named with the metaphysics of the early Greeks and may be ending, or fulfilling itself, in the present epoch, which is best described by the metaphysics of Nietzsche. At the birth of western philosophy, Being was understood as Phusis, which is usually translated as "nature." Being was later named, by Plato, the *Eidos* or Idea, and by Aristotle, form. Christianity took over Aristotle's metaphysics, adapting it to its conception of Being as God. Later still, the German idealists named Being Will (for example, Leibniz, Kant, and Schopenhauer) and Spirit (Hegel). At the "end" of metaphysics, Being is experienced as the Nietzschean Will to Power. Nietzsche's metaphysics, says Heidegger, marks the end of all metaphysics because it turns upside down the sensuous/supersensuous dichotomy that had essentially characterized all metaphysics, thereby exhausting the final possibility of metaphysics.

It is important to understand that, although Being has been named in different ways in the history of metaphysics, this does not mean that different philosophers have viewed the same existence in varying perspectives, for Being itself changes historically. In the history of western metaphysics, western Being can be seen to have inner movements that undergo changes over broad epochs. However, these changes are not the way various metaphysicians have conceived of Being, for Being is already, at any time, involved with all beings, including metaphysicians. It occurs over and above our knowing and doing. On one hand, metaphysicians do not dictate what is Being and, on the other hand, transhistorical Being does not determine the historical emergence of beings. Rather, Being as the historical emergence of all beings occurs through the relational matrix of humans and animals, earth and sky, in their historical spatiotemporal situations.[3]

Being has undergone various epochal transmutations, culminating in its final recurring form as Will to Power. For my purposes, I understand western Being as having a basic twofold structure, reminiscent of Phusis, the original naming of western Being, and I examine the Will to Power, the final form of western Being, in terms of this twofold structure. Phusis is the movement of life whereby emergent beings move forward into unconcealment and withdraw from unconcealment into concealment. Although these movements can be understood as manifesting themselves most clearly in the events of growth and decline and birth and death, respectively, they are to be understood as simultaneous movements that necessarily accompany each other to some extent in all movements. I am suggesting that this twofold ontological structure that has adapted to its various configurations broadly parallels the twofold clustering of gender characteristics within the West. Moreover, I argue that the Will to Power can be understood as a completed hierarchical configuration of this genderized ontological structure in which unconcealment completely dominates concealment.

For the pre-Socratic philosophers, phusis did not simply mean nature. It described the manner or way of a being, the appearance of something, and the "nature" of beings, although not in the sense of the primary substance or cause of things, which is a later development.[4] Etymologically, phusis means "growth," which thereby implies movement. The kind of movement fundamental to phusis is described by Heraclitus. He says, for example, "*Phusis* loves to hide *(kruptesthai phile)*.[5] We cannot help but find this a strange saying, since growth for us is a movement that never hides or conceals *(kruptw)* itself but, on the contrary, is continually coming forth into appearance.[6] Heraclitus, however, is here indicating an earlier understanding of the movement of Phusis as a self-unfolding that is simultaneously a rising up into unconcealment and a hiding or reclining back into the concealed. It describes the way particular beings come into being, change, and are already passing away in their very coming to be.

Readers have already been introduced to the notions of concealment and unconcealment in the discussion of metaphysical grounds in Chapter One. I pointed out that the word *truth* corresponds to the Greek word *aletheia,* which can be literally translated as unconcealment. Now we are in a position to understand this notion of unconcealment or truth in more depth.

Phusis is a twofold movement: it surges up into the unconcealment of appearance, and yet it rises out of concealment, reclining into concealment even in its rising. Rising into appearance can only rise, in fact, by bearing the reclining pull of concealment. This reclining pull, then, is the restraint of upsurgence. Reclining is not, however, a restrictive holding down of upsurgence but a protecting hold that shelters the blossoming into appearance. This reclining movement is the pull of the depths, the sheltering hold of the rising, whereas we might understand the upsurge into unconcealment as the ecstasy of the deep, a tremulous releasement from concealment. We might feel the complicity of these two movements by remaining with a being from phusis, such as a tree, and sensing its fundamental movements. On one hand, the tree soars up, extending and opening itself to the sky, and, on the other hand, it reclines back into its roots, hiding itself in the earth. It is precisely in this way that it grows and yet stays with itself. But there is no natural necessity that the growth of a tree, for example, be understood as only two movements toward earth and sky. In some cultures, there may be a multitude of movements, and they certainly may be gendered differently.

Heraclitus, in the fragment mentioned above, names this bond between rising and reclining, or unconcealing and concealing, "love" or "friendship" *(phile)*. Love is their closeness, their compelling attraction, their bending to each other, the jointure between these two different ontological movements. The two movements of concealing and unconcealing in their relation are not equalized in the sense of leveling out their differences but are conjoined through their belonging with, and difference from, one another. In the West, this relation of difference in sameness has undergone various epochal transmutations whereby the relation becomes a power struggle between two polarized forces. In western metaphysics, difference is not allowed to be *as* difference, but, rather, the one term, unconcealment, is constituted as the privileged ground by whose differentiation the other term, concealment, may be. The other of the privileged term is not given space to be itself. In our contemporary age, concealment, whose cluster of characteristics are similar to those historically associated with the feminine, is suppressed, feared, and understood as that which must be overcome and brought into the light of unconcealment. Thus, it seems to me, a pressing question for feminist philosophy is, as Luce Irigaray

(1985b, 345) in her fascinating deconstruction of Plato's myth of the cave and delineation of an act of matricide, puts it, ''How . . . can one return into the cave, the den, the Earth? Rediscover the darkness of all that has been left behind?''

Given the way gender has been constituted in metaphysics and society, the traditional gender paradigm of man and woman broadly parallels this ontological jointure. Men, in their stereotypical gender roles and culturally contextualized bodily movements tend to be more oriented to a rising forward movement belonging to unconcealment and women to a reclining movement belonging to concealment. Moreover, although appropriate relations of difference could be conceptualized as various forms of love or friendship, our very concept of love (and sexuality) tends to reify traditional heterosexual romantic love, where an obvious hierarchy is built into the gender opposition. Because sedimented heterosexual norms of love tend to dominate our conceptualization of appropriate difference, lesbian, gay, and bisexual relations have much to offer in our conceptualization of difference as such. Subversive genders not only have a freer rein to creatively transform sedimented masculine and feminine characteristics but may be more open to the quality of uncertainty, uncanniness, or let us say queerness, that saturates encounters with otherness.

This broad parallelism between traditional ontological and heterosexual structures that I am indicating is not to be taken as ahistorical and universal but thoroughly rooted in western culture and its metaphysical tradition. Even coming-to-be and passing-away should not be understood as a universal ontological structure but a historicized conceptual framework. It is important when moving in the region of ontology, which by definition is totalizing, to attempt to let in the unimagined differences of other times and cultures and, in keeping with this, to find ways of undermining the West's totalizing power.

Because of the strange parallelism between western traditional hierarchical gender division and the twofold ontological structure of western Being, gender may be most perspicacious in revealing the deep currents of western Being.[7] Thus, showing that the Will to Power is a power that thrusts forward toward pure unconcealment and is clearly characterized by Nietzsche as a masculine force (the topic of the few sections) is not to be understood as a marginal characteristic or a simple coincidence but as an important aspect of its dynamic.

Nature in Metaphysics

In order to show the phallocentrism of Nietzsche's Will to Power I will concentrate on relevant sections of two of Nietzsche's more mature and insightful works, *The Will to Power* and *Thus Spoke Zarathustra*.[8] Nietzsche's philosophy is well known as a philosophy that attempts to resuscitate the earth and the body. Thus, one would expect that, since the feminine has been identified with nature, earth, and body in western metaphysics, the Will to Power would be an ontological letting-in of the feminine. However, if we look closely at the relation of Nietzsche's metaphysics to nature, we see that Nietzsche's metaphysics, in fact, completely abandons nature as such and, at the same time, the feminine. It is most important to show the phallocentrism of the Will to Power in some detail because Nietzsche's philosophy is sometimes viewed as ultimately supporting feminist claims. One of the reasons for this is that Nietzsche's claim to resuscitate the earth and the body is taken at face value. My analysis will directly counter such views by showing the phallocentric character of the Will to Power and its destructive relations to the earth.

Nietzsche's poetic description of Zarathustra's supposed love of the earth will help us understand through metaphor how the Will to Power is phallocentric. This analysis of his philosophical metaphors will prepare us for the more difficult analysis of the Will to Power itself. But first we need to hear the story of the way nature appears in western metaphysics in order to put into relief the relation of Nietzsche's own metaphysics to nature.[9] As we recall, for the pre-Socratic philosophers, Being was named phusis, which is a simultaneous movement of unconcealing and concealing. Although phusis is a world away from the modern notion of nature, it is nonetheless connected to it and is our first western understanding of nature.

Phusis, as that which comes forth and appears in unconcealment *(aletheia)* from out of concealment cannot be distinguished from appearance or truth. However, even with the pre-Socratics (Parmenides in particular), a distinction was growing between that which truly is and that which in comparison is only apparently truth *(doxa)*. This distinction between Truth or Being and mere Appearance pushed the earlier Greek understanding of phusis into oblivion. The distinction between truth and appearance, which occurs with Plato as the opposition between the suprasensuous and the sensuous, marks the proper beginnings of metaphysical thinking. For Plato, truth is not appearance or the unconcealing-concealing sway of phusis, but, rather, truth is the unconcealment of the idea *(eidos)* which is the precondition for appearance. Phusis, through Plato, is ultimately reduced to a field of passive matter that can come into true Being only when exposed to the active, spiritual principle: the idea (*eidos* itself is transformed through Plato from its meaning as "outward aspect" to something supersensuous). Appearance now stands apart from Being and is true only insofar as it accords with the idea.

Moreover, through this emphasis on the *eidos,* thinking is no longer that which arises from phusis. Thinking is no longer a preserving of *logos* through attunement to the sway of phusis. (I discuss the intimate relation between *logos* and phusis in the final chapter of this book.) Rather, man possesses *logos* in his self-contained mind. Thinking is reduced to the penetration of the unknown by the light of reason. It reveals by ruling and setting chaotic (which now means disordered) nature in order by holding it directly in its light. Thus the light of reason becomes of greatest importance and is set off from the darkness of the concealed. The light of reason becomes the Platonic Good. In the glare of this light, nature can only appear as darkness and nothingness, whose meanings are dispensed with as mere opposites of light and Being. The bright light of the idea exposes the sensuous realm as that which has no *logos* and is in the service of the higher suprasensuous realm of ideas. Being, or the essence of everything, is no longer understood as nature but as suprasensuous. For Plato, Being is the *Eidos* or Idea; for Aristotle it is *Energeia* or Form.

The opposition between suprasensuous spirit and sensuous nature remains decisive for understanding nature in the history of metaphysics. In modern metaphysics, Being appears as Spirit. The notion of Being as Spirit is continuous with the *Eidos* in that it is unconditional, eternal, and self-affirming in comparison with conditional, transitory, sensuous nature. The human being is human insofar as he or she relates to beings in a manner that corresponds to the essence of that which truly is, now determined as spirit. As a result, nature is defined exclusively in relation to the human, the subject of spirit. Nature, then, is now objectified and represented as an impure, negative other that must be purified and conquered by the sovereign spirit. Through this process, spirit attains its essence and secures its autonomous self. If the spirit happens to look toward the otherness of nature (as in the Hegelian dialectic), it finds only itself in the other. Stability, permanence, unconditioned knowledge, representation, and purity become the general essential features of existence in this struggle for self-certainty. By contrast, the transience and contingency inherent in sensuous existence and the overwhelming immediacy of the senses, our unruly passions, and the spontaneous changes of appearance are devalued as incidental, deceptive, and inessential to Existence or Being.

Nietzsche in his metaphysics seems to come to the rescue of the sensuous realm with its passions and changing appearances by revealing that the transcendent world of spirit, which is set above sensuous being as a whole in order to determine its purpose, order, and meaning, was, in fact, collapsing. Its aim had become superfluous; its truth no longer quickened and supported life. Nietzsche recognized the impotence of that suprasensory world upheld by Christendom as God and by western metaphysics as the realm of Ideas and Spirit, declaring with his famous statement, ''God is dead.'' His philosophy claims to be the countermovement to metaphysics in that it turns metaphysics upside down. In this overturning, the suprasensory spiritual world is deposed and the sensory, earthly world is upheld as the true, genuine world. Nietzsche says that now all things of heaven and spirit are seen to have their source in the body and the earth. Human beings must be given back the courage for all their natural drives and for all those values that have been discarded—such as transience, chance, and change. The earth, for Nietzsche, is esteemed as the highest value, the richest source of power.

Zarathustra's "Love" of the Earth

It seems, then, that with Nietzsche's thinking, nature or the earth finally comes to the fore and is given its due respect. Can it be, however, that his thinking is not love of the earth at all and obscures itself in the dangerous illusion that it *does* love the earth in the most exalted and fullest manner? To examine the relation of Nietzsche's metaphysics to nature, I turn to that impassioned lover of the earth and Nietzsche's unforgettable creation: Zarathustra.

Zarathustra, who claims to serve the meaning of the earth, tells his disciples time and time again to remain faithful and true to the earth. He warns them of those "despisers of life" who speak of "otherworldly hopes" (Nietzsche [1954] 1978, 13).[10] In the passage entitled "On Immaculate Perception," Zarathustra criticizes previous thinkers, those men of pure knowledge, who loved the earth with "shame" and "a bad conscience." "Your spirit," says Zarathustra, "has been persuaded to despise the earthly; but your entrails have not been persuaded, and they are what is strongest in you" (p. 122). The metaphysical spirit wants to gaze at life at a distance like the moon. It wants to gaze on the earth without desire, to touch its beauty with eyes alone. Zarathustra criticizes this "immaculate perception of all things." "Verily," he says, "it is not as creators, procreators, and those who have joy in becoming that you love the earth" (p. 123). Zarathustra, on the contrary, as the virile creator that he is, wants to let the "river of [his] love plunge where there is no way!" (p. 84). He wants to "shoot the arrow of his longing beyond man" and "plant the seed of his highest hope" (p. 17).

We can note already the prevalence of metaphors associated with male phallus and male sexual activity in *Zarathustra* when Nietzsche is describing the relation of "man" to the earth. However, even if we forgive Nietzsche's traditional association of women with the earth and male with human being, questions remain. Has the earth, which in the metaphysics from Plato to Hegel was exposed and stripped of "her" most intimate nature and, indeed, abandoned as inessential, finally found a male lover in the figure of Zarathustra? Is it in comparison with Zarathustra's great love for the earth that previous metaphysics is characterized as having merely leered at the earth from a distance with secret lust and "moon eyes" (p. 123)? Or is it not, rather, as I suggest, his unrestrained assault on the earth that characterizes the difference? Let us listen to more of Zarathustra's teaching so that we can understand his kind of love for the earth and perhaps begin to understand what our relation to the earth has become in this modern age. Let us "test in seriousness whether [he has] crawled into the very heart of life and into the very roots of its heart" (p. 114).

At the end of part one of *Thus Spoke Zarathustra,* Zarathustra gives an important culminating speech similar to that of the prologue but now to an appropriate audience, his devoted disciples. He says to them: "Remain faithful to the earth, my brothers, with the power of your virtue. Let your gift-giving love and your knowledge serve the meaning of the earth. Thus I beg and beseech you. Do not let them fly away from earthly things and beat their wings against eternal walls. Alas, there has always been so much virtue that has flown away. Lead back to the earth the virtue that flew away, as I do—back to the body, back to life, that it may give the earth a meaning, a *human* meaning" (p. 76; emphasis added).

We have followed to some extent how the earth has undergone changes in meaning throughout history. We mentioned its original meaning as the concealing-unconcealing Phusis, its initiation to metaphysics and immediate degradation to passive matter, and its use as an object by spirit. That the earth should now be given a "human meaning" is, indeed, a strange twist. Some kind of activity and initiative is thereby thankfully restored to the earth, and yet mustn't we hesitate to call the earth "earth" if its meaning is "human"? Indeed, this transformation seems to cancel the difference between the earth and humans. How can the meaning of the earth be a human meaning?

Let us look more closely at the love described in the above passage. We learned earlier in this same speech that it is virtue which gives the earth its meaning. This virtue, moreover, is essentially power (p. 76). When this virtue is led back into the earth, then the earth is free to come into its supposedly true nature as that which wants to climb up above itself and create beyond itself. For, as we might have already guessed, according to Nietzsche, the earth's true nature is nothing other than the Will to Power which is a constant overcoming. With this bestowing virtue or power, "man" becomes a true lover of the earth. Yet, he loves the earth not by opening out in happiness to freely abide in relationship, but rather by compelling all things to come to him and into him that they may flow back from his well as gifts of his bestowing love (p. 75). The nature of this love, of this relation to difference is one that returns to itself. For feminist philosophers, this going out to the other in order to return to oneself sounds familiar. It is what Hélène Cixous (in Cixous and Clément 1986, 79) calls "the drama of the Selfsame" and is most apparent in the Hegelian dialectic.

To become a bestowing well, man must be in command of himself and the earth. The will of a lover is a will, says Zarathustra, that wants to command all things (Nietzsche [1954] 1978, 76).[11] Now this command is not simple domination, for in loving the earth, man becomes a gift and a sacrifice, venturing himself. However, this venturing of himself is only for the sake of the heightening and strengthening of *himself,* not, for instance, for the sake of opening himself to his lover, the earth. In this way of command, his will accords with the Will to Power that prevails in all beings.

This, then, is Zarathustra's love. Unlike the "emasculated leers" of the impotent mooning metaphysicians (p. 123) who gaze with benumbed will at the earth, Zarathustra, like a virile lover, takes command of the situation, penetrating the earth with his "sun-love": "Just look how it comes impatiently over the sea! Do you not feel the thirst and the hot breath of its love? It wants to suck at the sea and drink the sea's depths up to its heights: now the sea's desire rises with a thousand breasts. It *wants* to be kissed and sucked by the sun's thirst; it *wants* to become air and height and light's footpath and light itself! Truly, like the sun do I love life and all deep seas. And this I call knowledge: all that is deep shall rise up—to my height! Thus spoke Zarathustra" ([1961] 1976, 146–47).[12]

With the power of his bestowing virtue and with his commanding will, the virile Zarathustra will "plant the seed of his highest hope" deep within the fertile earth, thereby reaching his goal ([1954] 1978, 17). Zarathustra's highest hope, we learn from the prologue, is that the Overman shall be the meaning of the earth (pp. 16, 20). Can we now hear this proclamation of love as ominous, with a feeling of dread and an expectation of the worst? Such a violated earth bears in her secret womb our new and dangerous future.

Let us review what we have learned so far. The earth is loved by the commanding will. Moreover, it is power that gives the earth its meaning and this meaning is a human meaning, which Nietzsche calls the Overman. The will, power, and the Overman belong together. Their meanings flow into one another and form a circle: that "nuptial ring of rings"—eternal recurrence (p. 228). Eternal recurrence, metaphorically, is the terrifying marriage of man and earth in their transformed natures as Will to Power.

What "on earth" is happening here? Phusis as the ontological jointure of concealment and unconcealment has been radically transformed. Phusis no longer abides deep and secure within its mysterious concealment or density, freely bringing forth, but is driven to increased elevation and escalation. The silent, dark depths of the earth (a poetic way of describing concealment) are forcefully drawn up to the highest heights to become pure light. What we find happening with Nietzsche's metaphysics is that the ontological movements of concealment (movements like receiving, sheltering, holding, and reclining) are suppressed. Phusis is pushed to create beyond its limits, to overcome, expose, resist, and compel, for its character is now nothing else but Will to Power. Human beings, moreover, who take up Zarathustra's teaching do not respond to the enigmatic earth and life itself with respect. On the contrary, although Zarathustra wants to preserve the enigma of life and not impose thinkable truths on life, he teaches that one must command that "damned nimble, supple snake and slippery witch" with one's will and whip and thereby stamp a human meaning on her deep mystery (p. 226). Unlike previous suitors, Zarathustra manages to finally fathom the unfathomable mistress, Life. The romance ends with this marriage to Life, whom he renames Eternity. With Life's secret nature revealed, the earth is reduced to a flat table on which the gods play dice games, games in which mortal "men" can now participate (p. 229).

The Phallocentrism of the Will to Power

> All these interpretive modalities of the female function rigourously postulated by the pursuit of a certain game for which she will always find herself signed up without having begun to play. Set between—at least—two, or two half, men. A hinge bending according to their exchanges. A reserve supply of *negativity* sustaining the articulation of their moves, or refusals to move, in a partly fictional progress toward the mastery of power.
>
> —Irigaray 1985b, 22

Now that we are suspicious of Zarathustra's love for the earth and the planting of his seed (i.e., the Overman), thereby giving the earth a human meaning, let me continue the analysis by showing the phallocentrism of the Will to Power and the Overman. I begin by introducing the general features of Being as Will to Power.

Nietzsche's metaphysics is a description of existence as a constant becoming and overcoming: in other words, a constant rising up where the feminine reclining back is postulated as a negativity and lack of power. Everything that exists, from trees to human consciousness, says Nietzsche, seeks to grow stronger and is thus engaged in a continual struggle for more power. In every event of becoming or overcoming, there is a struggle between two elements of unequal power in which each fraction emerges with a different quantum of power (Nietzsche 1972, aph. 633). The sphere of each subject's power is, thus, continually increasing or decreasing. But it is most important to realize, and thereby avoid a common misunderstanding of Nietzsche, that an individual center of power does not selfishly gain power for itself and its own ends. Rather, in accordance with the Will to Power, it continually sacrifices all the power it has been able to command by discharging its power in overcoming a resistant and, thus, directing its power toward the furthering of Will to Power. Guided by the Will to Power, the center of the system as a whole, which is life itself, is constantly shifting, working toward the most economical arrangement of forces, and constantly wanting to surpass itself; for although its overall power remains constant, the system can always evolve into a greater potency through a more efficient establishment of power relations.

Life's power, thought Nietzsche, could be best economically managed by a new kind of humanity that would consistently, creatively, and consciously direct all power to serve the maximal enhancement, simplification, and escalation of the system's power. This humanity, which would consciously will itself in accordance with nature, now realized explicitly as Will to Power, would be the first "natural" humanity (1972, 120, 123, 124). It is this new humanity that Nietzsche calls the Overman. In order to suggest a possible understanding of this enigma, the Overman, let me put into relief Nietzsche's overturning of metaphysics and thereby describe that man of the previous metaphysics who is eventually overcome by the Overman.

As we have learned, Nietzsche recognized that the suprasensory world that was upheld by Christianity as God and by western metaphysics as Idea and Spirit was collapsing. His philosophy is a countermovement to previous metaphysics in that it overturns metaphysics: the suprasensory, spiritual world is deposed, and the sensory, natural world is seen as the highest value and the richest source of power. Now, as I have discussed, one would think that, since Nietzsche's metaphysics turns upside down the dualism between the suprasensuous and the sensuous and along with it, other traditional dualisms such as spirit/nature and mind/body, the feminine would finally come to the fore and be given its due respect since it is consistently identified with the sensuous side of metaphysical dichotomies. However, it we keep in mind that we suspect that metaphysics itself is inherently phallocentric, and if we remember that Nietzsche's countermovement to metaphysics remains intrinsically bound to metaphysics and can be seen to be, in fact, its final fulfillment, then it should not surprise us to learn that the feminine is finally ousted from even its traditional categorization as lowly nature and body, which is taken over by the masculine. With Nietzsche's metaphysics, a new, more virile form of the masculine now claims the traditionally feminine sensory realm for its own abode, redefining the now impotent suprasensory realm as feminine, or, rather, as non-masculine (i.e., since the feminine here is defined strictly in terms of the masculine rather than according to itself), and thus in terms of itself. The feminine, then, in this countermovement to previous metaphysics, is left to its own oblivion.[13] Let us now look at how Nietzsche uses the model of phallic power to describe the types of men corresponding to both the sensory and suprasensory realms.

The suprasensory realm was a "victory" of the "castrationist ideal," says Nietzsche (1972, aph. 204). This sexual description is apt because the suprasensory realm denied the source of true potency that lies in the "affects" or the natural powers of the body and the earth.[14] The man corresponding to this realm of previous metaphysics is thus described in numerous places as being "castrated," "severely mutilated," "emasculated," and "effeminate" (aph. 141, 204, 861, 951). Nietzsche notes that the man of the suprasensory realm has a "seductive charm" and a "morbid beauty" because of the "feminine sweet note" that he brings to the voice of virtue (aph. 204). It is this withering femininity *("marasmus femini-nus")* that Nietzsche saw as threatening to overrun Europe (aph. 125). He also names this emasculated man the "herd," that mediocre humanity whose will is directed toward morality, standstill, and equality.

Since the mass of humanity, still under the rule of the suprasensory realm, is characterized as being "a kind of castration of the seeking and forward-driving spirit" (1972, aph. 141) and thus as lacking true power, true power, to correspond to the model Nietzsche is using, must be phallic power. And, indeed, once one follows up on this indication, one is struck by the uncanny phallic sense of the Will to Power. It is consistently de-scribed as a kind of forward thrusting power that, through accumulation of foce, constantly seeks to overcome that which resists it by discharging its force and, thereby, gaining possession of its opponent.[15]

When Nietzsche describes how the Will to Power shows itself in the sex act as desire, it becomes even clearer that the phallus is very suited to the description of the way the Will to Power conducts itself.[16] Nietzsche directly links the increase of the feeling of power that is gained by over-coming a resistant to the feeling of pleasure achieved in the sex act (1972, aph. 699). The Will to Power is a "taking into one's service" "a great quantum of power to which one is able to give direction" (aph. 776). It ap-pears in sexual love, which, he says in the same note, is "fundamentally" "only love of one's 'instrument,' of one's 'steed,' " which "belongs to one because one is in the position to use it." Women's love, by contrast, is merely an "unbridled urge" (aph. 777). In case we have doubts, how-ever, about which sex enacts the overcoming, let us turn to another apho-rism: "For one party," Nietzsche says, "the sexual act is a symbol of unconditional submission and for the other a symbol of assent to this, a sign of taking possession" (aph. 732). In this "game of resistance and vic-tory" (aph. 699), we cannot doubt that it is the woman who offers "resis-tance" and submits. The man with his "instrument" is more suited to be the victor and take possession because he has phallic power, and Will to Power, we are beginning to understand, moves in a phallic manner.[17] Cix-ous (in Cixous and Clément 1975, 79–80) describe this "cuntditionality" of masculine desire as follows: "The good woman, therefore, is the one who 'resists' long enough for him to feel both his power over her and his

desire (I mean one who 'exists'), and not too much, to give him the pleasure of enjoying, without too many obstacles, the return to himself which
he, grown greater—reassured in his own eyes, is making.''

The feeling of power and desire to overpower that belongs to Will to
Power and appears in sexual love also appears in the artist as rapture
(rausch). The artist enacts the overcoming essential to the dynamic of Will
to Power by giving form to chaos, uniting Dionysian and Appollonian elements. In the artist, says Nietzsche (1972, aph. 852), "there must be a
feeling of plentitude, of dammed up strength," for this feeling of power,
this enhancement of force, allows the artist to form, to idealize, and to
perfect. Although women can serve as the object to be idealized and per-
fected by the artist's vision, they lack the artist forming power (aph. 804,
806, 811, 842). The only artistic impulse they have is that they "want to
please" (aph. 817).

I suggest that women are consistently characterized as weak and, at best,
serve as a mere object of resistance in Nietzsche's thinking because the
feminine lacks phallic power, with which the Will to Power is fundamentally identified. In this economy of power, the feminine, as Irigaray
(1985a) says, is understood "as lack, as fault, or flaw" (p. 89).[18] Her lot is
that of " 'atrophy' (of the sexual organ), and 'penis envy' " (p. 23). This
is not to say, however, that having an actual penis is a necessary condition for fulfilling the demands of the Will to Power. Although Nietzsche
typically assumes the inferiority of women as well as the feminine (1972,
aphs. 864, 1009), he indicates that exceptional women can join the rank of
the higher men as long as they don't attempt to "disrupt the status of
women in general" (aph. 894). Nor, of course, is having a penis a sufficient condition, since the majority of males are also in the herd mass.

Whereas the herd humanity is emasculated, having cut itself off from
its true source of power, the higher men are able to unleash gradually the
most powerful resources of the sensory realm; to take this natural, phallic
power into their service; and, thus, slowly to attain true manhood. The
higher men, as we would expect, given the phallocentrism of Will to
Power, are characterized by the typical manly traits of aggressiveness,
strength, hardness, indifference, and fearlessness (Nietzsche 1972, aph.
204). The higher men are only a bridge, however, to a still higher type of

humanity (and, moreover, I argue, a more traditionally masculine type of humanity), which Nietzsche calls the Overman. In mastering the ''affects'' or Dionysian resources of the sensory realm, the higher man does not tame or weaken them but maintains such superb Apollonian control that in the full freedom of their power they willingly obey his command like ''good servants'' (aph. 384). In the same way, the higher men would command humanity, slowly transforming it into an obedient, intelligent, consolidated mass (aph. 898, 955, 960). The higher men would consciously cultivate such a herd base not for the sake of domination or material gain but for the sake of creating the Overman.[19] Since the individual factors of the herd population would represent a minimal amount of force, such economizing of force would give rise to a tremendous stored up force, a surplus of energy within the overall system that the higher men could then consciously direct toward the service of the maximal economic management of the earth and all beings. The Overman, as Laurence Lampert (1986, 20), says, is ''an evolutionary phenomenon,'' the goal of a historic project that seeks to found a new and global people.

In aphorism 1050, Nietzsche (1972) speaks of the development of humanity in terms of gender. The ''further development of man,'' he says, is ''necessarily tied to the antagonism'' ''between the sexes'' (see also aph. 886). A distinct ranked order of power must be established between the potent masculine higher men and the weak nonmasculine or effeminate herd (aph. 861). The extreme polarization and antagonism between the masculine and the nonmasculine must be evolved further, rather than reconciled. The gulf, says Nietzsche, must be made wider and wider (aphs. 746, 886, 891, 898, 988); for the ever-widening gulf creates an ever-greater tension and an ever-greater accumulation of surplus power.[20] The human system becomes, says Nietzsche, like a ''bow with great tension'' (aph. 967), the release of which would ''give birth'' to the Overman.

In terms of gender, then, the Overman is not the reconciliation of the sexes but represents that which is higher than any reconciliation.[21] The Overman is a transcendent, absolute (in Hegel's sense) masculine that has no need to refer to even its negation for its meaning, since by restructuring everything to suit itself, it has no meaning outside itself.[22] The laughing shepherd who bites off the circle of time (Nietzsche [1954] 1978, 160; see also p. 147) overcomes all bounds and appears absolutely transparent to itself. Since, as I have argued, the higher men are consistently and purposefully characterized by Nietzsche by specifically masculine traits, the Overman establishes the masculine as the most unequivocally singular form of human existence. He represents a purified masculine humanity that, having overcome everything effeminate, including Life herself (Life is a female in *Thus Spoke Zarathustra*) is able to give birth to itself for all eternity.[23]

This dialectical movement that Nietzsche establishes between the herd and higher men is similar to the Hegelian dialectic of the subject going out to the other in order to come back to itself.[24] This "most commonplace logic of desire" is, as Hélène Cixous (in Cixous and Clément 1975) points out, both reproduced in theories of human history and "is commonly at work in our everyday banality" (p. 78). Implied in such a logic of movement and desire is that desire necessarily entails conflict and an overcoming whereby the inferior force is subsumed and destroyed. It is the inequality of forces that first triggers desire—a desire whose goal is for appropriation of the other (p. 79). In this power struggle, there is no place for difference as difference.

Thus, the phallocentric power of the Will to Power not only ontologically exiles the "other" as the feminine but is destructive to the "other" as earth and thereby to our deeper natures as human beings open to the movements of sky and earth and to the coming-to-be and passing-away of all beings.[25] Martin Heidegger (1982, 216–34) suggests that the Overman is a purified subjectivity that wills itself in the manner of Will to Power and that this anthropocentrism is already realized to some extent in this age. Today, human beings for the most part meet only themselves and their own products. Our being in the world-earth-home reduced to relations of power is not harmonious but "out of joint [*harmonia* in Greek]" (Heidegger 1976, 224). Nature is pressed toward a constant unconcealment that does not rise freely from concealment but is driven forward beyond concealment to serve in the all-encompassing, greatest possible perfection of power. As Michel Foucault (1980, 104) says, while the subjected forces are increased the forces that subject are themselves at the same time improved in their own force and efficiency. This economic perfection of power is best served

by objects that can be "counted" or calculated or, in other words, by entities that can be accounted for and fixed for the possibilities of calculation.
In this economy, nature can manifest itself only as fully transparent representations for the subject human being (see Heidegger 1974b). Devoid of
its own independent presencing, nature is transformed through technology
into a calculable storehouse that supplies power to increase the overall
economy of power. Human beings are equally caught up in this economy
of power.

If we accept this Heideggerean feminist interpretation of Nietzsche,
then we must understand the Will to Power as basic to the style of western
Being and as characteristic of the way human beings for the most part make
contact and sustain their relations to the human and nonhuman. It is the
way we tend to belong to the world and make our stand in it. Foucault, who
has done much work in showing the way power infiltrates the very modes
of our being, shows how, historically, new and more efficient economies
of power arise. From the seventeenth and eighteenth centuries, he says,
procedures and techniques were implemented that were "both much more
efficient and much less wasteful (less costly economically, less risky in
their results, less open to loopholes and resistances) than the techniques
previously employed which were based on a mixture of more or less forced
tolerances . . . and costly ostentation" (Foucault 1980, 119). It is important to see that these relations of power extend beyond the limits of the su-
perstructure called the state. They are not only out there in oppressive
institutions and government but also "in here" in our most local and concretized modes of being. As Foucault (1980) says, the state can only operate on the basis of a whole series of power networks that invest the body,
sexuality, the family, kinship, knowledge, and technology (p. 122).[26] The
growing economizing of power that Foucault describes is what Nietzsche
might have meant by the historic development of man toward the
Overman.

For Heidegger, our human being-there consists of responding caringly to
the earth and sky and its creatures, to other mortals, and to various historical directions emerging from our situation within the world-earth-home.
The Will to Power, as an overcoming and overpowering, Heidegger argues, is presenting us with the unique, deep danger that human beings will

remain oblivious to their more earthy natures as crucially responsive and response-able beings, understanding themselves only through relations of domination. The contemporary threat that Will to Power poses is all the more insidious because it is disguised as a modern technological challenge for human beings to gain command of nature as a whole, including their own natures, and thereby order, restructure, and secure everything according to anthropocentric and, I would add, androcentric needs and goals. If this were fully accomplished, Heidegger points out, human beings would respond to nothing but themselves, and moreover, through such human lack of openness, history would in some sense end. He suggests that this successful human command of the earth is what Nietzsche unwittingly meant by the ''Over-man'' (i.e., the overcoming of ''man'' who had always been bound by the earth) and that the temporality that overcomes historicity is Nietzsche's ''eternal recurrence of the same.''

Implications for a Feminist Ontology

> Therefore, the feminine must be deciphered as inter-dict: within the
> signs or between them, between the realized meanings, between the
> lines . . . and as a function of the (re)productive necessities of an inten-
> tionally phallic currency . . . a sort of inverted or negative alter ego—
> ''black'' too, like a photographic negative.
>
> —Irigaray 1985b, 22

Where are feminine kinds of presencing in this overpowering of the Will to Power? (And, moreover, where are appropriate masculine and other possible gendered presencings that emerge through difference?) I would now like to indicate some of the directions thinking with the concept of feminine might take in lieu of this analysis of Will to Power as phallocentric.

Given that anything which comes to appearance can reveal itself almost only according to the dominant western Being, which holds sway in a peculiar phallocentric way, new gender presencings cannot be free to show themselves unless Being ''turns'' out of its present manifesting.[27] Being's turn depends on the interconnected web of relations within the world-earth-home. In order for those of us who are in the grips of the Will to Power to

respond to the world-earth-home in a nondestructive way, we need to
"step back" from the current Being as Will to Power. Such stepping back,
however, can only be marginal and fraught with error, since the way in
which we relate to the currents of earth and sky and other human beings is
under the sway of Will to Power. As Foucault (1980) has shown, power
infiltrates the very modes of our being and is not simply localized in the
state apparatus and in institutions. Each of us in our very being has been
"constituted" to a large extent by relations of power, down to our gestures, discourses, and desires.[28] "Nothing in society will be changed,"
he says, "if the mechanisms of power that function outside, below and
alongside the State apparatuses on a much more minute and everyday level
are not also changed" (p. 60). However, whereas Foucault as a neo-
Nietzschean understands that the only way to end this war of relations of
power is by a "final battle" (p. 91), I would suggest that the attempt to
step back in minute, everyday, localized ways from the constituting effects
of power can already enact a change in the very nature of power itself. I
work toward such a politic and an ethic of place in the final chapter.

One way of stepping or reclining back from the Will to Power in philosophical thinking (which I believe is intimately tied to our doing and thus
is not mere cognitive reflection on a certain subject) is, like Luce Irigaray
and Hélène Cixous, to think on the absencing of the western feminine in
western metaphysics and the cultural symbolic. Resuscitating the feminine
as an absencing (rather than as a positive and previously hidden essence) in
metaphysics can help subvert and undermine the phallocentric and ecodestructive forces that guide this age. It would seem, moreover, from this
analysis of the Overman that resuscitating feminine absencing would at
least partially involve the positive project of redefining the feminine
through the effeminate or nonmasculine region revealed in metaphysics.
For example, the very attempt to open ourselves to a releasement from the
Will to Power seems to involve the "effeminate" capacities that Nietzsche
rejected as weaknesses. Fostering an understanding of the positive qualities
of dependency and need, receptivity, passivity, and responsiveness might
help release ourselves from the binding power of the age while at the same
time working toward a reconceptualization of power. Such resuscitation of
traditional female values must not become a struggle to overcome mascu-

line values even with the sorely denied nonmasculine values, for this power struggle would still be operating within a relation of opposition and power that is in complete accord with the dynamic of the Will to Power. The trick is to let the feminine show up as concealed, not to unconceal it as a hidden source of power.

The more concrete danger of this gynocentric approach, well recognized in feminist theory, is that it could simply serve to reinforce the powerlessness of women and all marginalized peoples and promote political passivism. This criticism is well-founded and weighs heavily on me. Nonetheless I find a cautious, nonessentialist, gynocentric approach to the ontological matter of phallocentric Being an important way of working toward deep social change. The absencing of the feminine and all that has been deemed "other" in western Being at least offers *the hope* of *radically* different ways of thinking and being, and of transforming our cultural notions of power, gender, and politics. Unless the coming forward of marginalized peoples into concrete positions of power is accompanied by deep transformations in the methods, concepts, and comportments of thinking and acting belonging to the dynamic of Will to Power, unless, in other words, the step forward is at the same time a step back from the power relations of domination belonging to western Will to Power, then truly alternative ways would not seem possible. But, then again, as Nancy Hartsock (1987), says, "the 'center' will obviously look different when occupied by women and men of color and white women than it does now, when occupied by white men of a certain class background" (p. 201). Hitherto "marginalized groups are less likely to mistake themselves for the universal 'man' " (p. 205). My provisional answer to the question of political backwardness in my attempt to emphasize movements back is that it is only the extent to which one's acts, attitudes, and modes of everyday living are guided by movements of overcoming that there is a need for the kind of stepping back in the various ways I describe throughout this book. Because power does not only "weigh on us as a force that says no" but "traverses and produces things," "induces pleasure, forms knowledge, produces discourse," as Foucault (1980, 119) says, there is always a need for profound self-criticality in unmasking the working of power every step of the way. The political value of the gynocentric approach is its powerlessness—the fact that gynocentric attitudes, though in danger of naivety, romanticism, and conservatism, nonetheless offer a way to radically undermine normative power. We need "to convert a form of subordination into an affirmation" (and one possible way is through "mimicry"), as Luce Irigaray says (1985a, 76). This is not a simple metaphysical reversal but a deconstructive strategy. The affirmation of what has been excluded is radically disruptive. It subverts not by a phallocentric show of power but by a persistent tugging here and there at the loose threads of any system, and letting it unravel. The heart of this difficult task, it seems to me, is to do it in such a way that in the conversion, shift, or transmutation the nature of affirming, of power, of creating, of subjectivity, and of nature itself is therewith also transformed.[29]

To move warily into the neighborhood of what I am with some regrets calling feminine presencing, we clearly need to reflect on its ontological absencing in the history of metaphysics (for what appears in metaphysics is only the phallocentrically defined effeminate). The absence of the feminine is a kind of historical hole, a historical event that can disrupt the notion of history itself. For example, as a hole or a gap in the current of history, feminine absencing puts into relief the phallocentrism of continuous historical narratives. Absence, then, is not an emptiness but a kind of concealment that may be harboring important hints for radical change. As I understand it, this notion of concealment (appropriated from Heidegger) encompasses what the history of Western thought has associated with chaos, mystery, darkness, silence, movements back, the earth and the primitive.[30]

The absencing of the feminine seems to be the "truth" of the presencing of the feminine in western metaphysics. However, although I am understanding feminine presencing as an absencing, I am not affirming Derrida's (1977) analysis of the "feminine operation" in Nietzsche as distance, non-truth, simulation, and non-essence. Let me digress for a few pages to discuss this issue.

Derrida locates three positions of value with regard to women in Nietzsche's thought. For the most part, women are condemned as a power of falsehood. Woman is a lie opposed to truth, an appearance, adornment, and surface opposed to depth. Yet in the second position of value, Nietzsche also condemns woman as a kind of truth in the form of Christianity.

The "idea" during this epoch, says Nietzsche, becomes "woman." We have already seen this association of Christianity with the effeminate and with castration in Nietzsche. However, because Derrida emphasizes the alluring operation of the feminine idea in Nietzsche, the meaning of the effeminate is seen in a positive light. The "true" world of Christian belief, unattainable for now, is transcendent, inaccessible, and seductive. Woman as the idea, says Derrida (using the Freudian notion of the phallic mother), both castrates herself and feigns castration. I suggest, on the contrary, that for Nietzsche, the idea becomes woman not because she castrates herself but because the *male* idea in the Christian epoch castrates itself and becomes effeminate; in other words, it cuts itself off from phallic power, which Nietzsche recognized as lying in the sensuous rather than the supersensuous realm. Because woman, for Nietzsche, is essentially merely a castrated male, there is no confusion as to how the idea can become woman at a certain stage in history. Indeed, Nietzsche hopes that it will regain its power, its phallic instrument, at another historical stage.

Derrida is intent on developing the "feminine operation" in his own direction of undecidability. Woman, he suggests, is the distancing of distance, the divergence of truth from itself, the operation of separating herself from herself, the suspension of truth. He locates a third Nietzschean position with regard to women that confirms his own use of "woman." Beyond the double negation, woman is affirmed in Nietzsche as the power of simulation, of art, and of Dionysius. However, Derrida does not emphasize that this association of women with art and Dionysius is scarcely to be found and, moreover, full of ambivalence. There are, indeed, in Nietzsche's writings occasional associations of women with the Dionysian (for example, Nietzsche [1968] 1977, 109–10)˙indicating a certain ambivalence to women. In previous pages I have shown the more frequent exclusion of women from the artistic process in Nietzsche's thought. I have argued that this ambivalence is a result of the fact that the sensuous realm, which came to the foreground in Nietzsche's overturning of metaphysics, maintained habitual associations with the feminine. Christine Allen (1979), who also notes this ambivalence, argues that Nietzsche resolves his ambivalence to women's creative powers (associated primarily with childbearing capacity) by confining them to a lower level of Dionysian life.

One wonders why Derrida wants to associate the undecidability of difference with the feminine. Moreover, if woman is an undecidable, escaping every will to fixity, why is Derrida quite certain that this Dionysian woman is not a feminist? And, furthermore, that a feminist is someone who wants to oppose the truth of woman to the truth of man?

But perhaps the main difference between understanding the feminine as concealment as I am doing and understanding it as a Derridean undecidable *pharmakon* (which is both remedy and poison) comes down to whether one wants to emphasize the play of concealment and unconcealment in the contextualized event of truth *(aletheia)* or the more dizzying play of difference—a continual process of the divergence of truth from itself, Heidegger, the apolcalyptic *Schwardwelder,* or Derrida, the clever urban gadfly. But at a certain point, even this difference in emphasis becomes itself undecidable (Being's concealment of its self-concealment, for example, is rather dizzying to grasp). My attempt is to keep the self-critical humility of Heidegger and the self-critical humor of Derrida in a productive tension.

As Irigaray would say (see, for example, 1985a, 159), one plus a lack does not equal two. In moving into the regioning of the feminine we do not encounter simply a subject and its negative other but more fundamentally unimagined multiple relations of difference. The story goes something like this: the masculine in its historical essencing has appeared as that which is essential and has determined that which is inessential according to itself. The masculine, as it were, has claimed both sides of the difference (i.e., the masculine and its own negation), and the feminine has disappeared in the gulf between the two sides. The feminine has seemingly allowed of its own oblivion and has disappeared in the difference, leaving, let us say, the macho masculine and the effeminate to appear opposite one another in a relation of opposition. If we are to resuscitate feminine concealment in metaphysics, it seems we must follow it to where it has fled: into the abysses of difference itself. We thereby attempt to expose the relations of power that determine the age and meditate on the nature of differences or joinings themselves. Moreover, because the feminine has been unable to appear positively in the dualistic framework of metaphysics, we must suspect, along with Irigaray and Cixous, that the feminine already involves a multiple rather than binary sexuality.

Moving into the regioning of the feminine, then, may transform the phallocentric power that grips this age to a more relational (i.e., nondominating) presencing. For it would seem from this analysis of Will to Power that whereas normative man can be delineated without reference to woman, an exploration of woman brings us directly to the nature of relationship itself. Even in our stereotypical notions of gender configurations, man commonly serves as a neutralized universal to represent the human being and humanity, whereas *woman* traditionally leads us to think on the nature of the body and sexuality (gendered relations and sociality in general), on mothering (relations with dependent others), and on the nature of the earth (relations with all growing things). It remains an exciting and important question, of course, how the traditional concepts, masculine and effeminate, would change if, in Heidegger's words, Being "turned." I think there is some truth to Irigaray's notion that a new feminine is nonconceptual: "Can anyone, can I, elaborate another, a different, concept of femininity? There is no question of another *concept* of femininity. To claim that the feminine can be expressed in the form of a concept is to allow oneself to be caught up again in a system of 'masculine' representations. . . . If it is really a matter of calling 'femininity' into question, there is still no need to elaborate another 'concept' " (Irigaray 1985a, 123). But in any case the effeminate's absencing/presencing as relationality is not a weakness, for whereas the macho masculine has dominated appearing, the muted effeminate in its dis-appearance is drawing us back to the enigmatic nature of difference itself, and to the gathered matrix of all beings in their emergence.

Thinking with the western feminine, then, in both its past (and present) traditional absence/presence and possible future transformations and dissolutions is a way of reclining back from Will to Power, from the system, and giving thought to difference itself from which all relationality springs. Such cautious thinking must itself move more backward than forward, for attempts toward evoking the feminine out of its silence as though it were a positive presence reinforce the masculine/feminine opposition and perpetuate the dangerous perception that the system is only "out there" rather than also "in here." As Biddy Martin and Chandra Mohanty (1986, 209) say, in a Foucauldian vein, " 'The system' is revealed to be not one but multiple overlapping, intersecting systems or relations that are historically constructed and recreated through everyday practices and interactions, and that implicate the individual in contradictory ways."

A reclining back into difference needs to be first experienced rather than only theoretically worked out. It is a slow holistic process that involves uprooting prejudices in one's own psyche and immediate relations and attempting to take up a steadfastly self-critical stance in even the most mundane, everyday activities. It is, perhaps, especially in our most basic bodily activities like preparing our food that self-criticality is necessary, for the effeminate has been located precisely in this traditionally (i.e., from a phallocentric perspective) unhistorical and traditionally thought-less sphere of activities. Thinking with the feminine in any case is not a heroic, deliberate quest for a liberating power but is better described as a conscious waiting that endures to remain open to otherness of all kinds (i.e., all that, along with the feminine, has been categorized as other to the male subject).[31] Revealing feminine absencing may involve ways of living and thinking that are seemingly vulnerable, backward, inefficient, use-less in the face of the progressive external ordering of the world through phallocentric and anthropocentric methods; yet it is an ontological crucial attempt to become open to nonhuman otherness.

An essential strength of the feminist movement, as many feminist theorists have realized, does not lie in the struggle for more or equal power, though such struggle must continue for the literal economic, psychological, and cultural survival of women who are seemingly universally suppressed under Eurocentric male rule. A radical strength of feminism lies in its unique potential to slightly distance itself from compulsive participation in the phallocentric dynamic that drives this age. The persistent alienation of what has been deemed other by western thinking that continues to bring such wrenching conflicts to women of all colors who are shocked into questioning what it is to be a woman in a white man's world leads us to question ever deeper the mechanisms of western power relations and their operations in the seemingly most trivial aspects of our being in the world-earth-home.

Being Moved
Mlle Pogany, 1912–33, by Constantine Brancusi

Her neck rises and turns around her
round head, which rests gently on the
swaying sweep of her folded hands.
She is composed of three interrelating
parts that are qualitatively distinct and
lean toward each other in a delicate
balance: her rising neck, her full head,
and her reclining hands. Her rising
neck and reclining hands gracefully
cross each other and form a cradle for
her full head, which rests in the crux
of their movements. The sway of her
rising neck and reclining hands gives
the stilling of her rounding head as a
mother's cradling arms stills a baby's
distress. Her oval head, however,
though harbored by her neck and
hands, yet even more deeply holds
her rising neck and reclining hands, for
its gentle rounding is the rounding
rest of their sway. Her stilling head
gathers the sway into its bending protectingly over the deep. Her head's
repose is the gathering and stilling of
their movements, and it is this essential mysterious stillness of *Mlle Pogany*
that draws me to her.

Her curving neck supports her
head in a way that is uniquely different
from her hands. It rises up and forward, bulging slightly on the upper
side, showing a long, lean muscle. It

has the massive slow turn of *The Seal*'s large body and neck. Its slow rising resembles the gentle, thick rising swell of a responsive penis. Indeed, her head and neck resemble *Princess X,* whose phallic appearance is unmistakable. Her rising, curving neck gives her bending down a noble strength, offering her strong support, as a tree's trunk holds its upper leafy boughs. Its muscular rising is a skyey movement, what I would call a western masculine movement. It reminds me of the strong steady pull of growing entities upward toward the sky and sunlight.

In following her neck down, I see a large, earthy mass of unformed marble protruding at the beginning of her neck and shoulder. Her skyey rising neck, whose polished marble stands out markedly in contrast to the rough rock, comes out of this heavy, earthy mass. The emergence of her skyey neck from an earthy heaviness may well remind readers of *The Seal,* where the rising neck emerged out of, yet remained with, the large, heavy lower body and did not try to transcend or suppress its earthiness. The difference here, of course, is that the entire lower end and the protruding mass of *Mlle Pogany*'s shoulder remain in a raw, that is, an uncarved, stone state.

How are we to understand this obtrusive natural, unworked stone? At first it seems that Brancusi leaves the stone in its natural state to show the carving process in a way similar to Michelangelo's "unfinished" works. The natural stone that is left unworked here in *Mlle Pogany* is, indeed, reminiscent of the unworked stone of Michelangelo's "prisoners in stone" (*St. Matthew,* for instance). We must, however, be careful in thinking of Michelangelo's sculptures that we do not fall into the typical metaphysical traps of matter/form, and spirit/nature dichotomies. His method of carving is commonly understood as a struggle to liberate the spiritual form that is encased in the heavy, earthy mass of stone. Such interpretations, embedded in metaphysical prejudices, can be somewhat avoided only through a prolonged being with the works themselves and thinking *through* rather than *of* them. One can discover, for instance, through lingering with Michelangelo's works, that his forms emerge along with the particular qualities of the marble and not out of it, as though he were merely freeing a figurative outline from uniform matter.

We have already learned from *The Seal* that marble for Brancusi, like Michelangelo, is not a homogeneous passive material that the artist can freely form according to his preconceived conception. The natural stone is, rather, seething with movements which integrate with Brancusi's own bodily and cultural movements in the carving process and which are, indeed, shown up by his sensitivity to the stone. Brancusi respects the stone and lets the forms emerge along with the particularities of the stone; this is, indeed, similar to Michelangelo's way of working. For both Michelangelo and Brancusi, to form is to inhabit the stone through human touch. With the unworked marble of *Mlle Pogany,* Brancusi is showing how her form has emerged in accordance with the natural stone. However, he breaks the matter/form dichotomy, and more broadly, the culture/nature dichotomy in a completely unique way.

I notice by looking carefully at where *Mlle Pogany* touches the base that the earthy mass of rock does not provide a solid, wide foundation for the polished form; rather, she is balanced on only a small part of her unformed neck and on an even smaller part of the unformed end of one arm. Because the rough marble of *Mlle Pogany* stands out so boldly, she is clearly not only a carved bust but a balanced chunk of marble rock. In other words, the standing of the marble chunk shows the marble in its own being as rock. One can see through its earthy chunkiness that the marble rock belongs primordially to the originating order of phusis (nature). This belonging to phusis, moreover, is not displaced by techne or art (by the fact of its being formed into an artifact) but, surprisingly, reveals its belonging all the more through its being made.

One senses, for example, how *Mlle Pogany* is a broken-off chunk of a larger rock cut out of the rock face of perhaps a mountain. The marble chunk, moreover, achieves its own balance through its natural (phusical) density in relation to the earth's pull and through its unique rocky features. So far, what we have encountered here is not so different from the way that Brancusi, for instance, shows the grain of the marble, which is the stone's phusical ordering, by attending to it in his carving and polishing. The relationship between phusis and techne (or nature and art) is shown up uniquely, however, when we are attentive to *Mlle Pogany*'s other balance, which is given through the artist's techne, and when we notice, moreover, this other balance's relation to the natural balance that we have just described.

Mlle Pogany's three smoothly interrelated movements of rising neck, rounding head and reclining hands, which give her overall exquisite stillness, is also a balance, a most delicate, refined balance that is quite different from the balance of the chunky, earthbound rock. We might call the balance of these three parts of the composition an aesthetic balance or, perhaps, if we sense her disposition given by the movements of the forms, a spiritual balance. Now, this aesthetic or spiritual balance, though clearly different from the earthy balance of the marble rock, since it is ordered through techne, is not in opposition to the phusical balance of *Mlle Pogany*. On the contrary, what one notices is that the rising neck, bending head, and reclining hands together remarkably shelter this natural balance of the rock; for the deep center of gravity of the marble rock that appears to be somewhere in the dark crux beneath her chin is also, at the same time, the axis where all three elements of the composition meet. This dense, impenetrable center, which secludes the rock's ownmost phusical balance, then, is surrounded by the distinct movements of her neck, head, and hands, and in their surrounding they hold this self-seclusion as their axis.

The skyey rising of her neck draws us back to its origins in the earthy mass of her shoulder which, in turn, has guided our thinking on the overall balance of *Mlle Pogany*. Her overall balance, I am saying, can be understood as an overlay of two kinds of balances or originating orders (*arche*): the balance belonging to phusis, given by the marble's earthy gravity, and the balance belonging to techne, given by the artistic integration of forms. Though these two balances are qualitatively different, they are enigmatically at the same place. *Mlle Pogany* not only shows us a wonderful adherence of natural and artistic balance but shows us a sheltering of phusis by techne.

That techne here shelters phusis shows that visual art is a techne that can still respect phusis and, thus, might show us how techne could generally work in accordance with phusis. In this techn-ological age, where modern techne works against phusis with a view to conquering it, finding a techne that could coincide with phusis is crucial. We have seen that *Mlle Pogany* lets the earthiness of the marble be in its earthiness and reveals it as such. Great art, indeed, has a way of uncannily bringing us close to a sense of the earth's own *logos* (or order), which is phusis. We have learned from *Mlle Pogany,* moreover, that letting the earth be as earth does not entail leaving it to itself but coinciding with it and sheltering it. It would seem, then, that we humans shelter the earth not by merely setting off protected wilderness regions from urban and industrial regions, in other words, separating phusical regions from technological regions, but by coinciding in our unique human way (which is precisely that of techne) with the way of phusis. What such coincidence with and sheltering of phusis by techne could be in this age is a difficult but essential question that involves the place of humans in the world-earth-home. Since the present relations of humans to the earth are undoubtedly ecodestructive, it is important to understand how our dwelling on the earth might change to become more ecoconscious. To offer concrete advice for building a new world order, of course, would not only be presumptuous and highly speculative but would already assume that the world-earth-home lay solely in our human hands, rather than being an intertwining or dance of human and nonhuman elements. Nonetheless, through the presencing of *Mlle Pogany,* we can perhaps learn a little more about sheltering, which is a techne that is in accordance with phusis. It is a techne that I call, in Chapter Six, a cultivating or ecoconscious-building, in contrast to the phallocentric modern techne that dominates our technological era. We are now learning that this sheltering techne speaks of a gathering, sheltering stillness. Keeping this in mind, let us turn our attention to *Mlle Pogany*'s hands.

Her hands' supporting of her head is quite different from that of her rising neck, even though it forms with her neck the same crux upon which her head is cradled. Her head rests against her hands as we might do when we lie down to sleep and comfortingly let our hands pillow our heavy heads. Whereas her muscular neck provides strong support for her bending head, her hands' touching of her head is so gentle that her hands seem to accompany rather than physically support her head. She does not lean against one hand's open palm, as one might at first expect, for there are actually two hands that are directly pressed toward each other with open palms like the two that are one in Brancusi's *The Kiss*. Together in their resting against each other, they rest against her soft cheek. They do not touch her head directly, then, but rather the back of one hand rests against her cheek and the fingertips of the other hand, in overlapping its partner, incidentally touch her ear. However, though they are directly and fully touching each other, her hands are, nonetheless, guided in their reclining way by the rounding of her head. In this rounding of themselves to her head, we see that through their intimacy toward each other they together caress her soft cheek. *Mlle Pogany* is full of care in her grave gazing into the depths. The caressing hands are also full of care. They freely give sensuous and emotional support (in contrast to the more structural support given by her rising neck), bringing a softness and warmth to her grave demeanor. They touch her, not to take on the weight of her burden, but only to caress her head in a comforting way, to endure with her in her seeming sorrow.

Mlle Pogany's hands touch her caringly, and they delicately steady her contact with the deep. Their sensuous tenderness, however, contrasts starkly with the inexplicable tenderness of her own touching of the deep that wells up in the swelling of her eyes. In her hands' careful caress of her compassionate gaze there is a familiar human quality present, but her swelling eyes, which bulge and glow so mysteriously, are inhuman. Her Buddha-like gaze is farseeing and longlasting; the touch of her hands, close and immediate. Whereas the slight, soft touching of her head by her hands suggests mortal contingency, her enduring absorbtion in the deep indicates a nonhuman, immortal touching. Of course, *Mlle Pogany* herself is not an immortal, such as, for instance, a Greek cult statue in a temple where the early Greeks would gather to contact their goddesses and gods. Nonetheless, her still, farseeing gaze emanates a quality that one recognizes as distinctly spiritual and goddesslike. Thus, while her hands' touching of her head speaks of what is deeply human, her head's touching of the deep, by contrast, emanates an immortal meaning.

For the later Heidegger, Being is a dance of fourfolded Being, an interlacing of earth and sky, and what he called mortals and immortals or emergent history. Heidegger never explained his later notion of fourfolded Being in the manner of rational thought but, rather, turned to descriptive poetic prose to express his meaning. Thus, his later attempt to describe Being in a way that steps back from metaphysics has remained open, enigmatic, and undeveloped. We might meditate on the more puzzling relation between the two elements of Heidegger's fourfold (mortals and immortals) through the sensuous presence of *Mlle Pogany*. However, because Heidegger's concept of the immortals is too embedded in Christian prejudices, I will, when useful, refer to this element of the fourfold as historical-phusical emergence, which retains Heidegger's meaning without the supersensuous connotations. The relation of humans to the immortals is so enigmatic to some extent because anything nonhuman is itself so mysterious to us and, moreover, is dominated by humans in this age. In prehistory the immortals were often understood as variations of the Great Goddess; in ancient Greece they were the gods and goddesses of the patriarchal Olympiad; in Christianity, they are represented by the equally patriarchal God the Father and his Son, Jesus Christ. What our relationship to nonhuman emergence would be in a new world order is most hidden. Therefore, I follow up the general indications given by *Mlle Pogany* about the relationship of the mortals and the immortals with caution, but even in taking such care, I may well fall into error.

Mlle Pogany is thoroughly absorbed in the deep; yet she bends slightly to her hands' offering of a resting place. She appears to be listening to her hands full of mortal care, for the tip of her hands comes up and completely covers her one ear. She swells not only from the deep into which she gazes but also from this inner depth, which she listens to compassionately. We do, indeed, sense in the hands a capacity for a kind of speaking. The hands can articulate meaning (and in sign language this is explicitly conceptual meaning) through a wide range of complex movement. Their gestural dance is always an explicit touching of the world, a being-moved through their involvement in the world-earth-home, unlike linguistic speaking, which hides its embodiedness by directing us to the conceptual meanings signified. The hands of *Mlle Pogany,* however, are not currently engaged in a complex dancing but are layered on top of each other like the feathers of a wing pressed close to the body. They are not so much speaking hands as soft, fleshy hands. We see their complex speaking coming to a rest like a fluttering autumn leaf gently wafting to the earth. Her hands sway, resting against each other. Together they manifest a single gesture of simple fleshy touch like Brancusi's *Kiss*. They are not so much two hands touching each other but are more like a single sway, a single intercoursing.

Her hands manifest the simplicity of mortals touching each other, and it is this mortal, fleshy touching that *Mlle Pogany* appears to touch in her gentle listening to her hands. *Mlle Pogany*'s delicate hands pressed toward each other speak of humans who are mortal through their being-toward each other. A last human being surrounded by all that is nonhuman would no longer be mortal, for she would no longer be toward other mortals. We learn from *Mlle Pogany* that humans are sustained as mortal through their resting caringly against each other. This being caringly toward, moreover, is shown here in her resting hands as fundamentally nonlinguistic and fleshy, as touch. *Mlle Pogany*'s hands tell us that human caring touch informs every speaking of humans, from meaning-laden gestures to linguistic speaking. In other words, human communication is most primordially a fleshy communing.

Touch, however, is not to be understood scientifically as the physical impact of one object on another, nor is it restricted to a subjective feeling of another. Being touched and touching need to be understood here in a broad existential, and *psyche* (meaning breath), phusical sense. In touching each other, humans remain in touch with their own mortality (the phusical realm of birth, health, and death). Touching is a giving and a holding whose originating order is from phusis rather than from techne (as are artifacts). Yet for humans, touching always involves human techne, for we are essentially makers and builders. We build, however, through being in touch (from "making" love to building a civilization).

The hands of *Mlle Pogany,* in their intimate turning toward each other, do not only contact each other but, at the same time, touch the sheltering care of her immortal gaze that shelters the deep. They join with her gaze into the deep through their own sheltering care of her gaze. This subtle touching suggests that humans not only contact each other but that they contact the historical-phusical emergence through the intimacy of their mortal being with other mortals and through their sheltering care of the deep. In lending a hand to one another, humans are handed over to their emergent pathways. Contrary to our usual phallocentric notion that the movers of western history are only those who venture independently and courageously into the deep like traditional male knights in shining armor, *Mlle Pogany* shows us that history can also be moved by those who simply provide a restful space for contact with the unfathomable.

If humans contact the immortals through their gathering communion with each other, then, so too, the immortals come to inhabit those places where humans gather and contact each other. The immortals instill themselves in the vicinity of mortal crossroads of communication, that is, marketplaces, crossroads, temples and hearths. The immortals' enduring gaze into the deep, conversely, rests on humans' openness to the nonhuman. As in many Greek and Christian stories, myths, and fairy tales, the immortals often depend on the invitation of humans who welcome them as into a home in which to rest and feel a belonging.

Mlle Pogany's gentle hands offer a resting place for the welling up of her thinking into the deep and hold her thoughts in swelling stillness. It is as though care is needed by the immortals because it offers an abode, a resting place, through which they can vibrate with the deep.

Her hands hold her contemplation, not *up* as though on firm foundations, but through a kind of sideways gentle sway that crosses over her thick rising of the neck and helps her head rest back into her rising neck. Though both her neck and hands form a kind of cradling sway for her rounding head, the swaying movement itself is seen most clearly in her reclining, caressing hands. Her hands recline gently together, swaying in their caress of her cheek like a softly falling leaf in the wind. This sway is a rocking, nurturing sway, the sway of human caring. Her swaying mortal hands are a kind of intermediary between her head and the deep, for their gentle, slight holding of the side of her head in its pull down lightly cushions her immortal touching of the deep.

This gentle support is like that of caryatids (and of Greek temple pillars in general) who gently hold up and cushion the pediments upon which the Greek immortals are depicted. The many folds in their dress (which are like the fluting of Doric and Ionic columns), the noble gentle gaze, and the way they easefully bear the sheltering roof by means of their head and one swaying hip that comes out to the side gives their supporting a kind of (traditional) feminine softness. They offer gentle, caring support with their contingent bodies. The swaying caryatids, like the mortal hands of *Mlle Pogany*, are an intermediary between the immortals, who come from the deep of the sky and who alight on the temple pediment, and the heavy, deep earth below.

Mlle Pogany's hands show human beings as those who caringly touch. That humans are shown to be essentially about touching and holding is foreign to us, for we are accustomed to distinguish humans from other life forms almost exclusively through their capacity to reason, which through Plato became the essential characteristic of techne. Our reliance on rationality as the defining characteristic of the human being, however, reflects western and androcentric prejudices. As some feminist research has shown, supposedly universal human traits, such as the way we understand reason, are, in fact, biased in favor of the masculine. *Mlle Pogany,* however, shows humans in their more feminine aspect (or at least nonphallocentric aspect), as caring, touching participants in the world-earth-home. This touching care of humans, this mortal sheltering, is a kind of techne, a "nurturing building" that is in keeping with phusis.

Mlle Pogany is deeply involved, deep in thought, deep in feeling. When I look at her, I am faced with her forehead and cannot look directly into her eyes. The flatness of her forehead and her smooth round head give me the impenetrability of her thoughts, which seem to be absorbed in origins. She holds to herself, and those who look at her are held off. Thus my eyes slip around her smooth rounding. I cannot penetrate her private wisdom held by her rounding head. Its dense simplicity blocks my thoughtful gaze, and I slide round the rounding. However, when I look down at the softly swelling eyes, they hold me. They do not hold because they are looking at me, for they are oblivious to anyone's gaze. Nor can I see what she sees. (In the bronze *Mlle Pogany,* if one looks into her eyes, one sees only oneself reflected.) Rather, I am held because I can feel her gazing into the depths. Though I cannot touch the abyssal depths directly as she can, I can touch her touching of them. Like the gentle caress of her hands, which share in her gaze an almost incidental way, my own eyes touch her deeply open gaze. She is approachable despite her farseeing divine look because of the gentle touching of her soft cheeks by her hands, for I recognize and can empathize with this familiar gesture of her hands, expressing simple human care. The touching of her hands manifest my own eyes' caress of her touching of depths beyond my comprehension. I can feel intimate with her, though I cannot see what she sees, and I can come near her in her communion with the deep, though I cannot enter her communion and penetrate the deep.

Let me now turn from her delicate, restrained hands, which hold her tender gaze, to this head, which bends over the deep. Perhaps what strikes one most forcefully is *Mlle Pogany*'s gathered stillness. We have discussed how *Mlle Pogany*'s hands gently hold her head and accompany its still repose. Now her head, for its part, *stills* the trembling sway of her hands. This stillness of her head, moreover, which tends over the deep, portends an inexplicably deeper gathering stillness, which lies in an unfathomable abyss.

Mlle Pogany's sheltering care of this deeper stillness is revealed by her own gathered stillness, by her composure. It is evident that she is in contact with depths and holds what she touches close to herself. Her stillness is not the stopping of movement or the equalization of opposing forces. It is not the aftermath of activity or the potential for future movement. Rather, it is the gathered concentration of movement in the sense of Aristotle's *en-tel-echeia* (which, literally translated, is "the having-of-itself-in-its-end"). It is not a stagnant stillness but intensely alive, not flat and empty but well rounded and full. Gathering stillness is the sheltering care of abyssal depths. It depends on the deep of earth and sky, on the caring sway of mortal feeling and building, and on the immortals who gaze into and shelter the deep in their own enduring way. What is the nature of this sheltering, enduring gaze that bends to the deep?

Mlle Pogany's luminescent, white round head glows thickly, opaquely, like a full moon. The polished marble shines. She gazes down toward the earth intimately tied to what she muses over, yet distant from it. Her eyes swell from the drawing pull of the earthy deep. Her head's fullness holds, shelters, and draws back into an inner depth in the deep recess below her chin. She is a moon goddess swelling from the holding of the earth's depths.

The bending down of her round, moonlike head is not a falling down. It is not that the strong rising of her neck begins to falter and goes limp at her head, for her head is not the culmination of the rising but, rather, bends with strength from a compelling pull toward the earth. Her head does not grow out of her neck in the way that her neck, for instance, grows out of and stays with the earthy, unformed mass of her shoulder. Her head seems to have a life of its own. Her still, round head is so full in its presence that her neck's holding of it and her hands touching of it appear somewhat incidental; indeed, she is so absorbed in contemplation that she seems oblivious to her hands. Her neck and hands attend to her rounding head, but her rounding head and swelling eyes attend to the depths.

Mlle Pogany, then, moons over the deep in blissful belonging. The deep glows luminescent in her uncanny swelling eyes. She touches what is far away and brings it near for us to contact. However, the deep is not revealed or brought near in such a way that its depth is canceled. The deep remains deep in her contact with it; she does not expose the dark deep to broad daylight but, like the moon, is drawn to and reveals the earthy otherness through her soft glow. To moon over another commonly means that one's emotions are weightily drawn toward the other, rendering one listless and aimless. It has negative connotations because of the lack of aim and will. *Mlle Pogany*'s bending over the deep is, indeed, a kind of mooning, for it is not motivated through a will of her own but clearly through a drawing pull toward the deep. However, it is precisely this passive being-moved which *Mlle Pogany* holds so quietly that is of vital importance for this age of Will to Power. In mooning over the deep, she holds the drawing pull for us to sense. In her gazing longingly, lovingly, sadly toward the deep, I see the pull of the deep sky's deep belonging to the deep earth.

Guided by *Mlle Pogany*, let us think through this moonlike, passive contacting, which is in truth an active holding or sheltering. (I will retain the concepts *passivity* and *activity* even though they are sedimented metaphysical dichotomies or relations of opposition that I work to disperse, since my thinking, though hoping to undermine metaphysics, must nonetheless work with its concepts until they yield to a new naming.)

Mlle Pogany sees much but says little. If she can be said to be speaking, it is sensuously with her eyes. They swell and hold in place a feeling contact. Her eyes are wide open, unfocused, and bulging. They swell recliningly, pregnant with the deep. Her mouth, by contrast, is small and closed. The only sound she might make is a soft humming that would stay in her throat. Her whisper of a mouth withdraws with her chin into her neck. She with*holds* words. Her silence is not a mere refusal to speak, however, but harbors and shelters words. Words, perhaps, come too quickly to us. Our words tend to lay bare. We forget that true words come from this silent deep, this swelling round. Words are not originally mere signs commanding, directed forward, stripped of concealment.

Mlle Pogany listens and touches what she hears. Words have not yet been born. There is only this rounding, stilling swell. And roundness stills, shelters.

Mlle Pogany's relation to the deep, we have said, is that of a passive being-moved. She listens rather than speaks; she holds the deep and does not expose it. She can be pulled in this way precisely because of her softness, her capacity to yield and receive another. Passively being moved, yielding, and receiving are movements that have been traditionally aligned with the feminine and traditionally degraded. Looking at *Mlle Pogany*'s inexplicable shining softness, one is shown that so-called feminine yielding is not a submissive giving way to a conqueror but is a human way that gives. In other words, it is a path or way that involves a certain kind of giving to an other.

In *Thus Spoke Zarathustra,* Nietzsche ([1961] 1976, 101), understands giving as essentially power over an other. As I discuss in Chapter Three, it is a creative act of bestowal like that of the sun's overflowing light (a metaphor that Nietzsche uses), but one that is overpowering. *Mlle Pogany*'s giving, on the contrary, is now a power that emanates from her but is rather a releasing of herself in accordance to another's rhythm. She releases herself not by falling into the other, away from herself, but by feeling outside herself and following through the other along the lines of contact. She empathetically releases herself into the attracting pull. Such yielding or giving of herself happens through her steadfast remaining in empathy, in feeling contact with otherness.

This "other" human way or path is not valued as a way because it does not have a clear aim in view—and is thus aimless, or in other words, meaningless and unproductive. It moreover appears to be a momentary experience rather than a way, or method proper, which has certain steps that can be passed down and repeated (i.e., a techne as Aristotle defines it in the opening book of his *Metaphysics*). But perhaps most important, such opening of oneself to an other is completely alien to this culture, which is geared toward protecting itself against, and conquering, otherness. Otherness in the history of western metaphysics has been understood as an opposition to the subject itself. It is the in-itself that mysteriously holds to itself in the light of the known, transparent self. Traditionally, we westerners have felt threatened by the unpredictability of otherness, variously naming it chaos opposed to order; nature opposed to culture; and irrationality, unconsciousness, and darkness opposed to rationality, consciousness and light. We have worked to conquer otherness in order to feel "at home" in the world. Might we perhaps learn about a different mode of relation with otherness through this way that gives, and about a different way of being at home?

Mlle Pogany, in her musing over the deep, welcomes otherness. She goes outside herself and is absorbed in it. She lets it into herself, absorbing it. She rests in a quiet ecstasy.

There was a time when female *ecstasis* was understood as a way of contacting the mysterious otherness. The incoherent ecstatic voicings of women who entered the Korykeion cave of Mount Parnassus, for instance, are the ancient historical source of the Delphic Oracle. As the myth says, Apollo, the god of reason and of the sun, took over the oracle by killing the chthonic Pythia who dwelt in the Korykeion cave. Although women still gave oracle in Apollo's temple at Delphi, now their inarticulate ecstatic cries, supposedly induced by fumes from a stream flowing under the temple from Mount Parnassus, were interpreted by a politically powerful Delphic priesthood and translated into hexameter verse. Through this political priestly control, the oracle lost its meaning and was rapidly reduced to a mere instrument of power politics.

Mlle Pogany absorbs and holds, stilledly swelling from contact. She is pregnant with the deep, which means its otherness remains other, even as she holds, shelters, and nurtures it deep within her, and indeed, otherness remains other precisely because of this deep sheltering. It is thus unlike Hegel's *Aufhebung,* where what is useful in otherness is absorbed by Spirit, but cannot maintain its otherness in the absorption.

Though *Mlle Pogany* is outside herself, absorbed in the deep and given over to it, at the same time, she is wrapped roundly with herself in gentle intimacy. She has not lost herself in the other but holds to herself even in her holding. Her intimate self-holding and privacy are startlingly clear. We are self-conscious in looking at her, for our gaze feels intrusive of her privacy. Her openness to the deep is neither an exposure of the deep, then, nor an exposure of herself. It is not, however, that she avoids exposure by protecting herself from otherness that is, by staying back from it or concealing herself from it. She is open, intimately, passionately open. She is compassionately full with the deep and is pulled out of herself by it; yet, at the same time, she is complete in herself. This gentle diffusion of her being inside and outside is like the intimacy that occurs in the intercoursing of lovers, where they give themselves yet find themselves in the giving; or like a mother, who not knowing whether she sings for the sake of her sleeping baby or for herself, remains humming lullabies, caught up in the sleepy sway.

Mlle Pogany muses. She contemplates the deep like Brancusi's *Muse* and *Sleeping Muse*. Her head is round and large and looks bald even though she has a hairline. Her swelling eyes are Buddhalike, and her bending head and retreating small mouth give her a humble, wise appearance. She has a peaceful inner strength, a quiet wisdom. Her egg-shaped head hangs ponderously over an abyss. She is thinking, but not with a furrowed brow. She is not figuring out a problem, not looking for solutions, remedies, conclusions. Her wisdom is not that of exact scientific knowledge, which predicts and produces formulas. It is not a Cartesian cogito which produces "clear and distinct" ideas. Her thinking is so diffused it lacks words and images (though this is not an actual lack but, as I have discussed previously, a way of holding and sheltering that which has yet to be born as words). She thinks passively, diffusely through a yielding absorbtion. She is concentrating on the deep but not in a willful directedness. Rather, she is drawn that way. She does not think on the deep so much as think along the same lines as it.

If we look into her swelling eyes, her thinking, seeing, and feeling into the deep seem diffusely fused. She muses in a cognitive-emotional-perceptual twilight. Vision and thought here are not focused on an object but are immersed in feeling otherness. Her thinking is saturated with feeling. She communes, vibrates with the fullness. She pulsates in the contact, like snakes copulating. Such communing is not only a way of emotionally contacting the deep but is shown here as a way of thoughtfully contacting it. In this thoughtful contact, her thoughts are hardly her own; she provides a place for their emergence through contact. This meditative communion, which has no aim in view and which is not even in possession of its own thoughts, is more vital ontologically than all our computations (from the Latin *putare:* pure, clear), for it is a phusical thinking, a thinking that remains continuous with the e-motions of the body and the movements of the earth.

The *Mlle Pogany* we have been thinking through is the first *Mlle Pogany,* which was made in 1912. In 1913, Brancusi made four bronzes of this first *Mlle Pogany,* keeping essentially the same form as the marble but working the metal in each one quite differently. In 1919, Brancusi did a second version of *Mlle Pogany* in marble, and the following year he made four bronzes of this second version. Now in this second version, *Mlle Pogany* is noticeably changed. She has become more abstract, stylized, and has a hard, impersonal look. Nearly twenty years after the first *Mlle Pogany*, Brancusi made a third version in marble and later, in 1933, cast two bronzes of it. *Mlle Pogany III* continues even further along the path that *Mlle Pogany II* had taken. To conclude this meditation on *Mlle Pogany*, it seems appropriate to turn to the last *Mlle Pogany* of 1933, for her startling transformation bears on my previous understanding of the earlier *Mlle Pogany*. But before turning to the later work, I would like to bring to the fore an aspect of *Mlle Pogany* that gathers many of the themes I have been discussing and that perhaps constitutes the most significant overall change in the later *Mlle Pogany*.

If we linger with the early *Mlle Pogany*, what likely strikes us above all is her compassion. Her twilight meditations are enfolded in a compassionate bliss. She gazes with swelling eyes, which are fleshy, vulnerable, welling with compassion, like a mother gazing upon her troubled infant. The lower portion of her eyes merges into her cheeks, and some of the marble veins flow down from her eyes like tears. In the early bronze, reflected people walking by slide down from the outside corners of her eyes and run down her cheeks. Her sorrow is not a dramatic pain, such as the penetrating pain of sudden loss, but an enduring, diffused pain. Compassion is a twilight emotion. She is pulled gravely down through empathy. Her enduring softness is almost too vulnerable. What is it that she endures with such tender vulnerability, hears and sees with such compassion?

I have described the intimacy of *Mlle Pogany*'s mortal hands, which accompany and comfort her compassionate communion with the deep. She is listening to these hands full of mortal care as she gazes out. In listening to her caring hands, which are pressed toward each other and rounded to her head, her compassion pours out. She touches their tender vulnerability, and their own unique weight, which is their mortality. She listens, it would seem, to the deep of mortals. As humans, we are uniquely pulled to the deep. We are in the drawing pull of coming-to-be and passing-away as all earthy entities; but, unlike other entities, we are mortal, which means that being in the drawing pull *is* our sensitivity, our constant weight. We have, then, a unique openness to the depth's drawing pull. What *Mlle Pogany* shows is that this openness to the deep gives us over to compassion, for the compassionate gesture of her hands is reflected and intensified in her gaze.

Perhaps, before all rationality, compassionate touch is the distinctive mark of being human. We are *gentle* flesh. To be truly mortal, we must hold our being-toward-birth-and-death as dear and close as her hands cherishingly hold her head. It is our intimate mortality that draws us to the deep and lets us tremble with life. Our mortality is not an illness but our essential health, our participation in the hale of the fourfold's round dance. We are held close in being through our being-toward-death. But this hold tightens into a terrifying vise when we, instead of enduring our mortality, fight for immortality. To endure our mortality, we are needful of soft compassion and gentle care. Enduring mortality gives us over to our compassionate human being as that which shelters and cares for. In our openness to sky and earth, we care for nonmortal others, and in our being-toward-birth-and-death, we shelter both other mortals and historical-phusical emergence. With others, in the enduring passion of our mortality, we build compassionately.

The later *Mlle Pogany* looks out in stark contrast to the early *Mlle Pogany*. She has lost her compassion, her gentle care. Her eyes, above all, have changed dramatically. They are not softly swelling but are deep cuts whose heavy ridge shoots back, curving along each side toward the back of her head and continuing down to form a line for her ear. Her nose is a sharp beak, almost transparent at its end. She has no mouth at all. She does not lean protectingly over the deep, but hunches over and squints as though out of a visor. The wide half-circle of her eye, which cuts into her cheek, clearly encourages us to see her forehead and nose as forming a kind of medieval war helmet.

She is no longer drawn compassionately to the deep but is withdrawn into her back as a hard shell whose stepped arcs spiral down from the back of her head, elegantly swerve to the side, and are completed by her propped-up arm, which forms the opening flap of the shell. In the earlier *Mlle Pogany,* we recall, her body emerged out of unworked marble rock. The later *Mlle Pogany,* however, is a self-contained form. The previous unformed mass of her shoulder has become a hard, stylish shell, a sleek armor in which she is fully contained and protected. She withdraws in gradations along the regular, progressively smaller circles of the shell's space. She folds back into herself, but not in a harboring self-seclusion. Her being with herself here is not the self-sequestering privacy of the earlier *Mlle Pogany* but a defense. She protects her inside against the outside. The inside and outside are not diffused but rigidly defined. One feels, moreover, in looking at *Mlle Pogany III,* that inside there is not a fullness but a tense rigidity, as fear tenses the body. Her shell encases her, entrapping her as well as protecting her. Such protection of the inside from the outside is not a sheltering. Sheltering is not a defense against something but an enduring hold, which is an openness, a giving that involves care-full feelings.

Her defensive strategy, moreover, could easily turn into an offense. Perhaps this is why she appears both pathetic and ominous. She is like *Flying Turtle* (1940–45), Brancusi's last work, which is both a completely helpless turtle on its back and some kind of missile or arrowhead.

Mlle Pogany III's hands no longer touch her head and provide a resting place. Her hands have collapsed into each other and are more like a single arm against which she is propped. Her rocklike, rigid arm lacks the gentle sway of the early *Mlle Pogany*'s hands. What we see instead is a kind of frame-by-frame representation of a swaying motion in the regular receding circles of her shell-like back. Her arm, moreover, is more like a telephone handle than a human arm. She, indeed, appears to be on the telephone. She is not contacting the deep, giving oracle and listening to her mortal hands full of mortal care. She does

not touch what she listens to. She
no longer muses, communing with
the depth. Rather, she appears to be
plugged into a communications network, receiving signals and transmitting information. She is not fleshly
listening or speaking but appears to be
operating through a model alien to
the flesh: perhaps through electricity
like a computer. In fact, the grayish
marble is highly veined with darker
gray, forming a patterning that resembles an electrical network.

Mlle Pogany III retreats, withdraws.
This withdrawal is not a reclining. Reclining, as we saw in the earlier *Mlle
Pogany* with regard to her hands, is a
soft sway, a being drawn intimately to
otherness. The hands in their unique
reclining sway, softly accompany her
enduring compassion. In their reclining, they offer a resting place to softly
hold her own soft compassion. It is
important to see that reclining is not a
negative movement in contrast to the
rising into the unconcealed. Reclining
bears a negative sense of declining
when put into opposition to rising. In
reclining into herself, the early *Mlle
Pogany* is not declining but is gathered
to herself. Such gathering is not a
withdrawal or negative turning-in on
herself as an independent self opposed
to another. She is not closed off against
the outside but swells softly, thick
with concealment.

Mlle Pogany III, however, no longer swells and sways. She is thin and tight. The swaying movement of her neck and arms has shrunk into a thin twist. Though her neck is still somewhat soft and bulges, this bulge is not a soft swell but the result of a strain from the strangling knot that her neck and arm forms. She does not sway and bend, holding otherness, but is retreating, declining, collapsing into herself.

Mlle Pogany III reveals the psychological plight of the feminine in this age. She turns against herself because she is now no longer in relation to the soft depths but in relation to her own vulnerabilities. Her previous openness that enabled her to contact the deep has become weakness in the new relation of opposition between the inside and outside, subject and other. Her retreat from what is now an external otherness does not even bring her to an enclosed belonging with herself; for though she is turning in on herself to protect her softer parts against the threatening other, she is, at the same time, turned against herself in self-destruction. Despairingly, she strangles herself with those same soft inner parts that once had enabled her to receive the deep. Her compassionate yielding and openness become in this new light a gaping wound. She becomes a hole that no longer holds. Her efforts to protect herself fall in a vortex of nothingness.

Positive reclining is not this destructive retreat. The earlier *Mlle Pogany* is reclining into contact, yielding and releasing of herself into unconcealment. The gentleness and softness of the earlier *Mlle Pogany* informs all her movements: her bending, curving, swelling, and swaying. Her reclining is not a negative decline, essentially because of this gathering, resting softness. Reclining must be saturated with such mystery and softness. Such softness, moreover, is not a weakness but a rounding strength. Reclining is an enduring of the heavy weight of being saturated with concealment, an enduring of rounding fullness, a pregnancy that all mortals bear.

Chapter Four

Deconstructing the Culture/Nature
Dichotomy: Preparations

> I want to grasp things with the mind the way the penis is grasped by the vagina.
> —Marcel Duchamp (in Schwartz 1969, 114)

I am inquiring into the origins of the oppression of women by describing the interlinkages of oppression with the metaphysical movements of western Being. I move into the region of a feminist ontology, then, by specifically describing basic ontological movements or currents in historical Being. This focus on movement is a helpful way to work toward a feminist ontology. Movement is a concept broad and indeterminate enough to be comprehensive yet open to the many ways general movements can vary when concretized in particular actions and methods. Unlike the abstract notion of a feminine principle, which suggests a fixity and certainty of gender delineation that I believe is false, the notion of movements is rooted in the ruptures and irregularities of nature, in the motility of our corporeal bodies *within* a social-historical context. As I understand it, moreover, such metaphysical movement shows up in what Irigaray calls the cultural/symbolic; that is, the art, symbols, mythologies, philosophies, and literature of western culture. Thus, although what I am calling feminine and masculine movements are vaguely "given" movements that lay out general tendencies and predispositions, they are nonetheless changeable according to various cultures and historical periods and are always indeterminate. These general styles of movement vary tremendously, moreover, in their particular historical and cultural embodiments as, for instance, archetypes, cultural stereotypes, and gender symbols as well as in their more diffused concretization in social relations, practices, and institutions. They can be understood to intertwine, moreover, in the particular lived comportment of men and women, the young and old, and in the multidimensional psychophusical web of a single human being. In other words, they body forth in innumerable particular ways. I am not, then, working toward a feminist ontology in the sense of a totalizing theory that attempts to universalize particular modes of being, but as an attempt to undermine traditional general descriptions of our western being in the world-earth-home by letting in movements that have been excluded in western ontologies. The process of letting in movements that have been conceptually marginalized will result in a cracking of rigidified concepts and letting new meanings grow through the cracks. Once this starts happening, working toward a feminist ontology becomes itself a suspect project. If we can understand western metaphysics as a kind of solidifying of the play of movement because it attempts to grasp Being as a fixed structure and stable stuff, then I am attempting to disrupt this fixity, in the manner of Derrida, and let in the movements of change, chaos, and becoming. However, given the technological thrust of western Being, I also understand present Being as a constant going forward (a Nietzschean becoming as interpreted by Heidegger), that is not truly a *becoming,* a *growing,* because it denies, suppresses, and overpowers the pull of the body, earth and of the past.

The general "movement" of western Being can be broadly described as an emergence into unconcealment from concealment. I have borrowed this part of ontological movements of unconcealing and concealing (also described as rising-reclining, emergence-withdrawal, presence-absence) from Heidegger's analysis of the Greek notions of *poiesis* and *aletheia* in order to help characterize the currents of the masculine and the feminine and the characteristics that have clustered around them. I am not claiming that this dynamic of unconcealing-concealing is universal and fixed for all time or a cross-cultural phenomenon. Rather, I understand it to be rooted in the locality of traditional western culture and thus, like gender structures, to change its style over broad epochs or even to be unrecognizable in other cultures.

The ontological movements of unconcealing and concealing, as I see them, are highly influenced by the well-known western metaphysical dichotomy of activity/passivity. This dichotomy has played a key role in western phallocentric descriptions of the genderized movements of the sperm and the egg and of sexual intercourse between the male and the female. The female's supposed passive sexual receiving of the male has been consistently viewed by western culture as inferior to the male's penetration and seeming overcoming of the other. This sexual dynamic of female re-

ceiving and male penetration, moreover, has served as an important paradigm of our western conceptualization of power, creativity (see Hartsock
1985), reason (see Lloyd 1984), and cultural production. It has also been
used for describing the psychology of men and women (see Irigaray 1985a
and 1985b) as well as for describing the more metaphysical movements of
spirit and nature, form and matter, self and other, and the phallocentric
movement of western Being itself.[1] The dichotomy of male activity and female passivity, however, is by no means a cross-cultural one. In the culture
of Australian aborigines, for example, the sperm are considered passive
and are associated with the moon, calm water, and temperate weather.[2]

I attempt to undo this key hierarchical binary of movement throughout
this book (and especially in the art writings) by giving positive senses to
the subordinate term, passivity. In a manner similar to Irigaray, I mimic
the traditional characterization of the feminine and exceed those descriptions in order to show its hidden revolutionary strengths. For the characterizations of the feminine, which are to a large extent derived from sexual
reproductive differences, are noncharacterizations in that they are constituted according to an economy of representation that revolves solely
around the male phallus. As the unrepresentable other and as absence in a
metaphysics of subject and substance, the feminine offers the possibility of
undermining that ontological system.

Thus, in this chapter on phusis and techne, I emphasize the sheltering
and holding involved in the "passivity" of concealment. Moreover, I put
concealment into relief by stressing the movement of going-back-into-itself
involved in the bringing-forth of phusis (nature), and the movement of
gathering involved in the bringing-forth of techne (art, culture). In the final
section of this chapter I continue to describe the phallocentric movement of
the Will to Power, which, we learned in Chapter Three, is the culmination
of a way of Being that is presenting a particularly dangerous style of the
ontological dynamic whereby the masculine ontological movement of
coming into the unconcealment of appearance dominates emerging and the
feminine reclining back into concealment is suppressed and devalued.

In Chapter Three I suggested that thinking on the feminine in its absence
or ontological exile may help us step back from the destructive Being that
guides this age and may help us cultivate a new kind of relation of differ-

ence other than that of a hierarchical opposition between concealment and unconcealment and between the masculine and the feminine. I mentioned that a provisional way of making a space for difference and for the feminine (as a multiple sexuality) in particular is by mimicking the traditionally effeminine from its entrapment in metaphysical relations of opposition. In this chapter and the next two, I take up this method by specifically analyzing the culture/nature dichotomy, which I see as a central metaphysical dichotomy for understanding not only the roots of the historical dominance of the masculine over the feminine but the nature of the Will to Power itself. Given that the very meaning of culture appears, in some degree, to be locked into an antagonistic relationship with nature, we are encouraged to look here for an important source of the devaluation of woman, since women have historically been identified with nature. We are also generally encouraged to question the way we, as human beings, are on the earth and to search for a possible way of being on the earth that is not intrinsically opposed to nature, yet allows for our unique relation to it.

Letting in the feminine is fundamentally a process or method that does not end with a description of the feminine as a saving power or as a presencing freed from its absencing of phallocentric metaphysics. The results of the process are more in the method or process itself. Releasing the feminine from its metaphysical absencing may help open the nature of gender to fresh determinations and conceptualizations, but that can be realized only through the methods of undoing sedimented gender characterizations. As I mentioned in Chapter One, to skip this process of redefining the feminine and moving immediately to a postmodern gender multiplicity (whose leading theorists are male thinkers like Derrida and Baudrillard) reinforces the feminine as lack and non-essencing. So, too, the deconstruction of the culture/nature dichotomy will hopefully help reconceptualize nature and our human relation to it; however, the extent to which our deconstructing is successful can be determined by whether we find ourselves looking at nature, on the one hand, and culture, on the other, or in the midst of something quite different. Moreover, in undermining western ontology by letting in the feminine, it may be that the very project of developing an ontology is itself undone.

In the following three chapters I deconstruct the concepts of nature and culture by resuscitating the original meanings from which they arose. I investigate the culture/nature dichotomy, then, by going back to its ancient roots in the Greek understanding of the difference between techne and phusis. *Techne* and *phusis* are normally translated as "art" and "nature," respectively, but since these translations cannot do justice to the original meaning, I leave these words in their untranslated form. I have already discussed the notion of phusis in Chapter Three. I relate techne to our modern, broad concept, "culture." "Culture," as it is used today, is a complex concept that has three basic meanings. It can refer to a general process of intellectual, spiritual, and aesthetic development. It can indicate a particular way of life, whether of a people, period, group, or humanity in general. And it can mean the works and practices of intellectual, and especially artistic, activity.[3] I use the term in a broad way that includes all three meanings. However, my interest in this notion is primarily in its relations to nature. Thus, by "culture" I am essentially referring to the products of consciousness by means of which we attempt to transcend and control nature in some way.[4]

In the next chapter, I explore the relationship between techne and phusis within the context of generation. I turn to Aristotle's metaphysics to find both a source of their antagonistic relation and indications of the benign relations from which the culture/nature dichotomy has turned out. My guiding question will be, How do techne and phusis figure in that pointed moment of generation when the seed is "placed" in the womb? The tool (stylus) of my unraveling, then, will be the pricking point of the male penis. (As Derrida [1977, 176] pointedly points out, the question of style and method is always the question of a pointed object.) Using this crochet hook, as it were, I will attempt to uncrochet the oppositional relational threads between techne and phusis in Aristotle's analysis. I work toward retrieving the subordinated thread, nature, and releasing the feminine holes that have been fixed in place by the weave.

In this chapter, then, I lay out the nature of this phallocentric "crotchety" weave between techne and phusis in preparation for the decrocheting that will take place in Chapter Five. In Chapter Six I attempt to recrochet the nature of our natural-cultural human being using a new tool, the "fork" of gender difference, and paying special tribute to the crux of the matter, or rather the "crotch" of the mother matter, overlooked in the metaphysical race toward the self-same.

Women and the Culture/Nature Dichotomy

> Where I live as a woman is to men a wilderness. But to me it is home.
> —LeGuin 1989, 46

The influence of the culture/nature dichotomy on the oppression of western women is well known in feminist studies. A woman has been seen in man's culture as being "closer to nature" than a man primarily, it seems, because of her "mothering" body. A woman's body not only drips and bleeds but swells roundly; it holds and gushes new life as well as nurtures with white milk.

If we go back to the beginnings of the story of the West in early Greece, we find women placed in a social sphere of activities that were also seen as closer to nature, and that were, at the same time, increasingly distinguished from the activities of the state or *polis*.[5] Although women have taken on the primary responsibility for nurturing children in their growth, most likely because they give birth and give milk, there is of course no phusical necessity that this care, even for the very young, needs to take place primarily in a domestic sphere segregated from the public, political sphere or, any necessity that, after the initial lactating period, women continue to take on primary care of infants. The public/private dichotomy is not cross-cultural, inevitable, or biologically based. Yet, the home since the Greeks has been the place of "women's work" and has been put (more or less and in quite different ways depending on the different historical periods) into an opposition with the public, political sphere. The home is understood as a sphere of activities that deals with so-called lesser natural functions in opposition to more essential cultural projects and public sites of power.[6]

An important reason for this opposition in the West is its conceptual associations with the metaphysical opposition between nature and culture.[7] If we go back to the historical beginnings of the development of the public/private dichotomy in the West, it seems to begin with the rise of the *polis* and reaches clear articulation at the founding of the Athenian democracy. In archaic Greece, kinship structures of the aristocratic feudal society were deteriorating through the rise of a new middle class. As Marilyn Arthur (1977, 67) describes it, "The small household emerged as the productive unit of society and any head of a household (who was simultaneously a landowner) automatically became a citizen or member of the state. Conversely, the state itself, the *polis,* was defined as the sum of all individual households." She argues that as the integrity of each individual household came to possess political significance, the sexual activities of women, which could potentially violate the integrity of individual households and thereby disrupt the political order, had to be more carefully controlled.[8] Such political factors, however, interweave with already sedimented conceptual associations. An examination of Homer's *Iliad* and Aeschylus's *Oresteia* reveals that the *polis* as a concept is established through its opposition to nature and to unruly female forces that are identified with nature (see Hartsock 1985, 186–209), an identification that goes back to prehistory. By the time of Aristotle's *Politics,* the male is clearly identified with the *polis* and the woman with the home, the inferior realm of natural necessity (see Elshtain 1981). Hegel, following on the Greeks' notion, identifies the home and women with particularity and merely natural existence (man's first nature), and men and the *polis* with the sphere of universality toward which man aims (man's second nature).[9]

It must be emphasized that the association of women with nature and men with culture is not universal or historically homogeneous. Many ancient societies had androgynous deities, for example, that revealed an association of both male and female principles with natural and cultural forces.[10] In Greek mythology (as with the ancient Sumerian), the feminine is identified particularly with the earth and the masculine with the sky. However, in some other cultures, the Iroquois and the ancient Egyptian, for example, the sky is considered feminine.

Moreover, just as the association of men with the public, political sphere and women with the private sphere is culturally specific, so is any development of the public/private dichotomy itself. In some non-state societies, for example, most vital collective decisions are made within the domestic grouping. And in most simple societies, political leadership does not confer power or prestige.[11]

In those early non- and pre-Greek societies where deities were female and women were associated with nature, women often possessed significant social status. However, in early Greek societies where male deities increasingly dominated the religious pantheon, the association of women with the earth and the self-closing mystery and inner darkness of the earth affected women's lives in a profoundly negative way. Women, for the most part, were confined by the male-dominated society to insular domestic homes away from the open public world.[12] As Ruth Padel (1983, 8) argues, "Athenian life seems to have been functionally divided between two gendered roles that were themselves defined by the spaces inhabited: one at ease among marble buildings and public spaces like the agora, gymnasium and assembly, and the other confined to the inmost part of the mudbrick 'home.' " The division between dark inner spaces and open public spaces was reflected in the architectural space of Greek buildings. Most Greek buildings, both sacred and domestic, were constructed in such a way that they had a dark inner center. In the temple, there was a dark inner shrine lit by torches and unenterable except to those properly consecrated. In the domestic house, the dark inner space was the hearth, presided over by a female deity, Hestia. The inmost part of the mudbrick domestic home was called the *muchos,* meaning the "women's quarter," and had very limited entrance.[13] *Muchos,* as a hidden recess, can also refer to Hades and to a prophet's shrine. The *andron,* the "men's room," by contrast, was a room for social (and extramarital) intercourse and was easily accessible from the street. It had the most lavish anterior of the house, and the floors were often decorated with mosaics. It was here that the well-known social *symposion* took place. As Meg Miller (1991, 28) notes, the only females who would enter the *andron* were female slave attendants.

Confined domestically, women in Greek culture, moreover, could participate in public social life only under male control. Their participation in religion (one of the rare forms of public activity), for example, was usually confined in the cult buildings or cult procedures in a similar way to their confinement in domestic homes. An important point to be made here is that women's participation in Greek culture, which was limited and carefully controlled by men, also reflects a deep cultural association of women with the earth, darkness, and what I have been calling, following Heidegger, concealment. In early Greek societies, women were assigned ritual presidency over the transitional experiences of birth and death, which were culturally perceived as passages into and out of concealment. Dying was understood as a going into the dark, and being born, as a coming into the light. Although darkness and concealment were understood as having a sense of sanctity, they were already culturally feared as something that could negatively affect one. Thus, not surprisingly, the supposed female aptitude for aiding passage out of or into darkness was culturally linked with a supposed female aptitude for making contact with what was generally "polluting." As Padel (1983, 5) says, "In Greek as in some other cultures, concepts of the sacred [were] interwoven with concepts of pollution: *hagnos* or *hagios,* 'sacred,' is cognate with *agos,* 'pollution.' " This also helps explain why aspects of female biology were perceived as polluting to men even though women at the same time functioned as a focus of sanctity.[14]

Men of early Greece made use of, and carefully controlled, the supposed kinship women had with the earth and with "the darker, polluting side of divinity." On behalf of men, women were to make contact "with potentially contaminating objects and forces" (Padel 1983, 6). Thus, women sometimes, for example, guarded sacred objects that were normally hidden and revealed under strict ritual conditions, like the *arrheta,* "unspeakable things" in the Panathenaic festival at Athens; or they made contact with the sacred under carefully controlled conditions, as did the priestess at Delphi, whose cries were patterned by the male priests into hexameter verse.

Given the obvious harmful effects of the historical association of women with earth, darkness, and chaos, many feminists attempt to remove the association of the feminine with nature so that gender differences can be thoroughly reworked. Gynocentric feminists are more concerned with reworking the association of the feminine with nature, understand it in new, positive ways (for example, Irigaray, Cixous, O'Brien, King, Hartsock, Griffin, Daly, Ruddick). In different ways they affirm an identification of the feminine with nature, emphasizing, for example, the cultural need to rediscover the nurturing power of the mother or the *jouissance* of the female sexual body and to socially take up degraded women's work in order to create a nonsexist and/or ecoconscious society.[15] Exploring the historical association of women with nature and the culture/nature dichotomy that is informed by this association is a crucial way of revealing the dynamic of phallocentric western Being and of disrupting normative concepts. That is not to say, however, that the traditional association of women with nature should remain intact. The current popular association of mother with nature in environmentalist advertising, for example, tends to simply reinforce the perception of nature as a storehouse of riches for man's use.[16] The culture/nature dichotomy helps frame traditional feminine and masculine characteristics that in turn enforce an oppressive heterosexuality. Turning to the age-old links between the feminine and nature and uncovering the various motivations for the associations will provide ways to better understand not only gender difference but also the gap between "man and nature" and how this gap may be transformed into creative differences.

One of the main problems in using the traditional association of women with nature, even as a strategy to describe our present being, is that of essentialism. As I discussed in Chapters One and Two, the problems involved in advocating a kind of female specificity (such as affirming an association of women with nature) can be alleviated by understanding the feminine as a presencing that is historically and culturally contextualized and the female body as a phenomenological body that is nourished and influenced by natural-cultural determinants. In Chapter Six I suggest that to further help in this regard we need to return to the Greek notion of phusis to understand nature itself as growth and becoming and we need to step backward and sideways from the culture/nature dichotomy that frames the current feminist debate on gender creation. By understanding gender as a phusical becoming, we can recognize both cultural and natural determinants in the creation of gender and thereby allow for a dehiscence of gender styles that celebrate the body.

A major problem that gynocentric feminists face is that of conservatism. In affirming, for example, that women have more experience of continuity with, or rootedness in, nature (because of, for example, women's mothering body, traditional processes of socialization, and women's home labor), gynocentric feminists are in danger of reinforcing traditional gender roles and stereotypes. Although I might agree that aspects of women's historically lived being in the western world-earth-home (for example, "women's work") has in some ways enabled women to remain aware of the body and the earth to a greater degree than many men, I would not agree that women are intrinsically or transhistorically "closer" to nature because, for example, they give birth or menstruate. The event of birth can definitely bring a laboring woman in contact with rhythms of nature, but one can also experience these rhythms of nature in the changes of the moon, for example, or in the death of someone near. I must stress that my hope is not to keep women segregated in the home away from public institutions and positions of power where they are so badly needed, or to reinforce heterosexuality, but, rather, to undermine and transform our destructive cultural attitudes and concepts so that the sites of power and privilege themselves change. In this regard, I am working to understand and to attempt to change the concept of power itself, for example, as domination over otherness.

Feminists do not need to choose between the following extremes: *(a)* to join the transcendent projects of the traditionally male spirit and reason and, thereby, deny our bodies, dominate the earth, and perpetuate the western metaphysical substructure that underlies all our dualisms, or *(b)* to retain the traditional "earthy" feminine and remain politically and culturally inactive and psychologically and economically suppressed. This dilemma that has persisted in feminist theory in different forms at various times is already an effect of the culture/nature dichotomy. It seems to me we need to go back and question and criticize basic assumptions of western society so that we can find indications of new relations of difference that are nonoppositional and that would help not only the feminist project but the world-earth-home as a whole.

I would suggest like many gynocentric feminists that in western beginnings, domestic activities—for example, the birth, nurturance, and care of the young and old—became devalued and separated from the site of power, the public political sphere (the *polis*), to some extent because domestic activities were involved with the sphere of natural change and becoming. The home generally came to be seen as that sphere dealing with processes connected with nature and the mortal body in contrast to the public sphere, which takes over the main responsibility for cultural projects. These projects came to be understood as projects of an "immortal" spirit and resulted in products that transcended the individual, the body, and the coming-to-be and passing-away of natural entities.[17] It seems to me that if this more fundamental and more ancient metaphysical opposition between nature and culture were to change into a new relation of difference, then the home and the workplace and the gender division of labor would themselves undergo profound changes.

In the light of the male *logos,* the earth can only show itself as silent, dark, wild, and threatening. How would it be if we could show the earth in a new, nonoppositional light—in a way that lets the dark be dark and the wild be wild rather than dispensed with as irrational? How would it be if we could show that seemingly threatening wilderness not as other and not segregated to the male institution of the domestic, but as "home," in other words, as belonging-place?

Art (Techne) and Nature (Phusis) as Ways of Bringing-forth

> The beasts have nothing more to do but to pick up the materials required to satisfy their wants: man on the contrary can only satisfy his wants by transforming, and as it were originating the necessary means.
>
> —Hegel 1973, 46

To unravel the culture/nature dichotomy I am returning to the sources of our philosophy in the Greeks. My return to the Greeks (and most particularly Aristotle) generally involves a twofold analysis. I critique aspects of Greek thinking that were taken up by later metaphysics and developed into the present metaphysical dualisms of this age. At the same time, I put into relief those aspects of Greek thinking that were left behind, excluded, and suppressed in order to allow this evolution of western dualisms. The former investigation will help me critique the inner logic of the binary opposition between nature and culture, and the latter investigation may indicate ways to let the subordinate term *nature* presence in its own right.

There are a few points in Heidegger's philosophy of history that must be emphasized before I begin in order to avoid misunderstandings in my analysis of the Greek way of thinking. First, both the "beginning" and the "end" of metaphysics are long processes full of diversity.[18] Second, western Being is not a causal process where one stage necessarily leads to the next. History could have taken many different directions than the paths it has happened to take. There are not direct causal links from the Greek age to our own modern one, but, rather, historical pathways are fluid, full of shifts, contingency, indeterminacy and open to new interpretations. Finally, the difference between Greek thought and our own cannot be overemphasized. The difficult task is to attempt to get into the Greek way of thinking through the layers of modern concepts and ideas. Since we cannot completely cancel out our historical perspective, we do not hope to encounter supposed original Greek thought. Instead, in the process we are looking for ruptures in our worldview.

Let me now introduce the concepts of techne and phusis, which are so crucial to the deconstructive analysis I am undertaking. To approach the profound depths of meaning involved in the Greek terms *techne* and *phusis,* it is helpful to understand them in a Heideggerean way as modes of *revealing* beings (Heidegger 1977b, 5–17). The following description of these concepts is not meant to characterize their meaning exhaustively but, rather, to give vague indications of the depths involved in these terms. I attempt to recover forgotten Greek senses of the terms, foreign as they may sound to our modern ears. The previous discussions of concealment and unconcealment will be of considerable help.

For the early Greeks, according to Heidegger's story, that which appears is something that comes out of concealment into the unconcealment of appearance. It is not, as we moderns might think, that beings appear because they have been exposed by the light of reason and thereby freed from the darkness and chaos of the unknown (for Apollo had not yet gained ascendancy over the Greek consciousness). Rather, that which emerges shines in its truth precisely because its being there shows its mysterious coming from out of concealment. Its shining unconcealment points back to its mysterious origin in the concealed, just as a newly born baby shines with the wonder of its origins, as a gushing-out from a hidden or concealed source. Truth as *aletheia* is literally as un-concealment (emphasizing a pointing back to concealment).

That-which-appears, moreover, is released in such a way that the releasing shows up as a holding-release. It is as though concealment were continually pregnant with, and yet continually giving birth to, unconcealment.

The mystery of existence is that at the same time we receive the flourishing of existence, we feel the inexhaustibility of its giving. We can witness, describe, examine, and reflect on that which comes up for us, and yet we can never expose the depths of its fullness with our thoughts or with our feelings.

This way that beings come forth in their holding release is a revealing of their Being. The Greeks named this way of coming-forth from concealment into unconcealment *poiesis,* which Heidegger translates as "bringing-forth-here" *(Hervorbringen).* They distinguished between two different ways of bringing-forth, or *poiesis:* techne and phusis.

Through techne, beings reveal themselves in a way that is dependent on human beings, for only humans have the ability to let something appear through techne. Techne is not so much the action of making or creating something, as we would tend to think today, but it is more a kind of knowledge in the sense that techne gathers and lays out something. When a carpenter builds a table, for instance, she lets the table "show" itself as a table. In other words, she lets the table come into its being through her knowledge of the wood, her knowledge of the appropriate shape into which the table is to come, and through her knowledge of the ways in which the table is to be used. This knowledge that guides her actions is more fundamental to the meaning of techne than the manual skills involved. For us moderns, on the contrary, techne is understood as an art, as a kind of *making,* which is how the Greek word *poiesis* is commonly translated today.

Another way in which beings reveal themselves and are brought forth is through phusis (nature). That nature is a way of bringing-forth is more familiar, since in our cultural myths nature was often imaged as female. Just as females were seen to give birth to new beings, so nature was understood as the source of all living things, from flowers to fruits to animals and people. For the early Greeks, Heidegger stresses, the way of bringing-forth that belongs to phusis is not merely another way of bringing-forth that is equal with that of techne; it is a bringing-forth in its deepest and most original sense. Beings from phusis have the originating order *(arche)* in themselves, whereas beings from techne do not bring themselves forth from themselves but have to come forth through human beings.[19] For example, a table comes forth by means of the carpenter who is external to the table, whereas a seed grows from itself. (This distinction will become crucial when we get to our discussion on the coming-to-be of a baby.) Phusis is thus the most fundamental mode of bringing-forth, and techne should be understood as ultimately a mode of phusis and not in opposition to phusis. Techne for the ancient Greeks was the way that humans within phusis uniquely brought forth.

If we think on human beings with regard to this distinction, we can see that they are placed in a unique situation, for they participate in both ways of bringing-forth. They bring forth "man-made" entities through techne and they participate in the bringing-forth of phusis because they are phusical beings. Moreover, if we think on the situation of women in particular, we can see that, though it reflects the unique situation of all humans generally, the strangeness of their situation is brought into stark relief. As a human being, a woman participates in the uniquely human way of revealing through techne. Of course, the kinds of things she has brought forth through techne traditionally (e.g., weaving, pottery) have often been different from those brought forth by men. Moreover, as a human being, she participates in the bringing-forth of phusis in that she is born, grows, and dies. However, because she brings forth others from herself, she appears to participate in phusis to a much fuller extent than men. Ancient societies (before the turn away from the Great Goddess religions) saw nature as mother primarily, it seems, because a woman gives birth from herself like nature. Note that even though this capacity of hers was understood as phusical, it was, nonetheless, socially central and important to ancient societies, for the culture/nature dichotomy had not yet emerged.

The Coming-to-be of an Entity from Techne and an Entity from Phusis

> I am pulled-toward. In my hands is the exquisite found object. Around the exquisite object are my found hands.
>
> —Popescu 1991, 30

In order to continue an exploration of the concepts of techne and phusis in yet more depth and prepare for the discussion of the coming-to-be of a baby, it is necessary to draw a clear distinction between the coming-to-be of a cultural product and that of a natural entity. I describe the coming-to-be of entities by using Aristotle's four causes, which will prepare us for the dominance of the formal cause in Aristotle's treatment of the coming-to-be of a baby.[20] On one hand, the following analysis of the deep difference for Greek thinking between the coming-to-be of a cultural entity and that of a natural entity will help us reconsider our unthinking leveling of this difference in our modern anthropocentric age. On the other hand, in the following analysis I expose the central role played by the dichotomy of the inside/outside, which has helped bolster the phallocentric identification of the male with culture and the female with nature. Thus, I put into relief both the positive, nonanthropocentric attributes of Aristotle's analysis (which will be helpful in future discussions on environmentalism) as well as a phallocentrism involved in the distinction between techne and phusis.

Aristotle's four causes are commonly translated through the medieval Aristoteleans as the material cause, the formal cause, the final cause, and the efficient cause. Inevitably in any translation, something of the original meaning is lost. However, in the Latin translation of the Greek *aition* as *causa,* the transformation of meaning actually obstructs understanding, for it prevents us from comprehending how all but the efficient cause can be called a "cause" in a true sense. This is because *aition* does not mean the way something actively acts on another to produce an effect, which is our modern understanding of "cause" derived from modern physics. Rather, *aition* carries the notion of being responsible for another or indebted to another.[21]

When we think of what causes a building, for example, to come into appearance, we think only of the builder who actively makes the building.[22] However, let us think of the way all four causes as *aitia* manifest themselves in the bringing-forth of a building. The building is undoubtedly indebted to the matter from which is it made (material cause). The stones or wood of the building are what the building has come out of and thus are responsible for its emerging.[23] The building, Aristotle would say, is also indebted to the particular "look" into which it has taken shape (the formal cause). Now, this look is called the *eidos* and can be interpreted as the particular look of the building in terms of its shape and appearance, or in terms of its more abstract form such as one would find in its blueprint. As Heidegger (1976, 249) notes, the *eidos* was transformed through Plato from its earlier meaning as outward look to the form or mental look, which could divorce itself from concrete appearance. Aristotle most often intends the meaning of *eidos* in the sense of abstract form. However, in different contexts, the other meaning of *eidos* as outward look, or both meanings at once, seems to be implied.

The building is also indebted to its *telos*. *Telos* is usually translated as "end." This interpretation presents particular problems when we try to understand Aristotle's "final cause" because we understand a cause as being prior to an effect. In association with Aristotle's final cause, "end" is usually interpreted in the sense of the purpose for which something is produced. Although this interpretation escapes the difficulty of appearing as an effect rather than a cause, this interpretation is prejudiced by our modern instrumental thinking that all entities do not stand in themselves but "stand by" in order to serve some purpose. Although one can certainly find indications of this modern idea that all entities have a purpose in Aristotle, this was only one strand of a much fuller meaning that the word had in his thinking. Heidegger (1976, 231; and 1975, 85) points out that in order to grasp some of this fuller meaning of the word *telos*, we must understand it in conjunction with the Greek word *peras*, which means boundary or limit. *Peras* is the boundary or limit, not in the sense of that line between an inside and outside or between my property and yours, but in the sense of that regioning from which something can begin to emerge. This new interpretation of *telos* attempts to break the connotations of linearity and progression that this notion carries and that feminists have recognized as phallocentric. A building is indebted to its *telos* in that its *telos* provides the boundaries from which its matter and outward look *(eidos)* can begin to emerge. The *telos* of a building, then, would be the building's capacity to shelter. A building's coming-to-be must happen within the bounds of some kind of sheltering for humans or animals. To say that the building is built for the "purpose" of sheltering is not the same as saying that building occurs within the region of sheltering, for the former, modern view reduces the building to a mere functionality. In the ancient Greek sense, however, the *telos* is not merely an instrumental guidance but a recognition of the deep belonging of all beings to their ontological locales, and their regioning within Being.

The building is also indebted to humans who build (the efficient or moving cause). However, the builder of the building is not responsible for the building because he effects the building of the building, as we might first think, but because, as Heidegger points out, he gathers together both the matter and the look of the building with a view to its particular *telos,* the regioning of sheltering.[24] He gathers together the other three ways of being responsible and initiates the movement of building. Aristotle speaks of the efficient cause as that from which the motion originates (*Meta.* 983a30). The builder is the mover of the building, not because he can move things about, but insofar as he is the one who gathers the building together in its emerging. He gathers the other three causes through techne, which is not to be understood as a skill in doing something (i.e., in the narrow sense as a technical skill) but as knowledge of the *eidos.* The moving cause of the building is thus the architect (from the Greek arche and techne) and not the manual workers, for he is the one who brings the building to its completion *(telos),* with a view to the overall look or the *eidos* of the building, which guides the placement of materials.

It is not by accident that I began this discussion of the four causes with the example of an entity from techne, for Aristotle's four causes seem to be tailored to fit examples of human-made products. In fact, his favorite examples are human-made entities, even when he is attempting to demonstrate something about phusis, which already suggests a certain bias in his descriptions. Let me now, however, take the more complicated example of the emergence of a tree and discuss how the four causes manifest themselves in this event, with a view to clarifying the difference between cultural products and natural entities. The following analysis of the material cause will become especially important in the next chapter, for we will discover that mother does not "matter" even in this respect since the material cause is usurped by the father's "seed."

Just as a building is made from something (i.e., stones and wood), so, too, a tree is constituted from something.[25] However, if we think on the way a tree is indebted to its matter, we realize that we cannot merely say that the tree is constituted out of wood in the same manner that we can say that a building is constituted out of wood or stones. We would not say, for instance, that a tree is wooden, as we would say of a building or a table.[26] Aristotle, reflecting on this peculiar "matter," says that only human-made entities are indebted to matter in the proper sense of the word.[27] Matter as *hyle* is that which is suitable for or potentially *(dunamis)* the entity that is emerging and thereby participates in and has responsibility for the emerging. Potential matter is matter that has been formed to some extent (the necessary injection of what we will discover to be male potency). Only potential matter can be a true material cause. Thus, the material cause of a wooden building is not the earth, and not even the rocks or trees, but the stones or wood that have been cut into a suitable shape and are ready to be used in the coming-to-be of the building.

The example of a natural entity such as a tree brings difficulties with regard to the way it is indebted to its matter, because it is not really composed or made out of the raw wood and sap in the way that a building is made out of the suitable wood. If Aristotle were pressed to say what natural entities are made of, in the sense of raw matter to be formed, he would perhaps say the elements (fire, earth, water, and air). These irreducible elements consist of what Aristotle calls ultimate or primary matter and are the ultimate constituents of any entity, natural or human-made.[28] Primary matter is ontologically passive and identified with the feminine.

> She queries: passive virginal raw matter waiting to be formed; the underlying substratum serving as foundation for his erections?

However, the true material cause, the potential matter that is suitable for the coming-to-be of a tree and that is responsible for its coming-to-be, is not the wood and sap but the seed from which a tree grows. Though the earth is the ultimate matter out of which the tree is constituted, it is the seed out of which the tree grows that is the proper material cause of the tree. The tree's seed has been actively determined or formed in some way, in contrast to unformed primary matter.

> She thinks: I *object*, therefore I am?

Thus the problem of the material cause is solved: the seed is potentially the tree and the material cause. Just as a table is made from its suitable wood, so a tree grows from, or comes out of, its appropriate seed (we will return to this ''crutch'' of the matter in the next chapter).

The tree, like the human-made building, is also indebted to the *eidos* or to its particular look. The difference between the building and the tree in terms of *eidos* is that in the case of the building, as we have discussed, an intervening techne is needed to place the *eidos* forth, whereas in the case of a natural entity, the *eidos* directly places itself forth. A building can only come forth into its particular *eidos* if the architect gathers the materials into the look of the particular building. A tree, on the other hand, comes into the look of a tree without any knowledge of the look it is to take. The *eidos* or outward look places itself forth without artifice.

The way that the tree is indebted to its *telos* is that it grows within the bounds of its appropriate maturity, rooting itself ever more firmly in the earth and spreading its boughs outward into the sky. It comes-to-be within the bounds of this natural growing. The difference between a human-made building and the tree with regard to its *telos* is that whereas the tree is directed toward a phusis-like end, and thus toward its own phusis-like nature, a building as a human-made entity is not on the way toward *itself*, for its *telos* (i.e., sheltering), like the growing to maturity of the tree, is a "natural" rather than techne-logical end. *Techne* is "on the way" toward phusis (*Phys.* 193b12). The *telos* of techne is outside itself, then, whereas phusis is always on the way toward itself.

Finally, the tree comes-to-be by, or according to, phusis. It, then, has its moving cause within itself, whereas cultural products have their moving cause outside themselves. Phusis does not move its seed in the same manner as a craftsman orders the wood or stones of a building through his techne. The seed grows in a very different manner. It does not have the originating order of its movements for itself in a kind of nonconscious reflective way and can thus order or form its matter in its growth. Phusis belongs to the seed in such a way that the seed indeed enacts its own movement and growth, but not in such a way that the entity in its growing is making or producing itself. In other words, a tree does not grow through a kind of natural techne. A tree enacts its own being-moved in such a way that it continually and thoroughly stay with itself throughout every aspect of its growth. Its moving cause is not like an initial push that sets itself going, nor it is like a purposeful forming of itself. The tree's staying with itself means that it goes back into itself even as it unfolds and expands in accordance with its movement.

The movement of techne is quite different from the movement of phusis, even though both are ways of bringing forth. The movement of techne as it manifests itself in the building of a building is a gathering of materials into the look of a building within the regioning of sheltering. (This sense of gathering that is central to the movement of techne will become crucial to the discussion in the last chapter, for the notion of gathering is also central to the original meaning of *logos*. I put into relief the movement of gathering within the important notions of techne and *logos* as a way of feminizing these otherwise traditionally phallocentric metaphysical concepts.)

The movement of phusis, in contrast to that of techne, is a self-enfolding emergence that is simultaneously and inherently an unfolding out and a going back into itself. A tree grows by extending and opening itself into the sky and, at the same time, by reclining back with its roots and enclosing itself in the earth. It is through this rising-reclining movement that the tree stays with itself. A building, however, cannot grow from its blueprint, nor can it put itself back into its blueprint. The originating order of its coming-to-be does not inherently stay with it, because its moving or efficient cause is external to it. A central way of distinguishing between techne and phusis, then, is that the motion involved in the creation of a cultural product comes from the outside, whereas the coming-to-be of a natural being comes from the inside. The dichotomies of external/internal and active/passive blend into this phallocentric weaving of the Being of all entities and would seem to be themselves intimately interwoven.

The Challenging-out of the Will to Power

> A tree is a tree—how many more do you need to look at?
>
> —Ronald Reagan

I am describing the concepts of phusis and techne in detail in the attempt to undermine the culture/nature dichotomy. In order for this deconstructive analysis to take place on an ontological level, it is also necessary, however, to clarify how the movements of phusis and techne relate to the dynamic of Being, or historical Emergence itself. This one last hook in the conceptual weave we have been exploring makes the overall fabric of ideas *(begriffen)* harder to grasp. However, if one has been grasped by the unhealthy pathologies of our everyday cultural, social, and individual lives, then the following description of modern Being will not appear so abstract.

Techne and phusis, we have seen, both participate in the dynamic of *poiesis,* which is a free bringing-forth from out of concealment into concealment. In Chapter Three, when I discuss how Being in this modern age as Will to Power is the fulfillment of western Being as a whole and is essentially phallocentric, I characterized its movement as an unrestrained drive forward into unconcealment purified from concealment. This thrusting dynamic of Will to Power is not a bringing-forth *(poiesis)* but what I will call, borrowing from Heidegger, a challenging-out of entities.

In a well-recognized important essay, ''The Question Concerning Technology,'' Heidegger calls our modern Being *Gestell* and describes it in terms of the essencing of *technology. Gestell* comes from the German verb *stellen,* which has a wide variety of meanings. It can mean to set in place, to order, to arrange, to supply, and, in a military context, to challenge. Heidegger lets all these meanings have their connotative force in his use of *Gestell.*[29] *Gestell,* as Heidegger explains (1977e, 19), is a gathering of these actions, movements, and comportments to beings, just as *Ge-birg* (mountain range) is a gathering of mountains. That which gathers particular beings together into a way of being and courses through them in their coming to appearance is, in the language of metaphysics, Being. *Gestell,* then, is the Being of this technological age.[30]

For our purposes, we can note that *Gestell* as the essencing of technology shares the same thrusting dynamic of Will to Power but brings into focus the ontological significance of techne. If Being is the essencing of technology, then we are drawn to the conclusion that the bringing-forth unique to human beings has somehow taken precedence over the bringing-forth of phusis or nature and has come to characterize Being as a whole. But how can this be?

Technology, as we commonly understand it, is the various industrial machines and practical instruments made by man through the applications of science, especially physics, for the purpose of controlling nature in some way. We are aware that technology plays a key role in the progress of any civilization. Perhaps it is even clearer to readers, after the analysis of Will to Power, why technology is so crucial to our western culture. Under the guidance of the Will to Power, our western age works toward the continual escalation of power (political, economical, social, and individual), and we find the richest source of power not in the heavens of Platonic-

Christendom, since spiritual religions no longer guide the majority, but in our technological capacity to tap the earth's resources. Our culture, then, is fundamentally concerned with the attempt to assert complete control over nature. Moreover, our modern western management of nature, which is also taken up as quickly as possible by other world cultures, is based on the economic principle that we push the earth's energy toward maximum yield at minimum expense. This domination of nature is actualized through technology.

Although it is certainly true that technology is the key to power in this age, when Heidegger says that technology in its essencing describes the Being of our age, he is not referring to technology as machines and instruments that are in the power of human beings. Technology in its essencing or presencing is not the techne that is the distinctive feature of human beings but denotes the movements of modern western Being itself.

In order to present a fast sketch of how techne, which belongs to human beings, can come to describe Being itself, let us continue to reflect on our attempt to command the destiny of beings as a whole through technology, paying more attention this time to the being of entities. It is saddening that in considering ourselves the supreme subjects of the universe, we rarely encounter what is other than human but meet only ourselves, our own products, and what is useful for such production. Even in this so-called Decade of the Environment, the powers that be, guided by the global market economy, do not protect wild living beings and the living natural environment unless it is economically viable. Although we are now encouraged through the media to buy ''green'' products, to conserve energy, to recycle garbage, and even to compost, in our urban environment we are rarely motivated, for instance, to look up to see the changes of the sky. We are unlikely to have the time to stoop in order to make friends with a stray ladybug. It is rare to feel even our own presence as human beings because we have lost a sense of our mortality and of our responsibility to wild beings in the world-earth-home.

As I was getting on the ferry boat to go into the city today, after having written the above, the ferryboat captain looked up at the stormy spring skies, smelling the air. Contradictions allow for a refreshing gap in generalizations—a breath of fresh air.

For the most part, the earth is understood as a reservoir of natural resources, what Heidegger calls, a standing reserve of raw products strictly in the service of human beings.[31] Standing reserve *(Bestand)* characterizes the way in which things are when they are presencing according to *Gestell*. In this age, says Heidegger, things are not even objects, which in German is *Gegenstand* (literally, a standing against), for they have been further reduced to a manner of being in which their orderability and substitutability is of more account than their standing against the subject. In this coming to stand in appearance, earthly entities lose their own standing in themselves and are driven ahead of themselves to serve in the anthropocentric process of an "in order to." The ersatz earth is thereby given a human meaning, as Zarathustra prophesied.

Whatever comes into appearance in this modern age can only come-to-be (emerge or reveal itself) within the bounds of modern technology, which challenges out whatever emerges. Any entity, then, for the most part (and I say for the most part because Being is not completely characterized by *Gestell*), cannot appear as a natural entity that comes forth from itself and for itself but as a natural resource, a raw product to be used for the manufacturing of certain products.

For example, the tree in the forest appears in the light of its capacity to serve as an energy resource. It is challenged out by technology to serve as a raw product for the making of paper products, particle and chip board, lumber, and veneer. It may be that a particular forest stand is unsuitable to serve as raw material for even particle board or newsprint, because of its inaccessibility, for instance, but that does not take away from the fact that it stands there as a standing reserve of energy for possible future uses and does not stand in itself, shining forth from concealment.

Because natural entities can only reveal themselves within the bounds of *Gestell,* the world-earth-home is in danger. The deepest danger of modern technology does not lie in the fact that it is responsible for environmental pollution that threatens all earthly life or that nuclear power might get out of hand through an accident or through war but, rather, in the eventuality that the essence of technology comes to define existence as a whole, replacing phusis as the essential originating order (arche) of all beings.[32]

That modern western Being can now be described as the essencing of technology does not merely mean that now techne instead of phusis is the main way of bringing-forth. In other words, it does not merely mean that now human beings dominate the bringing-forth of things into appearance, that now perhaps, for example, they bring forth more products than nature and restrict and regulate nature's own bringing-forth. It is certainly true that humans are engaged in the technological management of the earth and thus regulate nature's own coming into appearance, as I have already mentioned. However, the essencing of technology is not even a bringing-forth in the ancient meaning of *poiesis* but is a dangerous ontological twist on *poiesis*.

Although the essencing of technology preserves a link with the ancient meaning of techne as a bringing-forth, it is a world away from that original mode of revealing. The essencing of modern technology or *Gestell* is a mode of revealing in the sense of a challenging-out-here. This means that under the sway of *Gestell,* beings are revealed, not by letting them come forth freely from concealment into unconcealment, but by aggressively challenging them out in their emergence, wrenching them from concealment.

The danger of *Gestell* is that in our age, entities are challenged out in their every emergence, rather than freely coming forth. Under the sway of *Gestell,* entities can only appear as products, either as already manufactured or as raw materials for them in the service of technology. When entities are only allowed to appear as products, then they have in a sense become human-made entities. A true ontological distinction, then, between techne and phusis collapses, and their relationship is reversed. Phusis is no longer understood as the most original mode of bringing-forth but, rather, as a kind of techne, as a producing of raw products. The free bringing-forth, the holding-sway of phusis is forgotten altogether.

The ontological movement of *Gestell* is not a bringing-forth that shows the wonder of an entity's coming forth from concealment into shining unconcealment but a challenging-revealing that is pressed to overcome the self-sequestering holding and gravity of concealment. This general ontological movement of challenging-forth in which concealment is suppressed bodies forth in innumerable different ways in most aspects of our being in the world-earth-home. By looking at our buildings, for example, we quickly get a general sense of the suppression of the pull back belonging to concealment. Most obvious in our cities are our modern office buildings, which rise effortlessly straight up into the sky, giving the illusion that they are light, floating entities that have transcended the need to be founded on the earth. They tend to be made of steel and glass or are veneered with reflective materials that help them appear as unearthly geometric apparitions. Because of their reflections on reflections and the resultant immateriality, it is hard to judge their actual size and to see them in depth. They are not built to weather and to show their enduring with time but, since it is culturally important to suppress signs of contingency and age, tend to be made of materials resistant to showing their age. They thus make their appearance as the transcendent mathematical idealities or abstractions upon which they are based, rather than as entities of the earth upon which they are grounded. That our modern architectual achievements such as skyscrapers, high towers, and vast spanning bridges tend to be admired for their seeming denial of the earth's gravity and density is not merely a passing aesthetic preference but, rather, reflects the deeper metaphysical values of our culture.

Techne today does not work for the sake of phusis. Building is not directed toward sheltering, which like the growing to maturity of a tree is a natural or phusis-like end. An architect, in the deepest sense of the word (arche-techne), should not be directed superficially toward the supplying of housing to meet the market demand or toward architecture for its own sake. She should, rather, be directed toward the phusical end of sheltering human beings and thus toward the needs of the human beings she aims to shelter. Our institutions, workplaces, and public housing, however, do not reflect social needs but economic and political pressures. They, moreover, declare a shocking lack of concern for the particular needs of women in relation to the built environment (see Matrix 1984).

Modern techne, under the sway of *Gestell*, is a challenging-revealing that takes precedence over phusis and attempts to replace it as the originating order of all living entities. Heidegger, in an early article on Aristotle, speaks of this danger of techne replacing phusis. In this particular passage, Heidegger is discussing an example that Aristotle was fond of using: that of a doctor who doctors himself and regains his health. Does the doctor regain his health according to techne or according to phusis? What we have here is a case where techne and phusis are interwoven in the same entity, for the doctor practices medicine on himself, which is a *techne,* and also regains health in himself, who is an entity from phusis. Is this a case where we cannot in fact distinguish techne from phusis? Even though the two ways of bringing-forth are in this case in the same being, Aristotle concludes that they are still distinct. Ultimately, the doctor regains his health because he is a living body that has the capacity for healthiness and not because of his techne as a doctor. His techne of medicine, explains Heidegger, can only support and guide phusis and cannot replace it as the originating order *(arche)* of health. Heidegger continues:

> Techne can only cooperate with phusis, can more or less expedite the cure; but as techne it can never replace phusis and in its stead become itself the arche of health as such. That could only happen if life as such were to become a "technically producible artifact. At that very moment, however, there would also no longer be such a thing as health, any more than there would be birth and death. Sometimes it seems as if modern man rushes headlong towards this goal of producing himself technologically. (Heidegger 1976, 235–36)

Heidegger wrote this article on Aristotle long before his careful analysis of the essence of technology. However, what he was to describe later as nature becoming a standing reserve of energy, we can see here in his concern that nature might become a technically producible artifact.

What strikes me about this statement is that he is pointing not so much to the danger facing phusis as a whole but specifically to the dangers facing what I would call the phusical aspects of human beings: our birth, death, and health. In other words, the modern collapse of phusis into techne, which is the poignant danger of this age, desensitizes and transforms our human "phusi-cal being." These crucial aspects of our human being have in varied and often oppressive ways been among the main responseabilities of women. The fact that our phusical human being is particularly threatened by the ontological demise of nature encourages me to turn to the nurturing care and phusical techne of the home for ways to conceptually heal the culture/nature opposition in our human be-ing despite the serious risks of essentialism and conservatism that such a turn could entail.

Chapter Five

Mother Doesn't Matter

> In fact, as soon as the question of ontology raises its head, as soon as one asks oneself "what is it?," as soon as there is intended meaning. Intention: desire, authority—examine them and you are led right back . . . to the father. It is even possible not to notice that there is no place whatsoever for woman in the calculations. Ultimately the world of "being" can function while precluding the mother.
>
> —Hélène Cixous (in Cixous and Clément 1975, 64)

The coming-to-be of a baby is an event that is experienced by many women and carefully considered sometime in their lives by most. By the coming-to-be of a baby, I am referring not only to the actual birth of the child but the whole region of watching over the growth of a human being. Improved birth control and the entrance of women into the workforce in western countries are major historical events that have affected many women's lives in a dramatic way. There is still a dire need for safer and more reliable birth control methods and legal, affordable access to abortions. However, western women, for the most part, are in a better position than their foremothers to choose whether or when to have children. This growing ability to consciously choose not to have children, rather than to have them happen one after the other, is a crucial historical change in the presencing of western women (see O'Brien 1983, 21–23).

Despite somewhat better birth control and access to safe abortion, however, the decision to have a child or not is still increasingly difficult for many women. Women deciding, for example, whether to continue a pregnancy must take into account the profound responsibility and economic hardship raising a child involves since the responsibility usually falls mainly into women's hands because of breastfeeding in the early months, traditional gender roles, and the increasing rate of marriage breakups. Moreover, on one hand, the social pressures on women to procreate are strong and restrictive, and, on the other hand, the widespread cultural presumption that mothering and activities associated with the care of the family and home are inferior activities has socially produced a suppression of mothering wisdom and a segregation of middle-class mothers to the home and has forced single and lower-income mothers to take on the impossible burden of working full-time and emotionally nurturing their needy young. Taking time off to bear a baby is often a dilemma even for many professional women because they are confronted with what boils down to a choice between fully participating in the sites of power and recognition, which demands long work hours, or sinking somewhat into the seeming powerlessness and anonymity of home and children. Such women who decide to continue a pregnancy usually try to juggle career and child at once, which they manage more or less successfully depending on the flexibility of their jobs, their economic resources, and their care support system.

I suggest that the concrete economic and social problems that revolve around mothering today (daycare issues and parenting roles, for example) seem to be at least partially entangled in the metaphysical domination of nature, the home, and the body, which help ground our cultural attitudes. Because the opposition between culture and nature is so stubbornly embedded in cultural thinking and, at the same time, is so intrinsic to the dynamic of *Gestell,* by not respecting nature's own presencing we not only place those who are considered closer to nature (i.e., women, "primitive" peoples, children) into a position of inferiority but transform nature into a commodity for the global market and perpetuate the nihilism of western Being. We can neither ignore the present need for technology and birth control in today's densely populated world-earth-home nor continue to presume that giving birth and watching over the phusical-cultural growth of children is of lesser significance to our human *being* than wage labor. Before truly radical change can take place we need to recognize our response-ability as phusical-cultural beings situated within the world-earth-home. Such recognition will emerge through a deconstruction of the recalcitrant culture/nature conflict.

The sexism of Aristotle's statements about the female and her contribution to generation has been described in detail by others.[1] I turn to Aristotle's understanding of the coming-to-be of a baby not simply to show that the cultural misogyny of his time had infiltrated his metaphysics, or to show that Aristotle was mistaken in his understanding of generation, but rather as part of a general project to help trace some of the metaphysical roots of the ontological misogyny and ecodestructiveness of western Being itself. Because Aristotle attempts to describe the originating order *(arche)* and causes *(aitia)* of the coming-to-be of a baby, he is describing this event in what he would admit to be metaphysical terms.[2] Thus, by analyzing in detail how Aristotle describes the coming-to-be of a baby, paying particular attention to the way techne and phusis figure in his description, I examine some of the initial antagonisms between nature and culture involved in the ontological exile of the feminine. I attempt to pull apart the aggressions that were coalescing between the concepts of techne and phusis, form and matter, and activity and passivity and show how gender has been involved in structuring the antipathy between nature and culture on an ontological level.[3] As Caroline Whitbeck (1984a, 69) has pointed out, Aristotle's use of the male/female dynamic as a model of the relation of form and matter (and I would add, techne and phusis) is not "just a quaint aberration" but crucial to his metaphysics. I mean to show how the growing metaphysical opposition between techne and phusis, which is centrally responsible for the narrowing anthropocentric and androcentric conception of our human being as formers of nature, is interwoven with the related hierarchical opposition of gender and importantly contributes to the general phallocentrism of western Being.

I have turned particularly to Aristotle for my analysis because the relationship between techne and phusis is a definite issue for him. He made the important attempt to return to the pre-Socratic notion of phusis, while other elements in his thinking on phusis point toward our modern notion of nature as energy. His position in metaphysics with regard to phusis, then, is somewhat unique (although one could, nonetheless, undertake a similar analysis with other Greek thinkers). On the one hand, his thinking on phusis in some way points back to the pre-Socratics (who in turn point back to pre-western conceptions), yet certain strands of his thinking on techne and phusis that indicate a relation of domination between them were similar to those taken up in western metaphysics. Aristotle, then, can reveal both a conceptual source of the present antagonistic relation between techne and phusis as well as help recover a more original and nonantagonistic relation to which his thinking points back and which in some ways is compatible with pre-Socratic thinking.

Aristotle's Analysis of the Coming-to-be of a "Man" from a "Man"

> It does not seem exaggerated, incidentally, to understand quite a few products, and notably cultural products, as a counterpart or a search for equivalents to woman's function in maternity. And the desire that man here displays to determine for himself what is constituted by "origin," and thereby eternally and ever to reproduce him (as) self, is a far from negligible indication of the same thing.
>
> —Irigaray 1985b, 23

In his *Metaphysics* and *Physics,* Aristotle does not directly speak of the coming-to-be of a baby but, rather, he describes the coming-to-be of a "man" from a "man." At this stage in the analysis we understand the term *man* to mean human being. However, we will soon have cause to question the supposed gender neutrality of this frequently used term. Already Aristotle's form-alistic description tends to lose sight of the phenomenon that is being described because it is so far removed from the actual existential situation.[4] The metaphysical superiority of form in Aristotle's metaphysics significantly contributes to his suppression of the mother and the newborn in this event and to his determination of the male as the sole contributor in generation and as the essential human sex.[5]

Aristotle uses the example of the coming-to-be of a man from a man in a well-recognized crucial statement in the *Physics* where he explains for the first time why it is that nature should be form rather than matter:

> Indeed, the form *(morphe)* is nature to a higher degree than the matter *(hyle).* For each thing receives a name when it exists in actuality *(energeia)* rather than when it exists in potentiality *(dunamis).* Moreover, it is from a man that a man is generated, but a bed is not generated from a bed. . . . So if in the latter case it is the art *(techne),* in the former too it is the form that should be nature, for it is from a man that a man is generated. (*Phys.* 193b7–12)[6]

We can see here that the example of the coming-to-be of a man from a man is centrally used as a way to explain why Phusis should be form rather than matter. The naming of Phusis as form in opposition to matter is a decisive event in the history of western Being, for this new conceptualization of Phusis contributed to the demise of a much older, pre-western understanding of Phusis as the Being or nature of all beings. The dominance of form remains in place as an important trait of western Being throughout the history of metaphysics and centrally participates in the changing conception of the human being as former and controller of nature.

Let us first examine just what *is* this coming-to-be of a man from a man. Our previous lengthy discussion of the four causes and the difference between techne and phusis will now be of considerable help. When Aristotle says here that ''it is from a man that a man is generated, but a bed is not generated from a bed,'' he is primarily pointing out how natural entities internally place the form in the process of coming-to-be, whereas cultural entities require an intervening crafts-''man'' to externally place the form.[7] We might think (as Heidegger 1976 mistakenly does) that Aristotle is pointing to the fact that in the case of the birth of a baby, a mother does not consciously shape the baby into form from her bodily material as a carpenter does the wood, nor does she need to master the science of reproduction in order to give birth. The baby in the mother's belly grows into its appropriate form by nature and not by artifice or techne. However, Aristotle is not thinking here of gestation and the actual birth experience; he is thinking, rather, about an abstract coming-to-be of the form of man from the form of man in which the mother and growing fetus are understood only according to the standard ''man'' (mother as an incomplete man and the fetus and, later, the child as an immature man).

A good place to start to unravel Aristotle's meaning of generation is with Aristotle's description of the sexual difference, which he describes in *The Generation of Animals:* ''For by a male animal we mean that which generates in another, by a female that which generates in itself'' (*Gen. An.* 716a14–15).[8] Now, Aristotle here is obviously suggesting that males contribute to reproduction by inseminating others, whereas females give birth from themselves.[9] This distinction is surprisingly similar to the distinction that he has made between techne and phusis. The craftsman or the one with techne, we recall, is the moving cause of the man-made entity *outside* himself, whereas an entity from phusis has its moving cause *in itself*.

One would think that because the female gives birth from herself and is thus participating in the coming-to-be from the inside, as it were, that she would be understood as being closer to the bringing-forth of nature. This was it seems in fact the case in almost all early civilizations.[10] For Aristotle, however, although the female is defined as the one who generates in herself, this is in fact no true generation at all, as we see from the qualification Aristotle adds farther on in the passage:

> Male and Female differ in their *logos*. . . . the male is that which is able to generate in another as said above; the female is that which is able to generate in itself and out of which comes into being the generated offspring, *previously existing in the generator*. (*Gen. An.* 716a20–23, emphasis added)[11]

The generator here is the male, for the male is the originating order *(arche)* of the coming-to-be itself, while the female, we read elsewhere, is merely the material cause (*Gen. An.* 716a5–8). The offspring is present in the generator because its form is present in the male seed. Thus the male is the mover and the one who brings-forth *(poioun)*. The father is the active moving cause, whereas the female merely contributes passive matter (*Gen. An.* 729a22ff). We will discover in the following pages through a closer analysis that the female does not ultimately even contribute the material cause.

It is important to keep in mind, for our purposes of exposing the culture/nature dichotomy, that the situation of the female strangely parallels that of nature. Nature in our modern age is a mere passive storehouse of energy that is challenged out and that has significance only through its serviceability for the active orderer and former, "man."

I now discuss the coming-to-be of a "man from a man" in more detail by examining this event in terms of Aristotle's four causes so that we can expose the dominance of form, male, and techne in this event. The four causes of Aristotle are often reduced to two, since the efficient cause (or mover) and final cause are identified with the formal, leaving the well-known distinction between matter and form. But, in fact, every type of causality finds its ultimate expression in the form, since form is responsible for the definiteness of matter, or the distinguishing of it from other things.[12] Form, thereby, is responsible for letting matter *be* something. In the coming-to-be of a baby, not only is every cause ultimately reduced to the formal cause, which will become obvious after I have discussed the complex matter of "matter," but this form is not the human form but more particularly the male form.

In *Physics B,* Aristotle explains why the four causes amount to one:

> The last three often amount to one; for both the whatness and the final cause are one, and the first source of motion is the same in kind as these (for a man begets a man), and, in general, that is so in the case of a moveable mover. (198a24–26)[13]

The last three causes amount to one because the formal cause (the "whatness") here is the form of man (i.e., the shape of man), for this is what comes-to-be; the final cause is also the form of man since that is what the embryo grows toward (i.e., a mature man and not, for instance, a mature horse); and, finally, the mover is also the form of man because it is the father who truly begets the child. Thus, all three causes are of the same kind, leaving only the material cause as something different. Let us leave aside, for the moment, the complex matter of the material cause and consider instead whether the form of man is the form of man as a male or as a human being. It would seem so far in the analysis that the form of man is referring to the human being. However, we will find as we look into this matter more closely that the term *man* here is not gender neutral.[14]

The word for "man" here is the Greek *ho anthropos,* which can mean both "man" as gendered and "man" as human being.[15] It should be noted that there is also a feminine noun, *he anthropos,* which is very close to the previous Greek word but means exclusively "woman." It is certainly true that a human being comes from a human being and by a human being. For Aristotle, however, the form and the final and moving causes here are not the form of the human being but, more specifically, the form of the *male* human being. We have already learned that the moving cause is not the human parents but strictly the father. He begets the child or is the moving cause, even though it is the mother who gives birth to the child, because he has the form of the male in his seed. The formal cause, then, is likewise not gender neutral, since the form in the seed is male. The final cause, more-over, is also not gender neutral because ideally only a male grows from the potential male form in the seed.

Thus, the form of a male (final cause) grows from the male form (formal cause) and by the male form (moving cause) in the male seed. But how can this be, since obviously sometimes females rather than males are born? In this case, it would seem the female and not the male would be the final cause. If the form is indeed gender biased, and the three causes of form, mover, and final cause can be reduced to the formal cause, then what happens when a female comes from a male form?

Aristotle realizes that there is a difficulty in saying that a man comes from a man because sometimes females are born. Thus, he makes the following qualification:

> For the seed acts just like things which act by art *(techne)* since it
> has the form potentially, and that from which the seed proceeds has
> the same name as that which the seed becomes, but only in a sense
> (for we must not expect the same name in every generation as in a
> "man" *(anthropos)* from a man *(anthropos)* since we also have a
> "woman" *(gune)* from a male *(andros)*. (*Meta.* 1034a35–1034b3)[16]

Here Aristotle clearly shows that when he uses "man" he is not using it in a gender-neutral way, since when he speaks of that from which the seed proceeds, it is clear from his preceding statements that he is speaking of the moving cause, which we have learned is strictly the father.[17] Moreover, when he qualifies the statement specifically in terms of gender, he does not say that a male or a female comes from both male and female elements but, rather, makes the strange statement that a woman can come from a male.

A female is obviously not born in a factual sense from a male. Rather, for Aristotle, a woman comes from the man in the sense that she comes from a form, and this form is male. The male seed has the form of strictly the male and thus should naturally (i.e., according to phusis) grow into the form of a male.[18] In other words, man is by nature male. When a female is born instead of a male, it is not that the seed is in this case potentially a female. Rather, the seed remains in all cases a potential male, but in the case of a female birth the seed has not grown toward its appropriate end. Only the male manifests the full development *(telos)* of the human being, "man." The female is an incomplete and, moreover, an infertile male. She has not reached the appropriate end, which is the male form.

When a female is born instead of a male from the potential male form in the seed, Aristotle calls this a "natural abnormality" *(Gen. An.* 775a15) and says it is due to a certain lack of heat.[19] It is natural because so many females are born that one cannot call them mere accidents of nature. However, it is an abnormality or, in other words, contrary to nature, because the essential form of the human being is male. "Man" is naturally male and is female only in a naturally abnormal way.

We must pause to wonder. One would think that the bringing-forth of phusis would be the appropriate guide for what is natural. How could it consistently do something unnatural? Yet, Aristotle says, phusis works against itself when a female is born.

The female does not fit easily in Aristotle's metaphysical system dominated by form over matter. In fact, the female would best be omitted altogether for nature to follow its proper course and achieve its appropriate end. Yet the female stubbornly persists in nature despite its ontological exile. It has not completely disappeared in the difference but appears in the western dynamic, disrupting its flow. The feminine, we recall, presented similar difficulties in Nietzsche's metaphysics. One must be cautious, however, in any project to develop a philosophy in the feminine that this feminine intransigence is not reduced to a mere resistance, to a mere stimulus for the growing empowerment of the Will to Power erection.

The feminine appears in metaphysics as an absencing, a lack, a passivity, and now, we discover, as a natural abnormality. The emergence of the feminine from out of its ontological exile will not involve a simple dissolution of its exile so that the feminine now stands (like a man) on the firm metaphysical foundation of presence and pure unconcealment. Instead, its emergence will open Pandora's box, letting out all those aspects of existence (otherness, the body, mystery, the earth, darkness) that have been disallowed in western phallocentric Being because their natures cannot be rationally represented as stable stuff, and that will reconnect us with the original difficulties of life (Caputo 1987).

The Ontological Demise of Nature

> And on the whole, Neolithic art, and even more so the more developed
> Minoan art, seems to express a view in which the primary function of the
> mysterious powers governing the universe is not to exact obedience,
> punish, and destroy but rather to give.
>
> —Eisler 1987, 20

When nature was understood as the Great Mother of all living things, it was a name for existence as a whole, for Being itself, in metaphysical terms. Our modern reference to "the nature" of something points to this premetaphysical conception. Describing the conceptual factors (interwoven with material, psychological, social, and political factors) involved in the transformation from the pre-western understanding of nature as Great Goddess to the modern understanding of Being as God the Father and the postmodern Will to Power is an important fiber in the general project to reweave a new philosophy that lets in the feminine and has been undertaken by feminists such as Merlin Stone, Riane Eisler and Marija Gimbutas. (The attempt to move into the region of a feminist philosophy is twofold, involving both exposing the phallocentrism of traditional structures and resuscitating other modes of being that have been ontologically exiled, devalued, suppressed, or lost in the western tradition.) In this chapter I unravel the conceptual knots that were forming between phusis and techne during the profound transformation in Being from Phusis to Will to Power by particularly exposing the buttressing offered by the concepts of form, father, and techne.

Let me now discuss the question of the material cause. We will understand that even this supposed contribution of the female to the coming-to-be of a baby is in the last analysis taken away from her and that techne sneaks in the back door to aid the male in this usurpation of the act of generation. The notion of matter is crucial not only because of its association with the female but because of its fundamental association with phusis. Thus the usurpation of the material cause by the male with the help of techne is a domination at the same time of male over female and techne over phusis.

Aristotle, in *The Generation of Animals,* teaches that in the coming-to-be of an animal, the female contributes "menstrual fluid," which is the matter needed for the coming-to-be, and the male contributes the seed, which has the form and which is the generating or moving principle (*Gen. An.* 730a26–27). Why is it, then, that in his more significant works, the *Metaphysics* and the *Physics,* that lay out Aristotle's metaphysics, this matter that the female contributes is *not* the true material cause?

Recall that in the case of the coming-to-be of a tree, in order to be a true material cause, the matter must be *potential* matter. Now the catch is that the menstrual fluid which the female contributes is not potential matter, but *primary* matter *(proton hyle)* (*Gen. An.* 729a33). Moreover, the menstrual fluid is what the female contributes, not to the baby per se, but to the semen or male seed, which once properly placed is itself the true potential matter. Thus, in the *Physics* and the *Metaphysics,* it is in fact the male seed, and not the menstrual fluid, that is given the privilege of being the material cause.[20] The seed is understood as that from which a man comes to be. It is the underlying subject and the material cause. Even the female's contribution of the material cause, then, is subsumed by the male, because primary matter, with which the female is identified, is essentially form-less and thus is lacking the very capacity to be a cause. Primary female matter is passive, lacking potentiality *(dunamis)*.

Let us examine more closely how the male seed becomes the true material cause in the act of generation, because it will reveal an odd concern of Aristotle's about the father's placement of the seed. The earth as a primary matter, we recall, is not potentially a tree until it is determined in some way, as a seed for instance. The same holds true in the coming-to-be of human being. The matter must be formed into the shape of a seed or sperm. However, the seed in this case is still not potential matter until it is properly placed in the womb and then can unite with the passive primary matter, which the female contributes and which the semen actively forms.

It is significant that the placing of the seed becomes a question only when copulating animals are concerned, and most particularly the human male. The fact that the seed of a tree must be placed by the wind in suitable ground is of no account when considering the nature of its coming-to-be. Aristotle's thinking on the placing of the male seed shows his own genuine puzzlement:

> We must now specify when something is potentially another thing
> and when it is not; for it is not potentially another at any time. For
> example, is earth potentially a man? No, but rather when it has
> already become a seed, and perhaps not even then . . . the seed is not
> yet potentially a man; for it must be placed in something else and
> change. And when it is already such that it can be moved by its own
> principle, it is then potentially a man; but prior to this it has need
> of *another principle*. It is like the earth, which is not yet potentially
> a statue, for it needs to be changed and become bronze. (*Meta.*
> 1048b37–1049a18, emphasis added)[21]

The human seed can be moved only by its own principle (i.e., its own originating order, which is from phusis) after it is properly placed in the womb
and can combine with primary matter. In other words, in order to grow in
a phusis-like manner, it is in need of another principle. This other principle
is none other than the father who, as a kind of motive cause, places the
seed in the womb.

Notice that in the important discussion of the nature of matter here in
The Metaphysics, the female menstrual fluid is not mentioned as an example of primary matter in generation. This is most unusual, since Aristotle
most often likens the female menstrual fluid to the primary matter of the
earth because, like the earth which needs the movement of techne to form
it, so the passive, formless female matter needs the active male seed (see,
for instance, *Meta.* 1071b29–32). The female in this excerpt, however, is
completely left out of the discussion. It is the male seed that is not yet
placed that is likened to the primary matter of the earth before it is determined as potential matter in its transformation from ore to bronze.

The omission of the female from true participation on an ontological
level in the coming-to-be of a baby is rather shocking considering how
much pregnancy and birth (not to speak of the tending over the growth of
children into maturity) often involve a woman's life and the large role they
have played in the oppression of women. The male's only concrete participation in generation is his (often uncontrolled) emission of semen in the
womb. Aristotle does not find the flesh and blood mother important to
the abstract coming-to-be of a form of man from the form of man, yet now

the father's placement of the seed becomes the necessary missing link that transforms female passive matter to potential matter.[22] Indeed, Aristotle at times names the father (with his movements) and not the seed as the moving cause in generation.[23] If the flesh and blood father's placement of the seed becomes so important in this metaphysical birth of a form from a form, then why do the bearing of the growing embryo for nine months and the actual labor of giving birth ontologically count for nothing?

Let us attempt to undo the knots of relations that have been woven together in the above excerpt from Aristotle's *Metaphysics* between techne, form, and the father with a view to creating a space for the mother. The one knotty problem that, if unraveled, will begin to unravel the tangled mess called the culture/nature dualism is the problem of the placement of the seed.

Natural entities move by their own principle. Man-made entities are moved by man. The seed of a tree grows by itself, but a lump of copper ore will not grow into a statue. In cases of natural entities, the form internally places itself, and in cases of artifacts, the form has to be externally placed.

Aristotle knits his brow. But the seed of man does not grow in his belly. It needs to be externally placed by man in something else, and then the form in the seed of man can place itself. (*That's* what this thing is for.) The form of man has to be put in the proper container.

Techne is brought in to help the male nature close the gap between the outside and the inside, to help fortify his resolve during the weak moment before the gates when uncertainty creeps in. The weak point: the rise or fall of the pocket signifier.

The "something else" waits quietly, all dark. Still. The unnamed she. The great round egg.

Action! Lights! Camera on the entrance. The technical difficulty is the placement of the seed. Aim in view: guide the long nose of the missile. Pickaxes pricking the earth for copper ore. Penetration through barriers. Courageous, brave, breaking of the sound barrier. Faster than the speed of light. Hi, ho Silver! To the moon?[24] To Baghdad? Adventurous voyage to the bottom.

(Mother is nursing the baby. Holding, rocking, swaying. No action there.)

Fire! The art (techne) of placing the seed. Father with his big pointed finger (reaching for Adam) is the other principle needed to set the seed on its way, the moving principle whose action determines, forms, transforms, injects potency. Potentiality. Father sets the coming in motion, spilling white consciousness. Creation. The Big Bang.

(Mother is doing the laundry, scrubbing out the salty stains. No techne there.)

Let's get real. Movement is the gush of white Will to Power. The white heat of man's fire. Melting the ore down. Pouring liquid bronze into the mold of man. The exquisite bronze *Charioteer* (Delhi Museum, 460 b.c.). *Poseidon* (Athens National Museum, 460 b.c.) all athrust with his pointy thing. Handy, randy man. Tools in and out of the earth. Fine, clever movements. Stick it in gear. Daddy, is this *drive* art or instinct?

Raw matter formed by man into a product for use. Man re-produced by man? Hey man, are you saying this is a *man-made* coming-to-be of a man from a man? (Now you've gone too far. Right through to the other side. Oh well. No use crying over spilt . . .)

All I'm saying is, There's got to be "something else" somewhere. And what I'm really wondering is, Why does the brief salty squirt count as the all-important movement and not the drawn out sweet receiving and holding? The penetration, and not the wide welcoming in?

My sweet milk comes down, drawn out by a hungry mouth. My great round waits for another rounding dance. My honey drips. I remember my panting, sweating body screaming to open wider for the great gush of life. Welcoming, receiving, waiting, dripping, pushing, crying, opening.

Doesn't matter. Mother doesn't even *matter* when it really counts. Because passive, impotent mother matter doesn't move.

But excuse me for that rather unruly outburst. Let me pull up my academic socks and answer the question. Is the placement of the seed from techne or from phusis? We have to go back to *The Generation of Animals* to find out that the tool of our unraveling, his thing, is not his to use as a tool after all but is the tool of phusis (not Phusis, the Great Goddess, but the Grand Crafts-man Phusis):

> Therefore, the birth must take place in the female. For the carpenter must keep close connexion with his timber and the potter with his clay, and generally all workmanship and the ultimate move-

ment imparted to matter must be connected with the material concerned. . . . From these considerations we may also gather how it is
that the male contributes to generation. The male does not emit
semen at all in some animals, and where he does this is no part of the
resulting embryo; just so no material part comes from the carpenter
to the material . . . but the shape and the form are imparted from him
to the material by means of the motion he sets up. It is his hands
that move his tools, his tools that move the material; it is his knowledge of his art *(techne),* and his soul, in which is the form, that move
his hands or any other part of him with a motion of some definite
kind, a motion varying with the varying nature of the object made.
In like manner, in the male of those animals which emit semen,
nature uses the semen as a tool and as possessing motion in actuality,
just as tools are used in the products of any art, for in them lies in a
certain sense the motion of the art. Such, then, is the way in which
males contribute to generation. But when the male does not emit
semen, but the female inserts some part of herself into the male, this
is parallel to a case in which a man should carry the material to the
workman. For by reason of weakness in such males nature is not
able to do anything by any secondary means, but the movements imparted to the material are scarcely strong enough when nature itself
watches over them. Thus here nature resembles a modeler in clay
rather than a carpenter, for she does not touch the work she is forming
by means of tools, but with her own hands. *(Gen. An.* 730b4–31)[25]

Aristotle wrongly thought that in some species the female fly inserted
a tube into the male in the copulation of insects (see Barnes 1982, 11).
Yet even if it were the case that the female physically entered the male,
her movements would not count as the moving cause. It is still the male
that sets things in motion because, like phusis, he is identified with the
working of techne. The female still only contributes passive material and
now receives, not the male semen, but his active "heat and potentiality
(dumanis)," which sets her unformed clay in motion *(Gen. An.* 729b24ff).

We can now answer our question. In the generation of a human being,
although the father has to "artfully" place the seed in the womb, he is act-

ing under the orders of phusis. Even though this placing is an external placing of form like the external placing of form involved in the creation of
man-made products, he is acting within the ordering of phusis. Thus, the
father, in the final analysis, places the seed according to his phusical nature
and not directly according to his nature as possessor of techne. But phusis
and the male, both being bearers of form, now have a most intimate relation. Once phusis is understood as form and metaphorically as craftsman or
former of matter, the male and not the female is seen as closer to nature.
For now the mysterious coming-forth of a baby from a mother's womb,
which identified the mother with phusis's bringing-forth from out of concealment, does not matter to the nature of Being. What matter now is the
active former.

Let me now return to the difficult statement of Aristotle's with which we
began, where Aristotle first names phusis form. We are now in a position
to see how the blurring of the distinction between man in his phusical nature and in his nature as possessor of techne or former of matter aids Aristotle's argument that phusis should be form and not matter:

> Indeed, the form is nature to a higher degree than the matter; for each
> thing receives a name when it exists in actuality *(energeia)* rather
> than when it exists potentially *(dunamis)*. Moreover, it is from a man
> that a man is generated, but a bed is not generated from a bed. . . .
> So if in the latter case it is the art *(techne),* in the former too it is the
> form that should be nature, for it is from a man that a man is gen-
> erated. (*Phys.* 193b7–12)

The first sentence in this passage is referring to the fact that a thing receives
its name from the form (which is also the moving cause) because it is in actuality. A thing does not receive its name from the material cause that is
only potentially.[26] For example, we name a man a man, which is the moving cause and has the form, and not a seed, which is the material cause.
The second sentence we looked at briefly at the outset of this discussion.
Aristotle is not pointing to the fact that a mother gives birth to a human being from her own flesh, whereas a bed requires an intervening craftsman
who possesses knowledge of form to make a bed from the original model;
but rather, he is saying that the form of man comes directly (internally)

from the form of man, whereas the form of the bed has to be externally placed. The rest of Aristotle's argument, which is indeed rather complex and concise, goes something like this: The form of man as phusis in the father is the moving cause of the man generated, just as the form of the bed as techne in the craftsman is the moving cause of the bed generated. Since the moving cause in both phusis and techne is form, and since actuality, which is form, is better and prior to potentiality, which is matter, then nature as a principle of motion should be form rather than matter.[27]

To follow the thread of the argument, then, we must focus on the notion of form. Tracing this thread we find that in the first case the form is from phusis, and in the second case the form is from techne. What sews the argument together is the fact that man possesses the form on both accounts. He possesses techne, which is knowledge of form, in his soul, and he possesses form according to his phusical nature in his seed.

Without the male who figures prominently in this argument, Aristotle's argument would lose its force, for the male craftsman serves both as the prime representative of the way phusis works and of the way techne works. The male tool crochets Aristotle's phallus-centered argument together, weaving in and out, leaving "her" out (because she does not have *one*). Father as the true moving cause takes over from the (genitally deficient) mother her active participation in the coming-to-be. Since he is not metaphysically closer to nature, he is no longer on the outside of the birthing event but, rather, on the inside, and he can claim the mystery of the coming-to-be as his own.

Aristotle's argument that phusis is form is an important indication for the history of western metaphysics of the general change that had been occurring in people's attitudes to nature in different regions of Old Europe (Gimbutas 1990). It helps conceptualize the broad, fundamental changes that had been occurring in early people's conception of nature (and in the social relations between the sexes) since at least as early as 2400 B.C. when the religions from the north subsumed the nature religions of the Great Goddess in the Near and Middle East and southern Europe (see Stone 1976; Gimbutas 1989 and 1990; Eisler 1987). The submergence of the Goddess religions was gradual and took place at different times and in different ways in the various regions. Often the various goddesses were assigned a *paredre* (male child or young lover) who then later took a dominant position and helped form the patriarchal Indo-European pantheon (see Saliou 1986).

The dominance of form in Aristotle, reinforced by its associations with the male as craftsman, with the father, and with techne, contributes to the long, discontinuous, and varied transformations from the premetaphysical notion of phusis as Great Mother to the present ontological decline of phusis into a standing reserve of energy in the service of techne.[28] Although phusis, for Aristotle, on the rare occasion still designated the fundamental relations human beings have with all beings and that beings have with each other, the conception of nature as formed matter became dominant in his thinking and was to remain vital for the West.[29]

In the Christian conception of Being, God is the grand craftsman and the former of nature. Phusis in this conception is merely the created work or passive matter formed by God. In the sixteenth and seventeenth centuries, with the advances in science, nature is still the formed matter of God but is now understood in terms of a complicated mechanism whose structure can be rationally known. With the advent of modern physics, which enabled scientists to explore the secret inner workings of nature, nature is understood as energy. During the industrial revolution of the mid-eighteenth and early nineteenth centuries, technology, depending on the advances of physics, was able to harness nature (newly understood as energy) for the first time on a broad scale. Now man (for it was the male gender), as master of the earth, deposes God and takes charge of God's creation through his own technology. Man becomes the grand craftsman and is himself the former of nature. Today we still understand nature as energy to be harnessed by technology. However, nature for us is not even a field of objects controlled by human subjects but is reduced to the objectlessness of the standing reserve. Because serviceability, usability and substitutability dominate nature's modern presencing, the stand of natural entities in the world-earth-home is not a standing against (*gegan-stand* is the German word for object) a subject. Rather, nature is reduced to a passive storehouse of energy resources, which does not stand in itself but stands by, ready to be of service to human beings.

Phusis has been understood as energy (from the Greek *energeia,* literally translated as "having itself in the work") since the industrial revolution. This uni-form for phusis offered by modern physics is a new, powerful synthesis of primary matter, potential matter, and form. Like primary matter it is that universal matter or substance from which everything is made. It is the underlying substratum that remains throughout all changes, for it can be transformed into mass, heat, or light while still remaining energy. Like potential matter, moreover, it has the power to do work. Aristotle's *dunamis,* taken up as *potentia* through the Latin, becomes for modern physics that force that can produce effects and can be acted upon by other forces.[30] Energy, like form, moreover, is also the actualizing of the power to do work, the being-at-work of force. Energy is mass in motion ($E = mc^2$). It is neither passive, formless matter waiting to receive form nor a fixed form but attains the flexibility and dynamism of becoming without losing the security, constancy, and fixity of being.

The ontological decline of nature as an independent presencing is at the same time a transformation of it into a passive reserve of active matter standing by to be formed through human techne. Thus today, techne is not understood as encompassed by phusis, which was once understood as the highest mode of bringing-forth. Rather, it is taken for granted by us through rapid technological advances that we are in opposition to, and in control of, nature. Nature, moreover, receives its meaning *from* our cultural productions. In other words, techne is no longer phusical but phusis in our modern age is technical.

Both the metaphysical dominance of techne over phusis and the material dominance of human beings over nature are bound up with the exclusion of women from contributing to the history of cultural production. Women's omission from western history has obviously not been necessitated by practical matters (i.e., that she had to stay at home to raise children). The material conditions of a woman's mothering body (pregnancy, birth, and most especially breastfeeding, which requires a relatively close physical proximity to the young) could have been accommodated by social structures in such a way as to enable women to wholeheartedly participate in the cultural production as they have in many other cultures at different periods and in different ways.[31] Early Greek women found themselves excluded from the sites of power at least partially because of the way in which cultural activity was and still is understood conceptually, namely, as a controlling and forming of passive nature with which they were identified.[32] If the work of caring for our phusical being, the young and old, and all living beings of the earth were recognized as crucial to the conception of our cultural being in the world-earth-home, then the sites of cultural production would both shift and change. For not only would more room be made for women's mothering body in cultural sites of power, but, as Nancy Hartsock (1985) and Sara Ruddick (1983), for example, suggest, nurturing practices themselves would profoundly affect the organizational principles of institutions and of political and social structures for the benefit of both men and women.

Although the conception of Being as Great Mother is undoubtedly more benign and encourages a respect for nature in contrast to that of God the Father and his Creation, and although this early expression of simple societies' relation to nature corresponded with a higher status of women in those societies, the Great Goddess religions cannot be realistically reinstated on a broad scale in our contemporary societies since our material and spiritual conditions are so radically different today.[33] Attempts to evoke the various Goddesses and reclaim their wisdom by Starhawk (1979) and Mary Daly (1990), for example, are nonetheless refreshing and invigorating. Such invocations may be helpful along the path, not toward reinstating Mother or Father, Goddess or God, but toward responding to the breathing ground, to living animals, to our own bodies, and to human beings in a more response-able manner. We mortals need to recognize that we are not supreme subjects in command of the earth but are part of an embodied ''round dance'' of Being.[34] The step back from the phallocentric power that guides this age is not a step back into feminine power. Although the step back lets in the feminine, it is a step back into our belonging-place *(topos)* as human beings in the world-earth-home.

In Chapter Six, I feminize the culture/nature dichotomy by introducing the notion of phusical techne, which is best understood through home-oriented or nurturing arts. This notion of a cultivating techne attempts to let in the feminine and allow the traditionally subordinate category of nature to resume its original encompassing of culture. Through this discussion I work toward the ecofeminist project of revisioning our natural-cultural situation as human beings in the world-earth-home.

Soft or Hard? Or? Or How to Philosophize with Breasts: The Minoan Snake Goddess, 1600 B.C.

"Why so hard?" the charcoal once said to the diamond; "for are we not close relations?"
Why so soft? O my brothers, thus I ask you: for are you not—my brothers?
   Why so soft, unresisting and yielding?
                              —Friedrich Nietzsche, "The Hammer Speaks"

Love seeketh not Itself to please, / Nor for itself hath any care; / But for another gives its ease, / And builds a Heaven in Hells despair. / So sang a little Clod of Clay, / Trodden with cattles feet; / But a Pebble of the brook, / Warbled out these metres meet. / Love seeketh only Self to please, / To bind another to Its delight: / Joys in anothers loss of ease, / And builds a Hell in Heavens despite.
                              —William Blake, "The Clod and the Pebble"[1]

She stands with a firm stance that holds authority. She is transfixed yet not rigid, for the strong writhing movements of the snakes in her hands flow through her arms and body. Her flounced dress is like a snake's skin that can move and flex despite its rigidity. It holds in the fluid movements of her hips and gathers tightly at her waist. By contrast, her breasts positively bulge out of her dress, spilling out freely and nakedly like a snake breaking out of its skin. Her hair, too, is snakelike as it flows down her back in springing curls. Her head is still, still enough to hold a wild cat like a crown on her head. The cat poises, motionless and elegant, proudly arching its back in contrast to the wild wriggling of the snakes.

Who is she? She is commonly known as the Snake Goddess. She is one of the pre-Indo-European "fertility" sculptures of the Goddess religion that was prevalent during the Upper Paleolithic period to the second millennium B.C. in the Near East, Europe, and the Mediterranean area. Her history as Snake Goddess can be traced as far back as the combined snake and bird goddesses of the Magdelenian culture of the Upper Paleolithic period (12,000 B.C.), and memories of her persist in the later

173

goddesses Hera and Athena, who were themselves transformed in the Greek Olympiad (Gimbutas 1982, 150). Sometimes the Snake Goddess and the Bird Goddess are separate figures and sometimes they are a single divinity. Each cultural area had its own various methods of portraying her, but the symbolic signs associated with her and the general conception of her image were the same (p. 142). She is mistress of diverse life-generating forces, especially the life-giving force of water. Her presence is felt in the earth as well as in the skies, in the lower and the upper waters. Her influence in southeastern Europe was cut short by the invasion of seminomadic northern tribes of the Indo-European culture during the fourth millennium B.C. The colorful pottery and art of these peoples also quickly vanished. However, around the more southern Aegean area and on the Greek islands, the traditions of the Goddess survived to the end of the third millennium B.C., and on the even more southern Crete, with the Minoan civilization her influence lasted into the mid-second millennium B.C. The Minoan Snake Goddess, then, is one of the last vestiges of the old Goddess's presencing.

Although the Minoan culture has often been referred to as a matri-

archal culture in contrast to the
patriarchal Greeks, there is no evidence for an actual dominance of
female power in the culture.[2] The
notion of a matriarch seems to me in
any case a patriarchal afterthought
since its dynamic is modeled on the
structures of patriarchy.[3] However,
while the sovereignty of the female
principle in the Minoan religion and
the custom of maternal descent in
the Minoan society do not prove the
existence of a matriarchal power
structure, they do show that women
had considerable freedom and status.

The Minoan Snake Goddess does
not fit the prevalent image of a fertility goddess, which is typically
portrayed by the so-called obese, steatopygic stone figures of the Upper
Paleolithic period. She upsets our
common impressions of a fertility
goddess because she has narrow hips,
a small waist, and firm rather than
pendulous breasts; in other words,
she has an overall modern eroticism.
Her hairstyle, dress, and imposing
authoritative stance, moreover, show
her to be a "sophisticated" lady. The
overriding homogeneous categorization of prehistoric female images as
fertility figures limits their diverse
meanings and dismisses their unique-
ness and mystery. The very word
fertility at best presupposes the giving

of nature as a kind of unrestrained fecundity in contrast to the controlled productivity of culture. It thereby also, however, creates a rift between female
reproduction and cultural production. With the help of this form of the culture/
nature dichotomy it is commonly explained that divinities were female in the
infancy of civilization because foraging and early agrarian cultures depended
wholly on the productivity of nature, which in turn was associated with female
productivity. This modern, western way of thinking about fertility, however,
depends on an instrumental means and ends model that distances us from the
wonder of bringing-forth. In trying to come near to a non-western flourishing—a spilling-over with fullness (that we see in the Snake Goddess's breasts,
for example)—we need to think not on the notion of fertility (or the capacity
to produce) but on the wonder of bringing-forth itself. For, it seems to me, it
was not so much the end result of their efforts that evoked peoples' wonder
and thankfulness but, rather, the mystery of nature's coming-forth itself. As is
evidenced by their well-recognized exuberant and happy artwork, the Minoans,
for example, delighted in the gifts of the sea and the land and the gift of bodily
openness. This expression of their delight is a testimony not to an economical
pushing of material production to maximal yield but to their attunement to,
sheltering of, and sharing in, the life-giving swirls of nature's coming-forth. So,
too, in the Snake Goddess's full breasts it is not fertility in the modern sense
that is celebrated but, rather, the "It gives" *(Es gibt)* of Emergence itself.

She stands with a strange, balanced fullness. Looking at her from the side
we notice that she leans surprisingly forward from her feet, although her heels
are flat on the ground. She balances this forward incline by sharply arching her
back (like the arching cat on her head) and pulling her shoulders back. As a
result of this peculiar stance, her most vulnerable parts, her soft breasts, are
thrust forward. This thrusting forward, softly, erotically, while at the same time
pulling back and giving way is a wonderful image of the body's capacity to
deeply bend to difference.

This athletic arching of the back, which gymnasts, for instance, take after
their performances, is a stance peculiar to the Minoan culture.[4] From many
bronze figurines of worshiping men and women (sixteenth and fifteenth centuries B.C.), and from various figures depicted on small seals, it is clear that the
stance with the arching back often occurs when someone gives respectful salu-
tation to another. Generally, the figure arches back with a closed hand touching

the forehead and/or chest. The athletic Minoan culture admired this odd way
of holding up the body, which shows both the body's flexibility and strength
and, at the same time, the body's softness and vulnerability. In this stance, the
body's vulnerable protuberances, genitals and breasts, protrude all the more.
Marija Gimbutas (1990, 95) suggests that bodily protuberances were associated
with the sprouting dynamism of the snake in Neolithic art because special attention was given to inscribing snake motifs on every convex roundness of the
female body and on the male phallus.

That the Minoans delighted in responding to difference and, as it were, getting into the swing of an other's movement is quite evident in a major Minoan
cultural sport: bull leaping. In this sport (in which both men and women would
participate), a skillful acrobat would grasp the bull's horns just at the moment
when the bull lowered its horns for an angry toss and then spring off the horns
with a backward flip over the back of the bull. The point of these rather dangerous acrobatic antics, it seems, was not to show mastery over the bull but to
take up and extend an other's movement by swirling with it through the body.
Contact with otherness (here the nonhuman movements of the bull) is shown
up with a flourishing swirl through the human body. The Minoans deeply loved
swirling movements. On their magnificently swelling pots, they drew swirling
octopuses, lilies, crocuses, dolphins, and swirling lines. The swirl can be understood as expressing the Minoan's bare openness to and delight in being-with
otherness (which here is the same as nature). Their happy, swirling pots show
an enjoyment of the flourishing of life itself. In other words, they brought
human joy to the flowing swirls that burst out abundantly all around them in
the fish of the sea, the birds, flowers, grasses, and trees.

The Minoans, then, in contrast to our western culture, which is founded on
a relation of domination of nature, made openness to nature an art or techne.
Although I will not discuss the Minoan culture in detail here, it is evident from
their pottery, which expresses a joyful, exuberant, yet easeful contact with the
wildlife of the sea and land; from the architecture of the Minoan palaces, which
are oriented to the sunlight and wind and are arranged according to smaller,
particular spatial locations that give way to and respect human sociality rather
than being arranged according to an overriding uniformity and economy; and
from their sport of bull leaping and their arched-back stance, that this culture as
a whole had a down-to-earth openness to their environment, the wildlife of the

sea and the land, and their own fleshy, social bodies. Their delight in swirling with difference was central to their culture and was cultivated in various artistic ways.[5]

As far as we can gather from the remnants of the Minoan culture, only the snake priestesses (rather than the priests) ritually dance with the snakes. One wonders whether we would call this holding of the snakes a dance if the figure were a male. Calling this activity a dance, for example, could be partially the result of sexist associations with dancing girls who danced for the pleasure of princes and kings. Yet, there is evidence from fresco fragments that a dance seems to be an appropriate name for the priestess entwining with the snakes and that the audience may even have been composed exclusively of women.[6]

Unlike the Indo-European and Near Eastern mythologies where the serpent symbolizes evil powers, the snake was an important animal in the various cultures of southeastern Europe. The snake and its derivative abstract forms such as the wavy line are the dominant motifs of the art during the Neolithic period up until the Minoan civilization. It is strongly associated with life-giving water, likely because of its spontaneous dynamic movement and the periodic shedding of its skin, which is an image of the cyclic rejuvenation of nature as a whole. Because of their shedding of their skin, snakes are also linked to healing. Even later after the Indo-European invasion, the influence of the snake as healing and awe inspiring persists. At Delphi, for example, the mythic Pythia was the source of oracular prophecy. However, reflecting the growing dominance of the patriarchal religions of the northern invaders, the Pythia in Greek mythology is killed by Apollo in his infancy, the new male god of prophecy. In this same Apollonian light, the serpent is well known in Judeo-Christian mythology as that evil lowly creature who conspires with Eve against the first created man.

The Snake Goddess bends to the snakes, not by imitating their snaky movements, but by holding their movements and letting them vibrate through her. Responding to the wild sinuosity and energetic spontaneous movements of the snakes would have required great flexibility and full bodily concentration. Her dance is a joyful celebration of openness to difference, of the wondrous softness and openness of the human body, of its ability to bend to the swirling lines of nature.[7] In fact, perhaps her dance manifested more of the snakes' own dance than it did her own human body's response to the snake. In the same way that the spectators saw the strength and swirl of the bull's tossing head through the extension of it in the acrobat's body, the audience of the snake priestess would have witnessed the taking up and extending of the snakes' own sinuous movement, which was put into relief through the responsiveness of her flexuous body. Because we westerners tend to stress the subjective side in all contact with otherness (as indeed the term *otherness* implies), it is a strange thought for us that in the dance of the snake priestess, it may have been the snakes' movements that were beheld with wonder and that were shown through her fluid openness to the snakes, rather than her own movements making use of the snakes' power as a kind of inspiration. Yet, from the presencing of this artwork, it would seem that her sacred taking up and holding of the snakes' sinewy movements is a celebration of the swirling writhing of the snake. Letting the other fill one with its otherness is not feared by the Minoans but welcomed and celebrated. Her dance shows the art (techne) of taking up another's movement, altering it, and being altered by it.

The snakes look straight out on either side of the Snake Goddess, mesmerizingly. They are held straight out away from her head in each of her hands with the unwavering strength of her upraised arms. The still, proud cat on her head, the wriggling snakes in either hand, and her jutting breasts form a strong triangular stance that commands respect. We assume she is a goddess or high priestess of some sort because of the seemingly powerful command she holds. But what is the deeper nature of this command?

Her firm holding of the snakes does not seek to control them. She allows the snakes to wriggle freely and, by holding them up, exhibits their wriggling that longs to entwine around. The Minoan delight, as we have discussed, is not in the mastery of another but in the taking up and holding of another's movements. Although she tightly grasps the snakes as she dances, they are not imprisoned by her firm hold on them. She is neither showing power over the snakes nor threatening others with the snakes, using them as some sort of weapon. Rather, by being held up in the careful dance, the snakes are free to writhe all the more vigorously, wildly seeking something to wind around.

Recall that the command of Will to Power, is a command of the natural powers of the body and earth, which had been suppressed in previous Platonic-Christian metaphysics. These natural affects must be tapped in such a way, says Nietzsche, that their wild power is not "tamed," thereby draining the affects of their power. They must be commanded in all their wildness for the sake of the enpowerment of power. This Nietzschean command and grasp of nature (which he images as a wild woman in *Thus Spoke Zarathustra*) thereby allows nature to retain its full force while nonetheless humanizing, transforming it into an energy resource in the service of man. Is the Snake Goddess's command of this kind (i.e., a tapping of their untamed power)? In other words, is there a difference between her holding of nonhuman otherness and modern technology's hold on nature?

The Snake Goddess is undoubtedly afire with the wriggling energy of the snakes. Holding the snakes out in the air like this would be like holding live wires. One's body would shake and vibrate with the current of movement. She stands, one might think, like a hydroelectric tower, gathering and distributing energy. Electricity is indeed a wild energy, immediately channeled and distributed for use. The wild energy of the snakes, however, by contrast is not channeled and apportioned but gathers and swells in her body, which alters according to this energy. Moreover, she does not contain the energy of the snakes but endures their movements. Because she cannot endure their movements for a predictable length of time, she cannot turn their movements into a stable and secured supply of energy.

The snakes are obviously not tamed since they remain vigorously writhing in her hands in all their wildness. Yet, they are not untamed, if this means an attitude of hostility toward her. On the contrary, there appears to be an intimate relation between the Snake Goddess and her snakes. The snakes are her wild pets. They are wild, threatening, yet have a secret bond with her.[8] The Snake Goddess's hold on the snakes is not a Nietzschean command from the very outset because she is not in a power struggle with the snakes. She is not unlocking or tapping their power, controlling them in a top-down way, because she herself is altered by contact with the serpents. She dances with and through them. Just as Merleau-Ponty says our bodies are *of* the world, so her dance is so involved with the movements of the snakes that it is *of* the snakes. Her tensed body is not motivated by a will to power but by a concentrated openness to hold the serpents' vibrations more deeply. She herself becomes serpentine as the wriggling snakes writhe about her body.

She lets their wild writhing flow through her body. The wonder of the Snake Goddess is that she lets in and holds the spontaneous, life-giving force of the snakes, like a storm cloud holds impending rain. Thus she holds their powers

in a way that is not an overpowering of them and, thus, in a way that is so foreign to the movements that guide our western age. She lets in, absorbs, holds.
These movements have traditionally been viewed in the West as inferior and
passive in contrast to active penetrating movements because of the implicit cri-
teria of judgment: power, which in turn is understood as the ability to compel
obedience. Given that our western Being is based on power relations, the
Minoan Snake Goddess, who is at a remove from our western age, may help us
understand how the receiving and holding of another's movements is a strength
that is repressed in this western age and how this movement is a crucial way
of ordering in its own right. This movement must be understood if possible
from its own particular manner of being.

Before I continue with these descriptions, it will be helpful to contrast her
stance, which is representative of the Minoan culture, with that of Apollo, the
god of reason belonging to the neighboring, but later, Greeks who were to
emerge as the powerful culture that gives birth to the West. Let me turn to the
famous relief sculpture of Apollo on the western pediment of the Temple of
Zeus at Olympia, made during the transition from the Archaic to the Hellenistic
sculptural style (460 B.C.). The battle on the pediment depicts the mythic battle
between the Lapiths and the centaurs. According to the myth, King Perithous
of the Lapiths wanted to celebrate his wedding to Deidameia, and he invited his
neighbors, including Theseus and the centaurs. During the feast, the centaurs
became drunk, and the king of the centaurs, Eurytion, offended the bride,
Deidameia. A battle ensued, and the centaurs were defeated by the Lapiths
with the help of Theseus.

Apollo, the god of reason, stands calmly in the center of the pediment; his
right arm stretches out imposingly, making a right angle with the vertical line of
his body. He is the still point of order in the twisting, struggling, chaotic movements of violence surrounding him. With his clear, farseeing gaze and his arm
that stretches and points out and across the battle scene, he commands the
action. We know that honor and justice will prevail because Apollo's order
infuses the bodies of the men, directing their ability to fight the centaurs.

The bold, naked men, who fight the centaurs and are on the verge of completely defeating them, are clearly fighting under Apollo's direction. Unlike the
struggling, pushing, grasping, scratching, biting, and pulling of hair in which the
centaurs and women are engaged, the men fight with weapons. One Lapith

man, for instance, stabs a centaur quite cunningly from behind, under the centaur's arm and into his chest as the centaur, unaware, holds a woman with both arms. Another raises his sword to deal a centaur a clean blow. Theseus raises his axe to kill the centaur king. These weapons (sword, knife, and axe) all require a well-aimed, quick blow in order to be effective. In other words, the skill required is the calm rational ability of Apollo, which can pinpoint the goal ahead and direct itself straight to that goal. The men's premeditated, rational blows are starkly contrasted to the immediate, physically close, animal-like fighting of the centaurs (and, moreover, the women). The centaurs, though larger than the men and physically stronger, as half-animal beings, lack the ability to plan ahead that is needed to see the aim in view and lack the rational distance between oneself and one's goal, which is needed to strike one's mark with a straight, skillful blow.

The women, like the half-animal centaurs, are also oblivious to Apollo's calm rationality, which flows through the whole scene, restoring order. The bodies of the women are turned toward us, closest to the front and larger than the men, putting into high relief their piteous struggle. The swirling lines of the women's drapery contrasts both with the naked bodies of the men (for the men have let their robes fall to the ground) and with the centaurs. The drapery gives the women a sinuous grace but also emphasizes their being dragged down and their inability to defend themselves against their aggressors. The heavy robes, while seemingly protecting them, fetter their movements, forcing them to defend themselves in a way that, like the centaurs', lacks Apollo's calculated, rational aim.

The swirling mass of drapery that clothes these women suggests that for the Greeks of the fifth century, the swirling line was certainly not a source of delight, as it was for the Minoans but, on the contrary, was feared because it evoked chaos, now understood as the absence of order and associated with the untamed presence of nature.[9] Although drapery is a definite cultural accruement, it is associated here with the fearful chaos and contingency of nature to wreak havoc on our clear, and often straight, cultural lines.[10] Because drapery relates so intimately and flexuously to the wind and movements, it so easily swirls out of control.

It is the wit of the men, their agility, and their rational, sure blows that secure the victory over the centaurs. The women are merely passive victims who struggle vigorously to get free, but to no avail. From this pediment it would seem, however, that women do not need the male warriors' protection because they are thought to be softer and weaker. The women appear larger than the men, and the men, moreover, have cast off their robes, clearly exposing their own soft, vulnerable penises. Surely a blow here would be even more debilitating than a blow to a woman's breast. I suggest that the penis is so obviously exposed because it symbolically manifests the forward thrust of the rational (understood as male), rather than the physical, power in the fight. Apollo's rational order in this pediment clearly speaks to the men's naked bodies and their skillful bearing of weapons and not to the women's bodies, heavily clothes in swirling masses of drapery.[11]

The Minoan Snake Goddess's stance is clearly not Apollonian.[12] The phallic snakes in the Snake Goddess's hands, in contrast to the medium of Apollonian reason, are not weapons that cut straight lines through the air to their victims but wriggle in all directions unpredictably. If her eyes are transfixed, seeing straight ahead, moreover, it is not because they stare at a goal posited straight ahead of her through an act of rational consciousness but because they are expressing her ecstasy. They stare wildly, letting in rather than focusing out. Their wide-eyed openness invites us to come near to her. Her ecstasy is a result of being full of the snakes' power (the snakes, for their part, are also relishing her powerful hold). Though she is powerful, she is not aggressive, for although her distant gaze is somewhat fearful and intense and the snakes are undoubtedly threatening, the softness of her naked, swelling breasts draws us near. Their whiteness, roundness, and smoothness and the fine veins of the polished faience invite the touch.

The movements of the phallic snakes orient her whole stance. Their movements vibrate down her arms, expand through her attuned body, and finally swell into her breasts. It is her swelling breasts, then, which have no muscle and whose tensity can only be seen in their peaked thrust, that absorb the mad wriggling of the snakes. In these softly swelling breasts we feel the strength of the snakes' wildness. Her breasts, then, manifest a different kind of power than that of the Greek phallic reason, as do the Minoan snakes themselves. Her breasts gather and locate the swirling movement, like the backwash of a streaming current, like a recess pool that gathers the torrent of a waterfall.

We cannot ignore these breasts, which do not merely fall out of her bodice but positively burst out like flowers. They are like perfectly ripe fruit bursting with fullness. Whereas her skirt is rather stiff and bends only along predetermined joints, her breasts are soft and swelling. The voluptuous fullness of her protruding white breasts is so bold that one is somewhat taken aback. In our western culture, breasts are prevalently rather passive objects of male desire. Thus, women cannot freely bare their breasts in public because of their sexual value. Moreover, even though from the common viewpoint of male desire, a mothering body loses its sexual desirability, women cannot freely breastfeed in public places but must do so furtively. That the nurturing capacity of breasts is markedly separated from their sexual significance, particularly in white western culture, and that this nurturing capacity is nonetheless repressed (have you ever seen a white woman breastfeeding on television?) indicates a deeply unhealthy repression of sensuality.

The Minoans, by contrast, it would seem from the open-bodice dresses of the women, openly enjoyed the sensuousness of the female body just as they clearly enjoyed the sensuousness of nature as a whole. The fullness and whiteness of the Snake Goddess's breasts suggest they are full with milk. This liquid fullness seems to enhance her erotic appeal rather than cancel it out. At one and the same time, as mother and erotic lover, she is voluptuous and sensual. Her nipples are erect. The spilling out of her breasts is a releasement of the snakes' wild, passionate movements. It is a giving of nature's sap, of milk, and of life-giving rain.

Her breasts show most perspicaciously contact with what is wild and nonhuman. They stare out with wild, inhuman eyes. Indeed, her breasts seem more expressive than her face, for her eyes stare without seeing, mesmerized, and mesmerizing her audience, but life and movement gather here and express themselves in her breasts. That the breasts can be the gathering place of so much movement and, moreover, can be a gathering locale for cultural celebration is strange for us. The Snake Goddess's breasts, however, are unmistakeably alive with the vibrations of the snakes. They swell whitely, firmly, toward us. Her hair, too, snakes around her breasts in a kind of adoration of the full swelling. It ripples down like life-giving rain, like milk spilling over.[13]

Phenomenologically, the soft roundness of the Snake Goddess's breasts is so obvious because of her squeezed waist. Her tight bodice holds her in at the waist. So, too, she tightly holds the phallic snakes with her hands. Yet her tight grasp on the snakes is not a show of dominating power, for as I have said, it is really her breasts that fully hold the snakes. Her breasts that softly swell and bulge in their holding are almost the inverse of her hands tight grasping of the snakes. Can we come any closer to understanding this elusive holding that is not an overpowering or indeed in the region of power but is an openness to difference, a giving of oneself over to another? Perhaps we can by staying here with her breasts.

Her hold and command are not oriented to the hand and eye but, we discover as we attune ourselves to her presencing, manifest most clearly in the tremulous swelling of her soft breasts. The snakes' vigorous wildness, then, is not held by human willpower but by human softness. Is it not startling that these soft breasts epitomize her command? Power and authority for us are something hard rather than something soft. Yet the power of the Bird and Snake Goddess was often epitomized by her breasts. Breast-decorated and nippled vases emerged in the sixth millennium B.C., and this motif did not diminish in importance until the invasions of the patriarchal northern religions. Breasts are powerful because they are a source of life-giving milk, and, more broadly, of life-giving moisture. The command of the breast, then, is that of deep openness, of giving, and of nourishment (and for early people, this nourishment was not only for the living but for the dead, for how else to explain breasts that are found on funerary monuments?).

It would be a mistake, however, to think of the giving of life-giving fluids as matriarchal power, for the Snake Goddess's dance is not a Nietzschean dance of victory over an inferior power. She is involved with the snakes and turns with their convolutions. She swells and alters with her holding. This nourishing power undermines the nature of our contemporary notion of power as stable reserve of force with which to dominate others.[14] The Snake Goddess, it is true, has a firm grasp on the snakes and a firm footing on the earth. She is entranced, transfixed, concentrating. Her movements are not loose and wild like the snakes, for she tenses her whole body in order to let the writhing vigor of the snakes enter her. Holding the snakes' movements, moreover, requires her whole bodily strength. Yet her rigidity is not the fixity of an iron will directing power, but it simply provides a locality for the overall writhing movement. Even though her body is tensed, her posture is relaxed as though in a yoga asana. This flexuous ease of her pose is seen in the overall rhythms that shake and vibrate through her soft flesh and play in her swaying hips.

Might this flexuous pose, nonetheless, be a form of the supreme command belonging to the Will to Power? Let us return again to her breasts. Her breasts, like the movement of the Will to Power, thrust forward, but the thrust forward of her breasts lacks true direction. They thrust roundly, blindly, begging for touch, and not straight out with a goal in view. She is in an attitude of open-eyed attention, of full concentration, not on what she sees, but on what she feels. Her breasts swell roundly and rest back in their fullness. The movement of Will to Power, by contrast, does not recline back to rest and delight in the fullness of holding. It delights only in the victory of conquering another, in the overcoming of another's power for the sake of empowerment.

Her breasts, however, do not store the wild energy of the snakes, just as breasts do not store milk. Their surprising softness does not reveal a protecting in the sense of containing (for containing requires a resilient exterior), but rather, the softness of her breasts belies a giving, a spilling out. They jut out as a kind of offering, a wanton giving that is not a teasingly coming forward but coming forth with a strong, round fullness and softness. Her breasts, then, not only gather, absorb, and shelter the movements of the wriggling snakes that flow down her arms, but her breasts release them with a soft flourish. This releasing is a giving that does not return to empower the self.

Her giving of her breasts is like the giving of nature: it offers, spills out disinterestedly. However, a woman giving birth and giving milk, and human giving over to the movements of another in general, are not purely natural activities in the modern western sense of animal bodily functions that exist on a lower plane of being than cultural activities. Human giving is a phusical event continuous with that of animals, but a bringing-forth distinguished by our humanly embodied being. We humanly participate and guide those given rhythms that constitute our mortal life; we make love, give birth, give milk, bury our dead, and eat food in uniquely human and variously historical and cultural ways. Perhaps the beginnings of human culture lie not only in the intelligent "invention" of fire and tools but in our embodied capacity to be flexuously open and thoroughly sensitive to difference, in other words, to our artful delight in bodily opening out. It is not surprising that in some early societies the breasts expressed a human responding to nature. For the flow of milky giving from the breast and the corresponding open neediness of the babe expresses well an originary nourishing artfulness of our embodied being in the world-earth-home.

We of a mass media technological culture forget that human techne is steeped in mortality. Techne is not a courageous independent making of self-sufficient, and hopefully eternal, products flung defiantly in the face of the swirling chaos of nature. A well-grounded human techne is the giving of human sap, a way of responding to, participating in, and being within the Giving of the There *(es gibt)*. Can we understand mortal techne as an overflowing of rich sap, an expressing of warmth and wonder, rather than phallocentrically as an active producing of "man-made" products, mentally directed and often violently erected? (Can we understand the phallus itself as soft and giving rather than hard and penetrating without losing the erection?)

Chapter Six

Toward and Backward: An Ecofeminist Revisioning of Human Be(com)ing

The pastel sky expands wide at the day's decline, opening for a fierce setting sun. Pelicans, making a continuous soft line, move between sky and sea. A long, beauteous dip down, then up again, fluid and gentle on their way home.

My eleven-year-old daughter is digging a hole in the sand with her cupped hands, as deep down as she can reach. Long quiet pubescent earth-work. She makes a deep channel to connect sea to hole. The tide is coming in.

Is it a whale that makes these big waves? No, it's the moon. The moon? Yes, the gravity of the moon pulls at the earth, draws its waters back.

The Question of Tools

Those of us who stand outside the circle of this society's definition of acceptable women; those of us who have been forged in the crucibles of difference—those of us who are poor, who are lesbians, who are Black, who are older—know that *survival is not an academic skill*. It is learning how to stand alone, unpopular and sometimes reviled, and how to make common cause with those others identified as outside the structures in order to define and seek a world in which we can all flourish. It is learning how to take our differences and make them strengths. *For the master's tools will never dismantle the master's house.*

—Lorde 1984, 112

I am changing my metaphors in order to let in otherness. In this chapter I will not attempt to reweave the relations between phusis and techne with the fork of sexual difference, as I promised in Chapter Four. It is not that this fork is clumsy or that I may have had more than two gendered prongs with which to contend. I would not have minded the fork's inefficiency as a sewing tool since its pronged nature at least lets in sexual difference, un-like the unicolumnar phallus that helped crochet the metaphysical nature/

culture dualism. But I have come to question the emphasis on external tools (especially pointed ones) to help bridge the gap between culture and nature. Why do our western definitions of the evolution of culture, artistic creativity, and cultural productivity and development rest on notions of activity, externality, mediation, and transformation or domination of nature to the exclusion of notions such as receiving, internality, empathy, and caring for otherness?[1]

Given the gap between ourselves and nature, reweaving the relations between phusis and techne would be better accomplished if we could weave from our bodies like spiders, spinning the threads anew, connecting us to the web of the nonhuman world. Or if we attempted to inscribe this difference not with the pointed stylus, but with the "milk of human kindness" that springs from our bodies and hearts in our relations to dependent others. Or maybe instead of a fork, which after all can be used as a hunting weapon (and so-called male hunting tools have been viewed by androcentric anthropologists as founding our culture itself), a spoon would be a more apt tool for my gynocentric philosophical purposes to gather and hold, rather than to penetrate and overcome. But then perhaps my metaphor would still be privileging a traditional hierachical conception of the culture-nature difference (i.e., a raw/cooked food distinction for instance).

If they could be joined, phusis and techne would best be sewn with a joining that brings together without external tools altogether, and without already completed linear threads. But then how to join? And, what is being joined? I do not want to participate in reweaving new tapestries of metaphysics if this means "beyond the earth" or in reweaving new ontologies if this precludes the differences of personal experience. Nor do I want to get involved in a historical project in the sense of a projectile that has a straight aim in view and that relies on a notion of history as a linear, forward-directed progression or process of maturation, for this phallocentric movement of historical Being is intrinsic to our contemporary nihilistic, earth-denying situation.

Even the metaphor of weaving is working against me in this process of deconstructing. In choosing this metaphor at the beginning, I have already privileged certain kinds of movements and have already made certain assumptions about culture and nature. If I am unweaving what has been woven, in the unweaving I am already preparing for the reweaving, and without being able to question the nature of weaving movements and the prejudices concerning the practice of cultural activity that I am bringing to the work.

My threads are getting tangled, my activity confused. And my writing, after all, is still being written with a pointed pen. Still. Still, I have to begin from here: my phallocentric situation.

All these gynocentric metaphors (from the Greek *metaphora* meaning to carry over from one place to another), of Mary Daly's and Andrea Nye's spiders spinning, of Hélène Cixous's writing with mother's "white ink," and of ecofeminist gathering, do help avoid the alienating gap between culture and nature by carrying something valuable from the exiled region of activities, traditionally considered not truly human because they were identified with nature, to the region of cultural activity and thinking. They help us move back into the neighborhood of what is in question here: our cultural being as human dwellers in the world-earth-home.

Respecting the Earth's Drawing Pull

> The word is a hint, and not a sign in the sense of mere signification.
> Hints need the widest sphere in which to swing *[Schwingungbereich]* . . .
> where mortals go to and fro only slowly.
>
> —Heidegger 1966, 27

We all know the earth is in bad shape. We learn through the global media of the threats of nuclear catastrophes, spreading ozone holes, global warming, and the disappearance of rainforests and wildlife. We encounter the effects of industrial and automobile pollution, logging, consumerism, urban disregard for green environments, and the decline of wildlife in our own localities. The current drive of world governments to solve this deepening environmental crisis is toward an "environmentally friendly" global management of the earth's resources for human purposes. The widespread presumption is that to solve environmental problems we need only to come up with more powerful and suitable methods to reconstruct the natural. This supposed solution, however, involves the complete human control (and monoculturalization) of the world-earth-home. It is precisely this hu-

man disrespect for the integrity of the nonhuman that is a key cause of ecological destruction in all its myriad forms. Given our saddening earth
situation and our deepening obliviousness to anything but ourselves, there
is a need for an ecoconscious rethinking of what it is to be human.

The present western conception of being human has been informed by
phallocentric and ecodestructive metaphysical dualisms such as those
of culture/nature, human/animal, reason/emotion, mind/body, self/other,
subject/object, activity/passivity, form/matter, and man/woman. I have
shown how the culture/nature dichotomy in particular dominates the androcentric and anthropocentric conception of our human be-ing because, following Heidegger, I understand this dichotomy to be central to the nature
of western historical Being. All these dichotomies, however, are so closely
interwoven that they confirm and support one another.

Thus, the following ecofeminist revisioning of our human be-ing involves an attempt to give weight to nature and to the consistently viewed
"inferior" sides of the above metaphysical dualisms. As Val Plumwood
(1991, 18) argues, it is these tranditional qualities excluded from conceptions of being human that can help provide continuity between ourselves
and nature.[2] My understanding is in keeping with what Karen Warren
(1987, 18–20) calls "transformative feminism. It attempts to make interconnections between all systems of oppression, to open a theoretical place
for the diversity of women's experience, to acknowledge the social construction of knowledge, to rethink what it is to be human, and to recast
traditional ethical concerns to make room for marginalized values.

Western metaphysics and epistemology are based on a sense of human separation and alienation from nature, from all that is other to the human as subject. Metaphysical thought attempts to think, as Linda Holler
(1990, 6) puts it, "without the weight of the earth," to go beyond *(meta)*
the earth (phusis) in search for immortality, objectivity, transcendence, and
independence. The metaphysical systems found in the history of western
metaphysics tend to be expressions of an alienated "I" that equates connectedness with death, objectivity with autonomy, and transcendence of
the earth with freedom.

In western metaphysics, it is mainly the concept of reason (as *logos* and
later as *ratio*) that is said to distinguish, essentially, human beings from

other beings. Moreover, the notion of reason has been defined by excluding characteristics associated with the inferior, "natural" sides of metaphysical binary oppositions. One story of western reason, for example, goes as follows: In the very beginnings of western philosophy, the bright white light of Appolonian *logos* slowly dispels the dark, mysterious forces of the older, chthonic goddess religions. Plato refines the pre-Socratic notion of *logos* that was thought to suffuse nature by identifying *logos* with unchanging forms that can be contemplated solely by the human mind. He thereby devalues changeable matter and nature, relegating them to the realm of the nonrational. Aristotle explicitly names the human being as the animal with *logos*, contrasting it to our biological or animal part. Leibniz asserts the principle of sufficient reason that nothing can *be* without ground *(ratio)*, thereby accounting for all that is by relating it back to a representing subject. Descartes helped to further characterize reason as our essentially human characteristic by divorcing it from the untrustworthy body, confusing emotions, and the practical matters of everyday life.

This representing ego and disembodied Cartesian *Cogito*, which assumes an objective, representational view and denies the importance of finitude, locality, and particularity, is not an innocent misconception of philosophy that has little impact on the real world. On the contrary, it is operative, for example, in modern science's value of neutrality and distance from its objects of investigation.[3] This western philosophical account of human reason alienated from the natural sphere functions powerfully, moreover, in our model of technological development, which has forced itself upon so-called undeveloped countries in disregard of their often more ecologically balanced practices and which perpetuates a global economy that ravages the environment and feeds off the labor of the "Two-Thirds World" (see Shiva 1990).

The same characteristics associated with the natural sphere and excluded from definitions of human reason have been fairly consistently identified with the female (see Lloyd 1984; and Bordo 1990). Western traditional philosophical definitions of being human, then, reflect not only an anthropocentrism but, at the same time, a masculine bias (and we could add a white bias). This androcentrism of our human being is apparent in so many aspects of our daily life. Iris Young's (1990, 7) description of the corporate work world is a case in point: "Corporate and bureaucratic institutions presume a male model of behavior and life cycle of their employees—that professionalism requires detachment and impersonality, that 'success' requires old boy networking, impression management, and the willingness to devote many continuous years of more-than-eight-hour days to the job." It is easy to see how this androcentric corporate mentality, which is implemented by multinational corporations, contributes to the growing, ecologically destructive westernization of the world (and the oppression of non-western peoples).

When our human be-ing is construed in a white, androcentric, anthropocentric way, it creates cleavages between male and female, human and nonhuman, and white and colored and generates unhealthy conflicts within an individual's own psycho-phusical being. Such a be-ing, moreover, reinforces a purely instrumental relation to nature, for the gap between the alienated human "I" and everything else external or "other" to that self is bridged by tools and instruments, by a rational techne and a capitalist technology that assaults nature.

This instrumental approach to nature, which rests on our unquestioned alienation from, and domination of, nature, is central even to Marx's analyses of modes of production. All production, for Marx, involves the transformation of nature by human beings within and through definite forms of society. Human freedom is the movement out of "natural necessity" by means of the domination of nature. Corresponding to this, social progress is guaged by the extent to which nature has become human nature. What remains constant in all historically specific forms of production is the active subject, mankind, and the passive object, nature.[4]

Our contemporary human being lies predominantly in maximizing control of the basic rhythms of phusis both within ourselves and in the world, in disregard of our being situated as phusical beings on the earth. As a result, the ecological dangers that threaten the Being of the world-earth-home are not so much in humanly uncontrollable, apocalyptic ecological disasters but in the constantly deeper (and less visible) overtaking of the earth's own organic integrity and in the corresponding loss of our own human phusical being. In other words, *the* growing danger consists in our deepening human regulation and control of the diverse rhythms of nature for economic ends. In our global "man"-agement and monoculturation of the earth, the earth's wild beings appear only within the bounds of their human value, and the rhythms and diverse entities of nature are reduced to technically produced processes and energy forms that are controlled by a powerful white western technology and governed by multinational corporations for the sake of the consumptive West.

Our present understanding of the relation between culture and nature, which involves the domination of nature by culture, is a drastic though gradual narrowing of the ancient Greek meanings of techne and phusis in which they are partially rooted. Techne and phusis are ways of bringing-forth into the un-concealment (*a-letheia* translated as "truth") of appearance from out of concealment. This coming-forth into appearance is a ceaseless and often chaotic play of granting *and* withdrawal, of coming-to-be and passing-away. Nature as phusis is the most original and thus the source of all modes of bringing-forth, and techne is the uniquely human way of bringing forth in accordance with phusis.

In our present concepts of culture and nature, the seemingly passive letting appear of something from out of concealment and, moreover, the mystery of the "from whence" that lingers in the concept of unconcealing is absent. It is often assumed that our intrinsic role as human beings is to actively produce or create something by wresting its form from raw matter. It is often said that what marks our "making" as specifically human, distinguishing it from other animals, is precisely its active power to oppose, forcibly transform, or at least transcend natural ways. Essential to our contemporary making, moreover, is the *form* of the matter, the final completed product divorced from concealment, not the coming-to-be *from* something else. Unlike amphibilous entities like wedges, hinges, or crutches, for example, that are open to otherness, there is an emphasis on independence and clearly demarcated boundaries in our common understanding of what a thing is. We thus do not contact the integrity of entities presencing from out of concealment but divorce entities from their sources, transforming them into resources exposed as that which stands by to suit our human needs.

That the ancient Greek understanding of techne and phusis as modes of bringing-forth is a world away from our own can be seen even in Aristotle, for his writings not only point forward to present conceptions but seem to point back to more ancient understandings. In a passage from *The Physics,* for example, he makes the remarkable statement that "if a house were a thing generated by nature, it would have been generated in a way similar to that in which it is now generated by art (techne)."[5] This passage shows his turning out of the pre-Socratic understanding of phusis, rather than his turning into the modern era, which I emphasized in the last chapter. What is remarkable in this passage is that Aristotle assumes as obvious that if the moving cause of a house were phusis rather than techne, it would still come-to-be along similar lines. Such a thought is, for us modern thinkers, inconceivable because we take it for granted that the entire process of techne is not only foreign to phusis but is most often opposed to it. Building is understood as a way of protecting us from and against nature and not as sheltering us within and in accordance with nature. We distinguish ourselves from nature by drawing a firm line that separates cultural activity from natural ways. Techne, for us moderns, is understood as that which essentially controls and forms phusis, not that which supports, helps, or imitates phusis, except perhaps incidentally.

> I am having a difficult day. I stop and start, get into the sway of words and stop again. This getting pulled back from the smooth and regular temporal flow of writing to the idiosyncratic temporality of my living situation is the backward pull of writing.

There is an obvious need to reweave relations between culture and nature in a way that weaves with the gravity of the earth rather than against it. Given that the Greek notions of techne and phusis indicate some conceptual sources of the culture/nature dichotomy, it is helpful to go back to these concepts. This return to some origins of our concepts of nature and culture is not a romantic attempt to resuscitate idealized pre-western meanings as though they were the undistorted truth of the matter, but a hermeneutical circling back that attempts to be receptive to vague hints of alternative meanings in our western beginnings for the sake, moreover, of opening to difference. I look for indications of both the antagonisms that were developing between techne and phusis as well as aspects that were left behind and excluded in these concepts to allow for the western evolution of our destructive culture/nature dualism.

I have shown in Chapters Four and Five that the distinction between phusis as a bringing-forth in itself and techne as a bringing forth in another is used in Aristotle's description of sexual difference and human generation in a way that privileges externality, activity, form and the male over the internality, passivity, matter and the female. The familiar contemporary characterizations of cultural motion as bridging the distance between ourselves and an estranged, external, and seemingly passive nature by actively forming and controlling it it seems to me presupposes a similar masculine bias. The gap between our cultural selves and nature is bridged by a phallocentric motion forward. This movement involved in our conceptions of cultural activity, creativity, and productivity can be described as phallocentric because its dynamic privileges male sexual movements, male desire, and, moreover, reflects the external position of the male self in human generation. This phallocentric motion of techne, which is central to the traditional understanding of our being human, moreover, is continuous with the phallocentric dynamic of Being itself as Will to Power discussed in Chapter Three.

> As I write I am at war with the squirrels eating from my bird feeder. "Let me show you how ingenious I can be." I grasp a broom and poke at him (her?) with its end. The thrust forward of "the phallus" definitely has its uses.
>
> And, after all, this aggressive movement of my broom does not resemble his gentle penis last night. Yet, yet they are, culturally and historically, conceptually related movements.

I am pulled back to the Greek notions of techne and phusis, then, which are themselves pointing back to pre-western, premetaphysical, and nondichotomous relations between nature and culture, because they can help give positive senses to movements that, unlike the phallocentric thrust of metaphysics, draw back. To draw out new lines of difference we need to draw back from the dominant aims in view. (There is a close connection in many languages between the word for "draw" in the sense of to "pull physically" and the word for a "drawing" in a pictorial sense.)[6] By pulling our thinking back, we create rhythm. The Greek word *rythmos* originally meant, not flow or repetition, but pause, the steady limitation of movement. As Werner Jaeger says, "Rhythm then is that which imposes bonds on movement and confines the flux of things."[7] To reconceptualize our relation to nature in a way that is not hierarchical and oppositional, we need a new method of thinking that is not the straight-lined, goal-oriented, and unfeeling way of reason as characterized in metaphysics. We need a new pathway of thought that weaves its way by going back and forth. The gap between nature and ourselves is healed by attempting to sway as humans with the rhythms of nature, swinging to and fro with the coming-to-be and passing-away inherent in all life. The drawing pull back of the sway that has been exiled in western thought would seem, moreover, to help join us to the forgotten philosophies of those indigenous peoples who have lived and thought with the seasonal rhythms and ancient history of their land and who have not turned their backs on all that came before them.

> The baby is swinging back and forth, laughing ecstatically. His first experience in the playground swing.
>
> "He doesn't yet know how to be sad yet does he mom?" says my daughter.
>
> "No, sadness only comes with experience. Happiness seems to be there from the start." I muse on that, swinging back and forth, back and forth. But why am I always *pairing* things?
>
> We talk about her feelings. We are going to visit the loghouse where we once lived all together before the separation. She clings sadly to those memories of a complete family. She wants to go back to the past, for everything to be exactly like it was then.
>
> "No that's not healthy. You have to come forward to where we are now. When we go back, we will make new memories there," I find myself saying, pleased by the unexpected contradiction in my experience to what I had been emphasizing in my writing.
>
> The baby has nodded off, still slightly swaying.

We could say that given their historical ontological exile and our historical phallocentric hermeneutical situation, mimicking movements that draw us back to the earth is a presently useful strategy to undermine the relations of opposition in metaphysics.[8] This strategy, recognizable as belonging to Irigaray, does not involve simply privileging what has been excluded in metaphysics, for this move would merely reverse dichotomies without changing the relation of opposition or movement toward domination between concepts and the concepts themselves. The oppositional gap between nature and culture would remain intact. Rather, by letting in the sway back in our very method, we are already bridging the gap in a way that subverts the un*giving* dualistic relations of metaphysics. The extent to which we can change oppositional hierarchical relations between the two estranged concepts into a new relation of difference is the extent to which the concepts themselves will already metamorphose. In reweaving the relations between culture and nature, we need to recognize and become receptive to the drawing back movement involved in this reweaving.

We need, then, to be most critical and wary of our methods of investigation, our pathways of thought, and our styles of writing if we are to revision our human dwelling in an ecological and feminist way. The pressing need of our human dwelling is to weave *ourselves* into what I call, borrowing from Heidegger, nearness, which in the German *(Die Nahe)* is related to meanings of "neighbor" *(Nachbar)* and "to sew or stitch" *(nahen)*.[9] There is a global need to come near to the wild, to move into the neighborhood of our local earthy being, where we *already* belong as dwellers in the world-earth-home.

I was living in a log house way out in the woods. At night, the porcupines would gnaw at the outhouse, the handles of our tools, the floorboards and joists under the sauna for the salt from our sweat. Gnaw, gnaw, gnaw. Damaging my home. Keeping me up. I'd go out and yell at them, throwing rocks, but they would continue as soon as I stopped.

Then one of the larger ones started coming during the day. I had had enough. I taped my hunting knife to the top of an old broom handle, went outside, and jabbed with all my frustration and anger blindly at it under the house.

I still feel the soft flesh through the length of my weapon. The broom handle was suddenly pulled out of my hands. The porcupine running away, trailing the long pole. A trail of red, red blood and the rhythmic high-

pitched wheezing sound. Pain, life-threatening pain. Confusion. The
axe had to be used, blow after blow. A silent mess of blood and flesh
and quills.

I picked out all the quills to give to the native artisan center, trying to
repair the damage done. The ground was too rocky to dig so I took the
body out in the boat and dumped it overboard. Days later, its bloated
carcass washed up on shore, reminding me of my action. The maggots
cleaned it to the bone. I saved its skull.

O porcupine, why do I feel so close to you now that I hear your breath
in my ear as I write?

To weave ourselves into nearness means both to feel our continuity with
the nonhuman (and nonhistorical) from which we have traditionally divorced ourselves and to let the earth's wild living things contact us from
their own unique ways of belonging. It means to allow the wild to come
near, and to come near *as* the wild. This action is not a willful move from
us over here to the other over there, nor does it simply involve an external
making of some thing, work, or product (like a bridge) in the traditional
sense of cultural historical constructing. To let the wild come near as the
wild involves a twofold local release into nearness for which the exiled
feminine movements of metaphysics are needed. It involves release *from*
the Will to Power that guides our everyday social and personal being and
the global economy, and release *into* the healing movements of the wild.

To weave ourselves into nearness in diverse ways would help dissolve
the oppositional gap between ourselves and nature while still allowing for
difference. We cannot remove all boundaries (understood in the sense of
that from which something begins to be, rather than that which excludes
and cuts off) between ourselves and nature since unless we see ourselves as
distinct, we cannot be responsive to the wild.[10] In our contemporary dwelling in the world-earth-home, there is a dire need to feel earthly rhythms as
a source of refuge and health, to express our gratitude for and connection
to the land upon which we live, and to recognize our responsibility for the
earth's well-being. Attempting to merge our human being with nature to
the extent that we can no longer distinguish our unique receptivity to and
care for the wild ignores the possibilities inherent in our being human. We

have, moreover, already learned from phallocentric metaphysics, which privileges identity over difference, that canceling out difference and diversity although seemingly bringing us closer to nature actually cancels out the difference of nature. This phallocentric thrust of metaphysics has alienated us from our bodies and our feelings and from the ownmost particularity and difference of the earth's myriad beings and locations.[11]

Letting in feminine movements excluded by metaphysics can initially help in an ontological movement of release from our current challenging out of all that is into nearness. Resuscitating the unprivileged in metaphysics (i.e., concealment, dependency, need, receptivity, passivity, passing-away, darkness, locality) can help give indications of how we might rethink the nature of our human dwelling in a way that opens itself to the mystery of Be(com)ing. However, this gynocentric move to let in traditional feminine movements remains only as a hint along the way in this reweaving, a hint that needs the "widest sphere in which to swing." This hint given to us by Western metaphysics is enigmatic, beckoning both toward us and away from us. The historical absencing of the feminine beckons toward us to recover what has been lost. Yet, at the same time, it beckons us away from its metaphysical bind and the threat of fixity and conservatism. As John Caputo (1987, 263) says, every vision harbors within it "an exclusionary gesture, a repressive act, a movement of normalization and leveling" and "after a certain point every good idea becomes inflexible and repressive." The movement or path of releasement is a swaying to and from that will hopefully swing out of metaphysical oppositional distinctions and thereby also swing out of this peculiar genderization of ontological matters altogether.[12]

Playing in the Gap Between Culture and Nature: Moving into Nearness

This work on vision began, not with a vision, but with an experience of crying. Crying for the earth, the earth itself, whose devastation I see all around me. Crying over the plundering of the land. Crying from the depths of my ancestral body for the victims of the Holocaust. Crying for the Indians massacred in my country, for the last of the dying guardians of the earth. Crying *with* them. Crying in kinship with all suffering beings. Crying in participation, in sacrifice; but also in thankfulness for their spirit of sharing.

With the crying, I began to see, briefly, and with pain. Only with crying, only then, does vision begin.

—Levin 1988, 171–72

The paradigm of our human be-ing in western metaphysics is that of a rational male divorced from his earthy neighborhood. This conception of our human be-ing represses our bodies, our mortality, and our desires and emotions; dissociates us from the land beneath our feet and from the plants and animals in our surrounding world-earth-home; and pushes the majority of us to the margins of culture. It, moveover, gives rise to an understanding of the relation between "man" and nature that is central to the contemporary drive of our phallocentric worldly Being toward global economical development and management of the earth. The unrelenting, rationally controlled challenging-out of beings levels out their own particularity and difference and reconstructs them in terms of human use and value. To re-weave relations between culture and nature, we need a philosophy of the human being that welcomes our bodily being, that celebrates difference and diversity, a rationality that is open to contingency and passion, and a techne that works in accordance with the rhythms of phusis, that lets beings appear not only in the light of an instrumental reason but in their own wondrous coming-forth from concealment. To weave ourselves into nearness we need to question what marks us as human. But where to begin?

Today after writing I was cleaning a huge round black pot, our makeshift humidifier, after the long winter. The dark cavity was caked with accumulated mineral deposits and who knows what else from the waters of Lake Ontario. I turned on the kitchen tap and watched the sudden gush with suspicion. Dioxins, PCB's, DDT, and furans? Accumulating most especially, I am told, in my breast milk. Yet I am to take for *granted* that this is safe water. Can I really trust the white power that grants, that gives, this gush?

It comes down to a question of fresh water. Without life-giving waters we are nowhere. We are intimately fluid with nature through water.

It's a question of this fluidity beyond the barriers of inside and outside,
not the connection between the opposing solids: rational man and objective nature.

I begin, then, in this attempt at an ecofeminist revisioning of human be-
(com)ing with nature's fluidity and thereby help thwart the metaphysics of
solids.[13] I take my directive, my bearings, from a contingent, personal experience, an ad hoc local event. To begin with nature's fluidity speaks to
the popular poststructuralist claim that culture is fluid and nature is fixed
and solid. In some poststructuralist thought, the infinitely fluid configurations of cultural Becomings are contrasted with the suffocating fixity of Being, the metaphysics of presence, and with nature. As we saw in Chapters
One and Two, for example, in recent poststructuralist gender discourse,
the concept of the body as a biological fixity (and nature in general as an
unchangeable eternal presence) is contrasted with the concept of a body
constructed purely by social and cultural determinants and thereby as fluid
and changeable. This unfortunate current tendency toward polarization
within the gender debate is perhaps best encapsulated by de Beauvoir's
(1974, 249) statement more than thirty years ago, that "one is not born,
but becomes a women." and by Irigaray's (1985a, 212) more recent statement to the contrary, "How can I say it? That we are women from the
start. That we don't have to be turned into women by them." It seems to
me that, on one hand, to be feminist, we need to affirm with de Beauvoir
that gender becomes, that it is a process contextualized by history and culture. Yet, on the other hand, to be eco-conscious, we must also affirm with
Irigaray that bringing forth is part of our givenness. Our genderized body
is not formed solely by social and political significances but is motivated
by natural indeterminacies given because we are born of the world-earth-
home. It is important to recognize and reconstitute gender in a way that
gives weight to the body and evolutionary history.[14]

The poststructuralist account of the body leaves out what I have described following Merleau-Ponty as the anonymous noncognitive cleaving
of our bodies to the general incarnate structure of the world-earth-home.
Although poststructuralist thought rightly rejects the search of western
metaphysics for underlying foundations, for the permanence and presence
of Being, it tends to replace the solidity of metaphysical Being with the

fluidity of a Nietzschean Becoming that includes only human meanings. Some poststructuralism gender theorists seem to overlook the fact that the western metaphysical search for solidity was motivated by a will to transcend the fluidity of nature. For Parmenides, for example, who is often understood as the "father" of metaphysics, the look toward Being is a look away from all coming-into-being and passing-away.[15] The fluid changeability of nature appeared as negative (i.e., chaotic, disorderly, and uncontrollable) in the growing light of Apollonian reason and order. That poststructuralist accounts of cultural Be(com)ing often reduce nature to a fixity suggests a dangerous metaphysical reversal that keeps the domination of nature by culture and reason intact.

> Water? Another difficult day. I was searching for leads so hard today, I started sweating. This is no way to write with the earth. Meta-phusis is about men who *think* themselves and everything else to death.
>
> It's not that I don't like sweating. I enjoy an honest sweat that comes from heat or from physical exertion, but not from sitting over a desk *thinking*. Should I wait for inspiration or go out in the garden and dig?

Are we human in the way we sweat? That is certainly not a metaphysical question. Listen:

> I cried inside that sweat, it seemed as though I could never stop crying as though my heart was being tugged at and finally torn loose inside my chest. Other people cried too. So much emotion is expressed in the sweat and in the medicine lodge. And the weird thing about it is—you don't really know what it is you're crying about. The emotions seem to come out of some primeval cavity—some lonesome half-remembered place. It seems when I cried it was more than an individual pain. The weeping was all of our pain—as collective wound—it is larger than each individual. In the sweat it seems as though we all remember a past—a collective presence—our past as Native people before being colonized and culturally liquidated.
>
> —Valerio 1983

On the way toward a revisioning of our human be-ing, we need to pour healing libations to the forgotten earth, to give way to silenced peoples. Let rivulets of sweat run down our brow, between our breasts, around our

balls in remembrance of the thousand years where this cedar stood in the
Carwichan Valley before the clear-cutting. Cry like a baby for the Beluga
whales whose bodies are so contaminated that under Canadian and U.S.
law they are to be treated as hazardous waste. Release tears for the flooded
nesting grounds, the dry spawning rivers, the mercury poisoned waters of
Cree and Inuit land caused by the James Bay hydroelectric project. Wail,
loudly like women for the dead, for the forgotten in our own most local
neighborhoods.

For the love of wisdom (philo-sophia—the guardian of *logos*), for the
sake of earth wisdom, we need a moment of earthy fluidity and vulnerability in our thinking. We cannot weave ourselves into nearness by engaging
solely in rational, calculative thinking that has ignored its own motives and
desires and has pretended to be objective, measuring, for example, the
commercial potential of the land and weighing the economic interests of
logging companies against the needs of indigenous people and the objections of environmentalists. We need to *feel* our remoteness from the land
and from the philosophies of those indigenous peoples who know well that
if they lose their connection to the land their culture will cease to exist. In
our western homelessness, even the feeling of remoteness remains absent
(Heidegger 1971d, 166). We need to let our distance from nature and from
the philosophies of other cultures soften our thoughts as when we are distant from those we love. There is a need to let our thinking be first moved
by empathy rather than functioning according to the systems of power that
are currently in place and dictate what counts as reason. Do we dare let our
thoughts sink back meditatively, playfully toward chance and otherness?
Such artistic thinking does not need rule-governed procedures and fixed
grounds in order to make a move toward another. Rather, as Caputo (1987,
224) says, referring to Heidegger's poetic thinking, it is "the way one
learns to float only by surrendering every attempt to swim and remaining
perfectly still." But am I not confirming, for example, Hegel's misogynist
views on women's thought, knowledge, and action? No, hopefully not
confirming but mimicking to an overflowing excess that role that has been
assigned to me as a woman:

> The difference between men and women is like that between animals
> and plants. Men correspond to animals, while women correspond

to plants because their development is more placid and the principle that underlies it is the rather vague unity of feeling. When women hold the helm of government, the state is at once in jeopardy, because women regulate their actions not by the demands of universality but by arbitrary inclinations and opinions. Women are educated—who knows how?—as it were by breathing in ideas, by living rather than acquiring knowledge. The status of manhood, on the other hand, is attained only by the stress of thought and much technical exertion. (Hegel 1967, 263–64)

The forward progression characteristic of phallocentric rational thinking which essentially defines our western human being, has demanded a building up from *solid* universal foundations. The progression of rational knowledge has relied on fixed decision-making procedures, on a cognitive construction of premises by means of previously formed building blocks. As Edmund Husserl (1970, 363) says, it is because of this ability to rely on previously attained results that when a researcher returns to continue his work after having taken a rest, he does not need to run through the whole immense chain of groundings back to the original premises and actually reactivate the whole thing. A researcher makes new judgments on the basis of those already attained, and these new judgments, premises, and meanings, moreover, serve as foundations for still others. Rational thinking, as it has been traditionally defined, also depends on the capacity to encounter problems with as few presuppositions and prejudices as possible, for it is in this way that universal judgments can be constructed. In the sciences in particular, the construction of theories and universal judgments has been understood as necessitating a move from subjective experience to value-free objective knowledge. In this view of what thinking *is*, to let our thoughts be pulled back by fluid feelings is, at best, irrelevant and, at worst, dangerous.

> We all go into the water. The surf is magnificent, each wave very high and full. Unpredictably, waves come in very close and flood the shore. Several times, Una is knocked down by them, and her face is full of water. The waves pull back with a lot of force, and I realize that a small person could easily be washed away.
>
> —Lounder and Maestro 1990, 4

To attempt to "soften" our thinking is dangerous because the spontaneity of fluid feeling can give way to rash thoughts, and the lack of foundations and clear direction to a wandering, associational thinking that may not result in the formation of new meanings. The experiential locality implied by feelingful thoughts, moreover, can sink into thought too personal to be of theoretical value. To attempt to fluidly release our thinking from the institutionalized contraints of *ratio* is to play with fire. It is a thinking for lepers and nomads, for bats and nettles, "tender maggots" and earwigs, and the "odors of life" (William Blake, *The Four Zoas* 135:725–136:67 in Erdman 1982, 404). It is a listening to so many voices that one's thoughts can become almost mad. Yet, given our phallocentric philosophical horizons within whose boundaries reason (and democracy) has been determined, there is a need for thinkers to take the risk of fluidity and to fall back into the human capacity to enter feelingly into the life of the other, the life of all that has been assaulted by phallocentric western reason.[16]

We might picture this making soft of hard rationality as a gesture in the manner of the pop artist Claes Oldenberg. By softening what is normally practically hard, we are made aware of that to which we are attending beyond its instrumentality. Such humorous, softened thinking, however, is not in opposition to reason. Rather, it is to engage in a Derridean double gesture: "to insure professional competence and the most serious tradition of the university even while going as far as possible, theoretically and practically, in the most directly underground thinking about the abyss beneath the university" (Derrida 1983, 17). As Caputo (1987, 235), who also cites this statement, says, we need both "institutionalized reason" and the "free play" of reason, to let play and laughter infiltrate reason.

We may be released into nearness meditatively, through embodied heartfelt thoughts, and playfully, through communal celebration. The dire need of our present human be(com)ing would seem to lie more in this simple, flexible characteristic of our human be-ing to care for others, to dance, laugh, and sing in otherness, rather than in our ability to reason as we have known it. We need risk our institutionalized reason, not for the sake of irrationality (which would be a deeper needlessness), but for the sake of letting what has been deemed nonrational show itself in its integrity. It is through

a new human love and respect for oceans of difference, not through western indifference, that we are woven into the neighborhoods of the earth.

Culture as a Cultivating

> This turning from the mother to the father, however, signifies above all a
> victory of spirituality over the senses—that is to say, *a step forward in
> culture,* since maternity is proved by the senses whereas paternity is a
> surmise based on deduction and a premise. This declaration in favour
> of the thought-process, thereby raising it above sense perception, has
> proved to be a step with serious consequences.
>
> —Freud 1952, 153 (emphasis added)

> This highly disparate body of hazy, poorly formulated notions, metaphors,
> and irrational analogies [of ecofeminists] invites women *to take a step
> backward* to an era whose consciousness was permeated by myths and by
> mystifications of reality. It bodes nothing well for women . . . to follow
> in this regressive path.
>
> —Biehl 1991, 6 (emphasis added)

Stepping forward defines stepping back relative to itself. Active stepping
forward sets the standard for our thinking and doing, and gives the modern
measure for creativity. But might stepping back exceed the complementary
role assigned it in the dichotomies progressive/regressive, active/passive,
forward/back, developed/undeveloped?[17]

To muse further on an ecofeminist revisioning of our human be-ing, I return to the concept of techne, specifically to the notion of cultural building
or making. Building can be understood not merely as a technique of construction but in a broader ontological sense as one of the fundamental ways
we humans have our stay on the earth. As Heidegger explains in his essay
"Building, Dwelling, Thinking" (1971a), the Old English and High German word for building *(buan)* means "to dwell" or "to stay in place".
That building once meant "to dwell" is useful for ecofeminist thought because it undermines the modern view derived from phallocentric metaphysics that living or dwelling on the earth is a mere passive, natural existing
incidental to our specifically human be-ing, which supposedly lies in rea-

son and active cultural production. It also gets beneath the sociopolitical dichotomy of so-called domestic activities associated with "mere" habitual living, which take place to a large extent in the home, and cultural activities proper, which take place in the so-called public work world and are considered to characterize essentially the human being. By tracing building back into the domain to which everything that *is* belongs, we are going back into the neighborhood of our being that is prior to the culture/nature split and its attendant dichotomies.

Dwelling is never thought of as the basic character of our human being because "merely" being on the earth seems to be something that involves physical survival and not the "higher" human pursuits of the intellect. However, the etymological roots of "building" testify that the deeper sense of cultural building is to dwell. We build, says Heidegger, because we already dwell. In other words, we build from out of our dwelling. Indeed, we truly build in the full sense of the word only insofar as we are capable of dwelling. We weave ourselves into an "eco-centric"[18] nearness, then, into the neighborhood to which everything that *is* belongs, by rediscovering our capacity to truly dwell on the earth. (*Neighbor* [from the Old English *near-gebur*] means literally "the near-dweller"—the one who dwells near.) But then, what does the broader concept "dwelling" mean?

Going back to the etymological roots of other words that, like *buan,* mean "to dwell" (the Old Saxon *wuon* and Gothic *wunian*), we find that dwelling means not just to exist in any old way but to stay in a place by remaining in peace *(Friede)* by sparing and preserving things from harm. To keep something from harm and danger is neither just to leave something alone or to isolate it but to let something be free in its own nature.[19] We humanly dwell insofar as we protect the land upon which we dwell and allow those things and beings of our dwelling place the freedom to be in their own natures.

> We, the Henaaksiala (Haisla people) of Husduwachsdu (the Kitlope), have known, loved, and guarded the Kitlope Valley for untold, uncounted centuries. Here, our people have been born, have lived out their lives, and returned to the Earth, at one with the land.
>
> For we do not own this land so much as the land owns us. The land is part of us; and we are part of the land.

It is given to us only as a trust: to live within its boundaries in beauty and harmony; to nourish our bodies and our spirits with its gifts; and to protect it from harm.

We have a solemn, sacred duty to keep faith with those who came before us, who guarded and protected this land for us: we must do no less for ourselves and for those who come after.

—Chief Councillor Gerald Amos, on behalf of the Haisla Nation, to a logging company (in *Western Canada Wilderness Committee Educational Report*, 1991)

We build as a letting-dwell, says Heidegger, by sheltering the blossoming and fruiting, spreading out in rock and water, and rising up into plant and animal of the earth and by receiving the blessing and inclemency of the sky, not turning night into day, nor day into a harassed unrest. We dwell by keeping in touch with out mortal natures and by keeping watch for intimations of change in the broad pathways of historical Being.[20]

Dwelling reveals itself in our building activity in at least two ways: by nurturing things that grow and by constructing things that do not grow. Constructing is the way we normally understand all our building and making. We think, for example, of the constructing of buildings, towers, roads, and bridges and the manufacturing of cars, household goods, and industrial machinery. Cultivating is the caring and tending of growing things. It doesn't "make" anything in the usual sense because it lets something grow on its own accord. Yet, it is a building or techne, nonetheless, because it humanly attends to and takes responsibility for growing things. It would include activities such as tilling the soil, growing food, tending animals—in other words, the growing of those things we need for our phusical being. It would also thereby include it seems to me (although Heidegger reflecting a masculine bias does not mention them) activities such as cooking food, healing with herbs and medicines, educating the young, nurturing children, weaving clothes, and making containers for food and water. Constructing is the privileged mode of building. We immediately associate it with technologically "advanced" and more powerful industrial societies, whereas cultivating is associated with the more "primitive" pre-agrarian and agrarian societies. However, these modern associations remove constructing and cultivating from the neighborhood of humanly letting-dwell and into the current context of technological power.

Our contemporary building in both modes of cultivating and construct-ing is so destructive to the land upon which we live because, for the most part, our motives to build do not emerge from out of our earthy dwelling but for the sake of power and the development of the market economy. The fact that we tap natural resources with minimal consideration for the land, level the wild, and pollute the very waters from which we drink shows we are barely aware *that* we dwell. It is this prior lack of human dwelling in its deeper sense that is so ecodestructive. We need to learn from the rooted-ness of building in dwelling in order to think about a process of cultural building that works with the weight of the earth. In the following pages, I turn to the mode of cultivating building as a letting-dwell, then, for indica-tions of how techne as a whole might work for the sake of phusis because cultivating, it seems to me, is a mode of techne that remains especially attentive to phusis in its growth. This turn to cultivating building is well known in feminist studies through the ground-breaking work of Sara Rud-dick and Nancy Hartsock. Whereas Ruddick describes a specifically ma-ternal caring labor, Hartsock includes the production and preparation of food, healing, teaching, housework, and the care of the elderly as forms of caring labor. My discussion here is meant to contribute to their work in this area.

As discussed in previous chapters, the danger facing phusis as a whole is that its diverse structures and multifarious spontaneous rhythms of growth and decay are being regulated and replaced by the controlling powers of modern technology. The prevalent destruction of the environment and the desensitization of our phusical human be-ing to its dwelling in the world-earth-home are manifest results of the historical ontological demise of na-ture. It seems to me that it is the nurturance, rest, and growth of our phusi-cal being, in other words, our birth, health, and death, that is particularly threatened by our contemporary indifference to nature. This region of our existence, which is directly involved with the play of coming-to-be and passing-away, with healing and compassion, has often been in western cul-tures the region of ''women's work'' and has been generally regarded as insignificant human cultural experience. (Of course, aspects of this region

are sometimes taken over by men, whereby they become validated professions, and in the process become more and more removed from a holistic
understanding and care for our phusical being. Psychiatry is a case in
point.) Because the general region of cultivating involves technai that are
directly related to the care of our phusical being, it not only helps transform
our understanding of the institution of women's work, but it may help root
institutions like health care and education back in a holistic dwelling (as
they are for North American native peoples).

We have seen that the strong distinction between internal and external
modes of bringing-forth in Aristotle helped dichotomize creativity along
gender lines into an active cultural making and a passive natural material
for the making. From the outset, females are those who give birth internally from themselves like nature, and males are those who do the essentially human work of culturally bringing forth the form in things. Because
Aristotle privileges form and the external, active bringing-forth in another,
even generation comes to be seen primarily as a bringing-forth in another
(i.e., the active imposition of male form on female passive matter) rather
than as a bringing-forth in itself. The male, then, not only dominates cultural creativity but usurps the creativity of birth, which had associations
through Plato with the creativity of the intellect. The prehistorical association of women with nature is erased by Aristotle with relative ease (indicating the historical construction of this association). At the same time,
moreover, the making belonging to phusis becomes confused with cultural
making, which I have suggested is an important indication of the ontological decline of phusis.

The distinction between the internal bringing-forth of phusis and the
external bringing-forth of techne reinforces other dichotomies involved in
the concept of cultural making. For example, the externality of techne's
bringing-forth must be accompanied by the activity required to get from the
giver of form to that in which the form is brought forth. Thus, human making is conceptualized as an active informing of passive matter that, moreover, implies a certain amount of control over the material. Through this
need for control, moreover, the activity/passivity dichotomy can also be
seen to intersect with and sustains the self/other and subject/object dichotomies. Thus, cultural making as we understand it always originates in a

subject-self and informs an object-other. Moreover, because this making is understood as an activity whose performance has a finished structure or product as its result, the end product rather than the process or means becomes essential. The emphasis on external bringing-forth, then, helps support our common conception of making that involves a privileging of activity, self, and the end product.

In cultivating as a mode of making or building, however, there is not such a sharp division between the internal bringing-forth of phusis and the external bringing-forth of techne because when we nurture and cultivate, we neither bring forth from ourselves or in another but bring forth through the other. Cultivating thereby undermines the external/internal opposition and the dichotomies it sustains. A caretaker attends to the other's rhythms of growth and decline and is responsive to the other *as* other. S/he gets to know it and help it along, not by trying to control (or take over) the originating order of its growth, but by giving the other the space to rest and grow freely. Providing the space to live does not mean an indifferent allotment of physical space in which to live, but a kind of softening and rounding out of the space through relational bonds wherein the dependent other can support itself by belonging to that vibrating, swelling space. It is this attentiveness of the caretaker to the needs of the dependent other that helps bring forth the other into the ''hale of being.'' The success of the cultivater depends on such factors as thoughtfully anticipating the needs of the other and sheltering the other from possible harm. This forethought, empathetic intuition, and preventive care appear to be passive only in the light of externally obvious activities like engineering and construction in which the finished product is equally obvious. The bringing-forth in cultivating-building is not a matter of a subject-self who actively gives form to an external finished product but is a matter of the responsive care that develops between those who find themselves belonging together. Such caring labor, moreover, cannot be easily quantified in terms of money or prestige (Ruddick 1989, 215).

The developing relation of care belonging to cultivating building can be seen in a phenomena seemingly as purely physical as the relationship between a mother and the thoroughly dependent other growing inside her womb. I am choosing to describe this phenomenon, not because I think women by virtue of their capacity to become pregnant are better or even prime examples of nurturers, but because this region of embodied experience notably affects many women's lives and may be responsible for the still prevalent conception of women as inferior to men because of its association with the natural in opposition to techne. I should also note that I am relying on my own experiences and others where the conditions for the continuance of the pregnancy were favorable.

In turning to nurturing practices as a way to build ecocentrically from out of our dwelling, I suggest, like Ruddick and Whitbeck, that our social ordering needs to be organized more around nurturing practices.[21] Although I also affirm, with Hartsock and O'Brien, that women's experiences of reproductive processes and caretaking roles have historically kept women *in some ways* closer to the rhythms of growth and decay than men because, for example, women have had to deal with the needs of the body, and the young and old, in other ways men may historically be closer to these rhythms (for example, their contact with death on the battlefield). I put the experiences of the mothering body into relief, not because I understand them as intrinsically closer to nature, but because of the confluence of associations with nature that have defined these phenomena within the context of western metaphysics. Moreover, it is only because of our present phallocentric being that aspects of women's experience might be helpful in reconceptualizing cultural activity in an ecoconscious way. Because of this same phallocentrism of Being, presenting women's traditional experience as a model for cultural change and promoting exiled feminine movements could be used politically to reinforce gender stereotypes and cultural pronatalism as well as to promote political passivism. Given, however, the phallocentric Will to Power that predominantly guides our actions and everyday being, there is a need to work toward social change not only by entering into male sites of power through female empowerment (for which exiled feminine movements are debilitating) but to work toward social change more radically by attempting to change the actual sites of power and, moreover, the nature of power itself. Nonetheless, as Sandra Bartky (1990, 118) rightly cautions, "Clearly, the development of any ethics of care needs to be augmented by a careful analysis of the pitfalls and temptations of caregiving itself."

Pregnancy cannot be classified as either a passive repose or an active external making. In Derridean language, it is an undecideable, with respect to the dichotomies of active/passive, inside/outside, and self/other. It inhabits the slash, the joining between these terms. The pregnant woman is caught in a play of changes in which she participates with some uncertainty. She is alive with a new "temporality of movement, growth, and change" (Young 1990, 167) that pulsates through her mothering body and with which she continually reorients herself. She turns toward her swelling body, responding to it sometimes as a frightening other foreign to her, sometimes as a fleshly budding wonder, intimately a part of her, yet apart from her. Through this constant process of psychosomatic orientation, she bonds with "the not-me within me" (Cixous 1986, 90).

The dichotomy of the internal and the external is also inadequate to describe the phenomenon of pregnancy.[22] In pregnancy, says Iris Marion Young (1990, 163), "the inner and outer are continuous, not polar." Julia Kristeva (1981, 31) notes similarily that "pregnancy seems to be experienced as the radical ordeal of the splitting of the subject; redoubling up of the body, separation and coexistence of the self and of an other, of nature and consciousness, of physiology and speech." Sara Ruddick (1989, 191) also notes how the birthing experience undermines the individuation of self in opposition to an other.

A pregnant woman, moreover, is not a subject-self in relation to a created product that she controls in her womb, nor is her swelling belly a cancerous other out of her control. The fact that she is not in command of the wondrous growing and cannot order its formation does not mean that she is a mere passive (in the negative sense) receptacle to a growth. On the contrary, she fully participates in the event by watching over and nurturing the growth of that which grows of its own accord within her. She lets an other grow within her through a constant orientation of her phusical being that bonds her to the other and the other to her. It is this constant psychosomatic participation in the becoming of phusis that gives the flourishing-that-comes-to-be of self and other, which is called pregnancy. A heavily pregnant woman holds the unnamed that roots itself in her flesh and draws itself to its future. She continually orients herself to the changing situation by responding, receiving, holding, accepting, and enduring the new bodily situation. Moreover, as every mother and labor coach knows, a woman gives birth through hard work that involves, for the most part, relaxing as fully as possible into the rhythms that have taken hold of her. These movements can be considered neither activities in the usual sense, because they are not essentially external motions, nor passivities, because of the phenomenal effort involved. Such exiled feminine movements, rather, function outside the economy of the metaphysical opposition, passivity and activity.

The mode of being evident in pregnancy is neither a standing-in-oneself as a subject-self separated from the other nor a standing-by like a resource in order to deliver a product for an external other. In pregnancy, one stands-through, in other words, one endures. The self/other and subject/object oppositions are clearly inadequate to describe this unique existential bearing of an other. This mode of being of the mothering body is an enduring holding-round that is given by a belonging-together rather than by a self and an other.

The actual birth experience, moreover, which is a prime metaphor for creativity, is not the producing of a product fully apparent in the glare of pure unconcealment. The laboring mother is not producing a product (reproducing), for she is not a subject in control of the birth but has to give herself over to the powerful rhythms that flow through her and has to push in accordance with these already given rhythms. The newborn, moreover, is not a product stripped of concealment, for its open need points back to its dark strong-hold, to its mysterious origins. Its neediness draws its caretakers back from their everyday activities to shelter its vulnerability and care for its new emergence from the deep.

The developing relation of care involved in cultivating building, moreover, depends on knowledge of a different order than that of rational knowledge as it has been conceptualized in western philosophy. The attentive caretaker does not bring-forth through knowledge of form in the way that an architect, for example, plans a building, but through an intuitive attunement to the free play of chance and the interplay of the unpredictable rhythms of growth, rest, and decay. The birth and caring for children and the care for the mentally different, the emotionally disturbed, the ill, the aged, and the dying, for example, happens to a significant extent through a bodily orientation to, and emotional empathy for, another mortal. This knowledge that is acquired through living practice and feeling for another is not even clearly a conceptual knowledge, but as Maurice Merleau-Ponty describes it, it is more of a bodily knowledge and a tacit knowledge learned through the lived body.[23]

One might object that by embedding the knowledge involved in cultivating so deeply in bodily experience, cultivating building is no longer recognizable as a kind of techne. The knowledge involved in techne proper, as Aristotle (*Meta.* 980a1–82a3) describes it, evolves out of sensory experience into the realm of theory. Techne, he says, comes into being when we move out of the variety of knowledge gained by experience *(empeirias)* and form one category *(catholou)* concerning similar experiences. To say, for example, that a certain herb benefited Callias when he had a disease, and also benefited Socrates and many others, is a matter of experience. But to recognize that this herb will benefit all people who have a sickness of this kind *(eidos)* is a matter of techne. Experience is knowledge of individuals and particulars, but techne is a matter of universal knowledge. It is knowledge of form. The knowledge of techne is of a higher order than that of experience because, with the acquisition of forms or idealities, it can be passed down without the original experiences that gave birth to the meanings (see also Husserl 1970, 56).

But does knowledge need to enter a realm of *eidos* in order to be communicable and passed down? It seems to me that it is not only the ideality of the construction that allows a theory to be understood by all coming generations and to be handed down and reproduced with identical intersubjective meaning, as Edmund Husserl (1970, 37) says, but also the communality of embodied experience.[24] As Merleau-Ponty (1982, 385–86) stresses, formal thought feeds on intuitive thought, and theory on embodied intersubjective experience. Even the simplest axiom of geometry, for example, depends on notions of up and down, left and right, which refer directly to our lived bodies.

There is a dire need to pay attention to the dependence of universals on particulars, and of theory on bodily experience. Our contemporary practices, for the most part, do not build out of dwelling that involves our embodied and social experience and the rhythms of phusis but build from the blueprints of constructed idealities. Our dominant modes of thinking and doing, moreover, tend to be motivated by power and profit. They move according to the constant escalation of power and economic growth. Perhaps in Aristotle's day, wisdom consisted in seeking the first principles and causes behind experience that help stabilize the flux of experience because the ceaseless play of forces beyond human control was all too obvious. However, in our long western historical search for, and control of the "why" of existence, we seem to have become blind in our theories (from the Greek theōriā, meaning "sight") to the simple fact of existence even to the earthy ground upon which we live. For the sake of wisdom we need to think with the weight of the earth, which means in part returning to the immediacy, spontaneity, and contradictions of ordinary embodied experience, returning to the needs of people with a view to holistic phusical health and respecting creatures who may make pathways, unlike our own, high in the treetops or in the midst of the sea. We can help bring the smell of the earth to philosophy by thinking on cultivating building as a letting-dwell because in these unobtrusive kinds of human practices, the fact that we dwell within the often disturbing changes and movements of nature is most apparent. In particular, the reclining aspect of the holding-sway of phusis, or what I have referred to as concealment, which is suppressed in modern consciousness building, development, and action, is put into relief simply because it is this aspect of a being that requires the most care. Nurturing becomes most prominent when a child, for example, is ill, for then attentive care is needed to promote health. This care, moreover, must not be understood as pushing the child to a constant growth but as a caring attuned to the various changes and rhythms of a being. In caring, one confronts decay, change, facticity, and the limits of human control.

Human beings have a special relationship with passing-away. What would seem to mark us as human more fundamentally than reason is that, as Heidegger (1962) says "Being is an issue" for us. In our more authentic, fuller moments, we wonder about existence as a whole, questioning its origins and meaning, and are perhaps struck by the simple fact *that* it is. Everything passes away, but passing-away for us is a crucial existential issue of our own being. Although for the most part we hide the facticity of our being, the feeling consciousness of our mortality is an essential characteristic of being human. It helps keep us in motion.[25]

The suppression of passing-away inherent in our everydayness is also apparent in western philosophy's attempt to transcend the earth. As Friedrich Nietzsche insightfully recognized, metaphysics can be characterized as "the spirit of revenge" against passing away.[26] Perhaps philosophy has tended to favor reason over the body in accounts of what it is to be human because to recognize the body as "the corporeal ground of our intelligence" (Rich 1986) we necessarily encounter the fact of our mortality. In any case, the suppression of passing-away and the suppression of the earth and the body would seem to be related and to reinforce each other.

Nietzsche's ([1954] 1978) recognition of philosophy's suppression of passing away and his attempt to overcome it through the notion of eternal recurrence does not result in an acceptance of the passing-away inherent in earthly temporality. This is evidenced by the fact, for example, that passing-away is described by Nietzsche in negative terms as a "dreadful accident" (p. 141) and as an aggressive, heavy black snake that forcibly enters the mouth of a young shepherd (p. 161). The young shepherd, who can be understood as representative of the Overman, bites off the snake's head and thereby overcomes the force of the "it was" and the gravity of the earth. The earth is thereby renamed "the light one" (p. 192). The philosophy of the Will to Power, unlike previous philosophy, can affirm that passing-away is part of life but only by actively willing the past to return. Stamping this negative pull back with the seal of the will transforms the rhythm of coming-to-be and passing-away into an eternal recurrence, or forever coming. The newly conquered (rather than merely suppressed) movement of passing-away joins the phallocentric temporality of the will, which is a continual progression of power. The creative will (understood as exclusively active and forward thrusting since it is essentially an overcoming) thereby compels its worst enemy, the temporal movement of earthly passing away, "to dance" (p. 229). The "dancer's virtue," says Nietzsche, is to transform all that is heavy and grave to light (p. 230).[27]

Even the phenomenon of pregnancy, which one might presume would exclude passing away, can help us think *with* the weight of the earth rather than against. The mothering body, for example, is not adequately described in a traditional philosophic way as the medium of the will's transcendent projects because its newfound massivity draws it earthward. The forward progression of growth evidenced by the surprising, rapid development of the pregnant belly is obtrusively accompanied by a stronger pull of the earth's gravity. This pull back need not be experienced as a negativity. As Iris Young (1990, 165–66) says, "The solid inertia and demands of my body call me to my limits not as an obstacle to action, but only as a fleshy relation to the earth. . . . Pregnancy roots me to the earth, makes me conscious of the physicality of my body not as an object, but as the material weight that I am in movement." This pull toward the earth can give one new found strength. Hélène Cixous says a heavily pregnant woman walks massively in pregnancy and lives as if she were larger or stronger than herself (in Cixous and Clément 1986, 90).

Moreover, although a pregnant woman gathers herself with the other toward its future, she is not expectant in such a way that a direct aim in view, the birth, is the essentially defining factor because her present is already so full of unexpected change. Pregnancy is a straight-lined, teleological process only from an external, disinterested perspective. For the pregnant woman and empathetic others, there is a strong pull back to the sheltering, the holding-round of her present. Her swelling belly pulls the mother-to-be back to the mystery of origins, and she stands heavy with this mystery.

The event of birth, moreover, is not the opposite of passing-away but is, in fact, an important event for recognizing passing-away. In delivering the baby over to its mortal existence, the mother confronts the rhythms of contractions and expansions basic to our mortal existence in an accentuated, vital way. The mother labors in accordance with phusis. In a baby's first breath we hear a fragile, lusty sound that rings out from a concealed source and that marks us as alive and mortal. Birth, like death, speaks of our phusical connections. It embeds us in the earth and exposes us to our mortal situation.

To describe pregnancy and birth as modes of cultivating, in other words, as techne, is somewhat related to the classical feminist Marxian analysis that reproductive labor is a kind of productive labor. But I am attempting to understand the whole matter of the birth of a baby, not in the realm of production, which, I argue, tends to carry vestiges of the culture/nature dichotomy, but in the regioning of bringing-forth *(poiesis)*, which suggest nonmetaphysical concepts.[28] Thinking of human pregnancy and birth as the

producing of a social product, moreover, distorts the subjectively lived reality of the process.

Even the biological conceptualization of birth and pregnancy as reproduction loses touch with the experience of the event because the wonder
and mystery of bringing-forth from concealment is absent. One gets the
impression from Aristotle, especially because of his constant use of techne
as an analogy to describe phusis, that the forming of matter to produce a
baby is not so different from the forming of matter to produce a statue.
Reproduction, for Aristotle, is the reproducing of the species by nature
whereby the male form informs passive female matter. We might think that
Aristotle's analysis is clearly wrong because, given the knowledge of modern science, it is outdated and irrelevant to contemporary concerns. However, because modern science is rooted in many of the same metaphysical
prejudices, its more sophisticated understanding of reproduction cannot
help resuscitate the nature of this phusical event. Even though science has
now realized that the male and the female contribute equally to the genetic
formation of the baby, it still understands birth as the forming of certain
matter to produce a certain end result. To think of the coming-to-be of a
baby in scientific terms as purely reproduction, we distance ourselves from
wonder and repress our mortality.

The entrance of women and other exiles from the margins of culture into
the heart of culture is not just a matter of making more room for more
people but will involve profound changes in our cultural attitude to nature. These changes threaten the scientific and metaphysical foundations
upon which the West has been built. So too, profound changes in our cultural attitude to nature entails deep changes not only in our attitude toward
earth and sky, plants and animals, and the wild as a whole but toward
women, our bodies, our sexuality and mortality, toward peoples of color,
children, grandmothers and grandfathers, the wilderness, and perhaps most
fundamentally, toward the multifarious and often erratic movements of
growth and decline. I suggest that our uniquely human attunement to the
changes of phusis, which involves growing, cooking, and eating our foods;
bringing-forth, nurturing, and educating children; caring for our elders;
healing our bodies with herbs and medicines; caring for our friends; attending to our sexuality—in other words, caring for and cultivating the overall

health of our being—is as essential to the nature of our human cultural being as calculative rationality and its attendant dominant mode of building
as technological constructing. We move into nearness by personally and
culturally cultivating this phusical vigilance and respect.[29]

Constructing, I am saying, is a mode of building that has been central
to the conceptualization of our notions of culture and reason and to the
formation of western science and culture itself. It is a mode of building,
moreover, that builds up from foundations and that, as it has been conceptualized over the course of time, relies on dichotomous notions of externality, activity, and a separation of culture from nature. One might object that
cultivating is a techne that was central to preindustrial and, perhaps, agrarian societies but that it has little place in our urban technological societies.
However, we have seen that moving backward and sideways to cultivating
building is particularly crucial for these ecodestructive, phallocentric times
because of its fundamental respect for phusis and the phusical ground of
our intelligence. It may even be that constructing building depends upon
the phusical health that cultivating brings to our dwelling on the earth. Perhaps artistic, philosophical, and political work belong more originally to
cultivating building. (However, such activities are validated and funded insofar as they participate in, and can be accountable for, constructing objects, institutions, theories, and systems.) Perhaps without the health of
our practical phusical being to ground and disrupt it in an earthy way, constructing building smoothly shoots off into an unearthly realm of constructed idealities and, moreover, compels what *is* to conform to these
transcendent forms.[30]

We need to rediscover our capacity to dwell, to regain our phusical
health by fostering the arts of phusical cultivation. Although the professions of medicine and psychiatry are already well recognized modes of
techne and are concerned with health, the practice of cultivating health in
our human dwelling is not a call for an increase in these institutionalized
disciplines, since there is a need for the androcentric and often uncaring
professions of medicine and psychiatry themselves to return to the healing
arts they historically usurped.[31] The western approach to health separates
health from other aspects of life and fragments physical health into areas of
specialization. Because of western medicine's emphasis on curative medi-

cine to the neglect of preventive medicine (which involves our dwelling as a whole) the focus of western medicine in on fighting disease and on developing new medical technologies. The body, moreover, is viewed as divided against itself—as a battleground of forces that threaten health and counterforces that defend against infections. As Young (1990) points out, moreover, the normal healthy body is one that is unchanging and is modeled on the adult male body. The phusical rhythms of growth and decline are thereby suppressed. In particular, the often disruptive movement of passing-away is fought. Dying is never considered healthy. On the contrary, an important thrust of western medicine is to defend the body against death despite a patient's wishes to the contrary.

That the health of our phusical being is much more than a matter of western medicine is made apparent, for example, in a case study of the inadequacy of western medicine to improve the health of aboriginal peoples in the Sioux Lookout region of northern Ontario (near where I grew up) and the conflict between western and aboriginal understanding of health. Although western medicine has improved the infant mortality rate and lowered the death rate from infectious diseases in aboriginal communities, there has been a dramatic increase in deaths due to suicide, domestic violence, and injury often related to alcohol abuse. The loss of cultural and spiritual values and the breakdown of the traditional extended family due to rapid social, political, and economic change have resulted in an overall lack of health in individuals and in family and community life. Moreover, there is no indication that more physicians or treatment services will foster the health of these people, for clearly health must be understood as a relationship with community members, with nature, and with life as a whole. This understanding of health is outside the parameters of institutionalized western medicine but is in keeping with the aboriginal understanding of health.

While western medicine has conquered many threats to health, the nature of our health problems is changing and has become more a matter of our overall dwelling. Health, as the World Health Organization defines it, is not merely the absence of disease but psycho-phusical and social well-being. It is the capacity to interact with others in ways that promote cognitive and affective well-being. Human health, then, involves the capacity to communicate with and to care for human and nonhuman beings. We cannot appropriately build from out of our dwelling if our very dwelling is diseased and if we cannot fully feel our interconnections with human beings from other cultures who are within our own communities, with those that have preceded us those yet to come, and with the myriad diverse beings that weave through the lifeworld. In the face of the advances of the sciences, there is an overwhelming need to turn back and rest in our simple mortal embodied being-here in the world-earth-home with others, on the earth, under the sky and, from this nonrational ground of our simple being, to build with a most radical openness to the play of chance, change, and difference.

> IDENTIFY. i remember lying down on the bamboo floors. i hear the ocean slapping waves onto the shore. cool wind curls its way through the spaces in between, caressing my face and my hair. LOVED ONE. i roll my head to peek underneath, i can see the chickens pacing back and forth. the striped light cast on the earth. THEIR LOVED. a band of little chicks trot and nibble on the grain embedded in the soft soil. piggy and company hover about grunting and snoring as they sleep with their fat bellies. RELATIVES IDENTIFY. this floor, this bed, is good for kids who wet at night. . . . FEELING. the rain always makes us think of cold, we fantasize about cold weather. REMAINS. we walk barefoot and feel the warm soil. FEELING WHAT. chicken shit is soft and cold underneath the soles of my feet we climb up big baskets, six feet high, where they store the grain. we climb in and sit in its warmth. itchy, rough grain. after threshing this grain becomes rice. FEELING WHAT REMAINS. i love watching the white rice coming out of the threshing machine. it farts the husk on to one side. it is dusty. BY FEELING. we sweep
>
> —Lani Maestro (in Lounder and Maestro
> 1990, 8; written with a high fever)

Chapter Seven

The Being of Water
in the Hydroelectric Plant

> Quebec is a vast hydroelectric plant in the bud, and every day millions of potential kilowatt-hours flow downhill and out to sea. What a waste!
> —Quebec Premier Robert Bourassa

In the following pages, I think on water and continue thinking on the fluidity of nature by describing the being of water in the hydroelectric plant. I undertake this investigation by freely and spontaneously developing Heidegger's important description of how the ways or movements of *Gestell* reveal themselves in modern technology (these movements are mentioned by Heidegger in the context of a discussion of a hydroelectric plant set into the Rhine).

> The revealing that rules throughout modern technology has the character of a setting upon *(das Stellen)*, in the sense of a challenging-forth. That challenging happens in that the energy concealed *(verborgene)* in nature is unlocked, what is unlocked is transformed, what is transformed is stored up, what is stored up is, in turn, distributed, and what is distributed is switched about ever anew. Unlocking, transforming, storing, distributing, and switching about are ways of revealing. (Heidegger 1977e, 16)

These movements are to be understood not only in our usual way as the movement of beings that pass from here to there but in a broader sense as something changing from this to that, and ultimately as the dynamism of Be(com)ing itself.[1] Thus, my description of the being of water also suggests the way all entities under the sway of modern technology presence, such as, for example, live-stock.

Unlocking Energy

Unlocking, chronologically, is the first way of technological revealing, because nature must first be unlocked before it can be in any way trans-

224

formed for human purposes. Unlocking is also first in that it is the most important, for all other ways of revealing are dependent upon it. Like Aristotle's notion of coming-to-be discussed in Chapters Four and Five, unlocking is a kind of change or movement that indicates the way something wholly comes into unconcealment from concealment, and thus it encompasses all other kinds of changes or movements. In contrast to coming-to-be, which is a way of bringing-forth *(poiesis)*, however, unlocking describes the way something emerges under the measure of Being as *Gestell*. I here then understand the terms *locked* and *unlocked* as the corresponding *Gestell* categories for the concealment and unconcealment involved in a bringing-forth.

Unlocking is a forceful opening of that which has been locked away. In order for an unlocking to occur, something of value must be locked up, for that which is of little value would not be guarded and kept from sight. We know from Nietzsche's overturning of metaphysics that ontologically the new source of power and value is to be found in sensory nature rather than in the supersensory realm. This newfound power of the Will to Power is to a large extent what we generally today call energy. From a western perspective (which is forcing itself on the world as a whole), the greater a country's natural resources and the greater its technology to unlock and utilize its energy, the greater its affluence. Energy is not only material power (used to operate industrial processes; to artificially heat, cool, and light environments; to transport products and people; and to build up military defense) but is therewith economical and political power.

Under the sway of *Gestell* (or Will to Power), nature is shown as energy that can be unlocked by technology. Like the elusive, wanton figure of Life in Nietzsche's *Thus Spoke Zarathustra* ([1954] 1978, 224–27), who allures Zarathustra into a wild chase after her, so nature appears as that which challenges us to penetrate its seemingly inexhaustible riches and unlock its secrets. From our western perspective, an aggressive technological relation to nature seems to have been necessary for the growth and development of civilization. The decisive turn into the modern era occurred during the industrial revolution when the various uses of energy were discovered and harnessed on a massive scale through technology. However, this aggressive relation of challenging-out nature's energy through technology is not intrinsic to culture, techne, or technology but has developed in the context of western historical Being, whose "essencing" Heidegger claims is that of western modern technology. The concept of nature as energy and the corresponding aggressive unlocking of energy belong to the West. Many cultures of indigenous peoples such as North America's First Nations people; the Penans of Sarawak, Malaysia; and Amazonian tribes, for example, have not developed in the context of dominating nature but in close contact with the land.[2]

In the western unlocking of nature, energy is forcibly released and exposed. Energy is subservient to, and possessed by, the technology that can unlock it. To possess something is to redirect it toward ends that are external to its presencing and not to let it move from itself according to itself. A possession cannot give itself from itself and in its own time but might even be provoked to come out before its time. The movement of unlocking, then, is not a staying-with and sheltering of the unlocked but is an abandonment of it and a renouncing of allegiance with it.

> Cows live only three to five years in today's typical dairy.... This means it is economically necessary for producers to breed them as soon, and as frequently, as possible.... if she has not come into estrus by 16 months of age, she is a candidate for hormone implants to bring her into cycle.... In addition to having a significantly reduced life span (20 to 25 years under natural conditions), many dairy cows suffer painful side-effects from the industry's tendency to breed them for maximum milk production. High producing cows tend to be nervous and high strung because of their faster metabolism. Many are lean and drawn, with huge, heavy udders which may reach the ground; cut, bruised and infected teats are common.
>
> —Lambert 1986, 3

The bringing-forth *(poiesis)* belonging to techne and phusis in the ancient Greek sense, by contrast, is an ontological movement that involves an accompanying, a protective holding, and a guiding of that which is brought forth. In contrast to the possessive taking of modern technology, bringing implies a movement toward a site of fruition. The bringing-forth of a table, for example, or of a plant was understood as a kind of yielding of the entity, a giving of itself to be born.

Concealment under the sway of *Gestell* as the locked-up is not character-ized from its own integrity as a sheltering but is characterized externally as that which stimulates the ontological movement of rising. Its intensive self-closing aspect in the context of *Gestell* becomes a provoking, powerful resistance that demands an overcoming. For in its secrecy, the locked-up appears to be holding back and thus retaining power that needs to be dis-charged in order to serve the progressive unlocking of power. *Gestell* lays claim to nature's locked-up energy and exposes it by advancing upon it, breaking it open, and extracting that which is holding back. The tighter the self-locking of nature locks itself up, the more powerful and compelling is its resistance, and thus the more forceful the advance toward possession. Thus the relationship between the locked-up and the unlocked becomes one of a mutual challenge.

> Day after day, each bull is "milked" of semen by teasing him into mounting a castrated male or a dummy "cow." If the bull does not cooperate, an electro-ejaculator that delivers mild electric shocks may be used to stimulate semen production. The semen is collected, refrigerated, and stored in liquid nitrogen.
>
> —Lambert 1986, 3

To help our thinking on the difference between the movement of unlock-ing, which is a mode of modern technology, and the bringing-forth of techne as poiesis, let us turn to the difference between the waterwheel and the modern turbine (the modern waterwheel used in the hydroelectric plant). The waterwheel is the most ancient device known that harnessed a power source other than animals.[3] Like the turbine, the waterwheel is an entity from techne that reveals water in a new, human way. However, the waterwheel's manner of revealing water is not that of unlocking. A crucial difference between these two modes of revealing water is that in the turn-ing of the waterwheel, the water comes forth *as* water, whereas the turbine is oblivious to water as water.

The water's flow is shown in its surprising strength as it steadily and surely turns the huge waterwheel. What is this flowing water that can effortlessly turn the wheel? The stream's flow is a field of currents that intertwine, merge, break apart, and rejoin. These currents, each with their unique and every-varying speed, rhythm, spread, and direction, together embody the stream's current. However, the life of the stream is not given by a kind of closed internal relating of currents, for the stream's current is wondrously open to the earth and sky. The stream is a vibrating joining between earth and sky.

It is an earth stream. The stream hugs the earth closely, bending its way wherever the soil yields to its flow (by forming new rivulets or seeping underground). It is indebted to its source whether a spring or a parent river, to the slope of the land, and to the particularity of its banks and bed. The stream brings silt, plants, larvae, and fish along in its currents. In its bending to the earth and earth life, the stream, at the same time, reflects the sky.

It is a sky stream. The stream receives the sky's gift of rain and wind, which makes it grow and swell and rush in torrents to overflowing its accustomed banks. So, too, it receives the sky's bright sunlight and in yielding itself thus, it subsides and perhaps withers to a small trickle. The stream's flow changes with the daily weather, the broad seasonal rhythms of the sky, and the even longer rhythms that take place over decades and centuries. In its constant reception of, and surrendering to, the sky, the stream bears witness to the steadfast, yet multivariegated joining between sky and earth. This yielding and receiving of the stream in its relation to the sky is so quiet that it is easily overlooked as insignificant (just as sexual receiving is not seen as a movement when compared with active penetration especially in heterosexual relations).

The stream's flow in all its particular joinings of sky and earth turns the waterwheel. The wheel does not extract the flow from the stream, for the flow is not locked away in the stream. The flow gives itself freely to the waterwheel. It yields to the waterwheel, flows into it and around it. The waterwheel turns not according to itself but according to the stream's flow. Thus, the rhythm of the waterwheel's turning is that of the variegated rhythm of the stream's flow. The waterwheel lets the stream run its course and runs according to it, even when the wheel's turning turns a system of gears that turn the millstone that grinds the corn into stoneground flour. The miller would come to know through experience the rhythms of that particular stream's flow and each mill would run differently according to a particular stream's current (from the French *courant*, meaning "to run").

The waterwheel sings of the stream.[4] The waterwheel does, indeed, alter the interrelating of the current at that particular bend in the stream. However, although the waterwheel stays the stream, it does not stop it or transform the flow into something else. The stream continues on its way after it has splashed through and around the waterwheel. If we stand beside the stream we can see the water hit the paddles. In this rushing splash toward the sky, in that responsive spreading out, the water's relation to the sky is shown with a sudden surprise. As it hits the paddle and spontaneously yields to it, the water is held up to the light and expanse of the sky, singing of its relationship with the sky. However, this spreading is not an endless shooting up and off. Rather, along with the splashing out, there is a reclining back to the earth. The waterwheel, in fact, shows even more strongly the strength of the stream's pull toward the depths of the earth, and the stream's stubborn, undisturbed gathering to itself, for after it has rushed up and out with a white spreading skyey splash, it continues darkly on its original course. The stream, thus, responds to and is shown by the waterwheel in both its openness to the open sky and its strong holding to the holding earth. Its stretching out to the sky and its gathering to itself join sky and earth.

The waterwheel reveals the stream in a new way, and through the waterwheel the stream moves in a new way at that particular bend in the stream. However, though the stream is shown in the light of techne, the stream, nonetheless, moves from itself and according to its phusical originating order. At first glance, it seems that the hydraulic turbine is merely a more powerful and efficient waterwheel in its relation to the water. However, the techne here is not in accordance with the living current of the stream, for it attempts to replace the current's originating order (arche). It is not built according to knowledge of the originating order of the water's flow (i.e., phusis), like the waterwheel, but according to Newton's third law of motion, which states that for every action there is an equal and opposite reaction. This is not knowledge of phusis but knowledge of mechanical physics.[5]

The turbine does not exhibit an intimate knowledge of the stream's flow as a joining of earth and sky, but it manifests knowledge of a universal, homogeneous matter or substance called energy. The turbine is not in direct contact with the stream's flow at all but receives a flow of water that has already been modified by the penstocks (where it flows in a vacuum) and often by other pipes, a storage reservoir, and a hydraulic pump. The turbine is not responsive to the flow of water but merely reacts to the kinetic energy (from the Greek *kinesis,* meaning "movement" in a so-called stream of fluid by extracting the kinetic energy and transforming it into mechanical or rotational energy. The fluid is channeled through the turbine blades, which are ordered at an increasing size so as to harness the decreasing power of the water. This fluid that makes the rotor spin need not, in fact, be water but can be gas, steam, or another liquid, and although the turbine will be modified accordingly, the principle of movement is still the same. In a hydraulic turbine the fluid happens to be water. However, the water is shown not as water, but as fluid. The particularities of water, such as its tendency to evaporate and to corrode metal, are, in fact, hindrances to its operation as a hydraulic fluid.[6]

Water seen from a scientific perspective as a fluid is that that gives way before the slightest pressure and that has the ability to do work. Unlike the waterwheel, which strongly showed the water's inherent reclining to the earth, the turbine shows the fluid as having minimal capacity to withstand the slightest pressure and thus a minimal gathering-to-itself, which, we have seen, is a crucial aspect of reclining. Thus, fluid is most compliant to the demands of Newtonian mechanical physics, even when this demand is to serve as the greatest resistant (for instance, in the conversion of fluid to hydraulic pressure). Under the sway of *Gestell*'s challenging-out, reclining back becomes mere resistance and stimulus for the perpetual enhancement of power. The reclining back of the water is not present in its use as energy, for when energy is unlocked, it is immediately pushed toward increase and use.

> About 45 to 60 days after a calf is born, the mother cow is inseminated again. And so it goes—year after year—until the cow falters in her ability to produce either calves or milk at which point she is sent to the slaughterhouse and converted into the cheaper grades of hamburger meat that are sold to fast food chains. It is estimated that 80 percent of ground beef comes from "spent" dairy cows.
>
> —Lambert 1986, 2–3

Since, in its capacity to serve as fluid, water as water cannot be unlocked and utilized, the relation of water to sky and to earth integral to its being as water falls away as inessential. The water's being is reduced to that of being-for an other. The gathering to itself of water, for example, is reduced to the standing of mere passive matter whose ontological status is that of potential energy *(dunamis)* waiting to be transformed. In a hydroelectric dam, for instance, the water's inclination toward the earth is exposed as gravitational force that can be used. Dammed-up water is not water that tends toward the earth, and it is open to the sky; but it is reduced to potential energy in the dam's "head" (the level of water in a storage reservoir) that can be unlocked to run the turbines. Unlockable energy is possessed potential energy that stands on call to be pushed toward increase and enhancement. Such standing-by to empower the forward thrust of power cancels out the movements of receiving and of reclining back.

> A dairy cow produces about 20,000 pounds of milk per lactation period—usually about 305 days. She is milked two or three times a day during this time and then given a rest, or "dry" period for the six to eight weeks just before she is ready to bear another calf. This is done . . . for greater profits. Cows milked through their entire lactation period will produce about 30 percent less milk than those who have had a dry period. To start a "dry off," the dairy farmer shocks a cow's system by withholding her food and water for a day or so and by stopping her daily milkings. (Withholding water is an extreme hardship, as a dairy cow can consume 15 gallons of water a day.)
>
> —Lambert 1986, 4

In sum, what turns the turbine is not the variegated water's flow, which is an intertwining of earth and sky, but the uniform kinetic energy of the regularized fluid that has been discharged from the penstocks. The originating order of the fluid's flow is not the intertwining of earth and sky, not phusis, but the regulating system of pipes and machinery of which the turbine as a rotary machine is but a part. The turbine is an unlocking of the energy of the water rather than a bringing-forth of a new aspect of the water itself; in revealing the water as energy, the turbine divorces water from its concealed, protective origin in earth and sky and displaces the originating order of the water's own movement. Water is revealed as a fluid that has the ability to do work. In serving as a fluid, the water's own particular ways of being, such as its running flow given by the interrelating of sky and earth, are obliterated. The particularities of water do at times obtrude, but they are understood as obstructions to the ideal running of the power complex.

> Some female calves are born with more than the usual four teats—sometimes as many as eight. These extra teats are considered unsightly and a possible nuisance during milking, so before an animal has her first calf they are cut off and the wounds treated with a dab of antiseptic. The procedure is so common that anesthetics and veterinary assistance are not considered necessary. . . .
>
> Some farmers do it because they prefer the ease of handling hornless animals, claiming that they fight less and have fewer injuries. . . . The most common dehorning device is a large pair of shears like a giant nail clipper; it simply gouges out the horn—taking about a half an inch of skin around the horn with it. Obviously the unanesthetized calf has to be forcefully restrained.
>
> —Lambert 1986, 1–2

As we will see, the running of the power complex does not have its originating order in phusis but in the currency of the electrical current and ultimately in the currency of the economic system.

> The milk producing ability of the average Canadian dairy cow has more than doubled since 1961.
>
> —Statistics Canada 1991, 16

Energy as the Transforming Form

Unlocking, as a mode of challenging-out, is an advance upon concealment and a suppression of the ontological movement of reclining. Because phusical entities reduced to energy lack the internal originating order of their movement, the energy that is unleashed in an unlocking must be externally ordered. (Given this, the Gaia hypothesis, which understands the earth as a self-regulating system of energy transfers, is derived from a technological model of nature and reduces nature to a sophisticated technological system.)[7] In other words, it must be regulated and given direction by a masterful technological command. We can call the motion of external regulating the "transforming" of energy.

Technology unlocks only energy that can be externally regulated or transformed and thereby theoretically controlled and capable of being channeled into the service of human beings (sometimes unlocked energy presents challenges that cannot always be met). Energy is particularly suited to external regulation because energy is that which is continually transformed. In the hydroelectric plant, the potential energy in the water is transformed to kinetic energy, which is then transformed to mechanical energy in the turbines and is finally transformed to electromagnetic energy in the generators. It is evident that what is undergoing the transformations is not water, not even in its designation as fluid, but energy as such. Thus, the fact that water as fluid is the embodiment of energy in the hydroelectric plant is rather incidental to the energy transformations and is left behind when the energy is transformed into electromagnetic energy.[8]

The ontological movement of the transforming of energy is put into relief by contrasting it with the movement of bringing-forth that Aristotle called alteration *(alloiusis)*. Alteration involves a being becoming something other *(allos)* than it was before. A being "alters" by undergoing a change but still remaining the same being. In this way, it can be said to have undergone, experienced, or suffered something *(pathe)*. Alteration is a change of a sensible aspect of something that takes place along a path from one "contrary" to another. For example, the sky alters in the course of its changing from light to dark. Alteration is a movement or change in the manner of being in the sky and not a change in its essential being (which would be called coming-to-be). The tranforming of energy can be understood as a regularized alteration in that the path of change is mathematized. Unlike the Aristotelean notion of alteration, however, in this mathematized crossing-over from one energy form to another, the sense of an entity enduring or experiencing *(pathe)* the change, is absent. Transforming is thus a formalization of an alteration whereby formulas account for and predict the changes in energy. Transforming occurs along a sequence of frames or gradations that serve to measure the extent of the transforming.

What is this scientific stuff called energy that does not experience change because it is defined primarily by its ability to transform and thereby already to be useable? Energy for modern physics is that universal matter or substance from which everything is made. In this regard, the modern notion of energy can be seen as a return to those pre-Socratics who regarded matter as the underlying substratum that remained throughout all changes. Energy is called primary matter because it can be transformed into mass, heat, or light without undergoing essential change (it still remains energy). Even elementary particles, such as the neutron and the negative proton, that were presumed to be indestructible units of matter on which all other entities were composed can be annihilated and transmuted into radiation energy. Elementary particles are, thus, just different forms in which the more fundamental matter as energy can appear.[9]

In setting nature as energy into its conceptual schema, however, physics does not stop nature in order to represent it, understanding it, for instance, as stable, underlying substance or matter. Instead, physics represents the transformable uniformity of phusis in its very movement. Physics thus formulates laws of nature through experiments that represent the constancy of the transforming of energy in the necessity of its course.[10] Thus, for physics, nature is mass in motion, which is energy. Energy equals a mass times a constant squared ($E = m \times c^2$). Energy is a dynamic, transformable universal substance that conforms to the formulations of physics. It is the single dominant form or uni-form of nature. In physics, energy is not phusical since it represents only those aspects of phusis that can be mathematized.[11] All entities of modern nature derive their meaning from a single formula of modern physics: $E = mc^2$.

The notion of energy is part of a conceptual schema belonging to modern physics that overlays nature and enables nature to be used by technology on a massive scale. This conceptual schema is not, however, confined to a highly specialized field of modern science but has its roots in, and thereby radically participates in, our being in the world.[12] Modern theoretical physics has a direct practical application in that, for instance, the exact knowledge of the motions of bodies under the influence of acting forces forms the basis for the construction of machinery. From the physicist's notion of energy as mathematizable nature, especially that of Newtonian mechanics, we derive our more common notion of energy as the power of doing work. Thus, we understand energy as a vast commodity for industrial and ultimately consumer use but also speak of energy in reference to, for example, our own vitality.[13]

Energy, then, is not the fixedly constant, the underlying substratum, but entails a becoming. It is an underlying substratum that is continually crossing over from energy form to energy form, and thus it achieves both constancy of being and the dynamism of becoming.[14] It attains a new flexibility and dynamism without losing the security of its fixity.[15] Because matter as energy has attained a new dynamism, its usability as matter is much more powerful than Aristotelean passive matter.[16] In modern physics' understanding of nature as energy, a clear distinction between form and matter, *energeia* and *dunamis,* cannot be maintained. Energy as the power to do work is related to the Aristotelean *dunamis* and potential matter, whereas energy as the actualizing of the power to do work is a continual crossing over of energy from form to form and is related to the Aristotelean *energeia* and form. Energy is thus a synthesis of *dunamis* and *energeia,* matter and form.

When phusical entities are reduced to energy, they are not understood merely as objects in the sense of formed matter. The conception of nature as a field of objects under human control reached its height in the industrial revolution. Nature as a reservoir of energy resources is given a new ontological status. In its serviceability and usability, its "stand" or presencing in the world-earth-home is not a standing-against a subject (in German "object" is literally a "standing-against"), *Gegen-stand,* but falls into a kind of objectlessness that Heidegger calls standing-reserve.

> The white or prime veal trade . . . is directly linked to the dairy farming because cows must be forced to bear calves repeatedly in order to keep their milk flowing. On the average, half of the calves born are males. . . . Veal producers buy them up and raise them in strict confinement to produce a fancy, high-priced grade of veal. To get the best price, the flesh must be as pale as possible. To get the palest flesh, the calf is made anemic and restricted to a stall so narrow he cannot turn around or lick his flanks. (The restriction is necessary to prevent him from licking

his own waste to obtain iron.) No bedding is allowed, for that might be a source of iron. For fourteen weeks, the calf is thus confined and fed a liquid "milk replacer" (a mixture of powdered milk, fat, sugar, antibiotics and other additives) deficient in iron. No grain or roughage is fed as that would offer iron, relieve the controlled anemia and darken the flesh.

—Lambert 1986, 3

The Storehouse of Energy

James Bay 2 will affect watersheds the size of France and create reservoirs the size of Lake Erie. . . . Hydro Québec plans to borrow over $40 billion over a ten year period to dam, divert and destroy many of the last major free-flowing rivers into Hudson Bay and James Bay.

—Sierra Club of Canada 1991

Energy is unlocked, transformed, and then stored. The movement of storing, unlike unlocking and transforming, seems to be a harmless, necessary, and concrete activity rather than a dangerous ontological mode of technological being. It appears, for example, to be something in which both animals and human beings engage. A squirrel will store nuts for the winter, and this storing enables the squirrel to continue to live during a time when there is little food to be foraged from the woods. Humans through techne work the soil, tend crops, bring in harvest fruits, and then store them in some way, for example, in caskets and bins. Storing here would seem to be a cultivating building in the sense of bringing-forth, for the storing occurs in accordance with phusis and for the sake of the phusical end of nurturing our bodies.

It is tempting to regard the modern storing of energy merely as an extension of the storing of nature's fruits. There is a world of difference, however, between the storing that I have described here, which is a techne in the sense of bringing-forth, and the storing of modern technology which is a challenging-out. Let us compare, for example, the storing involved in blueberry picking with the storing of energy in the hydroelectric plant. The most obvious difference is that the storing of blueberries occurs as the result of a seasonal harvest, whereas the storing of energy in the hydroelectric plant is not at all dependent on the seasonal rhythm of growth and decline. In northern Ontario, blueberries ripen toward the end of July and last for about three weeks. Whether it will be a good year for blueberries depends on the weather. The storing of energy in a hydroelectric plant, by contrast, is a harnessing of an ever-present resource. It is a continual storing so as to ensure a never-ending supply of energy. In a hydroelectric plant, energy is mainly stored in storage reservoirs of water, for it is technologically difficult to store energy in its final form as electromagnetic energy.[17] The impounded water serves as stored potential energy, which can be maintained at a constant level, and thus its service as a power supply is guaranteed. Because of the stored energy in the reservoir, the engineering system need not accommodate itself to the variations of what is technically called the ''run of river flow'' but can effectively regulate the water head internally in order to meet peak energy demands. In its storing, then, the technological system is not attending to phusis and its rhythms. Storing energy is not a response to the seasonal flourishing of nature's fruits but is a response to the market economy and consumer demand. In fact, storing is technology's way of overcoming nature's rhythms of growth and decline.[18]

> Hydro Québec needs to release water through their dams during the high electricity demand period of winter. By spring, demand tapers off and they effectively close the dams to save water for other peak periods, often resulting in drought-like conditions in the rivers downstream. So, whereas natural rivers are at their peak in spring run-off, Hydro Québec reduces the flow in spring and in winter runs the rivers up to ten times their normal volume.
>
> —Sierra Club of Canada 1991

The storing of energy is a securing of the system's operational drive in the manner of Will to Power. A stable, constant reserve of energy that can be reliably grasped as something behind the dynamic of the system (which drives itself toward maximal output and optimal performance) guarantees the system's regularized forward thrust toward its operation's empowerment. The storing of energy thus enables the hydroelectric system to guarantee its services as a power supply to the consumer.

A crucial difference between the harvesting of nature's ripening and the modern technological storing of energy is that in the gathering and storing of fruits, for instance, there is a protective care that holds sway from the very cultivation of the fruit throughout the harvesting-storing work. This care is absent in the hydroelectric plant's storing of energy.[19] Protective sheltering or nurturing does not involve pushing a growing entity exclusively toward maximal increase in minimal time but attending to a phusical entity's seasonal flourishing and resting. The impounded water in the hydroelectric plant is not sheltered but measured and kept under control in accordance with the optimal measure required for the smooth running of the plant.

> In 1987, Manitoba Hydro diverted the Churchill River into the Nelson River and built hydroelectric reservoirs. Southern Indian Lake, the main reservoir, became an out-of-control flood. The flooding melted the permafrost and the shoreline slumped into the reservoir. The water then consumed more forest, more permafrost melted and the shoreline slumped again. This chain reaction may continue for centuries before it stops. Manitoba Hydro did not predict it.
> —Earthroots Coalition 1991, 1

The presencing of the water in the storage reservoir, like that of all phusical entities understood as mere energy resources, is that of a standing-by and a standing reserve for use. Nature as energy is not cultivated but economically managed. Even the water in the storage reservoir, like that of the water in the turbine, does not freely come forth to compose itself in an enduring presence as water but is challenged-out to stand by as a standing reserve of potential energy readily available to the turbines and on call for further ordering. It does not rest within itself, standing in fullness, but is fixed in place as potential energy. It is securely set before the hydroelectric plant's control systems, which can measure and represent it as a standing reserve of potential energy.

This kind of standing or presencing of modern phusical entities in the service of techne is similar to the standing of use-objects such as tools and equipment in that the material of use-objects is all the more suitable for use the less it obtrudes (see Heidegger 1962, 95–102, 130–36).[20] In contrast to a crafted thing or work of art, the material of a use-object ''perishes'' in the equipmental being of the use-object. For example, for a tool such as a toothbrush to function well, we must not be distracted by the material of the tool, but the tool must become an extension of our body and will. Materiality disappears in use-objects because the functionality of the form in tools and equipment overtakes the presencing of the material. The materiality of the water in the storage reservoir, for example, disappears in serving as head for the dam. The water is kept at a controlled height so that it is at hand for supply. It is measured either according to its height or according to the force of its fall, which is estimated in terms of the pressure on a unit of area called an acre-foot. This measurement is called the dam's head. The acre-foot storage required for the energy desired is calculated, and this measure determines the height required in the storage reservoir.

Water for the hydroelectric plant is a body of stored potential energy that can be measured according to its height from the level at the base of the dam, where its usability begins (the ground level is considered waste because of the debris mixed in with it), to the level it reaches at the top of the dam. Aspects of the water's presencing that we might think would escape this measuring, for instance, the water that evaporates or seeps into the earth, are nonetheless accounted for but counted out as being usable water. What matters for the hydroelectric plant is water purely as potential energy that is standing by to be transformed into kinetic energy in the penstocks. Thus, the water that goes over Niagara Falls (on the Canadian side) is categorized as fall's waste on the computer printouts at the Hydro-nypa Niagara River Control Tower since this water is not taken in by the intake pipes of the hydroelectric dams on both sides of the river above the falls. The water that is fall's waste for the hydroelectric plant is, on the contrary, a valuable resource for the tourist industry. However, the ontological status of the water in its capacity as water resource is equipmental or ready-to-hand whether it is being used to produce electricity or to gain the tourist dollar.

In the body of dammed-up water of a hydroelectric plant, the water is completely controlled by the technological purpose for which it is to be used. The artificial lake's shape, depth, movement, evaporation, and run-off are the result of a process of comprehensive planning and controlled shaping. Because the artificial lake or storage reservoir is dominated by its technical end, it is a product of modern techne rather than a phusical techne (or a natural phenomenon). As with the being of tools, usefulness is not a quality that is assigned to the storage reservoir of water after it has been made but is the fundamental characteristic from which it came to be.[21] The water as water in the storage reservoir is dismissed beyond itself to be used up in its serviceability. The that-it-is of the water does not obtrude in the storage reservoir. If we are struck by anything present, it is the massive engineering feat of the hydroelectric dam.

> To provide additional water to increase hydroelectric output, Hydro-Québec diverted three rivers into the La Grande River. This is the largest water diversion by volume on earth. The filling of La Grande hydroelectric reservoirs in the 1980's caused mild earthquakes at these locations.
>
> —Earthroots Coalition 1991, 1

Although Niagara Falls is considered one of the natural wonders of the world, it is so overpowered by technology and economic management that one is faced more with an amazing achievement of ongoing technological management rather than a natural phenomenon. Every cubic square foot of water of the massive flow is hourly accounted so as to record the Canadian and U.S. water shares of the mutually owned water. Moreover, the actual amount of water that goes over the falls has been calculated in advance according to the minimum amount required to accommodate the requirement of the Canadian tourist industry that the scenic beauty of the falls remains intact. This amount of water (one hundred cubic feet per second) is about *one-half* of the original amount that went over the falls before the new hydroelectric plants were built. The torrent of water going over the edge still makes a good photograph, however, and appears to be of much greater quantity than it actually is because the top of the falls has been leveled out and cemented (by turning the falls off in sections) so as to stimulate the appearance of the same amount of falling water.

Like the water in the hydroelectric complex, water for many urban dwellers, who mostly see water from the tap, presences as mere standing reserve belonging to technology. One might argue that if we stand beside the water in the storage reservoir and look at its relations to the wind, we can still say that the water moves from itself as a phusical rather than technological entity. However, even though accidental aspects of the water might escape its functional end, the water is essentially mere energy that stands by to serve the hydroelectric plants' turbines, and thus this service-ability defines its presencing.

One might further argue that though the water in the storage reservoir is so subsumed by the artificial lake and its standing by for use that it has become a use-object, the being of the water, say, ten miles upstream after it has been released from the turbines, having served its practical function and, moreover, the countless rivers that flow freely, do not derive their being from techne. However, in the context of the overall management of hydropower, even these waters have their primary being from techne. Most major rivers and their tributaries in North America, for example, are what engineers call regulated rivers. They are rivers that do not have the variegated flows of unregulated rivers because they are managed by flood controls, irrigation techniques, and storage reservoirs. The seemingly free-flowing river beside which we stand is really only a segment of the river that is allowed passage between the various types of valves. The river's movement, evaporation, and runoff, moreover, have all been measured and accounted for.

In fact, many rivers are no longer naturally in harmony with the land and natural entities that they meet but have become through technology a system that has to be managed. The river has become dependent on the guidance of techne. The fact that we might experience the river's receiving of the sky and reclining toward the earth despite techne's overtaking of the stream's movement is an important phenomena that shows that techne has not yet taken complete command of the earth's rivers. However, seen in the light of techne, which understands the river system as an energy resource (to serve hydroelectric, pulp and paper, and chemical plants; irrigation needs; and the tourist industry), its openness to sky is understood as evaporation and its reclining to the earth as runoff. Evaporation and runoff are both accidental features that escape the river's fundamental functional purpose or *telos* that essentially guides the river in its course.

> In 1984, 10,000 caribou drowned in a single incident on the Caniapiscau River in Northern Québec from water released by a hydroelectric reservoir. The Québec government's reaction was to call it an "act of God."
> —Earthroots Coalition 1991, 1

Thus these aspects of the river are incidental to the river's fundamental being. If it were technologically simple and economically viable to cancel our evaporation and runoff (and did not result in the destruction of other energy resources), then these supposedly accidental characteristics of the river's being would no doubt be erased, since the river could then be better controlled and regulated and assigned to its tasks.

> Probably the most devastating impact [of the James Bay 2 hydroelectric project] that is predicted for the freshwater seals is mercury poisoning.
> —Earthroots Coalition 1991, 3

We are entering a time when we will have the ability to take command not only of rivers but of most aspects of phusis by regulating and securing the earth's energies through technology. To a large extent, nature has already become a storehouse of energy standing by to meet our energy demands. By harnessing different forms of energy (potential energy of atoms, internal heat energy, kinetic energy of rotation) and by harnessing these energies in more efficient ways, we secure our energy supply. We ensure that we have light, heat, and food independent of the season, time of day, and kind of year. We live as though inside a global storehouse of energy, securing ourselves against the contingencies of our phusical being. Storing is not a gathering but an amassing. It is an attempt to hold mortal need and vulnerabilities at bay. However, even as our mortal needs, and thereby a sense of our mortality, are successfully held off through the storing of energy, our energy consumption insidiously increases. As the power-full West moves toward the possibility of setting up a new world order, challenging-out and economically ordering world energies, overpowering the ontologies of other cultures, and overtaking the integrity of the earthy being, the relational, multifarious bending of our phusical bodies in their playful relations to the earth and sky is thereby also regulated and taken over.

> In 1984, two-thirds of the Cree Indian community of Chisasibi in Northern Québec learned that it had been poisoned by mercury from eating fish, a mainstay of their diet, downstream of the first phase of the La Grande hydroelectric complex. Some elders developed numbness

of limbs, loss of peripheral vision, shaking and neurological damage. The Cree fought the project and lost.

—Earthroots Coalition 1991, 1

Distributing and Switching About

In the hydroelectric plant, potential energy, stored mainly in the storage reservoirs, is transformed via the turbines and the generators into electricity and then distributed through the power lines. The electricity is distributed over great distances by stepping-up the voltage through transformers, since power losses decrease with increased voltages.[22] When the electricity goes into industries and homes to service them, the voltage is then stepped-down. The distribution of electricity happens through power lines that run from one power station to another and that join a whole network of lines from other power stations across the continent. These lines form one vast North American matrix of electromagnetic energy (into which, moreover, nuclear plants in North America are plugged), enabling one power line system to feed off another system during peak energy demands.[23] Distributing is an ontological movement that apportions the electric current to towns and cities and, more specifically, to industries, office buildings, and households.

When energy is transformed from the potential energy in the water current to electromagnetic energy in the electrical current, a rather wondrous change has taken place, for water, which was considered by the pre-Socratic thinkers as one of the four irreducible elements, is transformed into its contrary, fire. This fire current or electricity is the currency of the hydroelectric system.

In the transformation from river current to electrical current, the current gains a new kind of gathering and order. We recall that the current of a stream or river is an intertwining of currents that merge, break apart, and rejoin, each with its unique, ever-varying speed and direction. The stream's current, moreover, is open to earth and sky, hugging the earth and bending to it, and yielding to and receiving the sky's clemency and inclemency. Like the river current, the system of power lines that holds the electrical current is an organized whole. However, in the power lines the currents are power lines that are externally bound to one another, regulated in their speed and direction, apportioned in regulated, measured amounts, and arranged according to the demands of the operation.

Companies and individuals join in the flow of power through their own form of currency: money. Energy is granted out, apportioned to those who are currently part of the system and have the currency to exchange for the electrical current. As in the market economy, keeping the power circulating through the system's circuits enables the system to remain in drive. The energy is kept in circulation through the Electric Power Transmission System, which consists of transformer stations that connect the lower voltage power generating equipment to higher voltage transmission facilities. These facilities consist of higher voltage transmission lines and cables and switch stations that serve as junction points for different transmission circuits. In the switch stations are circuit breakers and associated connection devices, which switch equipment into and out of service.

The external ordering of the electric current is, like all the other movements we have been discussing, from techne and involves regulating and securing power for human use. Distributing as a movement is associated with justice and laws, as in distributive justice. The law guiding the distribution of electromagnetic power through this vast grid, however, belongs to economics rather than to justice: the energy is maximally distributed at minimum expense in response to market demand.

Distributing not only has associations with justice but has even deeper associations with destining, for the early Greeks understood historical changes as sendings from Moira, the goddess of apportionment.[24] She spins the threads of life, granting measures for each mortal life, weaving their destinies. Moira, says Heidegger (1975, 98), is the bestowal of "luminous" presencing in which what is present appears. Distributing under the sway of *Gestell* is an assigning of power according to laws of economy. Economics guides the running of all our systems and guides what comes to light. Those entities and those aspects of entities that cannot be distributed according to this principle do not, literally, come to light. Thus, it is not merely that those who cannot afford to pay their hydrobills or to construct hydroelectric plants do not receive electric light, but in a deeper sense, only those who have this medium of exchange called energy (as natural resource, capital, or labor, for example) participate in, and are secured by, the historical power lines of the West.

> Trees that are cut down were once the shelter of hornbill, the home of gibbons, the home of langur, the home of every single kind of animal that lives up high. Where is their home now? Gone. Finished! No home for babui. No more home for saai. No more home for matui. No home for kuai. They don't like this. We don't like this. . . .
>
> The government says we are animals,—like animals in the forest. We are not animals in the forest. We are Penan. Humans. I myself know I am human.
>
> —Dawat Lupung

The electricity that is distributed is switched about in the high voltage transmission lines and cables by means of switch stations, circuit breakers, and associated connection devices that switch equipment into and out of service. This distributed energy, moreover, is, as Heidegger notes, "switched about *ever anew*" (emphasis added). When we switch on the light in our homes, we show ourselves as recipients of the light energy in the power line grid system. As consumers we are part of the system and are apportioned our light. However, given our modern Being of Will to Power, not even consumers are the true destination of the current. The distributed energy within the power line complex has no true destination or *telos,* for the current of energy in the power lines never finds its belonging-space but is, rather, forever circulating, switching about from one kind of energy consumption and transformation to another.[25] It is a standing reserve of energy that is constantly circulating in its objectless stand.

A natural entity, we recall, gathers itself and brings itself to a stand in its togetherness, whereas a human-made entity is brought to a stand by the craftsperson who gathers together the matter, form, and *telos* that are responsible for the entity's coming-forth. However, such human-made entities are natural in the sense that they are not opposed to nature because *telos* of a human mode is always phusical. Medicine, for example, should work for the sake of health. Modern arts and technology, however, in contrast to older forms, do not always appear to work within a phusical *telos*. Instead, they often move within technical boundaries, boundaries that are seemingly endless. They aim solely toward the continual empowerment and perfection of themselves.[26] This process of "willing" itself is endless. As Nietzsche (1956, 298–99) says, the will would rather will nothing than not will at all. Heidegger (1973, 107) warns that such endless circulating of power is an "unworld": "The circularity of consumption for the sake of consumption is the sole procedure which distinctively characterizes the history of a world which has become an unworld."

It is perhaps helpful to contrast this limitless willing, this destining that has no destination, with the metaphoric weaving of Moira according to which the early Greeks poetically thought entities historically emerged. Her linen threads, which bend and twist and are cut at certain lengths, give the determinations of an age's and an individual's lifeline or destiny. Her granting of boundaries is a giving of a destination, not in the sense of willing an endpoint to a journey, but in the sense of providing the boundaries according to which pathways emerge. This "whereto" or *telos* of one's pathway is not something that comes after the pathway has run its course, but guides the pathway from the very beginning. By contrast, modern power is switched about ever anew, continually circulating and continually being regulated by the distribution principle of economics, and has no destination. In the constant external regulating and securing of energy there can be no internal drawing-together and belonging-together, which are needed to help weave boundaries or limits. It is as though the multifarious possibilities of relating in Moira's fibrous weave of life were reduced in the electrical current to an "on" or "off" mode of relating.

Because the originating orders of the systems of power, under the sway of *Gestell,* are from techne rather than *phusis,* distributing cannot be bound to wholeness and rest. The unfolding of the system is not an unfolding in stillness and wholeness but is an external regulating and securing that continues endlessly. The word *system* originally comes from the Greek *sunistema,* which literally means a "standing-together." In a standing-together that still respects phusis, the relations between those elements brought together remain crucial, for they discover, through their gathering, the order of their belonging-together. In a system, however, that attempts to overcome phusis, it is not the gathering but the external regulating law that governs the elements brought together. What comes to the fore is not the relation but the law, plan, or schema that regularly arranges and organizes entities from the top down.

> Hatched by the thousand in artificial incubators, chicks are sorted by sex. The males considered uselsss, are gassed, crushed, or thrown into a garbage bag to suffocate. The females are all painfully debeaked. This prevents them from pecking other birds when stressed.
>
> Egg-laying hens are crammed five to an 18 by 12 inch cage. . . . Battery cages made of wire are stacked in long rows three to five tiers high with water and food available in troughs in front of the cages. After a year or two . . . they are taken from the cages and sold as "spent fowl." . . .
>
> Fryers and broiler hens cannot be raised successfully in small wired cages so they spend their lives on floors covered with shavings. Their . . . life lasts a maximum of 7 to 8 weeks.
>
> —Robbins 1991, 2

The horror of such a system is not only that its boundless challenging-revealing never comes to an end but that it insidiously grows, as Heidegger (1977d, 16) says, by "revealing to itself its own manifoldly interlocking paths and regulating their course." This system of life thus not only regulates and externally orders entities from nature, replacing their own originating order with technological controls, but, in fact, the system itself grows as though it were phusical. This growth of the system is not a growth that roots itself back into the earth but, rather, is one that increasingly goes forward. Moreover, this growth does not emerge through boundaries and regions given through its relations with earth and sky; it is, instead, boundless in its progression. It is placeless and homeless in its constant circulating and switching about. The end or destination of challenging-revealing is to be endless, to grant boundaries that are boundless. Everything is pushed ahead toward increase and productivity. There is no rest to the system's growth nor a sense of gathering and place. The "where" of a dwelling in the midst of this switching about is obliterated. The system, then, can be characterized as a homeless standing-by ready to be further ordered, where even the recognition of the homelessness of animal and human be-ing is itself replaced by the will to get ahead.[27]

The Holding Sway
Cycladic Figurine, 2800–2300 B.C.

Her swaying is ecstatic, blissful. The head raised back, rolling back, in ecstasy.
A gentle figure enraptured in the natural rhythms of nature.

The Cycladic sculptures all come
from the Greek Cycladic Islands, are
dated between 2600 and 1100 B.C.,
and all show a certain traditional pose.
They have tall bodies that are on their
toes and are slightly bending at the
knees. Their head is strangely raised
back, seemingly chanting upward to
the sky. Often the eyes and mouth
are not marked, but when they are,
it is thought they would have been
painted since there is faded paint on
some. The nose is a long, wedged line,
and the forehead is broad and sweeps
back. Most characteristic of their
stance is their folded arms. Their arms
go straight across the body from the
elbows, forming a strong contrast to
the vertical line of their body and
nose. Their arms are not actually
folded or crossed over one another in
a position of relaxation, but are holding the body itself.

   Their pelvic region, which, it
seems, was also often painted, is ac-
cented by a triangular shape. It is this
marking of the pubis and the small
swelling breasts that tell us they are
female. There is the rare exception

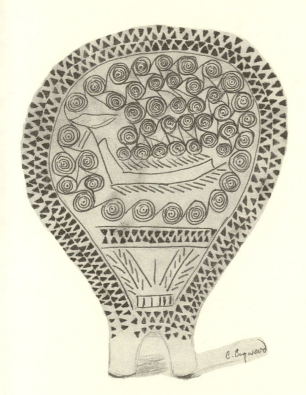

where we find a phallus instead of breasts and the pubic triangle, but these figures lack the holding sway that is so essential to the nature of the Cycladic female figures. The triangle is often quite large, going out to the hips and sloping down between the legs. There is also often a distinct line drawn around the neck. The toes, the fingers, and the hands that are holding the body are marked in relief. The body, which is usually quite long and flat, stretches downward, flows back, and tilts to each side. It would have been hard to make the body so tall, and indeed many have breaks in them. One can best see the bending movement in the profile view. One also sees from this side view that the belly swells out from the upper line of the pubic triangle. Some figures are obviously pregnant since the swelling belly is unusually pronounced.

The purpose of the Cycladic sculptures is a mystery. With a few exceptions, they are all females in a folded arm pose. Most of them were found in graves along with tools and jewelry, and most were hand-size. They vary in quality from rough schematized shapes to well-worked individualized pieces. The different qualities of the carving suggest that the sculptures were not just in the possession of an elite but were accessible to the whole culture. We must not think that these people were merely trying to represent the human body and got some features wrong or were restricted by their capacity to work with marble. We can see from their delicate marble vases that they could work the marble very finely, and from other sculptures, that they could render more naturalistic forms if they had wanted. Every curve of the traditional form hides a deep, living significance.

Reflecting their male prejudices, some archaeologists have postulated that perhaps the Cycladic dolls were sacrificial substitutes for the concubines of the dead husbands. (The fact that these sculptures were also found in the graves of females is brushed over as insignificant.) There is no doubt that in some way these sculptures accompanied the dead, but to assume not only that they are substitutes, which denies presence to the sculptures in their own right, but that they are substitutes for the husband's consort, which assumes the inferiority of women within the culture, is to degrade the female sculptures on two fronts. The more accepted theory is that the Cycladic sculptures are votive offerings to a fertility goddess, even though they lack the steatopygic shape that motivated archaeologists and art historians to name such figures in the first place. Although it is clear that in the early religions of that area, as in most parts of the world, the divine was understood as Great Goddess, I find the concept of fertility goddess to name "Goddess" objectionable, since it reduces the human relationship to the Goddess to utilitarian motives (i.e., "primitive" peoples worshiped a female divinity because the female produces new life like nature, and thus, by worshiping, her peoples hoped to ensure the productivity of their crops and the animals they needed for their survival). Moreover, the concept of fertility reduces the bringing-forth of females to a functional production. "Fertility Goddess" also becomes an overarching category that is supposed to explain the meaning of just about any prehistoric artifact that is female.

Even the term *Goddess* is problematic because it implies worship to a "higher" divinity, which in turn presupposes dualisms between higher and lower, heavenly and earthly. It is interesting, however, that whereas the concept of "God" implies a hierarchy of beings with God at the apex as the supreme being, the concept of "Goddess" implies a plurality. We can see this clearly by the fact that we cannot say "Goddess" in a way that implies the univocal singular, as we can when we say "God." We must way "*the* Goddess," which implies a pointing out of a specific entity among others rather than an all-encompassing, overarching Being. In any case, as I see it, the simplistic category of "fertility goddess" explains away the deep meaning these figures hold.

Perhaps the Cycladic sculptures are best described as offerings, not in the sense of a giving to appease a higher force or even in the sense of showing respect for a greater force (for these conceptions are locked into the spirit/ nature dichotomy of Christianity), but rather in the sense of giving themselves over to the pulse of life. The swaying Cycladic figure is a mortal drawing out of life's vibrating lines and movement.

This is not to say that early peoples were motivated by a need to put into images representations of who they were in order to help explain their world. The sculptures would indeed help them understand their being in the world-earth-home, but to understand this as the primary motivation, it seems to me, reflects a modern bias. Our modern thinking, says Heidegger, can be characterized as a representational thinking: a willful, self-reflective activity that essentially requires a placing-before, an aim in view. Images, of course, amply suit this need of representational thinking. As I show in the following pages, the Cycladic sculptures arise fundamentally from a people's being-moved by the movements of their fleshy being in the world-earth-home and, moreover, from being-moved uniquely as mortal beings to draw out the lines of that movement, not for a representational thinking, but in order to give themselves over in a fully mortal way to the holding sway of phusis or nature.

All of the Cycladic folded-arm sculptures are propped up with fasteners in the museum for display. They cannot be merely leaned against the wall, for they are quite tall; they "stand" on their toes (and the fact that there is a flat-footed musician points to the fact that their being on their toes was purposeful), and the curving back of the head resists being a good bracing for propping. We must, then, doubt whether they would have been propped up in their original context. The small figures, especially, were likely lying down and would be picked up to become upright only with the holding hand. If they were lying down, they would rest on the head and the buttocks, the legs going up into the air like a kind of handle. If the legs were pressed down, the head would rock upward. That the figures would balance on the tip of their head may have helped determine the odd flowing back shape of the head, though of course function would never fully determine form but would be only a layer in an inter-meshed network of meaning.

The hand-size figures invite the holding of the hand. This is especially clear in the earlier "violin" forms, which encourage the hand to hold the rather squat body (which has the Cycladic folded arms) around the waist and stroke the long, smooth, tapering necks. The long phallic necks of these earlier forms are carried over into the later forms, which also have long tapering necks; but in the later forms, as we have described, the unique heads are distinguished from the neck. The hand so wants to curve around the neck and the head, which tapers like the head of a chisel, following its wonderful flowing back. They were undoubtedly sculptures to be handled and not primarily looked at. Their meaning would blossom through being felt, experienced through the sensitive hand, and not merely through being eyed, worshiped as cult objects.

Now that we have an initial orientation to the Cycladic sculptures, I move into a closer investigation. My intention in this essay is not to solve the mystery of these strange figures, for their mystery, given not only because they emerge out of the depths of time but also because they emerge out of the depth of artistic creation, is intrinsic to their presence. My hope is that we can immerse ourselves in their mystery (rather than dispersing it) by paying close attention to their sensuous presence. By communing with their earthy presence, we can, moreover, hopefully step back somewhat from our distancing, modernist perspectives.

It is important to make contact with an individual artwork and learn from its particular sensuous manifestation of truth; otherwise, when dealing with these artifacts that bear strong stylistic resemblances to each other, one becomes locked into a mode of merely distilling their various features in order to define a single, overarching style characteristic of the group. Although this method can serve to orient one to the culture, as I have done above, it prevents one from contacting the art in a deep way, for deep contact depends upon particular presencing.

The Cycladic sculpture I have chosen to work with is one of the larger sculptures (1.4 meters) and is carved out of marble. The subtlety of its features and the fine carving of the marble are remarkable about this piece. Whereas one tends to look at the Cycladic sculptures as a whole and thus learn about the general Cycladic style, this piece, because of its outstanding sculptural quality, is strong enough to ground an investigation into the particularities of a single piece and thus to root our thinking in a particular sensuous presence rather than in a general artistic style. This work was not found in a grave and thus is called a cult statue. This gentle, refined sculpture shows the sensitivity of the sculptors hand to stone. It is superb in its carved lines, soft contours, and wonderful proportions.

Her head slopes back with mystery and nobility. Her eyes are not marked, but she appears to look far out toward a far horizon; though her broad, sloping forehead tapers back, her eyes appear to be on the utmost curve of the bending back, placing them in such a way that they seem to be stretching out toward the distance. Her head inclines slightly to one side. Her hip on this same side is slightly higher and tilts to the side, so we know that she is not only swaying up and down, as her slightly bent knees and the flowing back of her head suggest, but gently swaying her hips. What a beautiful sway, a movement so gentle and subtle, so full of deep, earthy mystery. Again and again one is drawn to this simple sway. She sways not only in one direction but completely, roundly. She sways with the deepest rhythms of earth and sky.

This essay is essentially a meditation on this sway. Before we flow with our thoughts into her sway, however, it will be helpful for us to orient ourselves this time to her culture as a whole. Thus, we look briefly at a kind of artifact that is also distinctive of this culture: the ill-named "frying pans" (so named because of their shape). These strange pans, which, like the Cycladic folded-arm sculptures, are also a key feature of Cycladic art, are anthropomorphic. They have two legs (forming the frying pan handle) and a pubic triangle, often with a slit down the center, marking the vulva. From the line across the top of the triangle that forms the beginning of the waist, the figure swells out into a round shape, which has raised sides that form contours similar to those of a frying pan (but upside down, for the incisions of the drawing are on what would be the back of the frying pan). Above the waist line most often are swirls connected with each other. In one, a single swirl swirls out into seven other swirls around it. Another typical design is the star within a star shape, and also a circle within a star shape. Often there is a boat with lines joining to fish within the mesmerizing swirls. The boats are placed horizontally across the body, in the same position as the folding arms of the Cycladic figurines. On one, the boats are not horizontal but slant down with a pronounced zig-zag line above the boat, evidently the movement of sinking. The patterns pulse with movement, expanding and contracting, and one's eye loses itself in this pulsing. These pulsating images would have perhaps evoked ecstatic states in a culture where images were rare and thus would have retained their magic.

On this particular pan at which I look, there is a long boat amongst the swirls placed where the arms fold on the Cycladic figurines. The swirls are quite mesmerizing, swirling in and out. The swirls are the waves of the sea. They depict not so much the look of the wave as the feeling of its movement when in a boat, the feeling of its churning rhythms. The swirls fill the face of the pan, and the long boat with its many oars seems almost lost in the swirls, yet it holds its own, moving across the swirling waters. These people must have loved and respected the sea, not only because it was the source of their main nourishment, but because of its mysterious depths, which hold so much life yet which pull mortals to their death. It is a mystery to which they could come close and which they feel through the rocking of their boats in the swirling water. Its rhythmic rocking sway would have touched their deepest sense of being.

The pubic area of the pan figure has no swirls. All around the round body and around the pubis, tiny triangles, like stars, are incised into the pottery. There are strokes in the pubic region resembling pubic hair but also reminiscent of the strokes of oars on the waters. Perhaps this region expresses the holding depths of a woman, the dense depths of the earth, the quiet depths of the sea, and the dark depths of the night sky that aided these peoples in their navigation over the equally dark depths of the waters.

The swirls appear to be swaying together because they are all interconnected, and not only each swirl to the swirl next to it. They are swirling pockets of movement, all joining, forming a large, swirling space. The long boats, by contrast, move horizontally across the swirling space, forming a straight line of movement, a mortal cut.

The Cycladic people were a seafaring people who had a huge fleet of ships that dominated the Aegean. However, in these pan figures we do not sense the military power of these people but their reverence for the mystery of the powerful sea. They make their mark, carve their human line in the sea with their boats. As they stroke the waters with their oars, their human line emerges and then submerges into the swirls spinning off from the oars, showing the waters as an immense sea of swirling movement all the more clearly.

The sway of the folded-arm Cycladic sculpture has a similarity to these long boats that move with a quiet buoyancy across the swirling sea. Her holding of her womb with her long arms, holding her body of mystery from which life is brought forth, is like the holding of these boats to the sea, the impenetrable depths from which wells so much life. She bends, sways, holds the mysterious source of mortal being. Though deeply embedded in the dark depths of mystery, she emerges into unconcealment through her mortal sway. She makes her line and gently carves the space around her with her sway, just as the long boats carve their line on the wide sea. Her sway is a gentle modification of nature's movements through her body.

Her long neck and chisellike head bend back, carve the gentle lines of her sway as a chisel carves wood. Her form itself is toollike because it fits so well with the hand. These people would have had such a close relation to their tools. They had equally important tools for carving stone and for making these votive offerings and beads as for fishing. Tools, as they are sometimes for us, were not so much a way of conquering the world but a way of touching it. They learned about the world through their tools. Their chisels made deep contact with the earthy stone, carving out human lines, which are natural in the sense that they are drawn from a bodily inhabitance. Only on a second-order level is the making of human lines a matter of techne. Their tools seem to confirm the fact that the bringing-forth of techne, which for us has become a bringing-forth that is in opposition to nature, is for some cultures a mode of the bringing-forth of phusis or nature. It seems, looking at these earlier people, that art and tools, for mortals, is as natural to our phusical growth as the spreading and bending of a tree's boughs. Techne is a mortal carving out of our belonging-place on the earth. To carve is to make human lines, to show the unique contact between mortals and the earth by carving out new lines that are nonetheless guided by the contours of the earth.

When men and women twisted their hair into new shapes and decorated themselves with the colorful stones of the earth or when they played musical instruments (indeed, perhaps even the pan figures were some sort of drum or rattle, having a skin stretched over it), this was perhaps a way to make contact with and to grow along with the earth, to show not only one's own inherence in the earth, but to bring to light the colors, shapes, and sounds of the earth. It was a way of giving back.

Her swaying is ecstatic, blissful. The head raised back, rolling back, in ecstasy. A gentle figure enraptured in the natural rhythms of nature.

She bends down to the earth, her forehead inclines back to the sky. She appears lost in the sway, humming blissfully.

She is not straight up and down but bends. Though her back is straight, her knees bend, her head reclines, her hips are loose. Her arms hold her body, gathering the gentle rhythm. Her legs incline down toward the earth, giving way to the earth, moving into it, but her forehead leans back, reclines back into the sky.

This reclining back of the forehead is so extraordinary for us. Our heads must be level; to recline back is madness, death. We are a level-headed people: we look straight out to assess, account for, stay on top of, situations. She yields, yields to a soft bliss, reclines back in ecstasy.

What is this yielding bend? It is a holding-yielding, reclining movement, a "feminine" movement. Her holding sway seems to be an ontological movement because it is not the movement of an individual but of a whole culture. It expresses the deepest movements of a people's being in the world-earth-home. This strange bending down of her body toward the earth and sweeping back of her head toward the sky expresses the Cycladic people's relations not only to the earth, sea, and sky but to other mortals and to the awe-inspiring mysteries of life itself. Her strange movement is a kind of techne or art that gathers a people in its relation to the nonhuman. No other being is so diversely open like ourselves to earth and sky, and to other beings. This capacity to be open does not put us above other creatures, but rather all the more among them and traversed by them.

Her gentle bending is a sacred dance that is so attuned to the rhythms of nature that it seems to have barely emerged as distinctly mortal. It is a movement grounded in the body and expressed through the body's swaying and bending and perhaps through her singing voice.

The Cycladic sway mourns, offers, dances, yields; it rises, reclines, and bends. The yielding bend is a giving way of her whole body, not a passive submission to a mastering force. It is a creative yielding that reveals the intimacy of intimate contact. This gentle rocking gently inclines up and down, back and forth, from side to side.

She is surprisingly long and narrow. She stands tall, enduringly, bending to the wide rhythms of life, carving the flexuous line of mortals. The rhythmic bending of her knees and reclining back of her head is a gathering, a joining of earth

and sky. She is a mortal line joining earth and sky, not a clasping of two separate regions together, but a true joining where the bringing-together stands
out clearer than what is brought together.

So peaceful, so gentle. Her somber serenity, however, is not the peace of
the grave. Cycladic people were not placed in this position at death. If she protects the dead, and indeed she is benign and protective in her stance, then it
is not a protecting that attempts to defend their souls against death but to ease
their passage into death, which is not the end of life's line but the reclining
back of the holding sway of life. She is in the sway of life, but life as completely
continuous, with a passing-away that we call death. Her long, enduring rhythm
is so unlike the rhythm of our modern age precisely because it reclines back
and admits of passing-away.

Death is not a mystery for us but a disease. The medical profession seeks to
prolong our lives as long as is technologically possible. Some wonder about an
"after" life. The aged and dying are usually hidden away. Women in particular
felt they must conceal their aging lines. To grow old is not perceived as healthy
but rather as an insult to our human intelligence.

For the Cycladic people, by contrast, death, it would seem, was not the end
of life to be repressed, for their cemeteries were near their dwellings. The
Cycladic figurines found in the graves, moreover, were sometimes obviously
pregnant. What kind of people were these who found no contradiction in wedding pregnancy and death in a single figure? They were a people who lived
close to the swirling sea. The sea gave them access to foreign peoples but could
also stop their passage and become their peril. They brought in the fish of the
sea's depths. They knew the rhythm of its tides, its flowing-in and receding.
They were a people who lived close to the land, watching over the forces of
its growth and decay. They lived close to the sky and were guided in their trav-
els by the moving constellations of the stars, and in their lives were conscious
of its overarching immensity. They lived, not always harmoniously with one
another, respecting the mysterious sway of coming-to-be and passing-away.

The Cycladic sway admits of the reclining back of the holding sway of life.
We see the reclining back of the sway not only in passing-away but in childbirth
as well, for though the newborn is vigorously pushed forward into life, the
laboring mother reclines back. This reclining back is not passivity but a laboring to endure the breaking forth of the newborn from her body. The bursting
forth of the newborn is not simply a cutting off from her body, for a bond of

continuity of flesh remains still, even after the umbilical cord is cut. Flesh nestles against flesh of its flesh.

As in birth, so, too, in death. Like the newly born, the newly dead nestle against the bosom of the earth, still continuous with it, though they are now wrapped in dark mystery and not in the unconcealed swaddling light of the living.

Her sway is a sheltering-holding of immense, slow rhythms with which we can barely make contact. One cannot sway by moving forward in one direction, but only by also reclining back. Our straight-lined ontological being-moved is dominated by a constant going-forward that represses passing away and that searches to store power for a motion escalating toward the acquisition of more power.

We can see now that birth or coming-to-be is not the pure rising up, the positive, active masculine movement and death or passing-away the negative, passive feminine movement. These two ontological movements belong together, and we see their belonging-together concretized in the Cycladic sway. A sway is codetermined by a rising and reclining, and what may appear to be a rising from one perspective is a reclining from another. To separate one from the other is to be left with two sides in need of a unifying force to bind them. Rather, the two are essentially codetermined by their single relation of belonging together. How can one separate the yielding from the pushing-out when one is in the sway of giving birth? Moreover, there are many kinds of movements present in swaying that we cannot conceptualize or even see because our thinking is so dominated by the contraries of active and passive.

The soft earthy-skyey undulations of her body bring together earth and sky by merging the movements of skyey rising and earthy reclining in a holding sway. She is not folding her arms but holds her swaying body. She hugs her body; her breasts and stomach swell slightly. Her arms rest on this gentle swelling of her belly. Her breasts are high, her womb area especially long, perhaps holding the first stirring of new life.

She holds: her head's swaying back into the sky, her swaying bend into the earth, the swaying from side to side of her hips. She does not hold with her hand and eye. It is a holding that is not localized, focused, that does not grasp. She holds with her body, her deep womb, the depth of her flesh.

She holds. Her holding of her trunklike body is a gathering of movements, as the movements of a tree's boughs swaying in the wind are gathered by the trunk.

She sensitively, gently rocks through her legs and head. Her holding is a holding in. We can imagine her humming, an internal gathering that vibrates with the movement. As the ships are rocked on the sea, cradled by swirls, so she cradles, rocks to sleep, soothes. As she holds, so she is held in a protective embrace, an immensity that shelters.

Her gentle stance and movements are affectionate. She might be cradling a baby, mourning the death of a beloved, or even giving birth. In any case, she is taking up a rhythm in order to endure, to bear the past and future. We who have suffered know that the gentle, earthy swaying helps us bear the uncontrollable flux and overwhelming immensity of being whether in labor or in other kinds of radical change.

Her sway is an attunement to the diverse movements of nature. It is the swaying of mortal flesh to the wind and waves, to sunlight, its bending to other creatures.

She sways, laboring to give birth. She sways, sinking into death. Her sway is the sway of passion, of compassion, of sorrow for what is lost, of celebration for what has arisen.

Her swaying is the swaying of life of the loved and wounded, the sway of coming-to-be and passing-away. No other being shows this rhythm of nature so lightly, so darkly, so lightingly, so heavily. It is our mortal flesh, its attunement to deep rhythms, that gives us our gentle, our painful, sensitivity.

She cradles, holds, sways in soft emotion. She stands enduringly, leaning into the earth, bending back to the sky. All gentle.

Chapter Eight

Ecological Be(com)ing in the World-Earth-Home

> We (with capital W) sometimes include(s), other times exclude(s) me.
> You are I are close, we intertwine; you may stand on the other side
> of the hill once in a while, but you may also be me, while remaining what
> you are and what i am not. The differences made *between* entities com-
> prehended as absolute presences—hence the notions of *pure origin*
> and *true self*—are an outgrowth of a dualistic system of thought peculiar
> to the Occident (the "onto-theology" which characterizes Western
> metaphysics). They should be distinguished from the differences grasped
> *both between* and *within* entities, each of these being understood as
> multiple presence.
>
> —Minh-ha 1989, 90

In this chapter, I am working toward an environmental ethic of place, what Jim Cheney (1989) calls, in his seminal article in this area, an ethic of bioregional narrative. It is an attempt to form an ethic that does not proceed by ahistorical universal principles but that arises out of different historical peoples and out of the local histories of the land. As Holmes Rolston III (cited in Cheney 1989, 124–25) puts it, "An environmental ethic does not want to abstract out universals, if such there be, from all this drama of life, formulating some set of duties applicable across the whole. . . . The logic of the home, the ecology is finally narrative."[1]

I am understanding an environmental ethic broadly and primordially as the description of an appropriate human attitude to the nonhuman. Heidegger (1977d) calls such basic thinking on human dwelling an "original ethics." For Heidegger, the traditional ethic of values relies on a metaphysics of subjectivity, in which we could include anthropocentrism. He wants to take us back to the roots of ethics in *ethos*. *Ethos* refers to the primordial bond of people with their natural, social, and historical existence, to the particular form that historical existence has taken and to which we are already bound (p. 246). At the center of my thinking in this chapter is the idea of creating a place from which to openly encounter difference, whether the differences be those between cultures, races, the past and present, genders, or between the human and nonhuman. I thus first use the

261

example of the current encounter between a supposedly coherent identity called the West and cultures deemed "other" to show up the need for a constant self-criticality in encounters with difference because of hidden motives like the metaphysical hopes for a secure well-defined self and secure rational grounds.

The overall structure of the chapter is given by my initial commitment to investigate the odd meeting of the seemingly oppositional concepts of ecology and economy in *eco* (from the Greek *oikos,* meaning "home"), in order to better understand how ecology and economy intersect. I go back to the etymological meanings of these concepts, uncovering, for example, an androcentrism in the development of the concept of *nomos,* and a sense of gathering in the notion of *logos.* I then give a perusary look at how the concept of home has been marginalized in the thought of some key western philosophers and attempt to understand home as a postmodern place open to difference.

This chapter, however, went wild, threatening to turn into a little book of its own. It moves backward and forward in a Gadmerian hermeneutic manner between the discursive horizons of self and other, reader and text, and past and present, but it also oscillates sideways in a Derridean undecideability.

I indirectly suggest that we go back to antiquity and prehistory in order to dig up and rescue any primordial ethical communities of people bound by shared attitudes, needs, hopes, and material goods, that we look at the ways their common ethos and cultural solidarity took the various forms of stories, rituals, and art, and that we try to understand how, with the advance of scientific thinking, the authority of these older views were undermined and their common ethos replaced by a marketplace of competing values.[2] I suggest that it is helpful to look again at what was overtaken by the western surge forward to the modern age, not so much in order to restore the structures of such communities, but mainly because it helps open us to productive differences. We might find, for example, unrecognized commonalities with, and differences from, other cultures that have been marginalized or overtaken by scientific progress and economic development. The further and more broadly back we reach, the more subtle, deep and ethnologically diverse will be our new nondominating movements forward.

This going back, then, is not to find an original mode of dwelling, un-contaminated by dominance. Every epoch has its dangers, is ambiguous in meaning, and is contradictory with itself.[3] I go back to the Greeks and yet further to simpler societies, not to find some secure happy time, but to open ourselves to differences, to crack our blind faith in scientific progress, and to disrupt that forward momentum. Going backward is an important move-ment given that as historical human beings of care and remembrance, we alone have the flexibility to reach back and gather.

Whitewashing the Earth

> At the end of the day, their [contemporary popular social anthropol-ogy movies] well-meaning attempts to critique modern civilization differ little from the neocolonialist laments for a vanishing culture familiar from the full-colour pages of *National Geographic*.
>
> —Wilson 1991, 151

An "obvious and striking feature of the late twentieth-century world," notes Sally Price (1989, 23) in her book *Primitive Art in Civilized Places*, is "the accessibility of its diverse cultures to those who enjoy membership in Western society." Westerners can travel with relative ease to even the remotest corners of human civilization or stay at home and watch exotic images of world diversity on the television and movie screen. The world market system assures those who have the financial resources that they can buy just about anything from anywhere. Heidegger (1971d, 165), also thinking on this phenomenon, says, "Yet the frantic abolition of all dis-tances brings no nearness; for nearness does not consist in shortness of distance. What is least remote from us in point of distance, by virtue of its picture on film or its sound on the radio, can remain far from us. What is incalculably far from us in point of distance can be near to us." Western technology and the market economy are shrinking the world, bringing the West closer to other peoples and other previously inaccessible regions of the earth. Yet this dramatic global change has not *opened* the West to dif-ference, either the nonhuman differences of the earth or the cultural differ-ences of non-western peoples. Advanced communication, transportation, and information systems have not released the West to the East, the North to the South, or the European to the "Indo."[4] They have not released the

world into neighborhoods of nearness. On the contrary, the expansion of
the West and the resultant "small world" is still, as in colonial days, primarily a movement of domination. It depends on the exploitation of the
land and organic life, and the exploitation of the labor and lives of the
majority of the earth's peoples. Because the oppression of the earth, of
women, and of those who do no belong to "the abstract dominant non-
group" called whites (Minh-ha 1989, 54) are intimately related and reinforce one another, caring for women and for the earth cannot be separated
from caring for diverse human communities.[5]

I have suggested, following Heidegger, that the dominating measure of
the present world, the dominant source of all value and meaning, is that
of western Being understood as the Nietzschean Will to Power. Like the
movement of technology discussed in previous chapters, so too, the dynamic of the market economy, where solid reserves are used as capital
accumulation to further profit and economic development, is one of will
to power. The simultaneous exploitation of the environment, women, and
non-western peoples by the industrial West and the market economy is
vividly described by Vandana Shiva (1990). Western economic development, she explains, is supposed to be a model of progress for the so-called
underdeveloped Third World that would improve productivity and growth.
However, western development, as capital accumulation and the commer-
cialization of the economy for the generation of surplus and profits and as
natural resource utilization, emerged in the context of colonialism, industrialization, and capitalist growth. This notion of economic development
has been falsely universalized and applied, with disastrous results, to the
entirely different context to attempting to satisfy basic needs of newly independent Third World peoples. Western so-called development in Third
World countries has generated profit for various multinational corporations, created internal colonialism, undermined sustainable lifestyles, destroyed local ecologies and has, as a result, created true material poverty.[6]
The increasing scarcity of water, food, fodder, and fuel, moreover, tends
to increase severely the burden of labor for women in particular because
they are the primary providers of bodily sustenance. As S. R. Barnet says
in his book on Africa, "The inextricable processes of agriculture industrialization and internationalization—are probably responsible for more hungry people than either cruel or unusual whims of nature."[7]

From a western perspective, Shiva continues, if a people do not participate in the market economy and do not consume western-style commodities produced for and distributed through the market, if they, in other words, eat home-grown foods, live in bamboo houses, and wear handmade, indigenously designed clothes, they are regarded as living in poverty. Because, moreover, from a western perspective, production and development take place only when mediated by technologies for commodity production and profit, such peoples are considered undeveloped and unproductive. But traditional lifestyles have often emerged in ways that are attuned to the land and local climate and are thus sustained by the land.[8] Not everyone desires capitalist productivity and growth in western terms. For most indigenous peoples, for example, maintaining an ecologically balanced connection to their land is much more essential to their being and culture than the land's monetary value and its so-called natural resources.[9]

Because of the critically destructive promotion of commodified relations with the land by western financial and corporate institutions, there is a dire global ecological need for guiding ways of being that do not have their roots in the cultural heritage and ideology of the West. (I emphasize *need* here and in the following pages to recall Heidegger's [1982, 197–253] description of the needlessness and homelessness of the present epoch.) We need to recognize the immense heterogeneity of Being and to let in those philosophies that have been born out of nondualistic, antifoundationalistic, and nonhierarchical relations and, moreover, those subcultures that have creatively and eco-sensitively adapted to radical cultural and environmental change. To cultivate neighborhoods of being that may help release us into what Heidegger calls nearness, there is a global need to modify and find alternatives to large-scale indifferent western technology, to the powerful capitalist market economy, and to reconceptualize such ethnocentric, sexist, and ecodestructive notions as rationality, knowledge, civilization, creativity, development, and growth. We in the industrial West, who are by far the world's largest consumers per capita, moreover, in particular need to relearn how to listen to our bodies and how to have respect for and celebrate with the earth. We need to take seriously and be joyously open to the concepts, stories, and knowledge of the world's diverse cultures, to find ways of being, modes of technology, and economies that are in accordance with, rather than against, nature. The West needs to restrain its competitive forward thrust for power and short-term profit, which is resulting in *irreversible* damage to the environment. It needs to, as it were, recline back with an openness that has no aim in view since straight-lined, goal-oriented, and visual-dominated processes are endemic to ways of western Being. A relaxation of the western upsurge would help clear a conceptual, economic, and social *place* for allowing the burgeoning diversity of differences to be in its own integrity, within terms foreign to the English ear, and according to (what Mary Daly would call) "a-mazing" measures.

Deeply different peoples in deeply different places have different kinds of knowledge. These kinds of knowledge have not attained anchorage in dominant institutional, social, political, and economic structures and have thus remained invisible (as have the people of these so-called minority cultures themselves), denoted as other than knowledge according to western measures. This silence, invisibility, and nonhistory (from the dominant western view) of other cultures, like the historical absencing of the feminine, the body, and the earth discussed throughout this book, hold much promise as alternatives to, and ways of disrupting the dynamic of, western nihilism.

But the overwhelming dynamic of Will to Power, which is both external and internalized, takes up what comes to light (for example, whatever is publicized; whatever comes into language, museums, and institutions; or whatever generally comes into the western view) and subsumes it within its own dynamic. As we have learned from Nietzsche, the Will to Power uses up dissident forces as resistances to ultimately increase its power and extend its dominance. Thus, the danger is that the current popular turn of the West to other cultures may ultimately subsume and absorb, for example, ecological economies within the western market economy or subsume the thoughts and practices of other cultures within the monocultural melting pot that belongs ultimately to the West. The danger is that these subjugated knowledges are insurrected, become popular, and are immediately recolonized. As Michel Foucault (1980, 86) says, the dominant "unitary discourses, which first disqualified and then ignored them [subjugated knowledge] when they made their appearance, are it seems, quite ready now to annex them, to take them back within the fold of their own discourse and to invest them with everything this implies in terms of their effects of knowledge and power." Thus these fragments of knowledge are no sooner brought to light, accredited, and put into circulation than they run the risk of recodification. We need to be on the lookout for what Gayatri Spivak (1988) calls the "historical dangers of a subjectivist normativity" (p. 151). For example, "in spite of their [Kristeva and others] occasional interest in touching the other of the West, of metaphysics, of capitalism," she says, "their repeated question is obsessively self-centered: if we are not what official history and philosophy say we are, who then are we (not), how are we (not)?" (p. 137).

The need for openness is not a call for an intensification of western anthropological research. Although the aim of anthropology may be the enlargement of the universe of human discourse, it risks being ultimately, as Minh-ha (1989, 65) says, mainly a conversation of the white man with the white man about the primitive native man. It is "the diary of the white man in mission; the white man commissioned by historical sovereignty of European thinking and its peculiar vision of man" (Stanislas S. Adotevi in Minh-ha 1989, 57). Because the presuppositions and expectations of western anthropology dominate most approaches to other cultures, we need to be profoundly self-critical in our approach to cultural difference, in other words, to question our own motives in wanting to open to the ways of other cultures. For example, images of the mingling of races has reached western popular advertisement and popular interest in aboriginal peoples is evident in the mass cultural media; but one can find in these advertisements, movies, television programs, and clothing styles vestiges of the "white man in mission." From "a Western point of view," says Sally Price (1989, 23) with regard to the new Benetton advertisements, for example, the new "planetwide closeness is permeated with the flavor of Unity, Equality, and Brotherly Love." Implicit in this popular acceptance of all colors, however, is the assumption that it is due to "an act of Western tolerance, kindness, and charity" and is not a reflection of human reciprocity or equivalence.[10] In our turn to the other, we need, then, to question "our most benevolent impulses" and remain vigilant about our "assigned subject positions" (Spivak 1987, 150 and 253). "However unfeasible and inefficient it may sound," says Spivak (1987, 150), "I see no way to avoid insisting that there has to be a simultaneous other focus: not merely who am I? but who is the other woman? How am I naming her? How does she name me? Is this part of the problematic I discuss?''

A noncritical turn of white cultures to the rich colors of other cultures and to vanishing peoples, could be motivated by a search for pure origins and grounds characteristic of western metaphysics epistemology, and we might add, colonialism. Just as with regard to nature the search is for ''virgin'' wild places and with regard to the body it is for original or natural bodily states, so with regard to other cultures the search is often for what is perceived as truly ''primitive'' and for some kind of racial and cultural purity. Typical of this approach in environmentalism, for example, is the tradition of setting aside wilderness preserves (thereby denoting their marginality) whose purpose is to serve western recreational and research purposes, thereby using the other as a resource of the wild and exotic.[11] In a similar way, moreover, ''other'' or ''foreign'' peoples are conveniently kept within western-drawn boundaries, made to conform to preestablished rules, and are ''packaged and predigested'' for western profit (Min, 1991).

Western valuing of the ''purely native'' (seen, for example, in the recent acceptance of ''primitive'' art by the western art establishment) effectively ignores the existence of ''the Third World in the First World,'' as Trinh T. Minh-ha (1989, 98) has famously put it. It helps keep invisible those persons of a multitude of cultures who have been brought up in white culture, yet who still feel connections to their mother culture. Such persons may be vocal critics of western ways yet are ignored because they do not serve as stereotypes of the traditional native (or, for example, do not make ethnic artworks). Central to an open turn to other cultures, it seems to me, must be the recognition of the diversity of cultures within one's very own neighborhoods. By turning to what is happening in our own alive neighborhoods, the oppressive categories of ''western'' and ''other'' may themselves begin to shift. If one looks at so-called western music, dance, and fashion, for example, one finds the profound influence of the African-American culture, which has been in the West a long time and, despite being separated from the main modes of cultural production, has developed popular culture by reversing trends of the dominant white culture (Michele Wallace, in Drobnik 1991, 28).

''Despite our desperate attempt to separate, contain, and mend,'' says

Minh-ha (1989, 94), "categories always leak." There are some hopeful indications that the monoculturalism of western identity itself is cracking. The multitudinous colors of the earth are showing through the whitewash. The dependency of the world market on the Third World and the existence of large immigrant communities within western boundaries, for example, can no longer be ignored. Moreover, despite the overtaking of their homeland and past attempts by Europeans to liquidate their peoples and cultures, indigenous peoples of western countries refuse to give up their land rights and are critically learning from their own cultures, which they have managed to keep alive. Environmental activists are joining indigenous peoples in realizing how much these cultures have to offer in alternative modes of inhabiting the earth. White feminists, too, are slowly becoming more aware (through their own cultural oppression and through the insistence of women of color) of the oppression of, and the deep contributions to feminism by, women who have been deemed other on two or three fronts. Western identity may crack in the face of its unmanageable heterogeneity.

Yet the "answer" to the dominant monoculturalism of the West is not a simple multiculturalism. This problem/solution approach is at the outset itself a western method:

> When the West finally recognizes the demands of its tremendous minority presence, it will perhaps reveal "multiculturalism" as its response. "Minority" voices (which, in the world, are not minorities, but in fact majorities), will say "We want a fair share of the wealth we produce, we want to see and create images that reflect our reality, we want to read and write a history that includes us, we want a share in running and defining this government's institutions, we want a share in directing the production of knowledge, and so on," and the West will answer, "Multiculturalism means we already have that. Come to us, you diverse, heterogenous people, and we will explain to you once again how multiculturalism reflects you." (Wallace, in Drobnik 1991, 24)

The concept of multiculturalism is becoming the quick western solution to a western problem. It "rebuts Western dominance by saying everything once thought to have only one version now has many different versions.

There is no one location for truth. But multiculturalism still suggests there is one way of providing an overview of all the 'Others.' It has yet to deconstruct itself as a category. It has yet to be a process that undermines its own authority'' (Wallace, in Drobnik 1991, 27).

A totalizing theory like multiculturalism, inspired by metaphysical anxieties for control, security, and power, implies an authoritative dominance over difference and therefore does not bring us nearer to difference as difference. Such universal theories tend merely to perpetuate existing power relations.[12] To really encounter difference on its own terms rather than on the terms of the dominant faction there is a need for theories and stories that emerge from localized places and continually bend back to it so as never to fly off into fleshless abstractions and subjugating universals. Such bioregional theories and stories that relinquish their supposed timeless authority for the sake of the gifts of localities, particularities, and uncertainties would bring about profound change in the modes of our being. I will return to this theme of a bioregional epistemology later on in this chapter.

Let me emphasize for now that to let differences emerge, it seems to me, we must be first capable of experiencing wonder in the face of difference rather than fear. Wonder turns into fear of the ''other'' only when a power-struggle develops between us and them, between self and ''other.'' ''To live fearlessly with and within differences'' (Minh-ha 1989, 84), there is a need for metaphors and paradigms of movements and actions different from those characteristic of western theory and practice. In western metaphysics, for example, historical and cultural change and action are understood only as the transfer of power and as taking place only in the male white centers of power. I suggest that the changes now needed may take place in the most unusual ways: from more localized places and through ad hoc bodily movements. As David Levin says, one way, for example, that new measures and *nomoi* for human be-ing may emerge that would help overcome the nihilism of Will to Power is simply and literally finding thoughtful and feelingful ways of ''walking the earth.''[13] We need to find ways of walking in our localities that open us to simple wonders and potencies beyond human control, yet that are within human reach. We need to rediscover those ways that dissolve upon contact with calculative thinking but that can blossom through human concernful cultivation. Such ''quiet intervention here and there . . . denies the ruling power systems their authority'' (Caputo 1987, 205).[14] Radical openness to alterity may take place through typically unhistorical ways, through bodily gestures and movements like receiving, gathering, greeting, releasing, and giving, through spontaneous movements like dancing, leaping, and skipping—in one's home, on the living earth, and under the sky, with neighbors and communities, and in the face of the past and the future. It may take place through strong recalcitrant movements that do not push, but like bonds of lasting friendship bide their time. Change may take place through seemingly insignificant sounds like laughing, singing, and crying; through the many voices of the drum and not of the public podium. It is my feeling that radical changes will likely take place behind our backs, away from the focal vision of the media, in rooms other than the classroom and boardroom, and by the likes of those who have not had the chance to surface. A first step toward recognition of radical alterity is to recognize the black silence that, as Nourbese Philip says in *Looking for Livingstone* (1991, 74), is all around ''waiting patient   content   willing to enfold   embrace everything   the Word, even.'' To let histories emerge different from that established through the white Word, we must first realize that there are different ways in which emergence itself takes place.

But, to go back again . . .

Eco-*nomos:* Backward
to Laws of Social Gathering

> I did not think that your edicts *(nomous)* held so much force that they permitted a mortal to violate divine laws *(nomima):* unwritten laws, these, but intangible. They have been in force, not since yesterday or today, but since the beginning, and no one saw their birth.
>
> —Antigone in Sophocles, *Antigone* 450–55

As Robin Atfield (1991) points out in his discussion of the causes of ecological problems, economic growth is the broader and more plausible candidate over that of affluence, technology, capitalism, or population. World ecological problems seem to be the result of exponential economic growth in population, food production, industrialization, pollution, and the consumption of nonrenewable resources. In the West, in particular, profit, for example, appears to be the measure of our system of values.[15] As Christine Spretnak says (1990, 10) ours is a "managerial ethos, which holds efficiency of production and short-term gain above all else." The current confrontation between the western market economy and the environment seems to be dangerously resolving itself in a global natural resource management and utilization. As deep ecologists have recognized, merely protecting natural resources within the guidelines of so-called sound economic practice is not only ecologically inadequate but dangerous because the market economy develops and administrates material resources in a way that disregards and destroys the integrity of the environment.

Economic relations work toward the goal of perpetual growth. It is this *telos* of perpetual growth that sets the limits for economic relations, but such a limit is limitless. Because of this perpetual forward motion, economic growth, then, is not phusical. Unlike the growth of natural entities, there is no resting, no receeding. People need to alter the current trend toward perpetual economic growth and establish "a condition of ecological and economic stability that is sustainable far into the future."[16] There is a "need for 'organic' or differentiated growth, the world being viewed as a system of diverse interacting regions, which need to co-operate, with growth in some regions and the abandonment of growth in others" (Atfield 1991, 17).

Because the global market economy so dominates all peoples' modes of being, to think on an ecocentric ethical being in the world-earth-home, we need to think on the nature of *economy* and its relation to ecology.[17] I will do this in an etymological way with a view to opening to difference.

That political, legal, and economic power are interrelated at a conceptual level is attested by the fact that *nomos* is not so much a matter of currency and exchange as a matter of authority and power. The main meaning of *nomos* is "law" or "statute." Moreover, although there is an ancient word, *nomisma,* that is derived from *nomos,* meaning "coin," *nomisma* indicated not merely usual currency but *legal* coinage made so by the authority of stamping the metal as proof of its weight and quality (Shipp 1978, 24). The interesting etymological fact about *nomos* that I would like to think about in the next few pages is that sometime between 625 B.C.

and 402 B.C. in Athens *nomos* came to replace another word meaning "statute," "law," "custom," or "rite," namely, *thesmos*. It is well known among Greek scholars, for example, that in Athens, Solon's laws of 594 B.C. that helped found Athen's institutions were referred to as *nomoi*, whereas the first secular written laws of the previous Draco (625 B.C.) were called *thesmoi* (from the Dorian *tethmios*). As Martin Ostwald (1969, 60) remarks, this change in terminology was fairly abrupt and reflects a deep change in Athenian thinking about "the nature of law and the attitude of the Athenians toward their laws." The sudden change in vocabulary can be explained if the concept of *nomos* accompanied some change in Athenian institutions. Ostwald, who attempts to pinpoint the change in vocabulary between 511 B.C. and 402 B.C., argues that the institutional change was the birth of Athenian democracy and was in particular due to the originality of Cleisthenes, who established Athenian democracy (507 B.C.), which was completed in 402 B.C. George Shipp (1978), who argues for a lengthier period of overlap in the use of *thesmos* and *nomos*, suggests that the replacement of *thesmos* with *nomos* was due to the growing importance of legal institutions during the early colonization of Magna Graecia and mentions as well the growing control of religious institutions by the state. A key factor that Ostwald and Shipp neglect to mention, however, and that I would like to discuss, for it also seems to have some bearing on the change in vocabulary, is the conflict between the sexes and the growing subordination of women that also occurred during this period of Greek history.

Ostwald concludes in his detailed work on *nomos* and *thesmos* that *thesmos* signifies laws or obligations imposed by the gods who are apart from, and above, the persons upon whom the laws are binding, whereas *nomos* signifies laws or obligations that are regarded and accepted as valid by those who live under them. The change from *thesmos* to *nomos*, he says, came about at a time when the Athenians no longer lived under the religious laws of the past, of the divinities, but instead decided to consider as laws only norms that they themselves had ratified and acknowledged to be valid and binding (Ostwald 1969, 53). From a feminist point of view, however, the fact that the written *nomoi* of Athenian democracy were a human rather than a divine dispensation did not result in a more egalitarian situation, for the so-called human authority here was strictly male, and the divine authority that it superseded, for the most part, had its roots in Goddess religions of old Europe. On the contrary, as Monique Saliou (1986) argues, the establishment of the "democratic" laws *(nomoi)* of Athens was the outcome of a process of female subordination that had begun several millennia earlier and, moreover, met with considerable female resistance. The new written laws firmly established those who were allowed to vote in the city versus those who were to be kept out of the civic body (women, slaves, aliens). Rules of behavior were also assigned in accordance with the inferior status assigned to these "non-Athenians." Saliou (1986, 193) points out that there was not even a Greek word to refer to female Athenians. There were only women of Athens or wives of Athenians. The rights transmitted by these new laws and the complex of apparatuses, institutions, and regulations responsible for the application of these rights put into motion new relations of domination.[18]

Athenian democracy institutionalized the silencing of women at a time when speech was the main political tool. It is thus not surprising, as Saliou (1986, 196) notes, that women adopted the unofficial cults in greater numbers than men and that in Greek tragedy (like Sophocles' *Antigone,* for example) women defend ancient values, those of kinship and maternal descent, those of old female deities, and those prior to the emergence of the written laws of the city.[19] The past had been undoubtedly more favorable to women.

I am not suggesting that the religious and social traditions that had been handed down through generations were in all ways, or even most ways, better than those formed by the new commercial class. The self-justifying ways of tradition can sometimes motivate and validate terrible injustices. Instead, given the rapid development of industrial arts and technology and the rapid social and political transformations occurring in Greece at the time, the general tendency to substitute systematically learned technical skill and economic measures for traditional practices and rules of conduct may have significantly contributed to furthering the oppressions of women.

It is noteworthy that the new laws, which came to have more authority than the unwritten laws of the past, were especially written laws directed to an elite literate class. Unlike *thesmoi,* commitment to writing was a distinguishing feature of the first *nomoi* (Shipp 1978, 16). Shipp suggests that *nomos* was first used as ''law'' in the period of the close of the Greek monarchy and the early colonization of Magna Graecia. In these colonies, as in early Greece, land settlement and land division were of the first importance.[20] There was thus a new necessity for lawgivers to embody in written codes, and publish in an official manner, the material of the previous monarchy and the laws governing the new deals to be had in the colonies, for established customs would not have been as sacrosanct in these new communities as in the fatherland. By the end of the fifth century, *nomos* signifies a usually written enactment that had either been embodied in the law code at the time of its completion in 403–2 B.C. or had been incorporated into it through the majority vote of the (male) assembly. These literally ''man''-made laws deprived legal validity of any laws that were not written and officially published in an authoritative manner (Ostwald 1969, 1). The *nomoi*, whose writing and publication were solely in the powers of the male Athenians, thus effectively and finally displaced the authority of the traditional unwritten laws of older religions and of kinship in which women had significant rights.[21]

A significant factor in the conscious (and political) replacement of *thesmos* by *nomos*, I suggest, is the connotations *thesmos* had with the authority of older female religions of non-Greek and pre-Dorian cultures that lay outside the growing phallocentric ethos. From the occurrence of the word in early Greek writing, we know that *thesmos* was not only the earlier term for law in Athens but was frequently used to denote religious connotations (Shipp 1978, 20). Many *thesmoi* were fundamental regulations sanctioned by divine rather than secular powers. When the later word *nomoi* is used to denote religious rules and customs, it replaces *thesmoi*, showing the increasing state control of religion in Greece (Shipp 1978, 18).

There are direct linkages of *thesmos* with goddesses. *Thesmos* is connected to the pre-Olympian Cretan version of the goddess Demeter, who is reduced to the function of agrarian fertility in the Olympiad. The Thesmophorion is the temple of Demeter, and the epithet of Demeter is Thesmophoros, the lawgiver. Given that Demeter is a chthonic goddess, one could speculate that the *thesmoi* of Demeter were bioregional laws, that is, rites and customs that arose out of human dwelling within the limits and gifts of the particular regions, unlike the man-made *nomoi* formulated, set down, and enforced by those who held the reins of political power and knowledge production.

Thesmos, moreover, is related etymologically to Themis, the goddess of social ordinance. This etymological relation of *thesmos* with *themis* is significant, for in *themis* there are strong connotations of social gathering and social justice rather than of subjugation and control. The word *themis* means laws or rights agreed on by common consent in contrast to statute laws, and *"themistesis"* is an utterance or ordinance of social conscience (*Lexicon,* 1982). The concept *thesmos* would seem to have older connotations of judging and justice rather than law, since a term even earlier than *thesmos* is *thesmosune,* meaning justice, and the later Athenian Thesmothetai were judges rather than lawgivers (Shipp 1978, 17).

So, too, the nature of the goddess Themis involves notions of social gathering and justice. Jane Harrison, in her book on Themis (1977), notes that a glimmer of the persisting authority of the old goddess Themis is seen in Homer, who recounts how Zeus cannot summon his own assembly but must depend on Themis to gather the gods and goddesses together. Themis, says Harrison (1977, 484), is the "spirit of gathering," "the social imperative incarnate." In tribal societies, Themis is the gathering involved in social conscience and structure, the coalescing found in common opinions that become sedimented conventions, and the kind of gathering involved in customs that are binding by common consent. Later, when the tribal system of kinship ties and earth reverence breaks up in favor of the *polis,* Themis is modified to become the abstractions of Law and Justice used by male Athenian citizens in the public agora and the assembly. The fact that already by the time of Homer (around 850 B.C.) the gathering of hearth and home is not considered a *themistes* (Harrison 1977, 484) testifies to its overpowering by the gathering of the *polis* (defined through an opposition to the domestic realm and to nature).

Social laws in their more ancient beginnings were not exclusively fabricated by an anthropocentric self and imposed on those deemed other by the dominant political group but tended to arise more deeply out of a community's enjoining order with its earthy-skyey, social-historical dwelling as whole and out of respect for earthly and skyey potencies beyond the reach of human control. (It is perhaps significant in this regard that the Latin *po-tens* derives from *potniai,* meaning "mistresses" or "sovereign" [Coontz and Henderson 1986, 201].) Although this kind of gathering and social ordinance that Harrison traces in tribal societies would not exclude the occurrence of ecological destruction, social domination, and oppressive customs within any society, one can at least say that this noncontractual gathering may have tended toward ways of sociality that were less sexist and at the same time more ecological because the social order was already respectful of the momentous and often disruptive movements of the death and regeneration of nature and thereby there was already a deep social acceptance of mortality. In this regard it is noteworthy that, as Harrison (1977, 465) puts it, the "crowning disability and curse of the new theological order is that the Olympian claims to be immortal (athanatos)." He sheds his plant and animal forms and rejects change and movements, renouncing the cycle of death and regeneration of nature (Harrison 1977, 468).

A fundamental difference between *thesmos* and *nomos* is that *nomos* is an authoritative external regulating and thereby a domination of others, whereas *thesmos* has the sense of an ordering that has emerged from one's earthy communal being as a whole.[22] *Nomos* is a regulation that is accepted or expected to be accepted as a valid and binding norm for citizens of the *polis.* In the first recorded use of *nomos,* moreover, the word is used to help draw a firm contrast between the natural and human realms. Zeus, says Hesiod, ordained for men the *nomos* in order that men would have justice *(dike)* in contrast to beasts who live without *dike* and devour one another. A well-known distinctive opposition between *nomos* and phusis develops in the second half of the fifth century.[23] By contrast, *thesmos,* in its relation to the goddesses Themis and Demeter, suggests a harmony between the natural and the social order. The goddess Themis is deeply connected to the orders and rhythms of the earth. Like Gaia, she is the presencing of the earth and of the prophetic powers of the earth. At Delphi, a renowned home of the oracle, she succeeds Gaia as the Pythia. Oracles, Harrison (1977, 511) explains, were places to be consulted for advice not so much for predictions of future events as for the practical purposes of the present. Such practical advice was not, in the early days of the oracle, formed and meted out according to political power and prestige. Themis gave social imperatives that came from deep within the earth. This communion and relationship between the nature and the social orders were accepted as obvious in earlier societies. Quarrels with one's neighbor or a river flooding its banks, for example, could equally be considered the result of human breaches of Themis. It is important to note, moreover, that Themis is the mother of the Horai (the seasonal rhythms of nature), one of whom is Dike, the Way or Necessity of all living things, later becoming the abstraction Justice.[24] But to come back to the present . . .

There is a global need for establishing human limits that do not function predominantly within western prevailing measures that are unjust and out of joint with the natural order. The natural order of the earth does not overstep its limits coming-to-be and passing-away. Only humans attempt to surpass their limits for only they have the will to transgress their limits.[25] (In this regard, it is rather ominous that for Nietzsche [1956, 298–99], the will of Will to Power is to will without limits.) We could understand *nomos* and *thesmos* as related fundamental ways in which human limits are established. The new emergent limits now needed are not those of *nomos*, understood as a top-down universal ordering of entities and anthropocentric creation of laws and generalizations. There is a need for diverse ecocentric limits and local *thesmoi* that may not be economical, for measures that are indeterminant rather than universal laws and that are truly egalitarian rather than motivated by a metaphysical will and desire to dominate and control. There is a need for ethics that emerge from nonhierarchical diverse ways of people's bodily being and their openness to unique localities and past histories.

But how do we begin to develop such limits, measures, ethics, and *thesmoi*? "More essential than rules," says Heidegger (1977d), "is that man find the way to his abode in the truth of Being" (p. 230).[26] The Greek word *ethos* means "abode" and "dwelling place" (p. 233). To move into the neighborhood of nearness, to let new *ethnoi* emerge, we need to come nearer to where we already are, to recover the places where we have been all along.[27] We could add to this Caputo's (1987, 255) insight that we can newly define "community," not by its convergence on one, as in a metaphysics of presence and unity, but in a postmetaphysical way, by its high threshold for tolerating dissent and by its respect for differences. The current *nomoi* tend to reduce our being in the world to an expenditure of time and labor, our sense of community and neighborhood to following rules that guide individual property interests and actions, and our being-at-home to doing "women's work" and managing material resources.[28] Given the degradation of where we are most locally, perhaps appropriate human limits could be given structure and direction in part by resuscitating and rethinking these devalued concepts of body and earth and of home, neighborhood, and feeling and the segregation of the private and the personal. For it is these concepts that underlie our most localized being in the world-earth-home. Rather than regulating and dominating the home, making it a place of closure, *nomos* is in need of being itself infiltrated by the relations that constitute being at home.

Regarding relations in this way as primary, rather than the elements in relation, is like reversing figure and ground, like stressing Being over beings (Evernden 1985, 133). If the western gaze relaxed its focus on objects and objectives, latent horizons may show themselves—the backgrounds without which western industrialization and technology could not have begun its historical thrust forward.

Carol Gilligan (1982), who from her case studies suggests that women commonly (rather than essentially) depend on a morality that is based on premises of connection rather than on rules, and Nel Noddings (1986), who offers a strong critique of a morality based on rules and principles, have made important contributions to developing theories of *relational* ethics. Jim Cheney (1987), moreover, who has developed a relational ethics in the direction of environmental ethics, argues that a moral community is already woven through the context of a networking of relationships *before* the emergence of laws and ideas of equality. "It isn't," he says, "that an abstract understanding of the interdependence of all members of the community (or ecosystem) generates an abstract obligation on the part of each person to preserve the community in health. What our responsibilities are is a function of where we happen to find ourselves in that web of relations which constitutes the community" (p. 136).

Just as Foucault undertakes an "ascending analysis of power," starting from its "infinitesimal mechanisms," which each have their own history and tactics and which are utilized and transformed by ever-more general mechanisms, so too, in our attempt to step back from power and its mechanisms we could start with the smaller, more subtle effects of power, its more regional and local forms in our everyday immediate lives. We should not concern ourselves with the "regulated and legitimate forms of power in their central locations," with "the general mechanisms through which they operate," but with "power at its extremities in its ultimate destinations" (Foucault 1980, 96). We could attempt to release the localized regions of our being that are marginal to the superstructures and institutions of power from the more oppressive global relations of power, thereby helping the dispersal of power clusters.

However, it is not a matter of attempting to return to the natural or fundamental limits set down by the passing-away and coming-to-be of phusis, for even this primary pulse, this inspiration and expiration of Being (Merleau-Ponty 1982, 167) is saturated with historical and cultural determinants. Even the gait and stride of my walk in a forest is at a fundamental phenomenological level unique not only to my personal and cultural milieu but to the tenor of this particular historical epoch (VonMirbach 1988, 25). Nature is not a predetermined, untouched force underneath the layers of our current *ethos*. There is no authentic prepersonal and transhistorical truth of Being or of nature that underlies our age. Indeed, nature has been so transformed by human *techne* that it is in dire need of care. Thus, the ecological crisis is not so much about conserving energy and preserving what is left but about irreversible damage to the environment. Nature is so out of joint that it requires human intervention to heal itself, for the "solutions" that nature may come up with could be more disastrous to organic life than the initial problems caused by humans.[29]

But to go back again . . .

Logos: The Laying-out that Gathers

> Every manifestation of a force in any form whatever is to be regarded as its speech . . . everything in the universe speaks. . . . If speech is strength, that is because it creates a bond of coming-and-going which generates movement and rhythm and therefore life and action.
>
> —Ogotemmeli, a Dogon elder (in Minh-ha 1989, 127–28)

Turning to ecology, the *logos* of the home, it seems at first that we find a discordance between *logos* and nature and home similar to that which we have found between nature and *nomos*. We quickly translate *logos* as "logic" or "reason" and just as quickly hear the discordance with nature and with home, for, as is common knowledge in postmodern thought, the phallocentrism of metaphysics is continuous with its logocentrism. Derrida has identified *logos* with the self-presence of speech and thereby with the speaking subject who is the guarantor of meaning, and feminists like Luce Irigaray and Hélène Cixous have taken up this notion in their attempt to displace male-centered structures of thought. Although I agree that western metaphysics is logocentric in the sense that it has hierarchized meaning, privileging, for example, presence over absence, reason over feeling, and unity over diversity, it is important not to make the concept of *logos* the scapegoat for this dominance. *Logos* like most of our central concepts has undergone profound historical changes, whereby certain characteristics have been taken up and developed and others have fallen away and are forgotten. There is a deep difference, for example, between the pre-Socratic *logos,* whose root lies in *legein,* and *logos* as the modern "word" and "logic" (and certainly the translation of *logos* as "speech" is rather narrow).

We can find an inner bond between *logos* and phusis by tracing the root meaning of *logos* back to *legein,* which means "to say," but more fundamentally to "lay-out" and "let-lie." In *legein* as in phusis (and *thesmos*) a bringing-together or gathering prevails. *"Legein,"* explains Heidegger (1975, 60), "properly means the laying-down and laying-before which gathers itself and others." "Saying," he continues, understood in the light of *legein* cannot mean "speaking" merely in the sense of activating the vocal chords, but rather, when we say something about something we make it lie there before us and let it appear. Saying, moreover, is itself only one way of laying-out and gathering, only one mode of *legein*.

Making something, techne, is also a mode of *legein*. Recall from Chapter Four that a carpenter, as the moving or efficient "cause" of a table, for example, does not "effect" the making but instead gathers the three other causes and lays them out into the form of the table. It is through *legein,* the laying-out that gathers, that the carpenter brings-forth the table into appearance. When form and functionality dominate the process of coming-to-be, however, then this sense of *legein* and gathering submerges and a forward-directedness takes over as the dominant movement.[30]

Understood as a letting-lie, *logos* is not in opposition to nature, belonging exclusively to human subjectivity, but already belongs to the gathering of nature.[31] In the fragments of Heraclitus there are traces of this inner bond between phusis and *logos*. As many Greek scholars would agree, for Heraclitus, *logos* is not merely discourse or reason but a name for the steady gathering, the intrinsic togetherness of Being. Everything that comes to be and passes away stands there in accordance with the enduring togetherness of *logos*. Heidegger argues that this steady gathering that Heraclitus says is common to all is the same as phusis.[32]

Logos is linked to *phusis* through the common trace meaning of gathering. Gathering is not like an accumulation of capital or a storing belonging to modern technology's standing reserves of energy because there is a fundamental sheltering and safekeeping involved in the concept of gathering. As Heidegger, says, when something is appropriately gathered, that " 'something extra' which makes gathering more than a jumbling together that snatches things up is not something only added afterward. Even less is it the conclusion of the gathering coming last. The safekeeping that brings something in has already determined the first steps of the gathering and arranged everything that follows."[33] By contrast, the amassing of both capital and energy is an economic securing of a stable reserve of power for the sake of furthering power. The securing of power is not a sheltering that guides an economic amassing, moreover, but is merely a step in a sequence of steps to a final goal.

Because the unity of gathering prevails through a relational sheltering rather than through a foundational building, a forward progression, or an external force, there is a sense of a communal holding-round in the movement of gathering.[34] However, the movement of gathering is not an ordering through a centralizing power that forces individuals to conform and that closes the circle but rather a gentle haphazard coalescing or clustering of multitudinous social relations, like that of gatherings as diverse as story-telling, meditating, demonstrating, sweats, singing, dancing, and jamming.[35] "It is not a geometric circle but a gathering of radical alterity endlessly displac[ing] its closure'' (Derrida 1986d, 271). Lame Deer describes the relational round gathering of the Sioux:

> With us the circle stands for the togetherness of people who sit with one another around the campfire, relatives and friends united in peace while the pipe passes from hand to hand. The camp in which every tipi had its place was also a ring. The tipi was a ring in which people sat in a circle, and all families in the village were in turn circles within a larger circle, part of the larger hoop which was the seven campfires of the Sioux, representing one nation. The nation was only part of the universe, in itself circular and made of the earth, which is round, of the sun, which is round, of the stars, which are round. The moon, the horizon, the rainbow—circles within circles within circles, with no beginning and no end. To us this is beautiful and fitting, symbol and reality at the same time, expressing the harmony of life and nature. (Lame Deer, in Levin 1985, 326–27)

Gathering is a diffuse intermittent coming together that might happen, for example, around a fire or in a kitchen where food is being prepared. The hearth is the original sacred altar even in our western cultural heritage.[36] In Greece, presiding over the primordial mysteries of the fire and the hearth was the oldest of the Olympians, the goddess Hestia.[37] Such ancient female goddesses were often associated with a gathering-round.[38] We can find traces of the importance of this sense of the sheltering-gathering round hearth and fire even in the Greek *polis* itself. Every *polis* had its own sacred fire that was kept burning and that, at the founding of the city, had been taken from a fire of an already established *polis*. This communal fire was a remnant of the older Goddess religions that stubbornly persisted in altered forms and in various revivals throughout the Greek period despite the growing dominance of the patriarchal Olympiad.

The primordial gathering of *logos* is attuned to, not separate from, our bodily being in the world-earth-home. *Logos* as a laying-out and letting-lie is bound to the gathering bringing-forth of nature. The gathering of *logos* is also not separate from the gathering of human heartfelt feeling.[39] For the Greek word *a-legein* means ''to care,'' ''to have a pain,'' and ''place of need.'' The *a* of *legein* here acts as an intensive. To be pained, to care, is here found to be a most intimate and intense kind of laying-out.

The heart's gathering is understood in our post-Cartesian world as ''mere'' feeling subordinate to the mind's gathering, but the mind was not always foreign to the heart. In Classical Greece, the intellect was popularly located in the breast and stomach along with the emotions (Padel 1983, 10). The generic word for the relevant organs was *spalanchna,* meaning ''entrails.''[40] Even Parmenides, often called the first metaphysician, speaks of having thoughts in one's heart.[41] A Greek word commonly translated as ''mind,'' the *noos,* is also linked to the heart in some Greek idioms. For example, *''en niao echein''* means ''he is glad at heart,'' and *''ek pautos noou''* means ''with all his heart.'' *Noein* (commonly translated as ''to think'') in its roots actually means ''to perceive,'' not, argues Heidegger, in the sense of passively accepting something that is sensed or felt; it concerns us in such a way that we take it to heart and keep it at heart.[42]

The gathering of *logos* in an earlier sense, then, is not a linking together of propositions in conformity to certain principles of correct reasoning. Such calculative logic divorced from the earth and body computes ever-new economical possibilities in the progressive systematization of Power. ''Logistics today is developing into the global system by which all ideas are organised,'' warns Heidegger (1972c, 163). Such computation races from one prospect to the next, never stopping to rest and wonder, to gather itself, to contemplate the giving of everything that is (Heidegger 1966, 46). It is not able ''to bide its time, to await as does the farmer, whether the seed will come up and ripen.''[43] Instead, contemporary instrumental thinking concerned only with the economical ordering about and systemization of world power is busily figuring out a way to quicken and genetically improve the seed's ripening.

Thinking separate from feeling is mind separate from body, and theory from experience. Many feminists are calling for a concrete knowledge that preserves connectedness with the earth, body, and feelings without destroying particularity and difference. In this vein, Sara Ruddick (1989) describes how abstract thinking leads to treatment of people as instrumental in war.[44] Many ecofeminists, for example, are calling for an understanding that is rooted in ''thinking feelingly,'' as Judith Plant (1990, 155) puts it, and for a *logos* or way of thinking grounded in the earth and thus not reducible to abstract reason, as Linda Holler (1990, 10) says. Traditional scientific analysis distances us from wonder and awe and from the emotional involvement and caring that the natural world calls forth (Spretnak 1990, 12). Our awareness of the earth cannot be merely scientific or abstract but must be a lived awareness connected by concrete loving actions (Kheel 1985, 137).[45] We need to remain true to our embodied experience that shows us that the world is, as Maurice Merleau-Ponty (1962) explains in detail, not what I think but what I live through. We are not separate from the world-earth-home but are *of* it to the very depths of our sentient being.

Thoughtful discussion in another culture can take place quite differently than that of contemporary western *logos* separated from the speaking of all that is nonhuman. Can we feel wonder in the face of the profundity of this difference? Can we enter into the region of differences that playfully gather without totalization and closure but that nonetheless communally gather rather than disparingly disperse in a Derridean fashion? (On careful analysis a Heideggerean gathering and Derridean dissemination are not simple opposites, however, as I am tending to set *(stellen)* them down here, but can be brought into a creative play, for an open gathering occurs only through both a differentiating and a dividing of itself.)

Listen: Trinh T. Minh-ha opens her book with such a gathering *logos:* ''In a remote village, people have decided to get together to discuss certain matters of capital importance to the well-being of their community. . . . On the day and at the time agreed, each member eats, washes her/himself, and arrives only when s/he is ready. . . . The discussion does not have to begin at a precise time, since it does not break in on daily village life but slips naturally into it. A mother continues to bathe her child amidst the group; two men go on playing a game they have started; a woman finishes braiding another woman's hair. These activities do not prevent their listening or intervening when necessary. Never does one open the discussion by coming right to the heart of the matter. For the heart of the matter is always somewhere else than where it is supposed to be. To allow it to emerge, people approach it indirectly by postponing until it matures, by letting it come when it is ready to come. There is no catching, no pushing, no directing, no breaking through, no need for a linear progression which gives the comforting illusion that one knows where one goes. . . . The conversation moves from the difficulties caused by rural depopulation to the need to construct goat pens, then wanders in old sayings and remembrances of events that occurred long ago. . . . A man starts singing softly and playing his lute. . . . Some women drowse on a mat they have spread on the ground and wake up when they are spoken to. The discussion lingers on late into the right. By the end of the meeting, everyone has spoken. The chief of the village does not 'have the floor' for himself, nor does he talk more than anyone else. He is there to listen, to absorb, and to ascertain at the close what everybody has already felt or grown to feel during the session. The story never stops beginning or ending. It appears headless and bottomless for it is built on differences. Its (in)finitude subverts every notion of completeness and its frame remains a non-totalizable one. The differences it brings about are differences not only in structure, in the play of structures and of surfaces, but also in timbre and in silence. . . . The story circulates like a gift; an empty gift which anybody can lay claim to by filling it to taste, yet can never truly possess. A gift built on multiplicity. One that stays inexhaustible within its own limits. Its departures and arrivals. Its quietness'' (Minh-ha 1989, 1–2).

This story *(logos)* lays out and gathers like a gift, received and in turn passed on, a story that does not exclude differences but that is nurtured through difference. Through the telling of stories, decisions are made consensually rather than hierarchically, which does not mean a harmonious agreement is reached but that the focal concern is the preservation of neighborly relations. It is almost inevitable that some conflicts are unresolvable according to usual adversarial means and this is why consensual decision making is so important. As Jim Cheney (1987, 132) from conversation with Karen Warren says, "Consensual decision-making takes relations seriously, it is a method of inclusion, and it is concerned to preserve community." Thoughts are not challenged-out as pertinent information to be accounted for in a decision-making process; instead, the thoughts and stories come out and sediment in their own time. The matter at hand is respected and allowed to mature until it comes into the unconcealment of the gathering of its own accord. To push the matter at hand would be callously to ignore the depths and dimensions of the matter and would result in the domination over the communal matter by certain individuals. In a willful attempt to assert control over the matter, to direct the flow of communal thought, some speakers would be subjugated by others. The discussion would then become an effect of power, a game of political strategies and tactics.

Speaking as a "saying" need not necessarily make propositional statements or provide proof and solid reasons. Singing speaks, silence speaks, voices of the past speak. Such speaking listens simultaneously, remembers, relates. It goes backward and forward and sideways to neighbors. The communal story gathers momentum and subsides, turns here and there, this way and that. It does not really begin or result in a closure but seeps back into the ongoing life of the village, sediments, rests in the rhythms of social life, of morning and night, of vital relations. The daily life of one's embodied being thus slips naturally into the varied temporalities, textures, and depths of the discussion. Because there is no linear progression in the discussion, no aim in view, there is no need for speed and efficiency, for predictions, or for clockwork precision.

But. But, it is perhaps here with this matter of time that we so-called moderns condemn this bioregional ethic and epistemology as naive and impractical. We need to allot a certain amount of time even for a pressing matter because, for example, the room we are using has been booked for a certain time, other appointments have been made, other work is waiting on the desk, or we have to attend to personal matters that have been excluded by the meeting. We no longer have the time to engage in such open, free-flowing discussions. After all, we would not be waiting until the moon comes up. There are too many voices to be heard, voices that have never reached the boardroom, the classroom, or any "room" of the dominant discourse. In fact there are centuries of unheard voices, or ignored, overpowered, and hierarchized differences. After all, one might say, practically speaking, there are always those who will step on others. Western ways have undoubtedly been proven to be the most powerful and efficient (economical) methods in the struggle for power. Yet, after all has been said by this "one," and done in this one way, there is an urgent need to become open to difference, to different ways of gathering, and to differences that gather. It is no longer a matter of *making* more time but, more vitally and radically, of *letting time be* in its life rhythms of coming and going. To live solely by clocktime is to measure our time as a regular series of intervals that are slices of the present and that move only in one direction: forward.

This homogeneous objective time of the purely present that is the same for everyone and for every situation dominates our lived temporal movements. There is a need to let the no longer present, the present, and what is not yet present, all presence in their own way, and to let them presence *near* to one another. In this neighborly way, time can be healing.

Letting thought and feeling interplay is an important way to open ourselves to mystery, magic, and the wonder of difference, for passion *(rausch)* is a rupture in our mood. It disrupts our complacency. Before anything is experienced as wonderful, one must resist the temptation to dismiss it as nothing but something else, that is, as something "unwonderful" (Evernden 1985, 140). To be in wonder is thus to start over-again (p. 141), to regain a certain innocence, maybe even to laugh. Through wonder we learn respect for nature, for other beings and for the magic tumultuous flows of existence beyond conceptual grasp. In wonder, we lose our breath and stop dead in our tracks (Caputo 1987, 214). Wonder, says Caputo (1987, 269), "inhabits the margins and interstices of everyday life. "There are certain breaking points, let us say, in the habits and practices, the works and days of our mundane existence where the flux is exposed, where the whole trembles and the play irrupts" (p. 269).

In wonder we gain a sense of something that is different from ourselves and our experience.[46] It is a rupture in our usual routines, an encounter with difference. However, difference can also inspire fear and subsequent will to dominate if difference in the first place is understood as conflict and contradiction.

Aristotle (*Meta.* 982b11 ff.) rightly said that the love of wisdom (philosophy) begins in wonder, but we have to question what his meaning of wonder entailed. Much later, Georg Hegel in his *Aesthetics,* recalling Aristotle, spells out for western philosophy more clearly the separations between man and nature, theory and practice, spirit and body, latent in Aristotle's thinking:

> Wonder only occurs when man, torn free from his most immediate first connection with nature and from his most elementary, purely practical, relation to it, that of desire, stands back spiritually from nature and his own singularity and now seeks and sees in things a universal, implicit, and permanent element. In that case for the first

time natural objects strike him; they are an ''other'' which yet is
meant to be for his apprehension and in which he strives to find himself over again. . . . There is present a contradiction between natural
things and the spirit . . . and the sense of this contradiction along
with the urge to remove it is precisely what generates wonder. (315)

The wonder that generates respect for otherness is, indeed, an experience
of difference, but unlike wonder in the context of a metaphysical desire for
sameness that motivates the cancellation of difference, wonder freed from
metaphysics is fundamentally an openness to the gifts of becoming that lets
the differences be. Difference is not a contradiction between spirit and nature, or self and other. There are differences grasped both between and
within entities, as Trinh T. Minh-ha (1989, 90) says. Thus, a precondition
for wonder is not wrenching ourselves away from our particular practical
inhabitance of a neighborhood, and from the *jouissance* of the body in our
desire for the universal and the spirit, thereby removing differences. This
desire for the selfsame as Irigaray would say, or for a secure subjectivity as
Heidegger would say, and for unity and presence as Derrida would say,
is a chronic condition of western metaphysics. Wonder does not have to
happen outside the gathering of our own ''homes,'' above passion, and beyond the needs of our phusical bodies, as the history of western philosophy
maintains. Sometimes in our ''most immediate first connection to nature,''
hauling water or gathering sticks for a fire, for example, we can be struck
by the profundity and beauty of that very connection and dependency.
Sometimes, in the midst of the familiar and the most humble circumstances, a most strange giving occurs: in the kitchen, for example, with a
freshly cut cabbage.[47]

Eco (Home): Gathering-Round

Ecology is permanent economy.
>   —a slogan of the Chipko movement,
>   women treehuggers of Himachel Pradesh, India

Having looked at the *nomos* of home and the *logos* of home, I finally
turn to *eco,* from the Greek word *oikeo* meaning to place or settle, to inhabit, to dwell, live, manage, and govern).[48] Ecology and economy meet

in that place where we are sheltered and gathered. In order to open to difference we need to start from some *place*. This place must not be a homogeneous foundation or goal that suppresses differences in favor of a unified stronghold but an opening, gathering sort of clearing, respectful of difference, yet still a particular place differentiating it from other places.

The Greek words for place *(chora, choros, chore)* are related to the word *chorizo,* which means "to separate."[49] We could say, then, with Derrida (1982, 324) that a place "gathers itself only in dividing itself, in differentiating [*différant*] itself." Place makes room for something by creating limits, boundaries that differentiate it from other places. The related Greek word *chorismos* means a differentiated place. The meaning of *chora,* then, would seem to confirm the thought in the preceding section that we make room for difference by creating limits, by creating boundaries, points of departure from which to act, from which to open human and nonhuman difference.

Such places cannot exist within an indifferent homogeneous Cartersian space. To accommodate differences we need not simply space (for which there is no Greek word) but belonging-places *(topos)* integral with the social, natural world. The poet William Blake describes such a living place.

> The Sky is an immortal Tent built by the Sons of Los
> And every Space that a Man views around his dwelling-place:
> Standing on his own roof, or in his garden on a mount
> Of twenty-five cubits in height, such space is his Universe;
> And on its verge the Sun rises & sets. the Clouds bow
> To meet the flat Earth & the Sea in such an orderd Space:
> The Starry heavens reach no further but here bend and set
> On all sides & the two Poles turn on their valves of gold:
> And if he move his dwelling-place, his heavens also move.
> Wher'eer he goes & all his neighbourhood bewail his loss:
> Such are the Spaces called Earth & such its dimensions:
> As to that false appearance which appears to the reasoner,
> As of a Globe rolling thro Voidness, it is a delusion of Ulro
> The Microscope knows not of this nor the Telescope. they alter
> The ratio of the Spectators Organs but leave Objects untouchd.

("Milton" 29 [31]: 4–18)

Spaces as belonging-places determine distances through relations rather than according to externally imposed measures. The creating of limits, from which belonging-places emerge, happen through an embodied dwelling, a self-critical inhabiting of where we are (historically, culturally, ecologically, artistically and personally).

Chora, "place," is related to the Greek words *chorea* and *choresomai,* which mean "make room for," "give way to," "to fall back," and "withdraw." Following this etymological trace, we can say that place or site consists not only in the emergence of boundaries but, at the same time, the emergence of an opening, a clearing, that receives, welcomes, gives way, and withdraws. Once a site emerges, other neighborhoods may also emerge, for it is only through a sense of belonging to a particular place that other places may become near or distant.

Such a living place is a point of departure for opening to difference. It is not a fixed place or point, although without self-criticality it can rapidly stagnate, become a constraining institution, a repository of a unified ideology, or an insular clubhouse.

> And what about my own possible desires for security and stability motivated by my migrant life as a child and by my uneasiness in university that the likes of me didn't belong there? No, I am emphasizing the notion of home, not because I am going to a dialectic extreme, but because, without a sense of belonging (whether it be under a protective tree beside the trans-Canada highway for the night, or with a new-found city friend showing me the ropes) I know I would go mad.

I am calling this belonging place of transcience and play, this strategy of survival, "home."[50] For many feminist theories, because the notion of "home" is so saturated with patriarchal domesticity, and because, moreover, the concept of home has been taken up by the rhetoric of the New Right, they argue it would be better to go some place else. However, it seems to me there is no other place to go than the most immediate *here* that we inhabit and where our habits are nestled. I turn, for example, to the "here" of the body, which Merleau-Ponty (1962, 100) says, "does not refer to a determinate position in relation to other positions or to external co-ordinates, but the laying down of the first co-ordinates, the anchoring of the active body in the face of its tasks." What are my fleshy tasks in my incarnate situation? I will find this out by remaining thoughtfully here: this particular patch of earth that I inhabit for a time, within unique historical and relational neighborhoods, where I take care of my body (and those that came from it, as well as those from which my own emerged), and where I find myself already engaged with neighbors and friends, the weather, plants and animals, pollution, death and birth, and where I find the excluded histories of oppression, conflict, and resistance (both social and ecological).

Home, as I understand it, is a nomadic place, an unfinished place of variable historical and geographical boundaries, but a belonging-place nonetheless. It is a "moral space out of which a whole and healthy self, community and earth can emerge" (Cheney 1989, 123). Home is not the site of a privileged subject or a self-same identity that excludes Otherness but a complex, contextualized multiplicity traversed by differences of race, culture, gender, and personal histories. We must get beyond the transcendental subject with its anxieties about unity and certainty and beyond the lienar, essentialized, self-certain identity (Cheney 1989, 123) to be even conscious of home as a crossroads of difference. We need first to take on a *feminist* subjectivity as Teresa de Lauretis (1986) describes it: "The female subject is a site of differences; differences that are not only sexual or only racial, economic, or (sub)cultural, but all these together, and often enough at odds with one another" (p. 14). These "differences not only constitute each woman's consciousness and subjective limits but all together define the *female subject of feminism* in its very specificity, its inherent and at least for now irreconcilable contradiction" (pp. 14–15).

If one attempts to move directly to a postmodern place of shifting grounds, to a home of nomads, with a modern stable subjectivity intact, one identifies only with those with which one has considerable personal contact and feels "at home" in the normative sense of the word, meaning customary, familiar. Warwick Fox's (1989, 12) criticism of Jim Cheney's emphasis on personal identification with a particular bioregion (rather than the cosmic identification favored by ecoholists) is a useful case in point. "The problem with this [personal identification]" says Fox, "is that, while extending love, care, and friendship to one's nearest and dearest is laudable in and of itself, the *other* side of the coin, emphasizing a purely personal basis for identification (*my* self first, *my* family next, and so on) looks more like the cause of possessiveness, war, and ecological destruction than the solution to these seemingly intractable problems."[51] This insular egoic self moves out to the other only from a secure base and only along interstices of familiarity. The feminist self, by contrast, has to be open to difference and constantly recontextualized (Martin and Mohanty 1986). She has acquired, through painful struggle both within and without, the "ability to coexist and cooperate in complex relationships rather than ability to kill, exploit, and suppress" (Naess 1973, 95, in describing an ecological egalitarianism). She attempts to simultaneously decenter the traditional subject and, moreover, traditional family—that Oedipal triangle of "mommy, daddy, and me," as Gilles Deleuze and Felix Guittari put it.

It will be noted that I am locating "here," on one hand, rather centrally in the narratives of the so-called "private realm"—the regioning of our emotional, sexual, and most basic bodily being rather than the "public" sites of power. I hope, however, that I am not simply reversing the hierarchy of public and private but instead displacing the opposition itself in the attempt to rediscover what being political means (and, after all, the personal is a political site and traversed by public institutions and systems). Perhaps by remaining self-critical according to my most basic historical socioeconomic inhabitance, new ways of thinking, making, and doing will emerge. Perhaps. On the other hand, I am locating "here" directly with my bodily inherence in nature. I believe it is most important to include nature in any notion of place, community, or identity and fully agree with Cheney (1989, 123) that to let local natural environments enter into the feminist notion of self may provide ways of "grounding narrative without essentializing the idea of self."

In western philosophy, where the concept of home has appeared as having philosophical significance, it has been regarded as subordinate to and often opposed to the historical, public, cultural world, to the theoretical realm of science and philosophy, and to human creativity in general. For Hegel, for example, the family is the sphere of "merely natural existence." It is man's first nature, which, though necessary for the human community, must be transcended by man in order for him to fulfill his second nature, which has to do with his activity in the political sphere of the state. In the dialectical process of historic development toward the univer-sality of the political state, the ahistorical immediacy of the familial sphere in a typical Hegelian manner is preserved and negated.[52]

Husserl makes a similar distinction between the home as the sphere of ''mere'' natural existence and the active, truly historical realm. In his dis-cussion of philosophy as the science of all sciences, for example, Husserl explains how the entrance of philosophy in the Greek world revolution-alized Greek culture as a whole. Science is different from other cultural forms already present in ''prescientific'' mankind because the products of science are not used up but are imperishable. The products of science are not ''real'' but ''ideal'' and, moreover, are serviceable as material for the possible production of idealities on a higher level. Those cultural forms al-ready present in ''prescientific'' mankind would be products and activities related to homelife and the phusical body that I have called ''cultivating'' *techne* (for example, agriculture, weaving, and pottery).

That the theoretical attitude is guided by the idealities and unconditional truths of science is derived in part from Aristotle.[53] Even though Husserl takes great pains to show that the theoretical attitude arises out of the life-world, ultimately, like Aristotle, he saw this new attitude as in conflict with that life. It was ''an intrusion into the course of 'serious living' either as a result of originally developed life interests or as a playful looking about when one's immediate vital needs are satisfied or when working hours are over'' (Husserl 1970, 285).

The western separation of the natural and the cultural and of the practical and the theoretical devalues not only family and home life but early and nonindustrial cultures.[54] In this view, which is the view that most west-erners take for granted, those arts that have to do with the health and care of the phusical body are understood as the mere satisfaction of one's prac-tical needs and as involving no, or little, theoretical component. Early cultures are thereby considered ''*pre*scientific,'' ''primitive,'' and ''*pre*-historic.'' Such concepts do not let these early cultures be in their own integrity but prejudge cultures according to western measures. From the western point of view, for instance, a culture without metal to create more powerful tools and weapons is ''primitive'' in the sense of being less intel-ligent and less articulate when compared with ''modern'' western culture.

If we take the time, however, to really look at the Paleolithic art of these "stone-age" people, we cannot help but be confronted with a refined artistic sensitivity and sophistication and a forgotten human openness to nature.

Heidegger, like Husserl, understands the philosopher as one who must separate himself from the sphere of the home. In *Being and Time* (1962), written in 1927, "being-at-home" is associated with the inauthenticity and stagnancy of the "they-self." Dasein comes to its more authentic self by feeling "not-at-home," which is the mood of *angst*. So too in *Introduction to Metaphysics* (1977c, 151), written in 1935, the home is "the customary, familiar, secure," and the philosopher is the solitary man who departs from these customary, familiar limits and makes himself a path in the midst of the overpowering power of phusis. These solitary paths of *men* (for obviously few women had and now have this privilege) lead to the *polis,* the city-state, which is where laws *(nomos)* are made and history happens. Creativity here is understood as a violent act where man wrenches himself from the familiar and sets out on a strange adventure. "Man," says Heidegger (1977c, 154), "disturbs the tranquility of growth, the nurturing and maturing of the goddess who lives without effort."[55] In "The Origin of the Work of Art" (1971c) of this same period, creativity is understood in a similar, rather violent way as a strife between earth and sky, although already there are indications of the importance of letting the differences of the earth *be* in the relationship.

In his later writings, however (usually recognized as sometime after 1940), Heidegger's attitude toward the home and the nature of creativity undergoes significant changes. He now thinks on dwelling as the fundamental characteristic of the human being, and of letting-be, not-willing, and releasement as crucial aspects of thinking and creativity. In terms of dwelling, modern human be-ing is characterized by a homelessness and needlessness, a homelessness that is, moreover, overlooked in the eagerness of human beings to attain the organized conquest of the earth as a whole (Heidegger 1982, 242–50).

I agree with Heidegger that placelessness, the lack of dwelling, is an important pathological condition of modern western be-ing, and with deep ecologists that reconnection with the land is crucial. There are also reasons why I want to reconceptualize the notion of home.[56] Our contemporary psychological feeling of groundlessness, of no meaning (i.e., nihilism) is connected to our cultural fear of the sometimes violent movements of coming to be and passing away, our cultural dismissal of plants, animals, and children as significant (Mary Midgley in Evernden 1985, 119), and our cultural suppression of the histories and voices of resistance and oppression. We cannot cultivate a sense of being at home open to difference without recognition of the earth as essentially related to our human be-ing, and without, moreover, letting the many histories, colors, and languages *of* human be-ing break apart our present complacent white fortresses of discourse.

By becoming attuned to the gifts and limitations, the celebrations and struggles of ourselves and others in our own particular place, we can reinhabit the land as a diverse people from deeply diverse pasts and reestablish contact appropriate to the particular character and possibilities of the area in which we find ourselves. Like environmental artists, we respond to the gifts and limits of a particular place with our own gifts and limits.[57] If we begin by attempting to care impartially for everything, we in practice can care for nothing (King 1989, 24). We could say that care begins in the home. It is there that we often learn the values of caring for and nurturing each other and our environment (Plant 1990, 160), and where social limits are established and relationships woven. Nomadic homes are particular rather than global because they are limited by how far our care can extend into our neighborhoods of being. Small communities, however, are linked to larger clusters of relations. As Val Plumwood (1991, 7) puts it, speaking of an environmental home, "care and responsibility for particular animals, trees, and rivers that are known and well loved and appropriately connected to the self are an important basis for acquiring a wider, more generalized concern."

Home is not only a place of care and nurturance for beings; it must at the same time be a place of self-criticism, a refuge where we question (sometimes with much anguish) our most immediate and intimate colored being. In our ownmost dwelling with others, we need to bear witness to those whose paths we cross, to listen to our grandmothers and grandfathers, and to learn from fellow travelers' experiences of oppression and of wonder. What is most important in such encounters in our particular time and culture is not so much the discovery of commonalities with others as it is the wonder and respect provoked by positive differences.[58] Our prime responsibility is to search out differences, those subjugated knowledges (as Michel Foucault puts it), to look for "the sweat and blood of people's lives that [have] been mortared" into the bricks of institutions (Minnie Bruce Pratt, in Martin and Mohanty 1986, 205, speaking of a market house in her neighborhood).

But, what about . . .

Giving and Power

> I demand that love struggle within the master against the will for power.
> —Cixous and Clément 1975, 140

Am I fighting against ending this book, or has everything really come down to the difference between giving and power, to the question, rather, of how to let giving infiltrate power? Is Heidegger's word *Ereignis* (appropriation) a name for the giving that gives presencing, the name for Being after Will to Power, the final master name? Or does he instead at the end let the names of Being "fly up in dissarray without thinking there is a single decisive meaning to be heard" (Caputo 1987, 107) and thereby expose us to the play of epochs? There are no transepochal truths, ethical imperatives, or golden ages that shine like beacons in this evening land. There is only the springing up and passing away of epochs (Caputo 1987, 115).

There is. In German, "there is" literally translates as "it gives" *(es gibt)*. According to Heidegger's story, western metaphysics has focused on the Being as the *ground* of beings to the neglect of Being itself because in the *giving* that gives presencing, the "It" that gives holds itself back and withdraws in favor of the gift, the sending of presencing. The gift, the sending of presencing, has shown itself in western metaphysics in various epochal transmutations: as the *hen* (one), *logos, idea, ousia, actualas, perceptio,* monad, as objectivity, as spirit, and as Will to Power. In these manifestations of western Being, the subjectivity of human consciousness increasingly comes to the fore, and the It that gives pulls back.

Another way of understanding what could be called a metaphysical lack of gratitude or perhaps even greed for presents/presence is western Being's "crav[ing] to persist" (Heidegger 1975, 46) in the present, denying the passing away of time. The phallocentric movement of western Being that I have been describing is a movement that privileges coming-to-be. In its perpetual secured forward movement, western Being (as it appears in metaphysics) uncannily denies becoming and secures itself as pure presence and stable stuff. Rather than relax and give way to the uncertain, groundless play of temporal flux, Being in western metaphysics aims solely for "continuance and subsistence." "It strikes the willful pose of persistence. . . . It stiffens—as if this were the way to linger" (Heidegger 1975, 42). Heidegger finds this peculiar tendency of western Being to persist in its presencing from Anaximander to the temporality of Nietzsche's eternal recurrence.[59]

To think on the play and uncertainties involved in giving rather than on fixed rules and solid metaphysical grounds, we have to recognize and accept passing away. Without this *pull back,* this harboring and sheltering-care, a gift after all is merely something one wants to throw away and not a true gift at all.

But let's change genders, times, and places, while still remaining with this theme of the gift. In an exchange between Catherine Clément and Hélène Cixous, Clément, reflecting a prevalent view, affirms that mastery is fundamental and necessary for transmitting knowledge, although she concedes with Cixous that one can conceive of societies where the conditions of access to knowledge would be profoundly different.[60] Cixous, on the contrary, believes that since only a privileged few have access to the (male) master's discourse and are therewith in a position of power, a way to bar dominance and power is to eliminate the notion of mastery in one's own practice and discourse so that "it will be given. Something on the order of a personal gift," says Cixous (in Cixous and Clément 1975, 140), "a subjective one."[61]

Giving establishes openness to, rather than dominance over, as primary.[62] Appropriate giving is not an expenditure, it is not the same as self-sacrifice, for self-sacrifice is a loss of self, whereas giving is an overflowing of self.[63] It is thus not a giving over of oneself to another subjectivity, although it can become this in the context of power relations or through the internalization of altruistic stereotypes. Giving is not so much a giving away as a giving to, letting something belong to another that already in a sense belongs to that other.[64] It is not a free-for-all but is a caring play whose rules are continually recontextualized and which takes place in a field of variable boundaries.[65] Giving is a form of postmodern play with an ethic of care attached to it.

Trinh T. Minh-ha (1989), who told the story of stories circulating like a gift, reflecting on a similar issue as Cixous and Clément wonders, "Can knowledge circulate without a position of mastery? Can it be conveyed without the exercise of power? No, because there is no end to understanding power relations which are rooted deep in the social nexus—not merely added to society nor easily locatable so that we can just radically do away with them. Yes, however, because in-between grounds always exist, and cracks and interstices are like gaps of fresh air that keep on being suppressed because they tend to render more visible the failures operating in every system" (p. 41). "Between knowledge and power, there is room for knowledge-without-power. Or knowledge at rest" (p. 40).

It seems to me that "knowledge at rest," and I would like to also add knowledge at play, is the kind of standing (*episteme* from *stame*, meaning "standing upright") that is needed to help open the discourse of white phallocentricism to contradiction and difference. It is the kind of knowledge that is given through experience and passed on through communal gatherings such as conversations and celebrations, through dance and music, through art gifts, through walks, through storytelling, through the voice of the drum. It is an attempt to "speak" of something that cannot quite be mediated through purely cognitive means and that tends to be subverted once institutionalized. Knowledge at rest, though not belonging to static forms *(eidos)*, is nonetheless passed on to others and sediments historically in its own way.

This playful, restful knowledge of a small village, for example, does not stands like the western standing preserve of knowledge that limits access to a privileged few. It is not resting on secure foundations with a view to building up from foundations. It is not an all-too-serious knowledge solidified into a firm, solid ground of reason that stands in opposition to our earthy ground, that excludes our emotional-sexual sentient being, and that gives the illusion of overcoming temporality, geography, personal history, and cultural specificity. It does not take its stand as information that informs, that is, that forms, organizes, and directs the western world in its increasing organization of itself and of the world. Resting and playing gives way to the movements of passing away. Such bioregional fecund knowledge seeps back into our incarnate dwelling, sinks back to the bottom of the heart, and ferments in those unruly depths of meaning that representational thinking, which can present only judgments and propositions, leaves untouched. It emerges from a vigilant lingering in the enigmatic supporting presence of becoming that is without a why and within which everything grows and decomposes.

I am describing this recollective movement back spatially as a movement back from the center to the margins, back to our hearts and bodies, to the particular land we stand on, and temporally as a movement back to our particular personal, cultural, geographic pasts with particular attention to suppressed histories. Going backward is not the same as going forward but in the opposite direction.[66] After modernity, there can be no going backward toward a stable truth, a primitive, natural, and native origin (or forward to a fixed goal). Derrida's critique, for example, has undone the notion of the meaning or truth of Being, of a primordial epoch that was granted a privileged experience of Being, of a postal service sending dispatches across the epochs of a primordial sender *(Ereignis)* and a privileged recipient (man) of a special message, which after a period of oblivion comes safely home again (Caputo 1987, 153). Nor am I simply saying that appropriate forward movement is at the same time movement in reverse. Such a linear understanding of *kinesis* or movement is defined according to a fixed point, understood as the present. From such thinking, we get both a linear-teleological movement of metaphysics and the circular eschatological movement of theology (Caputo 1989). Deconstructed moving backward is a stepping back, and an undermining not only of hierarchical order of the terms forward and backward but of the system of conceptual opposites (see Derrida 1986c, 329). The postmodern imperative to destabilize fixed truths and authorities, to overturn and displace the hierarchical order of concepts, set thought and action free. And if this freeing up of white theory is a frightening thought, well, perhaps we need to learn *rhythm* from the hip this time.

I am approaching the end of this book that purports to be working "toward'' an ontology with the hope that I have not begun an ''ontology,'' for an ontology is doomed to be totalizing, since it attempts to account for all beings. I hope that I have not worked ''toward'' but drawn back or rather remained in a certain place. I am attempting to listen toward something like the voices of drums that speak of the rumblings of the earth and of a fleshy sociality. If I am pointing, suggesting, indicating, going forward, it is to indicate the flow back within the powerful upsurge of historical and natural growth, and the need for each of us (here in the privileged writer-reader space of this text and subject matter) to turn back to our personal situations, our bodies, our cultural pasts, to seek out the silences, the stories of pain and of bacchanals, the darker places in our neighborhoods, and thereby perhaps discover *breaks* in our seemingly never-ending linear white narratives (which this book itself may have been) that allow us to really stop and listen to what ''suffers silently in the holes of discourse'' (Gauthier in Spivak 1987, 141), and, for example, to those ''millions of illiterate rural and urban Indian women who live 'in the pores of' capitalism'' (Spivak 1987, 135). I am attempting as well to move on a Heideggerean pathway of thought, but hopefully not with a view to going forward so much as to feeling the forest, the land, and the sky that gives this pathway, to sitting down and resting in the living ''nonhuman'' density from which the pathway emerges, and to enjoining the pathways of thinking with the pathways of the earth. I am approaching the end and will soon have to go back to the beginning to rewrite the introduction to a book that has not really gone anywhere but here. Well, let me tack on one of my painful stories.

Manitoulin Island: the Ojibways call it Heartbeat of Mother Earth. I liked to think of our little place on its western tip as the end of the world. It took a long time to get there, driving as far as we could, then walking in with all we needed on our backs. Once there, we oriented ourselves and established our boundaries as best as we could by walking lines with a compass, counting our paces. For many days we made our way with difficulty through miles upon miles of varied terrain—juniper bush, birch stands, red pine ridges, and cedar swamps. We felt the land. Sometimes we got lost. Our legs and arms got scratched. It was always such a relief to break out of the dense forest and feel the soothing expanse of Lake Huron. Through our counted paces we oriented ourselves to the new neighborhood and established a much-needed map, drawing our pathways, and sketching out the lay of the land.

We chose a nice place on the shore that, through our counted paces and compass readings, appeared to be still on our "property" and set to work. It seemed so funny, so uncanny, when we first started clearing out the thick cedar that in the midst of seeming boundless forest and endless shoreline, it was exactly here we would call "home." Yet soon through sweat and silent work, the clearing emerged. A strong log house was built during two summers and we lived there for over a year before moving back to the city.

I still muse about this worldly "clearing" that is established in contrast to the density of the forest. The clearing, says Heidegger, is not to be understood as pure light, pure unconcealment, pure world, but is inclusive of darkness. Yet, given the constant privileging of sight and light in western philosophy, the notion of Open continues to metaphorically favor light over darkness, sight over touch, consciousness (and language) over body, and certainly human over animal, male over female, the European over "other worlds."

But let me continue the story. There was this magical forest near my home, a place that I would never dare inhabit. Mossy wisdom. Wild stillness. Old, old, old growth. Perhaps it was that the passing of time presenced so clearly there in that immense quiet standing. Perhaps it had to do with the thick air, the filtered light, the deafening rustle of the leaves, the sheltering in that forest, the frightening openness to night spirits. That gathered place of trees. It commanded respect.

Here was a place I could actively and benevolently protect, I thought. One summer I went back to the end of my world and found the forest ripped out and a stark clearing in its place. The ancient trunks gone. The quite slow growth sucked out over one season by a new logging road. Open devastation.

Our body-maps were not so accurate. Who could have imagined that a road would have found its way through all that dense bush to that old, old forest that had been standing there so, so long?

I still feel the pain of the glaring light of that clearing as though it were gnawing at the very nerves of my being. What is this terrible pain? Years later hawberries and thistles have taken root. Thousands of daisies and wild strawberries cover the logging road. I am confused by the beauty.

But a deadly silence reigns in the clearing despite the increased chirping of birds. The bobcat, whose eerie screams would fill us with awe, has vanished and is almost forgotten.

Human clearings, as Heidegger has said, allow for openings that can be traversed; they establish a site. It seems to me, however, that in our human-dominated, world-dominated clearings, the playful flux of concealment, density, mystery, darkness, silence, and depth are taken for granted, as though this background were inexhaustible and will remain eternally waiting to be of service for our revealing. But maybe the earth's forests, for example, are not longer so dense that they can provide the background for human clearings. Perhaps the earth's density is losing its thickness; the deep of the sky, its depth; silence and concealment, its harboring; and even withdrawal, its "with." It is ironic that we in the evening land, the land of the setting sun, should so culturally fear, hate, repress, and conquer black silence to which even the most articulate and privileged of us return.

But I am taking things far too seriously and apocalyptically again. And still dragging my own heels to the end.

And well, I'm making it up as I go along. It's true:

I guess.

So—

Notes

Introduction

1. For the idea of beginning and ending the book with the word *but* as a way of undermining closure I am indebted to the art installation "But," Strutts Centre, Sackville, New Brunswick, September 1991, by Emmett Groane of Grup Nomad. (But. I'm lying, it's true. I changed my mind at the end.)

2. This is a word that Jacques Derrida uses to criticize Martin Heidegger.

3. There has been some work on feminist ontology, most notably de Beauvoir 1974; Daly 1985; Whitbeck 1984a; Vickers 1989, 27–47; and Reuther 1984.

4. I owe this way of phrasing the deconstructive project to Caputo 1987.

5. I use the term *muse* in the spirit of Allen and Young (1989, 1): "The muses, invoked by philosophers even prior to the time of Socrates as the source of philosophic inspiration, have been traditionally posited as the 'other,' forever outside the activity of philosophizing. . . . *The Thinking Muse* establishes, in contrast, a unity of inspiration and thought that moves within women's experience to the recognition and creation of more freeing modes of philosophizing. Beginning from women's perspective, philosophy need no longer get straight to the point, but consists in thoughtful wandering through the shadows of experience, not in order to bring them into light, but to reveal the ambiguous edges of things." For my own prolonged musing on the notion of musing, see "Being Moved" in this book.

6. De Beauvoir made full use of Sartre's existential philosophy of subjectivity and freedom in her book *The Second Sex*, one of the first monumental attempts to create a theory of women's oppression. More recently, other feminists have turned to existential-phenomenology, making critical use of its return to lived experience and its emphasis on the human freedom to change, while, at the same time, criticizing phallocentric biases within it. For feminist work in existential-phenomenology see, for example, articles in Allen and Young 1989; and Miles and Finn 1989, as well as Allen 1982–83; Young 1990; Butler 1989, 85–100; Daly 1985; O'Brien 1983; Weinzweig 1986, 139–60; and Graybeal 1990.

7. Unlike Nye (1988), and Finn (in Miles and Finn 1989, 209), I do not believe that it is hopeless to save any philosophical theories because the exclusion and denigration of women is integral to the system. I do, however, agree with Finn's excellent criticism of Sartre's notions of the in-itself and the for-

itself. His masculine sympathies and metaphysical biases do seem to penetrate far into his philosophy, and for that reason I do not find his philosophy useful for the development of a feminist ontology. Indeed, it was because of de Beauvoir's reliance on Sartre's distinction between the in-itself and the for-itself that she mistakenly viewed women's liberation to lie in joining in the transcendent projects of men.

8. See, for example, Allen and Young 1989; Nicholson 1990; Nye 1988; and Butler 1990.

9. In this regard, it is surprising to me that there is not more caution in the poststructuralist acceptance of Nietzsche, given that his philosophy helped validate the central ideological elements of the National Socialist movement.

10. This way of doing philosophy through art is based on the paradigms of Merleau-Ponty's (1982) interrogation of art and Heidegger's numerous meditations on poetry. It is established as an actual methodology which involves closely working in the presence of the artwork in Mallin, n.d., and 1983.

11. The initial selection of artworks I have used was made on the basis of works that compelled me to linger in their presence because they were generally relevant to feminist concerns and that were available in my immediate geographical location (Toronto, New York, Philadelphia). Later I traveled to Greece to study Greek sculpture but found myself drawn to the Cycladic and Minoan works.

Chapter One

1. This ontology might be understood to have some similarities with that of Whitbeck (1984a). Like her, I see the working out of nonoppositional and non-dualistic relations as a key to feminist ontology. Whereas she focuses on a self-other relation and contrasts it to the traditional self-other opposition, I work to deconstruct the culture/nature dichotomy.

2. Although at first my position may appear to be a simple dialectic in which I move toward a middle ground between oppositions such as nature and culture, it will become clear that I am attempting to tread on ground that is not constituted by two opposing terms. For though we find the dialectic well-suited to facilitate our thinking out problems, especially those of us whose thinking has been trained in the continental tradition, the dialectic intrinsically involves relations of opposition. I am attempting to step back from all relations of opposition and step into new relations of difference that do not progress through dominance and conflict but grow through a fundamental openness and respectful responding.

3. Others have also criticized poststructuralism. See, for example, Di Stefano, Harding, Benhabib, and Hartsock in Nicholson 1990.

4. Moreover, as Bordo (1990, 138) notes, marginalized feminists did not declare the theoretical impossibility of discovering a common ground among diverse women but, rather, encouraged feminist theoreticians to become sensitive to their prejudices and ignorance.

5. It is noteworthy that the very notion of the feminine as an unchanging essence reinforces the misogyny of metaphysics. Essences define a concrete thing by abstracting a thing's unchanging nature from its changing concrete appearance. Intrinsic to the notion of an unchanging essence is a whole host of metaphysical dichotomies such as that between the changing world and unchanging eternals, the abstract and the concrete, the rational and the irrational, the mind and the body, universals and particulars, and the supersensuous and sensuous. As is well known in feminist studies, the feminine is identified with the subordinate side of all these dichotomies, and thus the notion of the feminine as an unchanging essence perpetuates these sexist dichotomies.

6. The view that the feminine and the masculine are transhistorical universal principles can create problems other than that of ahistoricality. These principles, for instance, tend to misleadingly polarize the masculine and feminine, fixing for all time the battle of the sexes. The masculine tends to get understood as a negative force (i.e., aggressive, domineering, and destructive) and the feminine as a positive force (i.e., gentle, relational, and nurturing). This polarization and fixity leaves no room for other gender possibilities or for future change in the nature of the masculine and the feminine. Such an understanding of gender, moreover, seems to turn upside down the prevalent metaphysical understanding of the sexes in which the feminine is understood as negative, inferior, and evil and the masculine as positive, superior, and godly. As dialectics have shown us, merely reversing a philosophical dichotomy does not change the destructive relationship of opposition within the dichotomy and such a dialectical turn remains deeply bound to the dynamic of metaphysics.

7. See Fraser and Nicholson 1990, 32–33.

8. For example, Fraser and Nicholson 1990, 29–31.

9. Advocating nurturance as a female value, for example, without careful explanation and qualification risks perpetuating the conservatism of traditional family structures.

10. Some feminists, such as Chodorow and Dinnerstein, for instance, describe the extent to which they are the result of early childhood socialization and psychological gender formation.

11. In a similar vein, Fuss (1989b, 68) defends Irigaray against essentialism by suggesting that her essentialism at least has the political advantage that women will never be defined solely in masculine terms.

12. For other defenses of the importance of the body see Rich 1986 and Fuss 1989a.

13. See Levin (1985, 1988, 1989) for his excellent attempts to describe how we might open to Being through our bodily senses to counter the prevailing nihilism of our age. His work is a prime example of a thinker who is continuing the work of Heidegger and Merleau-Ponty in new fruitful directions.

14. From a liberal point of view, this political stance is legitimate, however. For, from this point of view, one struggles for the equal rights of a minority group, but once such rights have been attained, then the oppressed groups need no longer maintain their distinctive identities. I, however, find this stance unsatisfying because, as existentialists have pointed out, there is a need to integrate equality with diversity.

15. Gadamer (1989b) makes a similar point. Derrida, like many of the French neo-Nietzscheans, makes much of Nietzsche criticism that there is no preexistent meaning to be discovered and that all meaning is posited. Although Nietzsche is right in saying that there is no secure starting point from which knowledge can search for the universal law or principle, if one fully endorses his claim that all meaning is interpretation in the service of Will to Power, then Being is reduced to power relations, and all power is ultimately placed in the hands of human beings.

Derrida does not agree with Heidegger's interpretation of Nietzsche's devaluing and revaluing of all values as the culmination and fulfillment of metaphysics whereby thinking on Being is reduced to value thinking, and the earth is abandoned to its oblivion. I find Heidegger's four-volume study of Nietzsche, however, for the most part quite convincing, especially, for example, that despite Nietzsche's overturning of the metaphysical dichotomy between the sensuous and the supersensuous, he remains trapped within metaphysics and fulfills the phallocentrism and ecodestructiveness of metaphysics.

16. Bordo (1990, 135–36) argues that although the Derridean deconstruction rightly criticizes the metaphysical presumptions of a firm epistemological ground, it possesses its own fantasies of attaining an epistemological perspective free of the locatedness and limitations of embodied existence. Whereas traditional metaphysics can be said to be possessed by a dream of a "view from nowhere" or the ideal of an abstract universal reason without class, gender, or history, deconstruction is involved in a "dream of everywhere." Ultimately, she understands deconstruction as a new, postmodern variation of Cartesian detachment and disembodiment.

17. See Heidegger 1974b on Leibniz's principle of sufficient reason.

18. For a fuller explanation of Heidegger's translation of the term *wesen* see Heidegger 1977e, 3.

19. See Heidegger 1971e.

20. The notion of presencing, then, is in partial agreement with Butler's in that there is an essential incompleteness to the presencing of women, and there is no need to posit "woman" as a stable, unified, and agreed-upon gender identity. Gender is, indeed, a complexity that is "never fully what it is at any given juncture in time" and is "always an open assemblage that permits of convergences and divergences without obedience to a normative telos of definitive closure" (Butler 1990, 16). However, I would disagree that gender is a complexity whose totality is permanently "deferred," for then we fall into the endless game of perpetual bounding from sign to sign. Gender is not a self-identical category persisting through time as the same, unified, and internally coherent structure, as Butler argues, but neither is it a relativistic category, thoroughly constructed by culture and divorced from all associations with our living bodies and earthly life itself.

21. Of course, Hegel, too, insists that essence is not to be conceived abstractly and ahistorically but concretely as a process of historical becoming. For Hegel, essence is a dialectical development and unfolding of Spirit. However, unlike Heidegger, for Hegel history develops into progressively more perfect forms of Spirit reaching a final *telos*.

22. Irigaray (1985a) suggests that women are, in particular, the sex that is unrepresentable. Unlike the male sex, the female sex cannot be thought of in traditional metaphysics that has relied on a representational thinking because the female has eluded the requirements of representation, which demands a single, immutable subject. Because the female sex does not have a single erotic signifier (i.e., the phallus) but multierogenous zones, she is the "sex which is not one." The fact that the phallogocentric signifying economy of metaphysics is closed to such sexual multiplicity gives women a disruptive, revolutionary potential.

23. To find our way into the nearness of Being (the groundless ground), says Heidegger (1977d, 199), we "must first learn to exist in the nameless."

24. Feminists like Chodorow (1978), for example, who suggests that a cause of women's oppression is the fact that women are primary caretakers of infants, or like O'Brien (1983), who suggests that a cause of patriarchy lies in our different reproductive consciousness, in this view would be seen as theoretically misguided. Other feminists, moreover, such as Stone (1976), Gimbutas (1989 and 1990), and Eisler (1987), who explore the historic turn from chthonic to patriarchal religion, or Kristeva (1980, 1981), who, using psychoanalysis, explores what she calls the prediscursive maternal stage of early infant development, and Irigaray (1985a and 1985b), who attempts to return to recover the act of matricide that occurred at the beginnings of the western symbolic, would similarly be seen as misguided on theoretical grounds.

25. Derrida criticizes Heidegger's philosophy as still engaged in a "meta-

physics of presence,'' as relying on the assumption of an immediately available area of certainty. Derrida unfortunately tends to concentrate on Heidegger's earlier works and does not pay sufficient attention to Heidegger's own attempts to subvert metaphysics through his crucial notions of concealment, *a-letheia, Ereignis,* the Open, and the fourfold. Thus, when Derrida criticizes Heidegger for his entrapment in the ''metaphysics of presence,'' he suppresses Heidegger's understanding of presencing as an ambiguous flickering of absencing and presencing (which is similar to Derrida's own descriptions of meaning). When Derrida argues that Heidegger did not break through the ''logocentrism'' of metaphysics, he neglects Heidegger's understanding of *logos* (through *legein*), as ''a gathering that lets lie.'' When he criticizes Heidegger for still asking about the essence of truth and the meaning of Being (which Heidegger still understands meaning as something out there to be discovered), Derrida fails to keep in mind that meaning, truth, and Being for Heidegger are not stable unities and that, moreover, Heidegger in his later writings no longer speaks of Being or truth but of *Ereignis,* the fourfold and of *aletheia* or unconcealment.

Gadamer (1989a, 113), who also notes Derrida's neglect of the later Heidegger, says that ''because he reads Heidegger through Husserl, he takes Heidegger's borrowing of Husserlian concepts, which is clearly noticeable in the transcendental self-description present in *Being and Time,* as evidence of logocentrism.''

26. Heidegger meditates on the notion of the Open by turning to Parmenides' poetic statement on the ''untrembling heart of well-rounded *aletheia*'' (Heidegger 1972a, 67–73).

27. I owe this way of describing *aletheia* to Caputo (1987).

28. See Casey 1984 on this point. In my own work on art I have found it fruitful to turn to the beginning of western metaphysics, and even further to the prehistoric, in order to muse on feminist and environmental issues. Thus, I have looked for the beginnings of the culture/nature dichotomy in Aristotle and have meditated on prehistoric artworks. Although we must not romanticize a past matriarchal society or attempt to reinstitute such times, which would be impossible given our material conditions, technology, and gender history, it is, nonetheless, most useful to look at prehistorical, prepatriarchal periods, for they can show us different ways of being in the world-earth-home and working out such problems as gender structures.

However, as with any approach to the past, especially such an ancient past as the prehistoric, we must be painstakingly careful that our present prejudices are put into relief as much as possible so that we can be open to the radical differences from our present age that the work offers. We must, for example, avoid the modern tendency to see the notion of history as implying a certain continuity and *telos*. A common modern view, for instance, is that agrarian societies, which tended to be somewhat matriarchal, represent the infancy of history and that our technological urban civilization, which is patriarchal, represents the maturation of history. However, there is no necessity that history progresses toward an end. The broad lines of prehistorical time, for example, may have tended to recline back rather than lead forward.

Chapter Two

1. See, for example, Trebilcot 1981; and Ferguson 1981.
2. See, for example, Scott 1988, 45; and Butler 1990, 127.
3. I am not including here the French feminist poststructuralists (Kristeva, Irigaray, and Cixous). Moreover there are variations within the poststructuralist stance on the formation of gender and its relation to the body. I use Butler's Foucauldian–Merleau-Pontian analysis in *Gender Trouble* (1990) because it is the most thorough and convincing account I have come across. (All page references in the following discussion are to this book.) For other arguments that attempt to separate gender from the body see, for example, Flax in Nicholson 1990 and Scott 1988. For criticisms of poststructuralism see, for example, Bordo, Di Stefano, Harding, Benhabib, and Hartsock in Nicholson 1990.
4. De Beauvoir, says Butler (1990, 8), endorsing Sartre's dialectic between the for-itself and the in-itself, made the mistake of seeing nature as a resistant materiality, a medium, surface, or object, and the female body as that passivity that should be transcended by cultural projects.
5. Butler (1990, 79–81) criticizes (correctly, I think) Kristeva's prediscursive maternal body for the same reason.
6. Bordo (1990, 145) questions in a similar vein: "What sort of body is it that is free to change its shape and location at will, that can become anyone and travel everywhere? If the body is a metaphor for our locatedness in space and time and thus for the finitude of human perception and knowledge, then the postmodern body is no body at all."
7. Cultural construction is limited only internally by its own cultural discursive practices. Butler's notion of cultural construction is neither a cultural free will nor a cultural determinism. There are limits set to the construction of gender configurations which prevent both their capricious formation and their inevitability. Gendered configurations, Butler (1990) explains, are limited by the historical discursive analysis of gender (p. 8). Gendered bodies are "styles of the flesh" that are never fully self-styled, for styles are historically conditioned, which limits their possibilities (pp. 139, 145). The limits within which cultural construction must take place, then, are themselves thoroughly cultural.

8. We also thereby open possibilities for new cultural and technological manipulations of our sexual bodies. Although technological advances such as handing over our reproductive function to machines are perhaps unlikely and would be difficult to practically implement, by disconnecting gender from the body and ignoring its noncultural significance we are theoretically granting approval to any technological manipulations of our bodies that would serve gender fluidity.

9. Ecofeminists claim that the domination of nonhuman nature and the domination of women are intimately connected and mutually reinforcing. See, for example, King 1983, 16.

10. That the modern world reduces nature to a standing reserve of energy resources waiting to be further ordered is discussed extensively in Heidegger 1977e, 3–35.

11. This main claim of the deep ecology movement that the culture/nature dichotomy should be replaced with a relational, total-field image was introduced by Naess (1973, 95–100).

12. For an account of this see, for example, Lloyd 1984.

13. For an account of the body in Cartesian epistemology, see Bordo 1990, 143.

14. By ignoring the significance of nature and the body we would be ultimately joining the traditionally defined masculine side of all metaphysical dichotomies (i.e., mind, subject, rationality, culture) and abandoning the feminine side (body, object, irrationality, nature). The solution, however, is not to uncritically resuscitate the feminine side of these dichotomies but, rather, to reconceptualize both sides of the dichotomy and, more importantly, to disrupt the metaphysical opposition that operates within the dichotomy.

15. Bordo (1990, 144–45) also objects to their terminology. She finds deconstruction's metaphor of dance, for example, dangerous because it "obscures the located, limits of inescapable partial and *always* personally invested nature of human 'story-making.' " Deconstructionists refuse to assume a shape for which they must take responsibility and dream of limitless multiple embodiments. The true appreciation of difference, she argues, requires the acknowledgment of some limit to the dance beyond which the dancer cannot go. Whereas Cartesian epistemology is fixed on necessity and unity, deconstruction is intoxicated with possibility and plurality.

16. See, for example, Elshtain 1982; and Vickers 1982.

17. For a criticism of Foucault's notion of power, although from a different point of view, see Hartsock in Nicholson 1990, 157–75.

18. For example, Kristeva's prediscursive maternal body and Irigaray's notion of a multierogenous female body would be included here. Also included would be those feminists involved in countercultural spirituality who subscribe

to the cult of the Mother Goddess and believe that underneath history lies an alternative reality of harmony with nature, which is our true nature.

19. For example, McWhorter (1989), in her argument that Foucault does not hold a notion of a transhistorical natural body, presumes nature to be eternal and culture as fluid and changeable.

20. I do this in later chapters. I suggest, moreover, that the Greek notions of phusis and techne could be most valuable for reconceptualizing the notions of nature and culture, respectively, in a nonfoundationalist way. If we understood nature as phusis, as the changing realm of coming-to-be and passing-away and techne as a mode of phusis, we could find a way of describing the cultural construction of gender in a way that is determined by neither pure biology nor pure culture. We could affirm that gender is, indeed, a becoming but that this becoming is a phusical becoming that includes both natural and cultural determinants (although the division between culture and nature so dissolves as to render the terms ultimately impractical).

21. On one hand, science has discovered that, in fact, the physical, hormonal, and genetic differences between the sexes overlap to a considerable extent and have a wide range of flexibility, making it difficult to exactly pin down sexual difference. The main difference between the sexes seems to be reproductive functioning, which, one could argue, affects only a limited portion of human functioning. On the other hand, because of the reproductive function (i.e., because women carry the unborn during a nine-month gestation period, give birth, and often nurture the young through a significant lactation period), they are, nonetheless, seen from a biological point of view as "enslaved to the species," as de Beauvoir (1974, 41) puts it.

22. In philosophy, we can find the first attempts to resuscitate the body in Husserl's phenomenological descriptions of the lifeworld. The lifeworld is that natural, unreflective world that we immediately experience primarily as subjects who are bodily sensitive. Husserl (1970) saw that the world and the things themselves appear, or are given to us, most primordially before the explicit active operations of positing, judging, and doubting. His main aim in his discussion of the lifeworld is to show that the theoretical truths of the scientific objective world are grounded in these pretheoretical subjective experiences of the lifeworld that science takes for granted.

Merleau-Ponty takes up this aspect of Husserl's later philosophy, developing and altering it and leaving behind the idealist transcendentalism that tends to characterize Husserl's philosophy as a whole. Using Husserl's key notion of intentionality, Merleau-Ponty gives us a phenomenology of what he calls the body-subject. Intentionality, as Husserl describes it, is the relationship of consciousness to the world. Consciousness is not first a self-enclosed something in itself which then enters into relationship with an object. Rather, consciousness is codetermined by the object to which it is related. Thus every conscious act is already outside itself and directed toward something. This relationship is encapsuled by the saying that consciousness is always "consciousness of."

For Merleau-Ponty, intentionality is, as it were, more of a relationship of the entire bodily being than exclusively a relationship of consciousness to the world (even though consciousness is not for Husserl just a positing consciousness). Merleau-Ponty wants to restore all those intentional threads that unite our living body to its surroundings.

23. It is possible, for example, to use his phenomenology to help differentiate the female phenomenological body from the male. He describes, for instance, how the body moves in the face of its tasks. Although there are many motor-practical capacities that are present in both males and females by virtue of their being human bodies, there may be broad ways that each sex as a whole generally moves: the way it runs, sits, walks, and articulates itself in various natural-cultural situations; its bodily rhythms and sexuality. For interesting work in this area, see Young 1990.

24. See, for example, Butler's criticisms (1989, 85–100). I certainly agree with some of her analysis of Merleau-Ponty's masculine biases (and believe there are similar masculine biases as well as anthropocentric biases in his broader ontology). I do not agree, however, with Butler's claim that Merleau-Ponty relies on a "natural" body of biological subsistence that is removed from the domain of the historical. (All page references in the following discussion are to Merleau-Ponty 1962.)

25. Merleau-Ponty called it the body-subject, meaning that the body is the main subject of human activity and relationship rather than cognition. However, he dropped this term in his later writing because it was too easily misinterpreted as a kind of subjectivism.

26. This precognitive relation that Merleau-Ponty describes is better understood as a *non*cognitive relation, for the term *precognitive* is already prejudiced in favor of the cognitive since it implies that the relation in question is already destined for a cognitive articulation. The term *noncognitive*, by contrast, does not suggest a fulfillment in the cognitive but more or an independent existence or at least coexistence. For similar reasons, I will use the terms *nonlinguistic, nonpersonal,* and *noncultural.*

27. "It is impossible," Merleau-Ponty (1962, 189) concludes, "to superimpose on man a lower level of behavior which one chooses to call natural, followed by a manufactured cultural or spiritual world. Everything is both manufactured and natural in man."

28. It is, of course, significant that our modern western cultural practices attempt to divorce themselves from incarnate existence. Thus, if we compare, for example, Native American cultural dancing with white classical ballet, we

can see that whereas Native American dancing emerges out of a sensitivity to fleshy bodily movement and expresses our embeddedness in a matrix of relations with the nonhuman environment, classical ballet attempts to ignore our fleshy phenomenological being, cleaving to ideal cognitive forms.

29. Young (1990, 160–76) develops Kristeva's point that the subject is not experienced as unified in pregnancy, thereby offering a challenge to the subject/object dualism. I think, however, that even a split subject reifies the subject/object dichotomy. Young's chapter on pregnancy provides excellent phenomenological descriptions of pregnancy and birth from a woman's perspective.

30. As Young (1990, 167) notes, "Though she [the pregnant subject] does not plan and direct it [pregnancy], neither does it merely wash over her; rather, she *is* this process, this change."

31. Because breastfeeding is a social and, in a broad sense, a sexual activity and, moreover, demands a relative proximity to one's baby, it is perhaps the most culturally repressed aspect of the mothering body. Our western culture replaced breastfeeding with bottlefeeding in the late nineteenth and early twentieth centuries and later pushed substitute baby milk on the Third World, with disastrous results. Many women today do not receive the social support and knowledge needed to confidently take up this remarkable communication of the mothering body and, indeed, are prevented from involving themselves in it because the public workplace is geared to the male body.

Chapter Three

1. My project can be seen as following the line of thinking in Lloyd 1984, where the author proposes that the presumed inferiority of women if not due to merely superficial misogynist attitudes within philosophical thought but is a matter of the genderization of the ideal of reason itself. I push this notion further in suggesting that the woman problem is a matter of the genderization of Being itself.

2. For a concise discussion of Heidegger's philosophy of history, see Heidegger 1982, 197–252.

3. In his later philosophy, Heidegger attempts to transform the metaphysical, foundationalist concept of "Being," for example, by crossing it out and then replacing the concept altogether with his poetic notion of the fourfold of earth, sky, immortals, and mortals.

4. The meaning of *phusis* in pre-Socratic thought is variously interpreted by scholars. Burnet (1930, 10) argues that it meant a permanent and primary substance. Robinson (1987), along with Kirk and Raven (1987), translates *phusis* as "the real constitution of things." Charles Kahn (1987) similarly translates

it as the "character or nature of a thing." Beardsley (1918, 63) argues that until the close of the fifth century there is no direct evidence that *phusis* was used as a name for universal nature as an idealized or universal force. For more on the meaning of *phusis*, see Heidel (1909–10), who maps out a whole range of meanings originating from its earliest primary meaning of "growth."

5. Fragment 123 Diels-Kranz. The following thoughts on Heraclitus' fragment depend on Heidegger 1975, 113–15.

6. Moreover, elsewhere Heraclitus himself says that *phusis* is the "never-setting," in other words, that which never fails to reveal itself (fragment B. 16 Diels-Kranz). This fragment is translated by G. S. Kirk (Kirk and Raven 1987) as "The real constitution of things is accustomed to hide itself."

7. It does, indeed, seem that the woman question involves many of philosophy's most persistent problems: essence versus existence; the mind/body, culture/nature, and self/other dichotomies; and the problems of universals and particulars and the one and the many.

8. The following analysis of Nietzsche has been much influenced by Heidegger. See Heidegger 1979; 1982; 1987; and 1977f, 53–112.

9. See Heidegger 1977c, 93–206.

10. All page references in the following discussion are to Nietzsche (1954) 1978.

11. Thus, Nietzsche also says in *The Will to Power* (1972, aph. 362) that the "greatest lovers" are so from the strength of their will that wants to will beyond itself.

12. I have used Hollingdale's translation in this one instance since Kaufmann uses the female pronoun to translate references to the sun, which confuses the metaphor since it is the sea that has breasts. I prefer Hollingdale's gender-neutral translation.

13. This radical overturning in which the masculine now prevades both sides of the dualism helps us understand the enigmatic ambivalent attitude Nietzsche has toward women—examined, for instance, by Allen (in Clark and Lange 1979).

Given my analysis of Nietzsche's overturning of metaphysics in terms of what is masculine and feminine, what is feminine would be seen as inferior from the perspective of Nietzsche's new metaphysics; even in its banishment from the sensory realm, what is feminine retains its traditional characterizations that it had received from metaphysics ruled by the suprasensory realm, and, at the same time, it would be regarded with fear and respect because as the former ancient inhabitant of the sensory realm, which has become the new source of power, the feminine gains a privileged status.

14. The affect as a being-seized beyond oneself is an aspect of the Will to Power. Like the Dionysian rapture *(rausch)*, it is the capacity to extend beyond oneself and thus, when controlled and formed, is an artistic state.

15. See, for instance, Nietzsche 1972, aphs. 650, 658, and 704.

16. Freud follows Nietzsche in that he considers the libido to be masculine because of its active nature. See Freud 1952, 77. It is also interesting to note that he understands the sexuality of most men to lie ''in the necessity for overcoming the resistance of the sexual object'' (p. 21).

17. See especially Nietzsche 1972, aph. 658. In aphorisms 694 and 930 of this same work Nietzsche speaks of how the accumulated strength of desires seeks resistance. In aphorism 737 he speaks of the inability to offer resistance as a ''weakness,'' and in aphorism 777 he speaks of the weakness of women's love that, unable to offer resistance, sacrifices itself merely to an ''unbridled urge.'' We might gather from aphorisms 699, 776, and 732 discussed in the text and from these statements mentioned above that, at best, women might offer a good resistance, thereby fulfilling the phallocentric dynamic of Will to Power.

18. As Rich (1986, 67) says, ''The language of patriarchal power insists on a dichotomy: for one person to have power, other—or another—must be powerless.''

19. Although it is clear that capitalism operates according to the Will to Power's principles of power economy, in one note, Nietzsche (1972, aph. 764) suggests that the higher men would not be the owners of the means of production, for the power of the higher men lies outside the sphere of monetary exchange: ''The workers shall live one day as the bourgeois do now—but above them distinguished by their freedom from wants, the *higher caste:* that is to say, poorer and simpler, but in possession of power.''

20. The tension between the sexes is linked to that antagonism between Dionysius and Apollo in Nietzsche 1972, aph. 1050. Apollo, with his sun imagery and arrows, represents the more traditional masculine, and Dionysius, like his cult in ancient Greece, can be seen as aligned more with the feminine. Nietzsche appears to confirm this in *Twilight of the Idols* ([1968] 1977, 109–10), where in speaking of Dionysian sacrifice, he links the pain of women's childbirth experience with the pain necessary in all creating and becoming. Elsewhere, however, as I have discussed, he clearly denies women the forming power of artists.

21. See Nietzsche 1972, aph. 886; and Nietzsche [1954] 1978, 141.

22. This dialectic relation of opposition is perhaps best epitomized for feminists by Hegel's master/slave relation. That this relation is necessarily one between males is discussed in O'Brien 1983, 69–73; and Mills 1986, 74–98.

23. See Nietzsche 1972, aph. 796, which describes the world as a work of art giving birth to itself.

24. See also Mills 1991, 166, for a criticism of the Hegelian reconciliation of difference as one of domination.

25. Lampert (1986) uses Heidegger's interpretations of Nietzsche exten-

sively. However, he disagrees with Heidegger's analysis of Nietzsche's conquest of nature. Lampert argues that "Nietzsche's Zarathustra presents a teaching of loyalty to the earth, on man and woman, on morality, and on an order of rank that seems opposed to such conquest" (p. 100; see also p. 22). I think I have sufficiently shown, contrary to Lampert, that Zarathustra's "loyalty to the earth" in fact entails the earth's dominance.

26. This is particularly noticeable with the new technologies of power that arose in the seventeenth and eighteenth centuries, for they were exercised by obtaining social productive service from individuals in their concrete lives. A real and effective internal incorporation of power thus became necessary in the sense that power had to be able to gain access to the bodies of individuals, to their acts, attitudes, and modes of everyday behavior (Foucault 1980, 125).

27. The "turn" and the "step back" from metaphysics are Heideggerean notions. See Heidegger 1982, 197–252.

28. "It is already one of the prime effects of power that certain bodies, certain gestures, certain discourses, certain desires, come to be identified and constituted as individuals" (Foucault 1980, 98).

29. Irigaray attempts to do this at the level of discourse. "*What remains to be done, then, is to work at 'destroying' the discursive mechanics.* Which is not a simple undertaking" (Irigaray 1985a, 76).

30. The self-secluding and sheltering nature of earth, as Graybeal (1990, 143) discusses at length, has some similarities with Kristeva's semiotic.

31. See Rabuzzi 1982 for an analysis of the feminine mode of waiting as a positive alternative to the masculine mode of questing.

Chapter Four

1. In Nietzsche's metaphysics of the Will to Power, for example, the feminine is that which does not actively will to overpower but passively "wants to please" (Nietzsche 1972, aph. 817).

2. Maurice Godelier, Modes of production, kinship and demographic structures, in *Marxist Analysis and Social Anthropology,* ed. Maurice Bloch (New York: John Wiley and Sons, 1975). Cited in Coontz and Henderson 1986, 15.

3. The word *culture* is from the Latin *cultura,* from *colere. Colere* had a range of meanings: to inhabit, cultivate, protect, honor, and worship. The meaning of *inhabit* developed through *colonus* to *colony. Honor* and *worship* developed through the Latin *cultus* to *cult. Cultura* took on the main meaning of cultivation or tending. By the fifteenth century, the word had passed into English through the French *couture,* meaning primarily the tending of natural growth. See Williams 1976, 87–93.

4. This is how Ortner (1974) also defines it.

5. Arguments similar to this can be found in de Beauvoir 1974 and Ortner 1974, 88.

6. The so-called public/private dichotomy, of course, is not strictly parallel to the culture/nature dichotomy. The woman's socialization of children, for example, can be understood as a cultural activity, just as the male's hunting, for example, could be understood as an activity that is close to nature. In one sense, moreover, both the public and the private realms are cultural divisions, since animals, for instance, do not have this division. One also has to take into account the fact that the private realm today is thoroughly informed by the cultural public realm (consider, for instance, the influence of advertising on the modern home). For these reasons, the public/private and culture/nature dichotomies are better understood as two fluidly changing dichotomies that are linked historically through a dense web of associational meanings. What is important for my purposes here is that these dichotomies, interwoven with male/female difference, have helped to constitute a hierarchical social life that is evident on both manifest and latent levels and in which the feminine is consistently devalued.

7. Elshtain (1981), for instance, argues that the division between the basic notions of nature (phusis) and culture *(nomos)* made the more sophisticated differentiations within culture, such as that between the public and the private, possible.

8. See Nicholson 1984 for a fuller discussion of Arthur's position.

9. See Mills 1986 for an analysis of this. For an argument that the public/private dichotomy is found only with the advent of capitalism see Nicholson 1984.

10. See Coontz and Henderson 1986, 15.

11. See Coontz and Henderson 1986, 15–16.

12. See Pomeroy 1975, 57–92, on the restriction of women in classical Athens.

13. See Walker 1983 for archaeological evidence on this point.

14. There are taboos, for example, on touching women during menstruation or after childbirth and on entering a temple after intercourse, and in some periods of medieval European culture, women's aptness for handling the more polluting and darker aspects of divinity were seen as interdependent on the association of the darkness of the underworld with the darkness of the female womb (Padel 1983, 5–6).

15. The verb *jouir* (to enjoy, to experience sexual pleasure), and *la jouissance* (sexual pleasure, bliss, rapture) are terms that French feminists often use to emphasize feminine movements of fluidity, diffusion, and giving.

16. See Roach 1991 for an analysis of this.

17. Feminist criticisms of the search for immortality in Greek society can be found in Lloyd 1984, 18–22; O'Brien 1983, 116–39; and Hartsock 1985, 186–209.

18. Thus, although Heidegger will most often characterize Plato and Aristotle's metaphysics as a site that can serve to characterize the beginning of metaphysics, he will show how even Heraclitus can be understood as showing signs of the beginning of western metaphysics. Heidegger's effort is not meant to locate the exact beginning of metaphysics as a philosophical discipline but to think on the withdrawal of Being itself, which is a very vague beginning of western Being as it reveals itself in metaphysics.

For most Greek scholars, of course, Parmenides is usually understood as sowing the seeds of the philosophical discipline called metaphysics in that he, for instance, questions what we call "being" in metaphysics, though he does not name it as such but leaves the subject of his inquiry indeterminate. One could argue, however, as Owens (1959, 56–79) does, that Parmenides had no notion of any kind of reality above the sensible and thus hesitates to name Parmenides the first metaphysician.

19. *Arche* is a Greek word that can mean both the origin of something and that which holds sway over something. Heidegger (1976) thus translates it as "originating-order."

20. Heidegger (1976) in his early article on Aristotle argues that Aristotle does not collapse phusis into techne, emphasizing Aristotle's connection to the pre-Socratic thinking on phusis. I argue, on the contrary, through the analysis of the coming-to-be of a baby, that one can find in Aristotle the first glimmers of the modern western tendency to collapse phusis into techne, thereby thus emphasizing Aristotle's connection to our modern age.

21. I thus disagree with Owens ([1951] 1978, 162), who notes Aristotle's emphasis on being-responsible-for in his meaning of *aition* but believes that "the English word 'cause' renders the notion quite correctly."

22. The following analysis uses Heidegger 1976 and 1977e, 6–10.

23. Aristotle says that every entity must come to be "out of" something, "by" something, and must "become" something (*Meta*. 1069b35–36). The becoming of an entity has to do with both the formal and final causes.

24. I am using the male pronoun because that is what Aristotle uses.

25. "Constituted" is here H. G. Apostle's (Aristotle 1979) translation of the Greek word *en-hup-archov*. This word broken down into its root meanings means in, on, or according to *(en)* the beginning or originating order *(hupo-arche)*. See *Meta*. 1012b35ff.

26. We must remember, however, that the material cause is that out of which something comes to be and is not that which something is already composed of. It is true that we say the wood is in some way the matter of the build-

ing even after the building has come into being, thus calling the building wooden. However, the building has more precisely emerged *out of* the wood and *is* wooden.

Nonetheless, the case is very different with a natural entity. A tree comes *out of* its seed, but once it is standing forth as a tree, it is its matter in a different sense, for it cannot be named after its material cause. To add to the confusion, Aristotle will speak of the seed, on the one hand, as the determined potential matter or the material cause and, on the other hand, as the moving cause. This problem will arise when we try to determine the material and moving causes of the coming-to-be of a baby.

27. *Meta.* 1013b18–24. See also 1033a5–22. The Greek word for "matter" is *hulē*. *Hulē* originally meant wood, both in terms of a forest and in terms of wood for use (i.e., timber, firewood). Its meaning became extended to include matter in general, such as intelligible matter. Given the connotation of usefulness embedded in the meaning of *hulē*, it is little wonder that Aristotle insists that matter in the proper sense is potential matter. This meaning is similar to our own understanding of raw materials as natural resources.

28. Aristotle, then, will speak of matter *(hulē)* in two senses: on the one hand, it can mean the undetermined primary or ultimate matter, which is not a "this," and, on the other hand, it can mean a composite of matter and form, which is the substrate of accidents and is a "this." For a close analysis of Aristotle's uses of matter, see Owens ([1951] 1978, 330–45).

29. *Stellen* is also related to a family of verbs that make specific the various nuances of *stellen: bestellen* (to order, command, set in order); *vorstellen* (to represent); *sicherstellen* (to secure); *nachstellen* (to entrap); *verstellen* (to block of disguise); *herstellen* (to produce, to set here); and *darstellen* (to present or exhibit).

30. *Gestell* is translated by Lovitt as "enframing." However, I prefer to leave the word untranslated so that readers are brought directly to the depth of connotative meanings that resonate in the German.

31. The term *standing reserve* is a translation of Heidegger's *Bestand,* which in German ordinarily denotes a store or supply as "standing by" ready to be further ordered (Heidegger 1977e, 17–19).

32. Some contemporary environmentalists have criticized the fact that the twentieth-century environmentalists attempts at reform have resulted in mere natural resource management, leaving basic cultural assumptions about economic growth, human beings, and nature unquestioned. They are calling for a new ecological philosophy, which they call deep ecology. This new ecological movement shares some of the same concerns as Heidegger about the place of human beings on the earth and the need for a deeper ontological change. Some deep ecologists thus make use of Heidegger (and, moreover, Merleau-Ponty's

philosophy). See, for example, Abram 1988; Zimmerman 1983; Grange 1985; Foltz 1984; and Evernden 1985.

Chapter Five

1. See, for instance, Mahowald 1980, 60–69, and Thom 1976, 94–107.

2. The highest science, which is what we would call metaphysics today but which Aristotle calls first philosophy, is the investigation of the first principles *(arche)* and causes *(aitia)* *(Meta.* 982a1–3).

3. There are a number of feminists who have argued that the culture/nature dichotomy has figured importantly in the determination of the sexes. See, for instance, Merchant 1980; Stone 1976; and Lloyd 1984. What I am analyzing here is how this dichotomy operates on a metaphysical level.

4. Aristotle's emphasis on form is, nonetheless, not of course the disembodied self-sufficient Platonic Forms that Aristotle took great pains to reject. Aristotle's form is always, in sensible substances *(ousia),* tied to a particular "this." It is an *indwelling* intelligible principle of a particular entity and does not determine an entity's form from above.

5. The notion of form in Greek times, however, was likely already biased in favor of the male because of the prehistoric association of the female with the body and the earth and at least partially because of the dominant role the male played as former of temples, fortresses, weapons, and armor in the military-expansionist Greek society.

6. Aristotle 1980a, 27.

7. Recall that the main difference between natural entities and man-made entities is that natural entities have the originating order of their being moved *in* themselves, whereas man-made entities have the originating order of their being moved *outside* themselves, for example in the craftsman.

8. Aristotle 1985a, 1112.

9. In animals that move, the male and the female are separate, and thus the distinction between matter and form becomes more pronounced. However, even in plants there must be that which generates and that out of which it generates even though here the two are united in one individual. There is, then, a sexual distinction within the plant itself. What is surprising is that Aristotle says that it is better that matter be separate from form, as it is when the sexes are two individuals, because the superior principle should be separated from the inferior *(Gen. An.* 731b24ff).

This is reminiscent of Nietzsche's advocating that the gulf between the sexes (and between the effeminate herd and the higher men) must be made wider and wider. Aristotle's statement appears to suggest that it is better if form is purified from matter. Indeed, for Aristotle, nonsensible *ousia* are higher objects of contemplation than sensible *ousia.*

10. For analyses of the art and religion of the Great Mother, see Neumann [1963] 1974; Gimbutas 1989; and Stone 1976.

11. Aristotle 1985a, 1112–13.

12. See Owens (1951) 1978, 176–79, for a discussion of the dominance of form.

13. Aristotle 1980a, 36–37.

14. For a convincing argument that the use of *man* is generally gender biased, see Moulton 1981, 124–37.

15. Thus, we can already notice the dominance of the male in the cultural conception of the human being.

16. Aristotle 1979, 121.

17. He explains in the passage preceding this quotation that a thing from techne is generated by a thing that has the same name as itself. He gives the example of a house, which he says is generated by a house or by the intellect. As Apostle clarifies in his commentary (in Aristotle 1979, 334), Aristotle is referring here to the techne as it exists in the builder's soul, and this techne is the house because it is knowledge of the essence of the house or its form.

This statement is not to be confused with Aristotle's statement in the other passage we looked at from the *Physics* (193b7–12), where Aristotle says that a bedstead does not come from a bedstead; there he was referring to the nature of form in techne and phusis, whereas here he is referring to how we *name* the moving cause of such entities.

This passage should also not be confused with one that we encounter later in our discussion, in which Aristotle says that we name a man a man and not a seed. Here he is pointing out that we name an entity after its moving cause and not after its material cause, the seed.

18. It is strange that Aristotle here says the seed acts "just like things which act by art," for it would seem that though a seed has the form potentially like an artifact, which is what Aristotle is pointing out here, the way a seed grows and the way a building, for instance, comes from its blueprint are very different. In later pages, I will reflect on Aristotle's constant use of the analogy of techne to describe phusis.

19. See Aristotle 1953, xlv–xlvi, for the translator's notes on the problem with the notion of "natural abnormalities."

20. See *Phys.* 190b1–4, 191b22–25, 199b34ff, and *Meta.* 1049b4ff and 1034a9ff. The seed is both the moving and the material cause. In the seed the material cause and the moving cause are in the same thing, like the doctor who heals himself (*Meta.* 1049a15ff; *Phys.* 199b32).

How can the male seed be the material cause if, as Aristotle says in the *Generation of Animals* (737a11), "the physical part of the semen dissolves in the event of uniting with the menstrual fluid"? Even as the material cause, the semen does not truly contribute any matter as such to generation but, rather, only actively forms the passive matter of the menstrual fluid.

21. Aristotle 1979, 153.

22. That actual physical movements of the father are involved as well as the internal moving from phusis in the seed is suggested by *Gen. An.* 734b8–13 and also, for instance, in *Phys.* 261a1–9.

23. See, for instance, *Meta.* 1071a13–18 and 1013a31.

24. The correlation between the phallus and the conquering of space is obvious. As Garb (1990, 272) says, the whole drama is enacted along an axis of verticality.

25. Aristotle 1985a, 1134–35.

26. Aristotle uses this same example in the *Metaphysics* when he explains why actuality is prior to potentiality in time. There he says that there must be an actual man before the potential seed (*Meta.* 1049b17ff). Later in this same passage he says that actuality is also prior to potentiality in substance *(ousia)* and uses the example of a "man from a man," stating that a man is prior to the seed because the man has form of a man actually, whereas the seed does not (*Meta.* 1050a5ff).

27. See Aristotle 1980b, 205nn. 30 and 31, for translator's commentary.

28. Aristotle was obviously intrigued by the relation between techne and phusis, since he continually meditates on them in his writings. However, more often than not, he shows the similarities between phusis and techne rather than their differences. Though he undoubtedly understood phusis, in distinction from techne, as the highest mode of bringing-forth and was thereby reaching back to an earlier conception of phusis, it would seem from his constant use of techne to describe phusical processes that he also tended to understand phusis in terms of techne and thereby was pointing forward to our modern conception of phusis.

29. Aristotle generally understands phusis as one genus of Being (sensible *ousia*), but occasionally he reverts back to the broader, pre-Socratic understanding of phusis. See, for instance, *Meta.* 1003a27 where he says that Being is something like phusis. I owe this finding to Heidegger 1976, 268.

30. That there is a world of difference between the Aristotelean notion of *energeia* and the modern physicist's conception of energy becomes apparent when we consider that energy is linked to matter and *dunamis,* which is the contrary of *energeia* for Aristotle.

31. See the introduction to Coontz and Henderson 1986 for a discussion of cultural and historical variations of the public/private social structure.

32. I am not suggesting, however, that, for instance, Aristotle's naming of phusis as form is the "cause" of our modern devaluation of childbearing and rearing. I am not looking for direct causes of the problem and thus do not make

causal claims. I would not claim, for example, that if Aristotle had not named phusis form we would not have the culture/nature dichotomy today. The direction that history takes is always open and indeterminate. It is not the case that one historical event necessarily leads to another in order to achieve an implicit preordained end (as, for example, Hegel and Marx suggest).

33. Roach (1991) has shown, for example, that the association of the environment with the self-sacrificing maternal tends to reinforce a perception of nature as a storehouse of riches for our use. One could also argue, however, that the very notion of mother in the near future will undergo significant changes because of birth control and gay and lesbian parenting, for example.

34. See Heidegger 1971a and 1971e on this notion.

"Minoan Snake Goddess"

1. See Nietzsche (1968) 1977; and (1961) 1976, 214; also Blake in Erdman 1982, 19. Note that for Blake, Heaven and Hell are two contraries (which are both positives) that must be married, which he attempts in, for example, his "The Marriage of Heaven and Hell." In a like manner the clod and the pebble can be understood as both "positives."

2. See Saliou 1986 for a good discussion of this issue.

3. See Eisler 1987 for a discussion of this issue.

4. For the Minoans, it seems that bending backward was admired as a capacity for bending sinuously to another and would not be understood as a submission to another's power. Our expression of "bending backward" for someone, by contrast, means going too much out of one's way to accommodate another's wishes.

5. The extraordinary beauty of Minoan art and its celebration of nature is well recognized. For the importance of the Minoans as the last pre-Greek culture to live according to the nonwestern Goddess, see Scully 1982; Saliou 1986; and Eisler 1987.

6. There is a fragment of a fresco of a young woman's head with her hair flying out from her as she swirls around, indicating that she is dancing (1500–1450 B.C., from Knossos, Archaeological Museum, Heraklion). Since the fresco was found in an important room of the Knossos palace, the queen's Mergaron, we can assume that dancing was likely an important cultural event, as it is in so many cultures. There is also another fresco fragment (after 1600 B.C. from Knossos, Archaeological Museum, Heraklion) of many women gathered together dressed in open-bodice, flounced dresses and seated on a special viewing platform, talking gaily to one another. In the background are other women and men (although their sex is not clear) talking excitedly to one another. They have obviously gathered at the palace for some special event,

and one can only surmise that it is either in connection with the bull leaping or with the snake goddess dancing or performing some kind of ritual activity. (Tubular vessels with milk cups, moreover, which archaeologists believe were used for feeding domesticated snakes, were found at the palace at Knossos. This evidence suggests that snakes were indeed kept at Knossos.)

7. Every openness, it would seem, however, can become twisted, distorted into a means of overpowering another. Thus, we see the responsiveness of the flexuous human body geared to the overpowering of another in many Greek works; for instance, the famous bronzes of the same transitional period as the west pediment of the Temple of Zeus at Olympia, the statue of Poseidon (460 B.C.) in the Athens Museum, and *The Charioteer* in the Delphi Museum. Every muscle of Poseidon is guided by the direction of his eye and the aim of his weapon (which is missing but was likely a trident). He rocks back on his feet, readying himself to deliver his weapon, for the purposes of overcoming another, with the full force of his body, guided by his keen eye and sure aim. In *The Charioteer,* the well-recognized superb responsiveness of his body is also channeled along lines of power. He looks ahead over his horses, completely attuned to their movements. His feet lightly touch the chariot floor, responsive to the chariot's every jolt and turn, which require the achievement of continual new balances. The goal of *The Charioteer,* and of charioteers in athletic contests in general, is to win the chariot race, in this instance, the Pythian Games, by maintaining superb control of the wildly galloping horses.

8. Nietzsche, in his *Thus Spoke Zarathustra* (1976), also describes a wild but friendly relation to a snake when he gives us a memorable symbol of Will to Power: the eagle carrying a snake, who is his writhing friend, in his talons. The relation here, however, is different from that of the Snake Goddess and her snakes, for though the eagle does not attempt to suppress the snake's movements, it does not bend to the snake's wriggling but maintains its command, a command that is ultimately in opposition to the snake.

9. The first *Winged Victories* are images of swirling terror, depicting the chaos on the battlefield, and the chance involved in a battle's outcome more than the celebration of certain victory.

10. It is interesting to compare the drapery of the women in this pediment with the straight, controlled drapery of *The Charioteer* (470 B.C.). Such swirling robes are also found most prominently in the Greek *Winged Victories,* who were often mounted on the prows of ships or high on a rock in the harbor. The chaos of the drapery of these statues revelas the fragility of the *Winged Victories* momentary balance (victory) in the strong winds.

11. The athleticism of the Minoans, who delighted in arching and swirling into another's movement, is in stark contrast to this Greek athleticism, which is oriented to the overpowering of another. The Greeks admired the power and beauty of the controlled body and praised the will power of the athletes

and their competitive determination to win. The Olympic games of Greece were, for the most part, matches of military prowess that, moreover, excluded women.

12. Nor would I call it Dionysian. Dionysius reappears in the Olympiad in a revival of the older cthonic religion and in opposition to the cool rationality of Apollo. We know him as the demigod who inspired ecstatic revelries through wine and sexual play. The Dionysian rapture is a letting loose of dark earthly forces in direct opposition to the Apollonian rationality. However, we cannot call the Snake Goddess's ecstasy Dionysian, since the dichotomies of rational and irrational and chaos and order, which came to determine Dionysius's being, were not yet formed in the Minoan culture.

13. Chevrons (double or triple V's), parallel lines, zigzags, or wavy parallel lines are usual motifs on breasted vessels from the Paleolithic through the Neolithic, Copper, and Bronze ages. These motifs would seem to indicate streams of milk/rain flowing from the breasts. Moreover, on Buuk vases, breasts are shown in the midst of snake heads, and wavy lines emanate from them (Gimbutas 1989).

14. As Eisler (1990, 30) says, "Power was seen as . . . the capacity to create and nurture life. It was power to, rather than power over."

Chapter Six

1. The appeal of the western development project, which has usurped traditional practices that were often more connected to the ecosystem, to so-called undeveloped countries of the "Two Thirds World" gains its force from these western definitions of creativity and productivity.

2. Deep ecology similarily locates a key problem of our ecodestructivity in our anthropocentrism and separation from nature and advocates a reconceptualization of being human in a way that will reconnect us to nature. As ecofeminists have pointed out, however, because deep ecology is not sensitive to the androcentrism that is intrinsically linked to our contemporary anthropocentrism, it continues to rely on metaphysical dualisms that have been inimical to both women and nature. For some central articles on this debate see, for example, Plumwood 1991; Salleh 1983; Kheel 1985; W. Fox 1987; Zimmerman 1987; Cheney 1987; Warren 1990.

3. See Harding 1986; and Keller 1985, for feminist critiques of this method as androcentric. The (Kantian) view that desire, caring, and love are merely personal and particular emotions and are ultimately unreliable for founding a universal and impartial ethical theory also depends on this Cartesian separation of reason and emotion. See Plumwood 1991 for a feminist critique of neo-Kantian views used in environmental ethics.

4. See Nye 1988, 31–72, for an overview of the feminist approach to Marx-

ism, and Warren and Cheney 1987 for an ecofeminist perspective. Donald Lee (1980) argues, in contrast to the general Marxian attitude to nature that I have mentioned here, that for Marx nature is not an other but "man's body," and that to follow this aspect of Marx's writing to its conclusion would involve a stewardship of the ecosystem. Michael Allen Fox (1987, 171–72) also argues that in Marx's early essays on alienation, alienation from nature is to be included.

5. The passage continues. "So if things by nature were to be generated not only by nature but also by art, they would have been generated just as they are by nature disposed to be generated. So one stage is for the sake of the next. In general, in some cases art completes what nature cannot carry out to an end, in others, it imitates nature" (*Phys.* 199a12–17).

Aristotle uses this example to show how both techne and phusis work toward a *telos* or end. Both techne and phusis are "by nature [phusis]" disposed to move toward their end (*Phys.* 199a11). What Aristotle means by "by nature" is that the *telos* of a building, for example, is phusical, just as that of a tree. Phusis holds sway in both techne and phusis with regard to their *telos*.

Note, moreover, that because phusis always guides techne (at every stage because it works toward a phusical end), Aristotle does not imagine that things generated by nature could be generated by techne alone. He says, "if things by nature were to be generated not only by nature but also by art," thereby necessarily including phusis in the coming-to-be.

6. See Pollitt 1974, 223.

7. Werner Jaeger, *Paideia: The Ideals of Greek Culture,* 2d ed. (New York, 1945), 126, cited in Pollitt 1974, 224. As Pollitt (1974, 220–25) explains, modern scholars have fallen into two basic camps on the question of the etymology of the word *rhythmos:* those who derive *rhythmos* from *rhew,* meaning "flow," and those who connect it with *erhuw* and related words, either in the sense of "draw" or in the sense of "protect, guard, hold in honor." Eugen Petersen's account, which is explained in some detail by Pollitt and favors the latter position, would seem to be the most convincing. See Eugen Petersen "Rhythmus," *Abhandlungen der Kön. Gesellschaft der Wissensschaften su Göttingen, Phil.-Hist. Klasse* 16 (1917): 1–104.

8. Irigaray (1985a, 76) urges women to mime the traditional feminine deliberately and thereby to convert "a form of subordination into an affirmation, and thus to begin to thwart it." With a view to reinventing the relation of difference itself, she reappropriates the attitudes of the other, in order to subvert from the inside the appearances given by phallocentrism and unravel the oppositional relation altogether.

9. In German *nahern* means to bring near and is also related to *nahen,* to sew or stitch. See Graybeal 1990, 136–38, on this connection in Heidegger.

10. See Plumwood 1991, 15.

11. Some ecofeminists (see, for example, Cheney 1987; and Plumwood 1991) have criticized deep ecologists for falling into a "mystical indistinguishability" when attempting to reconceptualize our relations to nature and have pointed to possible androcentric biases in this account of the self. As Plumwood argues, we need a description of the human being that allows for continuity and difference.

12. See Heidegger 1966, 61, where the scientist and the scholar in the conversation say that releasement lies beyond the distinction between activity and passivity because releasement does not belong to the domain of the will. I understand the distinction of activity and passivity to sustain at one and the same time the Will to Power and sexual difference as opposition. See Cixous and Clément 1975, 64, on how passivity has been central to the traditional definition of women.

13. I agree with Irigaray that western metaphysics of Being is a metaphysics of solids. However, her reliance on physics to explicate the notion of fluid shows that she is not critical enough of the metaphysical phallocentric presuppositions upon which this science is founded. See Schor 1989, 48–55, for a criticism of Irigaray's use of Descartes and physics.

14. The natural determinants of the body are not fixed biological facts but, as I have described in detail in Chapters One and Two, are indeterminate fleshy aspects of our connatural body that open us to the world-earth-home. We find ourselves already born into an incarnate situation in which our body adheres through no effort on our part. Although this blind noncognitive adherence of our connatural body can only be separated from our cultural being in an abstract, artificial way and is difficult to describe because of its indeterminacy and ambiguity and because of the inadequacy of our dichotomous concepts, there is a dire ecological need to articulate such natural codeterminants of the body.

15. See Heidegger 1977c, 96.

16. In the next chapter, I discuss this relation between reason and feeling in more detail by turning to the Greeks.

17. I owe this way of describing the problem to Gatens 1991, 113, where she defends the theories of Irigaray and Cixous, describing their aim as showing the ways in which woman, the feminine, and female sexuality exceed the complementary role they have been assigned in gender dichotomies.

18. I use the term ecocentric rather than biocentric because the prefix *bio* refers etymologically to living organisms, whereas ecocentric has broader ecological connotations. For this distinction, see W. Fox 1987, 7–8.

19. *Friede,* the word for peace, means the free, or preserved from harm and danger, or spared (Heidegger 1971a, 148–49).

20. In all our dwelling, moreover, we dwell with things. A thing is not an unknown X to which perceptible properties are attached but is a gathering of the fourfold of earth and sky, mortals and history. See Heidegger 1971e, 165–86.

21. Because of the increased percentage of elderly people in our society, the care-giving burden of the elderly is far heavier today. This burden is usually taken on by women. As Post (1990) argues, this care giving must not remain as a female role but must become culturally important.

22. "When Una was inside me, her cells and my cells were shared, were flowing. Were we one person then? I ate, nourished her, my blood became hers, I drank milk and she grew bones. She is born and she is herself, but for a while, we still share those cells. She is outside me, and she is sloughing old cells, growing new ones. She is growing her own cells with milk from my body. Whose cells are they? Where do I stop and where does she begin?

"In a clear box I keep what is left of her/my umbilical cord, the part of us that dried up and fell away" (Lounder and Maestro 1990, 2).

23. For a description of how our bodies' acquisition of a new habit, such as learning to type, is a bodily knowledge, see Merleau-Ponty 1962, 142–47.

24. Even Aristotle qualifies the superiority of universal knowledge with the statement that unless a man has knowledge of the individual included under the universal category, he will fail to cure.

25. I would add to this that we are mortal not only because we can die but because we are born. We are not thrown into the openness of being, as Heidegger says in *Being and Time,* but are delivered over to our being. We are held in the rhythms of "contraction and expansion," as William Blake would say, or in the "inspiration and expiration" of Being, as Merleau-Ponty (1982, 167) calls it. As Mary O'Brien (1983) has suggested, we need a "philosophy of birth" to temper existential philosophy's emphasis on death and angst. In our everyday existence, we not only tend to be afraid of death but we also take our birth for granted. We tend to suppress the phusical rhythms of coming-to-be and passing-away, which are not merely single events at the beginning and end of our individual lives but are simultaneous lifelong sways of our phusical being.

Whereas Mary O'Brien contrasts the possible new philosophy of birth with what she feels in the western tradition has been a death-oriented philosophy, I would suggest that death and birth (coming-to-be and passing-away) are both essential to our phusical being. Thus, the emphasis on our being toward death in existentialist writings, which she criticizes, from my perspective is healthy, especially in the light of the suppression of death that we find, for instance, in Plato and that characterizes metaphysics as a whole. I would agree, however, that this emphasis on death must be tempered with a thinking on birth.

26. Revenge is "the will's ill against time and its "it was" (Nietzsche [1954] 1978, 140).

27. Body and spirit are not reconciled in Nietzsche. Nietzsche, rather, aims for that which is higher than any reconcilation, with the result that the body, like the snake writhing in the mouth of its supposed friend, the eagle, is taken away from its earthy habitation (Nietzsche [1954] 1978, 25).

28. Ruddick (1989, 49) also criticizes the notion of birth as a kind of production.

29. "When and in what way do things appear as things?" asks Heidegger (1971e, 181). "They do not appear *by means of* human making. But neither do they appear without the vigilance of mortals. The first step toward such vigilance is the step back from the thinking that merely represents—that is, explains—to the thinking that responds and recalls." For things to appear as things constitutes the "nearing" of the world.

30. As I see it, both birth control and abortion take place within the neighborhood of cultivating. It is not that pregnancy is "merely" natural, whereas abortion and birth control are cultural acts that transform nature for human ends (see Mills 1991, 167). This formulation is couched in the culture/nature opposition. Abortion and birth control have been conceptualized as cultural or technological control over the natural functions of one's body because of a variety of factors, some of which include the prevalent biological model of the body, our conceptualization of culture, and in the case of abortion, moreover, the control asserted by patriarchal legal systems, governments, and institutions over a woman's body. Even abortion (by choice) can be an act in accordance with nature rather than in opposition to nature since psycho-phusical health is usually the primary consideration (which includes such factors as the woman's economic circumstances, the needs of any other children, the availability of support from significant others) in the difficult decision. In the coming forward of the rapidly growing embryo, there must be respect for the drawing back of the mother who is faced with the realities of her phallocentric material circumstances.

If we as a culture were "closer to nature," women would have less need for abortions, not because they would "by nature" carry unwanted pregnancies to term, but because a healthier cultural attitude to nature and to our phusical sexual bodies would give rise to an open eroticism free of sadomasochism and repression (and thus less rape, teenage intercourse, and habitual intercourse) and to preventive measures (i.e., safer, more effective, and readily available birth control methods) that would decrease the number of unwanted pregnancies.

31. The androcentrism and uncaring practices of the psychiatric profession have been described, for example, by Elaine Showalter and Kate Millet.

Chapter Seven

1. This understanding of movement is recognizably Aristotelean. Aristotle understood movements as kinds of changes *(metabole)* from something to something else. *Metabole* comes from *metaballo,* which means to turn quickly or suddenly, as to turn earth over when one is preparing it for planting. In a movement or change, then, something that has been concealed and absent suddenly breaks forth into appearance, or something that is unconcealed and present reclines into concealment.

For Aristotle, there are three kinds of movement: movement with regard to place, movement with regard to how a being is, and movement with regard to how much or how great a being is. Sometimes he included a fourth kind of movement that encompassed all the rest: the coming-to-be of a being, which is a movement with regard to substance (the *ousia* or a being). See, for example, *Phys.* 226a23–36.

2. See Bookchin 1982, 43, commenting on this modern prejudice.

3. In the ancient waterwheel, flowing water was directed into cups of buckets attached to the perimeter of a wheel or to the ends of wide spokes. The waterwheel's rotating axle could be used to turn a millstone either directly or by means of gears and belts.

4. Some ancient waterwheels actually made music as they turned. There are some still singing today. I had the opportunity to visit one in Fayuum, Egypt.

5. See note 13 in Chapter Six, where I criticize Irigaray's reliance on mechanical physics to explicate feminine fluidity in contrast to what she calls the phallocentric metaphysics of solids.

6. According to one engineer at the Niagara Falls hydroelectric plant, the ideal hydraulic fluid would be mercury because of its density.

7. For a criticism of the Gaia hypothesis, see Cheney 1987, 125.

8. Physics understands electromagnetic energy as in fact existing independent of any kind of physical body. See Heisenberg 1962, 111.

9. The word *energy* comes from the Greek word *energeia,* which is a central Aristotelean notion for Being as *ousia.* However, there is a world of difference between the Aristotelean notion of *energeia* as a standing-in-the work, or a stillness that has itself in its *telos,* and the modern physicist's conception of energy. This becomes apparent when we consider that energy is linked to matter and *dunamis,* which Aristotle understood as the contrary of form and *energeia.* As Heidegger says, it is through *dunamis* and not *energeia* that we find the link with the modern physicist's notion of energy. *Dunamis,* already taken up as *potentia* through the Latin, becomes for modern physics that force that can produce effects and can be acted upon by other forces. In understanding energy as force, we have followed Plato, who thinks beingness as what condi-

tions and makes possible, which is *dunamis,* rather than following Aristotle, who regards substance as *energeia* and whose thinking is an attempt to swing back to earlier thought (Heidegger 1982, 172). See also Heidegger 1979, 64.

10. The precise mathematical formulation of these natural laws that determine the forms of energy in its transforming is not yet known. However, modern physics works toward this goal, and it is expected in the near future that a closed mathematical system of formulas will be found completely representing the natural laws for the transformations of energy (see Heisenberg 1962, 72 and 156). Heisenberg (1962, 72) believes that the final equation for motion of matter will probably be some "quantized nonlinear wave equation for a wave field of operators that simply represent matter."

11. Physics, says Heidegger (1977a, 118), not only makes use of mathematics but is itself mathematical. It proceeds only insofar as something is projected in advance as what is already known. In order for nature to be known, it must fit into a mathematical schema, which is interconnected so as to form a closed system. Each concept must be represented by a mathematical symbol, and the connections between the concepts are represented by mathematical equations. Thus, all possible phenomena can be represented by possible solutions. The nature taken up by modern physics, then, is only that nature that can be calculated in advance. The laws of nature, moreover, which physics establishes through experiment, are also accomplished with reference to this mathematized ground plan. To set up an experiment means to represent the conditions under which a specific series of movements can be controlled in advance by calculation.

12. In Husserlian terms, this can be understood as the relation between the theoretical world and the lived world. The relation between the theories of science and the lifeworld is not clear in Husserl's thinking. On the one hand, since the lifeworld is cultural, scientific theories must flow into the lifeworld. However, if this is so, then the pregiven lifeworld so affected cannot be "pretheoretical," as Husserl maintains. For a discussion of this problem, see Carr 1980, 190–211.

13. In the usual understanding of energy, moreover, unlocking the atom's energy was an important technological advance that we hope will provide a virtually unlimited supply of energy even as it presses us to the limits of our command. It is well known that our consumption of energy has increased dramatically in the last two hundred years and that westerners are by far the greatest energy consumers. The lack of nonrenewable energy forms and the resultant higher prices have encouraged western governments to rely more on renewable energy forms and the public to conserve energy (reduce, recycle, reuse).

14. Energy, as the transformable form, moves in the same manner as the

Nietzschean Power of Will to Power. The Will to Power is an imposing of the character of Being on Becoming. Its becoming guarantees constant enhancement of power, and its fixed principles of movement guarantee the constant economical conservation of power. The transformability and constancy characteristic of energy, moreover, are essential to the continual circulation of eternal recurrence. Thus aph. 1063 of *Will to Power* (Nietzsche 1972) reads, "The law of the conservation of energy demands *eternal recurrence.*"

15. This setting-in-place of forms is an essential characteristic of techne. For instance, the *eidos* of a table in the carpenter's soul is something that has to have been fixed or set in place beforehand so that it is steadily at his disposal in order to be used to make the table.

16. This new synthesis is similar to the synthesis of the masculine higher men and the nonmasculine herd that gives the Overman discussed in Chapter Three. In the manner of Hegelian dialectics, passive matter is simultaneously negated and joined to active form for the sake of furthering power.

17. An increasingly popular form of storing in the hydroelectric plant system is "pumped storage." Pumped storage is the storing of energy during periods of low demand in order to use it later to meet periods of high demand. The surplus of energy of the low demand period is used to operate pumps that pump water up to a storage reservoir. Pumped storage is becoming important not only as an economical way of operating hydroelectric plants but as a way of using entire hydroelectric plants as storage units to ensure the steady operation of nuclear plants, which are locked into the hydroelectric network. Thus, existing dams that are plugged into the energy system of other hydroelectric plants in the continent are converted to exclusively pumped storage plants, and new pumped storage plants are built alongside nuclear plants. Pumped storage is a more sophisticated form of the storage reservoir since the whole plant serves as a storage reservoir, but the principle of storing, which we are examining here, is the same.

18. Storing can also be used to overcome nature's lack of abundance. For example, lakes are stocked with fish to improve recreational fishing because the fish population has declined due to overfishing and industrial pollution.

19. I am not thinking here of modern agricultural production and the animal production industry, which are not guided by the rhythms of nature but are geared to the highest productivity that is technologically possible.

20. Evernden (1985, 65–67) points out this distinction that the early Heidegger makes between present-at-hand nature (which is the neutral and objective nature of science) and ready-to-hand nature (which is equipmental). However, Evernden mistakenly links Heidegger's later notion of nature as a standing reserve of natural resources to his early notion of nature as present-at-hand, leaving the notion of ready-to-hand as the more "authentic" nature. I would suggest, on the contrary, that the later Heideggerean notion of standing

reserve has crucial associations with his early notion of nature as ready-to-hand, in other words as "equipmental," and may be a synthesis of present and ready-to-hand. When we recall that a main characteristic of standing reserve is its insidious objectlessness, its ontological status as standing by for use, we can see both its associations with the chain of "in-order-to's" that characterize ready-to-hand tools and its dissimilarity with the standing-against *(gegenstand)* of the present-at-hand objects of science.

21. Heidegger 1971c, 28.

22. The discovery of alternating current in 1886 made electricity feasible as an energy source, for then electricity could be distributed from the point of generation over great distances without using much power.

23. Because of these interconnections, the actual electromagnetic energy that we use in Toronto to make our coffee may have been generated in the southern United States. Moreover, a short that might occur in one plant can affect other power stations across the country.

24. Moira is really a gathering of three moon goddesses (Moerae): Clotho, Lachesis, and Atropos. Clotho is the spinner of the linen thread, Lachesis is the disposer of lots who measures the thread with her rod, and Atropos, the smallest but most fearful of all the Fates, is she who cannot be turned *(tropos)* or avoided. She snips the thread of life with her shears.

Moerae means a share or phase. There are three goddesses because the moon has three phases: the new moon (the maiden goddess of spring), the full moon (the nymph goddess of summer), and the old moon (the crone goddess of autumn) (Graves 1960, 48–49). Zeus himself is subject to the Moerae because they are not his children but daughters of the Great Goddess Necessity, *Dike*.

25. I understand *telos* here as that which grants boundaries and determines the regioning of a coming-to-be rather than as a predetermined end or closure.

26. For Heidegger the immortals of fourfolded Being are absent in our age. If there is some correlation between the four causes and Heidegger's fourfold, which I believe is implicitly suggested in his writings, then the immortals are the *telos* of the fourfold. (In discussing the nature of a thing, Heidegger uses Aristotle's four causes as exemplifying an approach that reduces the thing to use object, and he offers his own approach of fourfolded Being as a way that resuscitates the thing as thing. His fourfold is rooted in Aristotle's four causes, but it is a fouring that attempts to make the step back from metaphysics. Earth roughly corresponds to the Aristotelean matter; sky corresponds to form; the immortals, to *telos;* and mortals, to the moving cause.) The immortals are that element of the fourfold responsible for the granting of boundaries to Being. Through this granting of various kinds of limits *(peras),* historical destining occurs.

27. See Heidegger 1982, 244–50.

Chapter Eight

1. Holmes Rolston III (in "The Human Standing in Nature: Storied Fitness in the Moral Observer" presented at the Values and Moral Standing Conference at Bowling Green State University, April 1986) argues, for example, that Aldo Leopold's famous holistic ethical principle that a thing is right when it tends to preserve the integrity, stability, and beauty of a biotic community should be understood as tied to the specific sand counties of Wisconsin. See Cheney 1989, 125, on this point.

2. My way of phrasing this is indebted to Caputo 1987, 240.

3. The Enlightenment, for example, as Caputo (1987, 254) points out, in asserting the autonomy of subjectivity also discovered the legitimate aspirations of the individual to be included in the common good.

4. As Spivak (1988, 140) says, in order for the difference between the Indo-European world and China to stand, the "splendid, decadent, multiple, oppressive, and more than millennial polytheistic tradition of India has to be written out of the *Indo*-European picture."

5. See Warren and Cheney 1991, 152, for how this is a distinctive difference between ecofeminism and deep ecology.

6. Shiva (1990) uses S. R. Barnet's (*The Lean Years* [London: Abacus, 1980]) distinction between poverty as subsistence living and poverty as misery resulting from displacement and deprivation.

7. "There are several reasons why the high-technology-export crop model increases hunger. Scarce land, credit, water, and technology are pre-empted for the export market. Most hungry people are not affected by the market at all. . . . The profit flows to corporations that have no interest in feeding hungry people without money" (Barnet, *The Lean Years,* p. 171, cited in Shiva 1990, 198).

8. For example, many African people in areas subject to drought used to grow millet, which is resistant to drought, and rotate it seasonally. Privatization of land and the expansion of wheat as a cash crop have replaced the growing of this local food in the name of development and have created famine (Griffin 1990, 95).

9. See, for example, Gwaganad 1989; and Plant 1989, 251.

10. As Minh-ha (1989, 54) says following Ivan Illich, "The perception of the outsider as the one who needs help has taken on the successive forms of the barbarian, the pagan, the infidel, the wild man, the native, and the 'underdeveloped.' "

11. For the similarities in the ideology of the wild between wildlife films and social anthropology movies, see Wilson 1991, 148–55.

12. "Trying to find the other by defining otherness or by explaining the

other through laws and generalities is, as Zen says, like beating the moon with a pole or scratching an itchy foot from the outside of a shoe'' (Minh-ha 1989, 76).

13. See Levin 1985, 264. He urges us to attempt to let go of ''the patriarchal body of moral law,'' or the ''nomological ego-body'' and retrieve our moral body of biopsychic wholeness laid down by matriarchal culture (p. 227). This is a *nomos* that ''sings.'' *Nomos* in its Delian meaning was a song in praise of morally exemplary heroic deeds (p. 246).

14. Caputo is here speaking of *Gelassenheit,* translated as ''releasement'' or ''letting-be.''

15. As Kheel (1990, 84) says, ''Our economy reflects our system of values, in which profit replaces inherent value as the ultimate measure of all things. If we saw ourselves as interconnected parts of the living being that is the earth . . . we could no longer justify economic exploitation.''

16. Donella H. Meadows et al., in *The Limits of Growth,* a report for Club of Rome's Project on the Predicament of Mankind (1972) (London and Sydney: Pan Books, 1974), p. 24. Cited in Atfield 1991, 16.

17. For an example of how ethical relations are developed on the basis of economic relations, see Cheney 1987. Individuals, he explains, are externally related bundles of interests protected by right. This possession of rights generates conflicts among individuals that are typically resolved by establishing some sort of pecking order among the rights or some rank of ordering of interests that can be satisfied by the individuals involved.

18. As Foucault (1980, 96) says, ''The system of rights, the domain of the law, are permanent agents of relations of domination and polymorphous techniques of subjugation, that function within the social organism.''

19. The first recorded political meaning of *nomos* occurs in Aeschylus's *Supplices,* where the chorus of female Oceanids, who have been resigned to live under the rule of Zeus, indicate that Zeus has won their acceptance because of his superior power. Although in Hesiod's first use of *nomos,* the early Zeus already has the authority to dispense general norms, in the *Supplices* what is regarded as valid and binding under the dispensation of Zeus is unprecedented, idiosyncratic, and enacted without the consent of the governed. Zeus's authority later becomes invested in human rulers (for instance, Creon in *Antigone*). Cited in Ostwald 1969, 21 and 44.

20. This first legal application of *nomos* would help explain the root meaning of *nomos* in *nemw,* meaning ''to distribute,'' as well as the relation of *nomos* with *nomos* (with the accent on the last syllable rather than the first), which means a pasture or place for cattle to graze or an abode alloted to one.

21. The Gortyn laws, whose inscription dates from the fifth century B.C. but whose antiquated laws (so called by Aristotle) applied mostly to serfs, de-

scendents of vanquished people, seem to reflect back to the Cretan civilization of one thousand years before. They display laws in which women had significant rights (see Saliou 1986, 177).

22. Jarret (1990, 36) contrasts *nomos* (in its later use) as social and political habits and customs that are socially constructed and historically specific with *logos* as the permanent or natural structure of law, rationality, or language. Because *nomos* is a discursive construction of changeable codes, it can be helpful in subverting the universality of *logos*. I argue on the contrary, that by following *nomos* and *logos* further back, that *logos* is a gathering rather than a universality and that *nomos* as an external ordering does not allow for difference.

23. Because *nomos* describes social norms and customs, there is a sense that these norms can be accepted without question. Thus, in the second half of the fifth century the "truth" of *nomos* is questioned, and *nomos* as mere convention is seen as inhibiting human freedom and is contrasted with what is natural. For example, in Plato's *Gorgias* (1982, 483b ff), Callicles in a Nietzschean fashion criticizes *nomos* as the work of the weak and the mere majority who are not capable of unleashing the power of phusis. Callicles is, in effect, attempting to sanction hedonism and egoism.

24. See Harrison 1977, 527, for the similarity of Dike to the Buddhist *rta* and the Chinese *tao*.

25. See Zimmerman 1983, 104 and 122, where this point is also discussed.

26. See Zimmerman 1983; and Evernden 1985, 69. Following Heidegger, these authors also describe the need for a new ethos.

27. Graybeal (1990, 139) also mentions this need.

28. Every Greek *polis* based itself on its *nomos*. The home, of course, in the sense of the nondiscursive private realm is also governed by the *nomoi* of the *polis*. However, the *polis* as a structured body politic developed specifically in contrast to home and in opposition to phusis (Hartsock 1985, 193). Thus, eco-nomics, the laws of home, express an external ordering that takes place within the body politic of power and often in opposition to nature.

29. This was pointed out to me in a conversation with Sheila McCusker.

30. The suppression of gathering can also be seen in archaeological/anthropological interpretations of the evolution of culture. New interpretations of the evidence suggest that gatherers rather than hunters were central figures in early social organizations, and that the first tools were containers, baskets, and bowls used to carry food gathered, not tools of violence. See, for example, Collard 1989, 40–41.

31. See Seidel 1964, 87–106; and Loscerbo 1981, 10–16, on this crucial issue in Heidegger. For Heidegger's own treatment of *logos* and phusis, see Heidegger 1977c, 126–32, and "*Logos* (Heraclitus, Fragment B 50)" in Heidegger 1975, 59–79.

32. Heidegger argues that Heraclitus (for example in B 1 and B 2) makes a distinction between hearing words and hearing the *logos*. When, for example, in B 50 we are cautioned to listen not to words but to the *Logos,* Heraclitus is indicating this broader and earlier meaning of *logos* that is connected with phusis.

33. "If we are blind to everything [in the grape harvest] but the sequence of steps, then the bringing-together follows the picking and gleaning, the bringing-in follows the bringing-together, until finally everything is accommodated in bins and storage rooms. This gives rise to the illusion that preservation and safekeeping have nothing to do with gathering. Yet what would become of a vintage which has not been gathered with an eye to the fundamental matter of its being sheltered [Bergen]? The sheltering comes first in the essential formation of the vintage" (Heidegger 1975, 61). I have changed the translation of *Zusammenbringen* to "bringing-together," since the translator sometimes translates it as "collecting," which seems to me a mode of amassing that Heidegger is criticizing here. Moreover, I have translated *Einbringen* more literally as "bringing-in," rather than "bringing under shelter" or "sheltering," to let the connotations of "bringing" come more into focus and because *Bergen* is also translated here as "sheltering," which in this instance is a more appropriate translation.

34. Although ultimately the forward-directed, aggressive, goal-oriented challenging-forth of *Gestell* is nonetheless a kind of historical gathering (the *Ge* of *Gestell*) and thereby a "granting" that holds the "saving" yet it is a gathering that has lost touch with the round holding essential to the ontological movements of presencing as *poiesis* (bringing-forth from concealment).

35. Truth too is imaged as round by Parmenides. In fragment 1.29 he speaks of "the unshaken heart of well-rounded truth" (*a-letheia,* "unconcealment") (Kirk and Raven 1987, 243).

36. Prehistoric houses (which were often round) were often built around a hearth, and many important artifacts from early peoples have been found in the hearth. The guarding and tending of the fire was crucial to early peoples' social and phusical being in the world-earth-home, since it was the source of warmth, light, and food preparation.

37. Every meal began and ended with a libation to Hestia, newborn children were carried around the hearth to bring them within the family circle, and all public and private worship invoked her.

38. Erich Neumann ([1963] 1974, 211–39) describes how the elementary character of Feminine appears in myths as what he calls "the Great Round."

39. In fragment 30 (Diels-Kranz), Heraclitus describes the deepest ontological structure of phusis or Being as an "everliving fire, being kindled in measures and being put out in measures." It is difficult for us to make sense of this

fragment, yet the importance of the fire for early people and its continuing sacred importance even in Heraclitus's day give weight to this thought. For Heraclitus, the fire is *to phronimon,* which can be translated as "thoughtful," or "meditative." The meditative fire is the gathering that lays open everything that presences, and shelters it in its presencing. "Its meditating," says Heidegger (1975, 118), "is the heart, i.e. the lighting-sheltering expanse, of the world."

40. The *spalanchna,* moreover, "speak," which helps explain the enduring Greek practice of entrail-divination (see Padel 1983, 11).

41. Fragment 6.6: "For helplessness guides the wandering thoughts [*noon, from noos*] in their hearts" (Taran 1965, 54).

42. Heidegger (1972d, 203) argues for the translation of the verb *noein* as "taking-to-heart" in Parmendes' fragment 6.1: "One should both say *[legein]* and think *[noein]* that Being is."

43. Heidegger 1966, 47. Graybeal (1990, 139) also discusses this kind of thinking.

44. See Ruddick 1989, 70, for how thought and feeling are linked in motherhood.

45. I would agree that thinking is shaped by practices, as Sara Ruddick says following Wittgenstein. But we must pay close attention to how these practices take place in a social and historical context.

46. Zimmerman (1983, 116) makes a similar point.

47. This feeling of wonder from slicing a cabbage was related to me years ago by Professor Sally Haag of the classical studies department at the University of Waterloo (Ontario).

48. The adjective *he oikia* means something proper to a thing, suitable, befitting, or naturally suited.

49. I have made these connections through Levin 1985, 331.

50. Home, then, is more than the place where we sleep; it is the place we inhabit, bodily and socially. As Brown (1990, 13) says, the "experience of being home must also be the telling, hearing, and re-ordering of the shared stories we cycle among each other. They concretely illuminate our place in the social and natural world."

51. See also Caputo (1987, 243), who argues that the formation of such subversive communities and subcultures are in danger "of retreating from the public in order to nourish one's virtue in private."

52. The family is preserved in order to offer man a "tranquil intuition of . . . unity" (Hegel 1967, 114). Man enters the spheres of civil society and state, where he struggles for recognition in a universal sense. See Mills 1979, 74–98 for a critique of Hegel.

53. See, for example, *Meta.* 980a1–982a4.

54. Husserl (1970, 359) goes so far as to say that because a "mature normal civilization" is established only through language, "the abnormal and the world of children" are excluded from civilization.

55. See also Heidegger 1977c, 126–32. As Zimmerman (1983, 111) points out, *logos* discloses the mysterious power of phusis and delimits it for the survival of human society. This world-founding (opening up of the world within phusis) is described as a rather violent activity by the middle Heidegger and thus in some ways reinforces the culture/nature dichotomy. In his later philosophy of the fourfold (which Zimmerman neglects), the "activity" of mortals is much gentler. Humans, moreover, are understood as only one element of the fourfold, not any more important than the other three.

56. I do not think it is intrinsic to our human be-ing to be placeless, as Evernden (1985, 117–20) maintains. Although it is true that we are indeterminate in our being, always awaiting resolution, and that techne continually changes our modes of being in dramatic ways, I do not believe we need to conclude as he does that we are worldly creatures not bound within a predetermined ecological niche, that we are "placeless creatures" unrelated to our environment. On the contrary, there have been and are many peoples whose modes of being and *techne* are most wonderfully related to local environments.

57. This notion of the gifts and limits of a place is from Plant 1990, 155.

58. Thus, it would be a mistake to image the gathering now needed in the many-worlded-earth-home as a round dance of many colored people around the globe. First, the image of the blue planet, current in popular environmental literature, is not ecological since it is a picture of the earth given from a distanced, totalizing, objective view, rather than from our lived experience. Moreover, the image of nations holding hands is not an image of openness to difference, since one cannot escape the implicit assumption that this mingling is due to (and controlled by) the neocolonialist benevolence of the West.

59. The oldest fragment of western philosophy (by Anaximander) reads: "But where things have their origin, there too their passing away occurs according to necessity; for they pay recompense and penalty *[diknv]* to one another for their recklessness, according to firmly established time" (Diels in Heidegger 1975, 13). In his essay on Anaximander, Heidegger describes how *dike*, the necessary order of the presencing of Being, occurs as a jointure between approach and withdrawal. This enigmatic fragment, says Heidegger (1975, 42), is pointing to a peculiar tendency of Being to perservere in its presencing. "It strikes the willful pose of persistence. . . . It stiffens—as if this were the way to linger—and aims solely for continuance and subsistence." Rather than release and give, it "craves to persist" (Heidegger 1975, 46). Coming to presence in the jointure of the while, what is present abandons that "jointure" and is thus out-of-joint *(adike)*. Nietzsche also recognized this

craving to persist in western philosophy, understanding it as an assault on passing-away. However, his overcoming of temporality, the eternal recurrence of the same, is not a releasement of passing away but an ontological movement let loose from the backward pull of time.

60. Jarret 1990, 36, also discusses this dialogue.

61. See Shiach 1991, 21–22, for a discussion of this alternative economy of femininity in relation to the concept of gift.

62. For example, in a gift-exchange economy of certain tribal societies where goods and services flow through the community (and between the human community and rest of nature) as gifts rather than as commodities, the giving of gifts leaves a series of interconnected relationships in its wake, and a kind of decentralized cohesiveness emerges. Giving is the mark of a successful person and the person's social status. Whereas in our market economy selves are externally related to one another and are defined by power, in a gift economy the self is defined by relations established through the giving and receiving of gifts. In the market economy, moreover, we find an atomistic concept of self and a correlative ethic of individual rights and justice. See Cheney 1987.

63. See Cheney 1987, 123, on this point.

64. Heidegger 1975, 43.

65. Even Derrida (1988, 148) says that "undecideability is always a determinate oscillation between possibilities (for example, of meaning, but also of facts). These possibilities are themselves highly determined in strictly defined situations (for example, discursive—syntactical or rhetorical—but also political, ethical, etc.)."

66. I do not agree with Caputo (1987, 169) that "the saving is the danger spelled backwards." Similarily, birth is not death spelled backwards. Rather, every radical turn is qualitatively different and moves in multitudinous directions.

References

Abram, David. 1988. Merleau-Ponty and the voice of the earth. *Environmental Ethics* 10 (Summer): 101–20.

Alexiou, Sylianos. 1984. *Minoan Civilization*. Trans. Cressida Ridley. Heraclion: Spyros Alexiou Sons.

Allen, Christine Garside. 1979. Nietzsche's ambivalence about women. In *The Sexism of Social and Political Theory,* 117–34. *See* Clark and Lange 1979.

Allen, Jeffner. 1982–83. Through the wild region: An essay in phenomenological feminism. *Review of Existential Psychology and Psychiatry* 18 (1–3): 241–56.

Allen, Jeffner, and Iris Marion Young, eds. 1989. *The Thinking Muse: Feminism and Modern French Philosophy*. Bloomington: Indiana University Press.

Allison, David B. 1977. *The New Nietzsche: Contemporary Styles of Interpretation*. New York: Delta.

Anton, John Peter. 1957. *Aristotle's Theory of Contrariety*. London: Routledge and Kegan Paul.

Aristotle. 1936. *Aristotle's Physics*. Trans. W. D. Ross. Oxford: Clarendon Press.

———. 1953. *Generation of Animals*. Trans. A. L. Peck. London: William Heinemann.

———. 1957. *Aristotlelis Metaphysica*. Ed. W. Jaeger. London: ETypographeo Clarendoniano.

———. 1962. *Aristotle: The Nicomachean Ethics*. 2d ed. Trans. H. Rackham. Cambridge, Mass.: Harvard University Press.

———. 1979. *Aristotle's Metaphysics*. Trans. Hippocrates G. Apostle. Grinwell, Iowa: Peripatetic Press.

———. 1980a. *Aristotle's Physics*. Trans. Hippocrates G. Apostle. Grinwell, Iowa: Peripatetic Press.

———. 1980b. *Physics*. 2d ed. 2 vols. Trans. P. H. Wickstead and F. M. Cornford. Cambridge, Mass.: Harvard University Press.

———. 1985a. *The Complete Works of Aristotle: The Revised Oxford Translation*. 2 vols. Ed. Jonathan Barnes. Princeton, N.J.: Princeton University Press.

———. 1985b. *Generation of Animals*. In *The Complete Works of Aristotle* 1. See Aristotle 1985a.

Arthur, Marilyn. 1977. "Liberated" women in the classical era. In *Becoming Visible*, ed. Renate Bridenthal and Claudia Koontz. Boston: Houghton Mifflin.

Atfield, Robin. 1991. *The Ethics of Environmental Concern*. 2d ed. Athens: University of Georgia Press.

Barnes, Jonathan. 1982. *Aristotle*. Oxford: Oxford University Press.

Barnett, William. 1938. *Aristotle's Analysis of Movement: Its Significance for Its Time*. New York: Columbia University Press.

Bartky, Sandra Lee. 1990. *Femininity and Domination: Studies in the Phenomenology of Oppression*. New York and London: Routledge.

Beardsley, John Walter. 1918. The use of *phusis* in fifth-century Greek literature. In *Early Greek Thought*, 1–126. *See* Taran 1987.

Berger, John. 1972. *Ways of Seeing*. London: British Broadcasting Corporation and Penguin Books.

Biehl, Janet. 1991. *Finding Our Way: Rethinking Ecofeminist Politics*. Montreal: Black Rose Books.

Birke, Lynda. 1986. *Women, Feminism and Biology: The Feminist Challenge*. Brighton: Harvestor Press.

Boardman, John. 1978. *Greek Art*. 2d ed. Toronto: Oxford University Press.

Bookchin, Murray. 1982. *The Ecology of Freedom: The Emergence and Dissolution of Hierarchy*. Pao Alto, Calif.: Cheshire Books.

Bordo, Susan. 1990. Feminism, postmodernism and gender skepticism. In *Feminism/Postmodernism*, 133–56. *See* Nicholson 1990.

Bowles, Gloria, and Renate Duelli Klein. 1983. *Theories of Women's Studies*. New York: Routledge and Kegan Paul.

Brentano, Franz. 1975. *On the Several Senses of Being in Aristotle*. Trans. and ed. Rolf George. Berkeley: University of California Press.

Brown, Lindsay. 1990. The trees here grow too slowly. *Harbour*. 1 (1): 13–14.

Buchanon, Emerson. 1962. *Aristotle's Theory of Being*. London: William Cloves & Sons.

Burnet, John. 1930. *Early Greek Philosophy*. Reprint. London: Macmillan.

Butler, Judith. 1989. Sexual ideology and phenomenological description: A feminist critique of Merleau-Ponty's *Phenomenology of Perception*. In *The Thinking Muse*, 85–100. *See* Allen and Young 1989.

———. 1990. *Gender Trouble: Feminism and the Subversion of Identity*. New York: Routledge, Chapman and Hall.

Cameron, Averil, and Amelie Kuhrt, eds. 1983. *Images of Women in Antiquity*. Beckenham, Kent: Croom Helm.

Caputo, John D. 1987. *Radical Hermeneutics: Repetition, Deconstruction and the Hermeneutic Project*. Bloomington and Indianapolis: Indiana University Press.

————. 1989. Gadamer's closet essentialism: A Derridean critique. In *Dialogue and Deconstruction*, 258–64. *See* Michelfelder and Palmer 1989.

Carr, David. 1980. *Phenomenology and the Problem of History*. Evanston, Ill.: Northwestern University Press.

Casey, Edward S. 1984. Origin(s) in (of) Heidegger/Derrida. *Journal of Philosophy* 81: 601–10.

Chen, Chunghwan. 1958. *Ousia and Energeia*. Tarpe: China Series Publishing Co.

Cheney, Jim. 1987. Eco-feminism and deep ecology. *Environmental Ethics* 9 (Summer): 115–45.

————. 1989. Postmodern environmental ethics: Ethics as bioregional narrative. *Environmental Ethics* 11 (Summer): 117–34.

————. 1991. Callicot's "Metaphysics of morals." *Environmental Ethics* 13 (Winter): 311–25.

Cherniss, Harold. 1962. *Aristotle's Criticism of Plato and the Academy*. New York: Russel & Russel.

Chodorow, Nancy. 1978. *The Reproduction of Mothering: Psychoanalysis and Sociology of Gender*. London: University of California Press.

Cixous, Hélène, and Catherine Clément. 1975. *The Newly Born Woman*. Trans. Betty Wing. Minneapolis: University of Minnesota Press.

Clark, M.G. Lorenne, and Lynda Lange, eds. 1979. *The Sexism of Social and Political Theory: Women and Reproduction from Plato to Nietzsche*. Toronto: University of Toronto Press.

Code, Lorraine, Sheila Mullett, and Christine Overall. 1988. *Feminist Perspectives: Philosophical Essays on Method and Morals*. Toronto: University of Toronto Press.

Collard, Andree. 1989. *Rape of the Wild*. Bloomington: Indiana University Press.

Coontz, Stephanie, and Petra Henderson, eds. 1986. *Women's Work, Men's Property: The Origins of Gender and Class*. London: Verso.

Cotterell, Arthur. 1979. *The Minoan World*. London: Michael Joseph.

Daly, Mary. 1985. *Beyond God the Father: Toward a Philosophy of Women's Liberation*. 2d ed. Boston: Beacon Press.

————. 1990. *Gynecology: The Metaethics of Radical Feminism*. 2d ed. Boston: Beacon Press.

De Beauvoir, Simone. 1974. *The Second Sex*, ed. and trans. M. Parshley. New York: Vintage Books.

De Lauretis, Teresa. 1986. Feminist studies/critical studies: Issues, terms, and contexts. In *Feminist Studies/Cultural Studies*. *See* De Lauretis, ed. 1986.

————. 1989. The essence of the triangle; or, Taking the risk of essentialism seriously: Feminist theory in Italy, the U.S. and Britain. *Differences* 1 (2): 3–37.

————, ed. 1986. *Feminist Studies/Critical Studies*. Bloomington: Indiana Press.

Demetrakopoulos, Stephane. 1983. *Listening to Our Bodies: The Rebirth of Feminine Wisdom*. Boston: Beacon Press.

Derrida, Jacques. 1976. *Of Grammatology*. Trans. Gayatri Chakravorty Spivak. Baltimore: Johns Hopkins University Press.

————. 1977. The question of style. In *The New Nietzsche: Contemporary Styles of Interpretation*, ed. David B. Allison. New York: Delta.

————. 1982. Sending: On representation. *Social Research* 49 (2): 294–326.

————. 1983. The principle of reason: The university in the eyes of its pupils. Trans. C. Porter and P. Lewis. *Diacritics*, Fall, 3–20.

————. 1986a. Differance. In *Margins of Philosophy*, 1–28. *See* Derrida 1986b.

————. 1986b. *Margins of Philosophy*. Trans. Alan Bass. Chicago: University of Chicago Press.

————. 1986c. Signature event context. In *Margins of Philosophy*, 307–30. *See* Derrida 1986b.

————. 1986d. White mythology: Metaphor in the text of philosophy. In *Margins of Philosophy*, 207–72. *See* Derrida 1986b.

————. 1988. Afterword: Toward an ethic of discussion. In *Limited Inc.*, ed. Gerald Graff. Evanston, Ill.: Northwestern University Press.

Devall, Bill. 1985. *Deep Ecology: George Sessions*. Salt Lake City: Gibbs M. Smith.

Diamond, Irene, and Gloria Semon Orenstein, eds. 1990. *Reweaving the World: The Emergence of Ecofeminism*. San Francisco: Sierra Club Book.

Dinnerstein, Dorothy. 1976. *The Mermaid and the Minotaur: Sexual Arrangements and Human Malaise*. New York: Harper & Row.

Donovan, Josephine. 1985. *Feminist Theory: The Intellectual Traditions of American Feminism*. New York: Frederick Ungar.

Drobnik, Jim. 1991. Michele Wallace interview. *Harbour* 1 (2): 24–29.

Dufrenne, Mikel. 1978. *Main Trends in Aesthetics and the Sciences of Art*. New York: Holmes & Meier.

Earthroots Coalition. 1991. Amazon north: Assault on James Bay. *Earthroots*, Spring.

Eisler, Riane. 1987. *The Chalice and the Blade: Our History, Our Future*. San Francisco: Harper Collins.

————. 1990. The Gaia tradition and the partnership future: An ecofeminist manifesto. In *Reweaving the World*, 15–22. *See* Diamond and Orenstein 1990.

Elshtain, Jean Bethke. 1981. *Public Man, Private Woman: Women in Social and Political Thought*. Princeton, N.J.: Princeton University Press.

————. 1982. Feminist discourse and its discontents: Language, power and meaning. *Signs* 7 (3).

Erdman, David V., ed. 1982. *The Complete Poetry and Prose of William Blake*. 2d ed. Comp. Harold Bloom. Berkeley and Los Angeles: University of California Press.

Evernden, Neil. 1985. *The Natural Alien: Humankind and Environment*. Toronto: University of Toronto Press.

Ferguson, Ann. 1981. Androgyny as an ideal for human development. In *Feminism and Philosophy*, 45–69. *See* Vetterling-Braggin, Elliston, and English 1981.

Flynn, Bernard Charles. 1984. Textuality and the flesh: Derrida and Merleau-Ponty. *Journal of the British Society for Phenomenology* 15 (2): 164–79.

Foltz, Bruce V. 1984. On Heidegger and the interpretation of the environmental crisis. *Environmental Ethics* 6 (Winter): 323–38.

Foucault, Michel. 1980. *Power/Knowledge: Selected Interviews and Other Writings, 1972–1977*. Trans. Colin Gordon et al.; ed. Colin Gordon. New York: Pantheon Books.

Fox, Michael Allen. 1987. Nuclear weapons and the ultimate environmental crisis. *Environmental Ethics* 9 (Summer): 159–79.

Fox, Warwick. 1987. The deep ecology-ecofeminism debate and its parallels. *Environmental Ethics* 11 (Spring): 5–25.

Fraser, Nancy, and Linda J. Nicholson. 1990. Social criticism without philosophy: An encounter between feminism and postmodernism, 19–38. In *Feminism/Postmodernism. See* Nicholson 1990.

Freud, Sigmund. 1952. *Three Contributions to the Theory of Sex*. 2d ed. New York: Johnson.

Fuss, Diane. 1989a. *Essentially Speaking: Feminism, Nature and Difference*. New York and London: Routledge.

————. 1989b. "Essentially speaking": Luce Irigaray's language of essence. *Hypatia* 3 (3): 62–80.

Gadamer, Hans-Georg. 1975. *Truth and Method*. 2d ed. Trans. Garret Barden and John Cumming. New York: Seabury.

————. 1989a. Destruktion and deconstruction. In *Dialogue and Deconstruction*, 102–13. *See* Michelfelder and Palmer 1989.

————. 1989b. Text and interpretation. In *Dialogue and Deconstruction*, 21–51. *See* Michelfelder and Palmer 1989.

Garb, Yaakou Jerome. 1990. Perspective or escape? Ecofeminist musings on contemporary earth imagery. In *Reweaving the World*, 264–78. *See* Diamond and Orenstein 1990.

Gatens, Moira. 1991. *Feminism and Philosophy: Perspectives on Difference and Equality*. Bloomington and Indianapolis: Indiana University Press.

Geist, Sidney. 1978. *The Kiss*. New York: Harper & Row.

―――. 1983. *Brancusi: A Study of the Sculpture*. New York: Haiker Art Books.

Giedion-Welcker, Carola. 1959. *Constantine Brancusi*. Trans. Maria Jolas and Anne Leroy. New York: George Braziller.

―――. 1960. *Contemporary Sculpture: An Evolution in Volume and Space*. New York: George Wittenborn.

Gilligan, Carol. 1982. *In a Different Voice*. Cambridge, Mass.: Harvard University Press.

Gimbutas, Marija. 1989. *The Language of the Goddess*. Foreword by Joseph Campbell. New York: Harper & Row.

―――. 1990. *The Goddesses and Gods of Old Europe Myths and Cult Images*. Berkeley and Los Angeles: University of California Press.

Gould, Carol, ed. 1984. *Beyond Domination: New Perspectives on Women and Philosophy*. Totowa, N.J.: Rowman & Allanheld.

Grange, Joseph. 1985. Being, feeling, and environment. *Environmental Ethics* 7 (Winter): 351–64.

Graves, Robert. 1960. *The Greek Myths*. Vol. 1. 2d ed. Harmondsworth: Penguin.

Graybeal, Jean. 1990. *Language and "The Feminine" in Nietzsche and Heidegger*. Indianapolis: Indiana University Press.

Griffin, Susan. 1989. Split culture. In *The Promise of Ecofeminism*, 7–17. See Plant, ed., 1989.

―――. 1990. Curves along the road. In *Reweaving the World*, 87–99. See Diamond and Orenstein 1990.

Griffiths, Morwenna. 1988. Feminism, feelings and philosophy. In *Feminist Perspectives in Philosophy*. See Griffiths and Whitford 1988.

Griffiths, Morwenna, and Margaret Whitford, eds. 1988. *Feminist Perspectives in Philosophy*. Bloomington and Indianapolis: Indiana University Press.

Gwaganad. 1989. Speaking for the earth: The Haida way. In *The Promise of Ecofeminism*, 76–79. See Plant, ed., 1989.

Harding, Sandra. 1986. *The Science Question in Feminism*. Ithaca, N.Y.: Cornell University Press.

―――, ed. 1987. *Feminism and Methodology*. Indianapolis: Indiana University Press.

Harrison, Jane. 1977. *Themis: A Study of the Social Origins of Greek Religion*. London: Merlin Press.

Hartsock, Nancy. 1985. *Money, Sex, and Power: Toward a Feminist Historical Materialism*. Boston: Northeastern University Press.

―――. 1987. Rethinking modernism: Minority vs. majority theories. *Cultural Critique*, Fall, 187–206.

Hegel, G.W.F. 1967. *Hegel's Philosophy of Right*. Trans. T. M. Knox. New York: Oxford University Press.

———. 1975. *Aesthetics Lectures on Fine Arts*. Trans. T. M. Knox. 2 vols. Oxford: Clarendon Press.

———. 1981. *Phenomenology of Spirit*. Oxford: Oxford University Press.

Heidegger, Martin. 1953. *Einführung in die Metaphysik*. Tubingen: Max Niemeyer.

———. 1954. *Was Heisst Denken?* Tubingen: Max Niemeyer.

———. 1958a. *The Question of Being*. Trans. Jean T. Wilde and William Kluback. New Haven: Twayne Publishers.

———. 1958b. *What Is Philosophy?* Trans. Jean T. Wilde and William Kluback. New Haven: Twayne Publishers.

———. 1962. *Being and Time*. Trans. John Macquarrie and Edward Robinson. New York: Harper & Row.

———. 1964. *Vortrage und Aufsatze*. 3d ed. Pfüllingen: Gunther Neske.

———. 1966. *Discourse on Thinking*. Trans. John M. Anderson and E. Hans Freund. New York: Harper & Row.

———. 1971a. Building, dwelling, thinking. In *Poetry, Language, Thought*. *See* Heidegger 1971d.

———. 1971b. A dialogue on language. In *On the Way to Language*. Trans. Peter D. Hertz. San Francisco: Harper & Row.

———. 1971c. The origin of a work of art. In *Poetry, Language, Thought*. *See* Heidegger 1971d.

———. 1971d. *Poetry, Language, Thought*. Trans. Albert Hofstadter. New York: Harper Colophon Books.

———. 1971e. The thing. In *Poetry, Language, Thought*. *See* Heidegger 1971d.

———. 1972a. The end of philosophy and the task of thinking. In *On Time and Being*. *See* Heidegger 1972c.

———. 1972b. *Holzwege*. 5th ed. Frankfurt am Main: Vittorio Klostermann.

———. 1972c. *On Time and Being*. Trans. Joan Stambaugh. New York: Harper Torchbooks.

———. 1972d. Time and being. In *On Time and Being*. *See* Heidegger 1972c.

———. 1972e. *What Is Called Thinking?* Trans. J. Glenn Gray. New York: Harper & Row, Colophon Books.

———. 1973. *The End of Philosophy*. Trans. Joan Stambaugh. New York: Harper & Row.

———. 1974a. *Identity and Difference*. Trans. Joan Stambaugh. New York: Harper Torchbooks.

———. 1974b. The principle of ground. Trans. Keith Hoeller. *Man and World* 7:207–22.

———. 1975. *Early Greek Thinking*. Trans. David Farrell Krell and Frank A. Capuzzi. New York: Harper & Row.

————. 1976. On the being and conception of *phusis* in Aristotle's *Physics* B, 1. *Man and World* 9 (3): 219–70.

————. 1977a. The age of the world picture. In *The Question Concerning Technology and Other Essays. See* Heidegger 1977f.

————. 1977b. "The essence of truth." In *Basic Writings,* ed. David Farrell Krell, 75–92. New York: Harper & Row.

————. 1977c. *An Introduction to Metaphysics.* Trans. Ralph Manheim. New Haven: Yale University Press.

————. 1977d. Letter on humanism. In *Basic Writings,* ed. David Farrell Krell. New York: Harper & Row.

————. 1977e. The question concerning technology. In *The Question Concerning Technology and Other Essays. See* Heidegger 1977f.

————. 1977f. *The Question Concerning Technology and Other Essays.* Trans. William Lovitt. New York: Garland.

————. 1979. *Nietzsche: The Will to Power as Art.* Vol. 1. Trans. David Farrell Krell. San Francisco: Harper & Row.

————. 1982. *Nietzsche: Nihilism.* Vol. 4. Trans. Frank A. Capuzzi. San Francisco: Harper & Row.

————. 1987. *Nietzsche: The Will to Power as Knowledge and as Metaphysics.* Trans. Joan Stambaugh, David Farrell Krell, and Frank A. Capuzzi; ed. David Farrell Krell. San Francisco: Harper & Row.

Heidel, William Arthur. 1909–10. A study on the conception of nature among the pre-Socratics. *Proceedings of the American Academy of Art and Science* 14: 77–133.

Heisenberg, Werner. 1962. *Physics and Philosophy: The Revolution in Modern Science.* New York: Harper & Row.

Hess, Thomas B., and Elizabeth C. Baker, eds. 1973. *Art and Sexual Politics: Why Have There Been No Great Women Artists?* London: Collier Books.

Higgins, Reynold. 1981. *Minoan and Mycenaean Art.* New York: Oxford University Press.

Holler, Linda. 1990. Thinking with the weight of the earth: Feminist contributions to an epistemology of concreteness. *Hypatia* 5 (1): 1–23.

Husserl, Edmund. 1970. *The Crisis of European Sciences and Transcendental Phenomenology.* Trans. David Carr. Evanston, Ill.: Northwestern University Press.

Irigaray, Luce. 1985a. *The Sex Which Is Not One.* Trans. Catherine Porter with Carolyn Burke. Ithaca, N.Y.: Cornell University Press.

————. 1985b. *Speculum of the Other Woman.* Trans. Gillian C. Gill. Ithaca, N.Y.: Cornell University Press.

Janson, H. W. 1986. *History of Art.* 3d ed. New York: Harry N. Abrams.

Jarret, Susan C. 1990. The first sophists and feminism: Discourses of the "other." *Hypatia* 5 (1): 27–41.

Kahn, Charles H. 1987. *The Art and Thought of Heraclitus: An Edition of the Fragments with Translation and Commentary*. Cambridge: Cambridge University Press.

Kahn, Robbie Pfeufer. 1989. Mother's milk: The "moment of nurture" revisited. *Resources for Feminist Research* 18 (3): 29–36.

Keller, Evelyn Fox. 1982. Feminism and science. *Signs* 7 (3): 589–602.

———. 1985. *Reflections on Gender and Science*. New Haven: Yale University Press.

Kheel, Marti. 1985. The liberation of nature: A circular affair. *Environmental Ethics* 7 (Summer): 135–49.

———. 1990. Ecofeminism and deep ecology: Reflections on identity and difference. In *Reweaving the World*, 128–37. *See* Diamond and Orenstein 1990.

King, Ynestra. 1989. The ecology of feminism and the feminism of ecology. In *The Promise of Ecofeminism*, 18–29. *See* Plant, ed., 1989.

Kirk, G. S., and J. E. Raven, eds. 1987. *The Presocratic Philosophers: A Critical History with a Selection of Tests*. 2d ed. Cambridge: Cambridge University Press.

Kramer, Hilton. 1979. *Brancusi: The Sculptor as Photographer*. New York: David Crob Editions.

Krauss, E. Rosalind. 1985. *Passages in Modern Sculpture*. Cambridge, Mass.: MIT Press.

Kristeva, Julia. 1980. *Desire in Language: A Semiotic Approach to Literature and Art*. Trans. Thomas Gora, Alice Jardine, and Leon S. Roudiez; ed. Leon S. Roudiez. New York: Columbia University Press.

———. 1981. Women's time. Trans. Alice Jardine and Harry Blake. *Signs* 7 (1): 13–35.

Lambert, Elspeth. 1986. The milking of cows. *The Animals Agenda*, April, 1–4.

Lampert, Laurence. 1986. *Nietzsche's Teaching: An Interpretation of "Thus Spoke Zarathustra."* New Haven: Yale University Press.

Lee, Donald C. 1980. On the Marxian view of the relationship between man and nature. *Environmental Ethics* 2 (Spring): 3–16.

LeGuin, Ursula K. 1989. Woman/wilderness. In *The Promise of Ecofeminism*, 45–47. *See* Plant, ed., 1989.

Levin, David Michael. 1985. *The Body's Recollection of Being*. Boston: Routledge and Kegan Paul.

———. 1988. *The Opening of Vision: Nihilism and the Postmodern Situation*. New York: Routledge.

————. 1989. *The Listening Self: Personal Growth, Social Change and the Closure of Metaphysics*. New York: Routledge.

Lexicon Abridged from Liddell and Scott's Greek-English Lexicon, A. 1982. Oxford: Oxford University Press.

Lloyd, Genevieve. 1984. *The Man of Reason: "Male" and "Female" in Western Philosophy*. Minneapolis: University of Minneapolis Press.

Lorde, Audre. 1983. The master's tools will never dismantle the master's house. In *This Bridge Called My Back*, 98–106. *See* Moraga and Ansaldua 1983.

————. 1984. *Sister Outsider*. California: The Crossing Press.

Loscerbo, John. 1981. *Being and Technology: A Study in the Philosophy of Martin Heidegger*. The Hague: Martinus Nijhoff.

Lounder, Barbara, and Lani Maestro, with Carol Laing. 1990. *Refuse* Catalogue. The Art Gallery, Mount Saint Vincent University, Halifax, Nova Scotia.

McWhorter, Ladelle. 1989. Culture or nature? The function of the term "body" in the work of Michel Foucault. *Journal of Philosophy* 86 (11): 608–14.

Mahowald, Mary Biody, ed. 1980. *Philosophy of Women: Classical to Current Concepts*. Indianapolis: Hackett.

Mallin, Samuel. n.d. Art line thought. Typescript.

————. 1979. *Merleau-Ponty's Philosophy*. New Haven: Yale University Press.

————. 1983. *Here to Zero*. Toronto: S. L. Simpson Gallery.

Marks, Elaine, and Isabelle Courtivron, eds. 1981. *New French Feminisms: An Anthology*. Amherst: University of Massachusetts Press.

Martin, Biddy, and Chandra Talpade Mohanty. 1986. Feminist politics: What's home got to do with it? In De Lauretis, ed., 1986.

Marx, Werner. 1954. *The Meaning of Aristotle's Ontology*. The Hague: Nijhoff.

Matrix. 1984. *Making Space: Women and the Man-Made Environment*. London: Pluto Press.

Merchant, Carolyn. 1980. *The Death of Nature*. New York: Harper & Row.

Merleau-Ponty, Maurice. 1962. *Phenomenology of Perception*. Trans. Colin Smith. London: Routledge and Kegan Paul.

————. 1968. *The Visible and Invisible*. Trans. Alphonso Lingis; ed. Claude Lefort. Evanston, Ill.: Northwestern University Press.

————. 1973. *The Prose of the World*. Trans. John O'Neill; ed. Clause Lefort. O'Neill. Evanston, Ill.: Northwestern University Press.

————. 1982. *Eye and Mind: The Primacy of Perception*. Ed. and trans. James M. Edie. Evanston, Ill.: Northwestern University Press.

Michelfelder, Diane P., and Richard E. Palmer, eds. 1989. *Dialogue and Deconstruction: The Gadamer-Derrida Encounter*. Albany: State University of New York Press.

Miles, Angela, and Geraldine Finn, eds. 1989. *Feminism: From Pressure to Politics*. Montreal: Black Rose Books.

Miller, Meg. 1991. When the Old Boys Met in Athens. *Rotunda: The Magazine of the Royal Ontario Museum* 28 (Fall): 26–32.

Mills, Patricia Jagentowicz. 1979. Hegel and ''the woman question'': Recognition and intersubjectivity. In *The Sexism of Social and Political Theory*, 74–98. *See* Clark and Lange 1979.

———. 1986. Hegel's *Antigone*. *The Owl of Minerva* 17 (2): 131–52.

———. 1991. Feminism and ecology: The domination of nature. *Hypatia* 6 (1): 162–78.

Min, Yang Soon. 1991. Mapping Asian-American cultural identity. *Harbour* 1 (2): 32–37.

Minh-ha, Trinh T. 1989. *Woman Native Other*. Indianapolis: Indiana University Press.

Morega, Cherrie, and Gloria Anzaldua, eds. 1983. *This Bridge Called My Back: Writings by Radical Women of Color*. New York: Kitchen Table, Women of Color Press.

Moulton, Janice. 1981. The myth of neutral ''man.'' In *Feminism and Philosophy*, 124–37. *See* Vetterling-Braggin, Elliston, and English 1981.

Naess, Arne. 1973. The shallow and the deep, long-range ecology movement: A summary. *Inquiry* 16: 95–100.

Neumann, Erich. [1963] 1974. *The Great Mother: An Analysis of the Archtype*. Trans. Ralph Manheim. Princeton: Princeton University Press.

Nicholson, Linda J. 1984. Feminist theory: The private and the public. In *Beyond Domination*, 221–30. *See* Gould 1984.

———, ed. 1990. *Feminism/Postmodernism*. New York: Routledge.

Nietzsche, Friedrich. 1926. *Gessammelte Werke: Der Wille Zur Macht*. Vols. 18 and 19. Munich: Musarion.

———. 1956. *The Birth of Tragedy and The Genealogy of Morals*. Trans. Francis Golffing. Garden City, N.Y.: Doubleday.

———. 1972. *The Will to Power*. Trans. Walter Kaufmann and R. J. Hollingdale; ed. Walter Kaufmann. New York: Vintage Press.

———. [1961] 1976. *Thus Spoke Zarathustra: A Book for Everyone and No One*. Trans. R. J. Hollingdale. Harmondsworth: Penguin.

———. [1968] 1977. *Twilight of the Idols: The Anti-Christ*. Trans. R. J. Hollingdale. New York: Penguin.

———. [1954] 1978. *Thus Spoke Zarathustra: A Book for All and None*. Trans. Walter Kaufmann. Harmondsworth: Penguin.

Noddings, Nel. 1986. *Caring   A Feminine Approach to Ethics and Moral Education*. Berkeley: University of California Press.

Nye, Andrea. 1988. *Feminist Theory and Philosophies of Man*. London: Croom Helm.

O'Brien, Mary. 1983. *The Politics of Reproduction*. London: Routledge and Kegan Paul.

Orenstein, Gloria Feman. 1990. Artists as healers: Envisioning life-giving culture. In *Reweaving the World*, 279–87. *See* Diamond and Orenstein 1990.

Ortner, Sherry. 1974. Is female to male as nature is to culture? In *Women, Culture and Society*, 67–88. *See* Rosaldo and Lamphere 1974.

Ostwald, Martin. 1969. *Nomos and the Beginnings of the Athenian Democracy*. Oxford: Clarendon Press.

Owens, Joseph. 1959. *A History of Ancient Western Philosophy*. Toronto: Appleton-Century Crofts.

———. [1951] 1978. *The Doctrine of Being in Aristotlelian Metaphysics*. Toronto: Pontifical Institute of Mediaeval Studies.

Padel, Ruth. 1983. Women: Model for Possession by Greek Daemons. In *Images of Women in Antiquity*, 3–19. *See* Cameron and Kuhrt 1983.

Palmer, Gabrielle. 1988. *The Politics of Breastfeeding*. London: Pandora Press.

Philip, Marlene Nourbese. 1991. *Looking for Livingstone: An Odyssey of Silence*. Stratford: Mercury Press.

Plant, Judith. 1989. The circle is gathering. In *The Promise of Ecofeminism*, 242–53. *See* Plant, ed., 1989.

———. 1990. Searching for Common Ground: Ecofeminism and Bioregionalism. In *Reweaving the World*, 155–64. *See* Diamond and Orenstein 1990.

———, ed. 1989. *The Promise of Ecofeminism*. Toronto: Between the Lines.

Plato. 1959. *The Gorgias*. Trans. E. R. Dodds. Oxford: Clarendon Press.

———. 1982. *Gorgias*. Trans. Walter Hamilton. New York: Penguin.

Plumwood, Val. 1991. Nature, self, and gender: Feminism, environmental philosophy, and the critique of rationalism. *Hypatia* 6 (1): 3–27.

Pollitt, J. J. 1974. *The Ancient View of Greek Art: Criticism, History, and Terminology*. New Haven and London: Yale University Press.

Pollution Probe Foundation. 1991. *Probe Post* (Toronto) 14 (2).

Pomeroy, Sarah. 1975. *Goddesses, Whores, Wives, and Slaves: Women in Classical Antiquity*. New York: Schocken Books.

Poovey, Mary. 1988. Feminism and deconstruction. *Feminist Studies*. 14 (1): 51–66.

Popescu, Beaty. 1991. Artist's statements. In *The Embodied Viewer*, 30–31. Catalogue. Glenbow Museum, Calgary.

Post, Stephen G. 1990. Women and elderly parents: Moral controversy in an aging society. *Hypatia* 5 (1): 83–89.

Price, Sally. 1989. *Primitive Art in Civilized Places*. Chicago and London: University of Chicago Press.

Probyn, Elspeth. 1987. Bodies and anti-bodies: Feminism and postmodernism. *Cultural Studies* 1 (3).

Rabuzzi, Kathryn Allen. 1982. *The Sacred and the Feminine: Toward a Theology of Housework*. New York: Seabury Press.

Reale, Giovanni. 1980. *The Concept of First Philosophy and the Unity of the Metaphysics*. Trans. John R. Catan. Albany: State University of New York Press.

Reuther, Rosemary Radford. 1984. Sexism, religion and the social and spiritual liberation of women today. In *Beyond Domination*, 107–22. *See* Gould 1984.

Rich, Adrienne. 1986. *Of Women Born: Motherhood as Experience and Institution*. New York: W. W. Norton.

———. 1978. *The Dream of a Common Language: Poems 1974–1977*. New York: Norton.

Roach, Catherine. 1991. Loving your mother: On the woman-nature relationship. *Hypatia* 6 (1): 46–59.

Robbins, John. 1991. Meat: Misery on the menu. Pamphlet. Toronto: Toronto Vegetarian Society.

Robinson, T. M. 1987. *Heraclitus Fragments: A Text and Translation with a Commentary by T. M. Robinson*. Toronto: University of Toronto Press.

Rorty, Richard. 1978. Philosophy as a kind of writing: An essay on Derrida. *New Literary History* 10: 141–60.

Rosaldo, Michelle Zimbalist, and Louise Lamphere. 1974. *Women, Culture and Society*. Stanford, Calif.: Stanford University Press.

Rothschild, Joan. 1987. *Machina Ex Dea: Feminist Perspectives on Technology*. New York: Pergamon Press.

Ruddick, Sara. 1983. Preservation love and military destruction: Some reflections on mothering and peace. In *Mothering*, 231–63. *See* Trebilcot 1984.

———. 1989. *Maternal Thinking: Towards a Politics of Peace*. New York: Ballantine Books.

Sachini, Angeliki. 1984. *Prehistoric Cycladic Figurines and Their Influence on Early Twentieth-Century Sculpture*. Edinburgh: University of Edinburgh.

Saliou, Monique. 1986. The processes of women's subordination in primitive and archaic Greece. In *Women's Work, Men's Property*, 169–206. *See* Coontz and Henderson 1986.

Salleh, Ariel. 1983. Deeper than deep ecology: The ecofeminist connection. *Environmental Ethics* 6 (Winter): 339–45.

Schor, Naomi. 1989. This essentialism which is not one: Coming to grips with Irigaray. *Differences* 1 (2): 38–58.

Schwartz, Arturo. 1969. *The Complete Works of Marcel Duchamp.* 2d ed. New York: Harry N. Abram.

Scott, Joan W. 1988. Deconstructing equality verses difference; or, The use of poststructuralist theory for feminism. *Feminist Studies* 14 (1): 33–50.

Scully, Vincent. 1982. The great goddess and the palace architecture of Crete. In *Feminism and Art History: Questioning the Litany.* Ed. Norma Broude and Mary D. Garrard. New York: Harper & Row.

Searle, John. 1983. The word turned upside down. *New York Review* 30 (Oct. 27).

Seidel, George Joseph. 1964. *Martin Heidegger and the Pre-Socratics: An Introduction to His Thought.* Lincoln: University of Nebraska Press.

Shiach, Morag. 1991. *Hélène Cixous: A Politics of Writing.* London and New York: Routledge.

Shipp, George Pelham. 1978. *Nomos* "law." Monograph 4. Sydney University Press, Sydney.

Shiva, Vandana. 1990. Development as a new project of western patriarchy. In *Reweaving the World,* 189–200. *See* Diamond and Orenstein 1990.

Sierra Club of Canada. 1991. *James Bay 2: The Monster Mega-Project that Must Be Stopped.* Otawa.

Silverman, Hugh J. 1984. The limits of logocentricism (on the way to grammatology). *Man and World* 17: 107–18.

Silverman, Hugh J., and Don Ihde, eds. 1985. *Hermeneutics and Deconstruction.* New York: State of New York Press.

Spelman, V. Elizabeth. 1988. *Inessential Woman: Problem of Exclusion in Feminist Thought.* Boston: Beacon Press.

Spivak, Gayatri Chakravorty. 1988. *In Other Worlds: Essays in Cultural Politics.* New York: Routledge, Chapman and Hall.

Spretnak, Charlene. 1990. Ecofeminism: Our roots and flowering. In *Reweaving the World,* 3–14. *See* Diamond and Orenstein 1990.

Starhawk. 1990. Power, authority and mystery: Ecofeminist and earth-based spirituality. In *Reweaving the World,* 73–86. *See* Diamond and Orenstein 1990.

Statistics Canada. 1991. *Farming Facts.* Ottawa.

Stone, Merlin. 1976. *When God Was a Woman.* London: Harcourt Brace Jovanovich.

Taran, Leonardo. 1965. *Parmenides: A Text with Translation, Commentary and Critical Essays.* Princeton, N.J.: Princeton University Press.

————, ed. 1987. *Early Greek Thought: Three Studies.* Vol. 14. New York and London: Garland.

Thiele, Bev. 1989. Dissolving dualism: O'Brien, embodiment and social construction. *Resources for Feminist Research* 18 (3): 7–12.

Thom, Paul. 1976. Stiff cheese for women. *Philosophical Forum* 8 (1).

Trebilcot, Joyce. 1980. Sex roles: The argument from nature. In *Philosophy of Women*, 288–95. *See* Mahowald 1980.

———. 1981. Two forms of androgynism. In *Feminism and Philosophy*, 70–78. *See* Vetterling-Braggin, Elliston, and English 1981.

———, ed. 1984. *Mothering: Essays in Feminist Theory*. Totowa, N.J.: Rowman & Allanheld.

Valerio, Anita. 1983. It's in my blood, my face—my mother's voice, the way I sweat. In *This Bridge Called My Back*, 41–45. *See* Morega and Anzaldua 1983.

Vetterling-Braggin, Frederick A. Elliston, and Jane English, eds. 1981. *Feminism and Philosophy*. Totowa, N.J.: Littlefield, Adams.

Vickers, Jill McCalla. 1989. Memoirs of an ontological exile: The methodological rebellions of feminist research. In *Feminism*, 37–56. *See* Miles and Finn 1989.

VonMirbach, Martin. 1988. In search of a Heideggerean praxis. Typescript.

Walker, Susan. 1983. Women and housing in classical Greece: The archaeological evidence. In *Images of Women in Antiquity*, 81–91. *See* Cameron and Kuhrt 1983.

Warren, Karen. 1990. The Power and Promise of Ecological Feminism. *Environmental Ethics*. 12 (Summer): 121–46.

Warren, Karen J., and Jim Cheney. 1987. Feminism and ecology: Making connections. *Environmental Ethics* 9 (Spring): 3–20.

———. 1991. Ecological feminism and ecosystem ecology. *Hypatia* 6 (1): 179–97.

Weinzweig, Majorie. 1986. Should a feminist choose a marriage-like relationship? *Hypatia* 1 (2): 139–60.

Western Canada Wilderness Committee. 1991. Western Canada Wilderness Committee educational report 10 (5). Vancouver.

Westra, Laura. 1985. Let it be: Heidegger and future generations. *Environmental Ethics* 7 (Winter): 341–50.

Whitbeck, Caroline. 1984a. A different reality: Feminist ontology. In *Beyond Domination*, 64–88. *See* Gould 1984.

———. 1984b. Afterword to the maternal instinct. In *Mothering*, 192–99. *See* Trebilcot 1984.

Whitford, Margaret. 1991. *Luce Irigaray: Philosophy in the Feminine*. London and New York: Routledge.

Williams, Raymond. 1976. *Keywords: A Vocabulary of Culture and Society*. London: Fontana/Croom Helm.

Wilson, Alexander. 1991. *The Culture of Nature: North American Landscape from Disney to Exxon Valdez.* Toronto: Between the Lines.

Wittig, Monique. 1978. One is not born a woman. In *Feminist Frameworks: Alternative Theoretical Accounts of the Relations between Women and Men.* Ed. Alison M. Jagger and Paula S. Rothenberg, 148–51. 2d ed. New York: McGraw-Hill.

Young, Iris Marion. 1990. *Throwing Like a Girl and Other Essays in Feminist Philosophy and Social Theory.* Indianapolis: Indiana University Press.

Zimmerman, Michael E. 1983. Toward a Heideggerean *ethos* for radical environmentalism. *Environmental Ethics* 5 (Summer): 99–131.

———. 1987. Feminism, deep ecology and environmental ethics. *Environmental Ethics* 9 (Spring): 21–44.

———. 1990. Deep ecology and ecofeminism: The emerging dialogue. In *Reweaving the World*, 138–54. *See* Diamond and Orenstein 1990.

Index

Active/passive dichotomy, 11, 116,
191, 196, 211, 329n.12; and hold-
ing, 181; pregnancy as undermining
214–15, 259; and sexual intercourse,
126–27; and stepping forward and
backward, 207. *See also* Passivity
Adotevi, Stanislas, 267
Aeschylus, *Orestia,* 131
Aesthetics (Hegel), 288–89
Allen, Christine Garside, 100, 316n.13
Allen, Jeffner, and Young, Iris Marion,
The Thinking Muse, 305n.5, 306n.8
Anaximander, 298
Anthropocentrism, 96, 103, 140, 191,
193; in metaphysics, 28, 192; of
poststructuralist description of gender, 31–32, 39, 44
Anthropology: Eurocentrism of,
267–68; social, movies, 263,
336n.11
Antigone (Sophocles), 274
Apollo: and Dionysius, 317n.20,
327n.12; in western pediment of
Temple of Zeus at Olympia, 181–83
Apostle, H. G., 320n.25, 323n.17
Architect, as efficient cause, 141–42,
323n.17
Architecture: disregard of women and,
132, 150; Greek, 132; Minoan,
177–78; sheltering and, 150; suppression of nature in, 149–50; and
temple of Zeus at Olympia, 181–83,
326n.7. *See also* Building; Dwelling
Aristotle, 9, 40, 78, 117, 217; my
approach to, 136; *energeia* and
dunamis in, 170, 235, 332–33n.9;
generation in, 154–71, 196, 211,
220; on *logos,* 157, 192; representation of Being in, 27, 83; sexism of,

153–54; on techne and phusis,
139–45, 150–51, 154–71, 194–95,
211, 216; on theory, 294; theory of
four causes, 139–45, 157–69; theory
of movement, 223, 224; on wonder,
288. *Works: The Generation of
Animals,* 156, 161–62, 165–66,
323–24n.20; *The Metaphysics,* 117,
155, 159, 163, 164, 181, 216,
324n.26; *The Physics,* 195; *The Politics,* 131. *See also* Efficient cause;
Formal cause; Material cause
Art: and environmental artists, 296;
Giacometti on, 64; Heidegger on, 60,
65, 295; method of thinking through,
7–8; Oldenberg on, 206; prehistoric, 161, 177, 310n.28. *See also
Aesthetics* (Hegel); Architecture; Artworks; Blake; Brancusi, Constantine;
Cycladic figurine; Desire, artistic;
Goddess, the, Snake; Nietzsche,
Friedrich, artistic desire in; *Poiesis;*
Techne
Arthur, Marilyn, 131
Artworks, 60; contrasted with
tools, 238; selection of, 8, 11,
310–11n.28. *See also names of
individual artworks*
Atfield, Robin, 271, 272
Athena, 174

Barnet, S. R., 264
Barthes, Roland, 7
Bartky, Sandra, 213
Baudrillard, Jean, 128
Beardsley, John, 316n.4
Becoming: and Being, 126; ecological,
261–303; energy as, 235; in gender
issues, 48–49, 202; as organic

359

Becoming *(continued)*
  growth, 9, 20, 214, 272, 313n.20;
  Will to Power as, 89, 203,
  333–34n.14
Being: crossing out of, 3; and culture/
  nature dichotomy, 11, 202–3; definition of, 3, 77–79, 297; as *Gestell*
  (Will to Power), 71–73, 75, 81–82,
  91–92, 94–97, 143–51, 224–47,
  264; as a giving, 29, 47, 82–84, 89,
  176, 284, 297–98; as God, 84, 90,
  161, 169, 171; as Goddess, 161,
  168–70, 171, 312–13n.18; as
  ground, 28–29, 32, 33, 297–98;
  human participation in, 32, 171, 217,
  278, 300; movement of, 29, 71–81,
  125–27, 145–51, 165, 297, 300;
  mystery of, 29; as ontological difference, 35, 65; phusis as, 145,
  146–56, 168–71, 339–40n.39; prereflective understanding of, 3; as represented in western metaphysics, 9,
  27–29, 77–81, 82–83, 248, 297,
  300; temporality of, 297–98. *See
  also* Heidegger, Martin, the fourfold
  in; Heidegger, Martin, philosophy of
  history
Being and Time (Heidegger), 295,
  330n.25
Birth, 55, 59, 151; as origin, 38, 155;
  giving, 59–60, 214–15, 219; philosophy of, 330n.25. *See also* Coming-
  to-be, of a baby; Origin
Blake, William, 290, 330n.25; ''The
  Clod and the Pebble,'' 173; *The Four
  Zoas,* 206
Body: as ambiguous, 54–55; biological
  view of, 2–3, 40, 48, 220; bodily
  knowledge, 215–16; bodily meaning, 54, 55; bodily openness to other,
  176–79; body/mind dichotomy, 11,
  46, 52, 90; Butler on, 41–44, 147;
  capacity of, to see things as unified,
  52–54; as connatural, 55–56; as cul-

tural construction, 23–24, 42–43;
  empiricist view of, 49–51; and
  essentialism, 16–23, 202–3,
  312–13n.18; feminist defenses of,
  308n.12; Foucault on, 41, 42–43,
  97, 313n.19; and gender, 8, 12–22,
  23, 24, 39–44, 57–58; as ground,
  42–43, 55, 221; idealist view of,
  49–51; Merleau-Ponty on, 49–58,
  60, 216, 285, 291; in metaphysics,
  32, 45–46; mothering, 58–60, 130,
  133–34, 170–71, 184, 212–16,
  218–20; Nietzsche on, 218, 331n.27;
  as noncognitive, 49–53; phenomenological, 13, 49–60; postmodern, 12,
  44, 308n.16, 311n.6; relation of, to
  nature, 14, 43–49, 50–60, 202–3,
  270; suppression of, 13, 43–49, 218;
  writing the, 8, 16, 190
Bordo, Susan, 307n.4, 312n.13; on
  deconstruction, 312n.15; on gender
  skepticism, 13–14; on postmodern
  body, 308n.16, 311n.6
Brancusi, Constantine, 2; balance in,
  61–62, 66, 108–9; carving in,
  63–64, 109. *Works: Flying Turtle,*
  122; *The Kiss,* 110, 112; *Little Bird,*
  70, 72; *Mlle Pogany I,* 105–23; *Mlle
  Pogany II,* 120; *Mlle Pogany III,*
  122–24; *Princess X,* 106; *The Seal,*
  61–74, 106
Breastfeeding, 59–60; suppression of,
  in western culture, 152–53, 315n.31.
  See also Dairy cows
Breasts, 39, 62; and breasted vessels,
  327n.13; of the Snake Goddess, 173,
  179, 183–86
Brown, Lindsay, 291
Building, 207–23; and constructing,
  199, 209–10; and cultivating, 114,
  209–23, 294; four causes of a,
  140–43; from out of dwelling, 74,
  208, 210; and nature, 195. *See also*
  Architect; Architecture; Dwelling

"Building, Dwelling, Thinking" (Heidegger), 207
Burnet, John, 315n.4
Butler, Judith, 32, 58; on body and nature, 41–44, 147; criticism of, 23–25, 43–49, 309n.20; on de Beauvoir, 311n.4; on Merleau-Ponty, 314n.24; on Kristeva, 311n.5; *Gender Trouble,* 23, 41; on origins of patriarchy, 34; theory of gender identity, 23–25, 41–44, 47

Caputo, John D., 305n.4; on *aletheia,* 37; on Being, 36, 297; on community, 278, 340n.51; on Heidegger, 204, 342n.66; on Nietzsche, 75; *Radical Hermeneutics,* 26; on thinking, 9, 206; on undermining power, 200, 271, 336n.3; on wonder, 288
Caring: *a-legein* and, 283–84; as cultivating of growing things, 210–23; in feminist ethics, 17, 278–80, 296; and giving, 298–99; and labor, 171, 210–23; in *Mlle Pogany,* 110–14. *See also* Compassion; Difference, respect for; Ethics; Feeling; Human being, as caring
Cause: as *aition,* 140; distinguished from origin, 34. *See also* Aristotle, theory of four causes; Efficient cause; Formal cause; Material Cause
Change, 68; need for unusual, 270–71; rejection of, by Olympians, 277; understood as transfer of power, 270. *See also* Coming-to-be and passing-away; Movement, backward; Movement, forward
Charioteer, The (470 B.C.), 326nn.7, 10
Cheney, Jim, 10; on consensual decision-making, 286; on ecofeminism and deep ecology, 327n.2, 329n.11, 336n.5; ethic of bioregional narrative of, 292–93; on gift-exchange economy, 342nn.62, 63;

on moral community, 292; on relational ethics, 279
Cixous, Hélène, 76, 77, 101, 329n.17; use of Derrida, 7, 281; *jouissance* in, 133; on knowledge and power, 298–99; on love and power, 91–92, 94; on passivity, 329n.12; on pregnancy, 214, 219; on the selfsame, 86–87; on writing with the body, 8, 16, 190
Clément, Catherine, 298
"Clod and the Pebble, The" (Blake), 173
Coming-to-be: of a baby, 152–71; of a building, 140–43; of a table, 281–82; of a tree, 142–45; as an unlocking, 225–27. *See also* Change; Coming-to-be and passing-away; Origin; Movement; Swaying
Coming-to-be and passing-away, 194; in dwelling, 210; and eternal recurrence, 218; feminine and masculine and, 76–77; as historicized, 81
Community, 296; caring for, 264; decision-making in, 256–57; as a gathering, 282–84; moral, 279, 292; nature as included in, 293; new definition of, 278; of simple societies, 262–63, 276–77. *See also* Gathering; Neighborhood; Place
Compassion, 210, 260; in *Mlle Pogany,* 110–14, 118, 120–21
Concealment: of Being, 79–80; definition of, 37, 99; dominated by unconcealment, 127, 149–50; in Heidegger, 37, 79–81, 99, 303, 309–10n.25; as the locked-up, 227; in Merleau-Ponty, 54–55; and mortality, 124; and nature, 37, 79–81; as resistance, 227; suppression of, 88, 149–50, 194, 217; women associated with, 98, 132–33. *See also* Sheltering; Wild, the

"Conversations on a Country Path"
(Heidegger), 36
Creativity: and active/passive dichotomy, 127; as eco-destructive concept, 189, 265; in Heidegger, 295;
in Nietzsche, 85–88, 91–92, 94,
317n.20; as phallocentric, 196;
in Plato, 211; and will, 72; and
women, 100
Crying, 200–201, 203, 204
Culture: etymology of, 129; meaning
of, 128–29. See also Building;
Dwelling; Making; Multiculturalism;
Techne
Culture/nature dichotomy, 11, 107–9,
189–91, 194–207; attempt to deconstruct, 44–46, 56–58, 128–29,
194–207; and Being, 9, 11, 128,
191, 202–3; healing gap in,
188–223; and home, 130–36, 151,
208, 294; in poststructuralist discourse, 39–40, 42–43, 47–48,
202–3; and public/private dichotomy, 130–33, 135–36, 170–71; and
techne and phusis, 152–71, 195; and
women, 46, 102, 130–36, 152–71,
211, 213
Current: change from river to electrical, 243; and courant, 228; and currency, 244; discovery of alternating,
335n.22; in stream, 227–29
Custom. See Nomos; Thesmos
Cycladic figurine (2800–2300 B.C.,
from Amorgos), 250, 253–54,
256–60; Cycladic peoples and, 255;
folded-arm style, 249–52; "frying
pan" figurines and, 254–55; giving
in, 252; holding in, 259–60; sway
of, 254–60; violin forms of, 253

Dairy cows: suffering of, in factory
farms, 226, 232; use of, for ham-
burger meat, 230; veal as by-product
of, 235–36

Daly, Mary, 16, 133, 171, 190, 305n.3
Dancing, 282; African-American, 268;
in Cycladic figurine, 257; Minoan,
178–79, 180; Native American,
314–15n.28; in Nietzsche, 218
Death. See Coming-to-be and passing-
away; Mortality
De Beauvoir, Simone, 76, 202, 305n.3,
311n.4, 313n.21; The Second Sex,
305n.6
Deconstruction, 25, 99, 300, 312n.15;
of culture/nature dichotomy, 44–45,
128–29. See also Derrida, Jacques
Deep ecology, 5, 45; and ecofeminism,
272, 295, 327n.2, 329n.11, 336n.5;
use of Heidegger, 321n.32
De Lauretis, Teresa, 10; on feminist
subjectivity, 292; on sexual difference, 45
Deleuze, Gilles, 7, 293
Delphic Oracle, 118, 178, 277–78
Demeter, 275–76, 277
Derrida, Jacques, 7, 46; criticism of,
7, 22, 24, 25, 26–27, 37–38, 285,
309–10n.25; on Heidegger, 3, 26,
285, 309–10n.25; on metaphysics,
22, 24–27, 34, 289, 300; différance
in, 25, 27, 34–35, 37; feminine in,
47, 99–101, 128; and gender skepticism, 14; on logos, 281; and Nietzsche, 26–27, 99–101; on place, 290;
origin in, 34; theory of language, 25;
on thinking, 206
Descartes, René, 46, 192
Desire: artistic, 85–88, 91–92,
317n.20; as disruptive force, 8, 288;
as male, 91–92, 152, 196; and power
in Nietzsche, 85–88, 91–92, 94,
101, 317n.4; for self in metaphysics,
289. See also Creativity; Feeling;
Jouissance; Willing
Development, concept of: as ecodestructive, 189, 192, 265; as western,
264–65

Dichotomies. *See under specific names:*
    Active/passive; Culture/nature;
    Inside/outside; Masculine/feminine;
    Matter/form; Public/private; Self/
    other; Subject/object
Difference: and Being, 35, 65, 80,
    127–28; between and within entities,
    261, 289; bodily openness to,
    176–79; cancellation of, 200, 289;
    Derrida on, 25, 27, 34–35, 37; and
    feminine, 101–2; Heidegger on,
    35–38, 65; home as open to, 262;
    and knowledge, 299–300; and need
    for self-criticality, 267–68; and
    need to let time be, 287–88; open-
    ing spaces for, 2, 10, 188, 195,
    261–63, 270, 290–93; origin as,
    34–35; respect for, 206–7, 222–23,
    285–89, 296–97; sexual, 32–33,
    45, 48, 156–67, 204–5; wonder
    in face of, 288–89. *See also*
    Dichotomies
Dike (necessity, justice), 277, 278,
    335n.24, 341–42n.59
Dionysian/Dionysius, 100, 316n.14,
    317n.20, 327n.12
Drum, voice of, 301
Dwelling, 68, 71, 295; and Being's
    turn, 68; and *ethos,* 278–80; etymol-
    ogy of, 207–8. *See also* Architec-
    ture; Building

Earth: and concealment, 303; as femi-
    nine, 132–33; as ground, 33, 67; in
    Heidegger, 35, 295; suppression of,
    136, 218. *See also* Concealment;
    Matter; Nature; Phusis
Eco (home), 10, 289–90
Ecofeminism, 10, 16; and deep ecol-
    ogy, 327n.2, 329n.11, 336n.5;
    definition of, 312n.9; as irrational,
    207; and redefining human being, 9,
    191–223, 207–23; and thinking feel-
    ingly, 114–19, 203–7, 283–85,

288–89. *See also* Culture/nature
    dichotomy; Shiva, Vandana
Ecology: and ecoholists, 199, 292;
    ecological dangers, 193–94; and
    economy, 289–90; ecosystem, 66;
    etymology of, 262; and gender,
    39–40; as narrative, 261; and simple
    societies, 277. *See also* Culture/nature
    dichotomy; Deep ecology; Ecofeminism;
    Environment; Nature; Phusis
Economy: as dynamic of Will to Power,
    147, 264, 317n.19; and ecology,
    289–90; etymology of, 262, 272–75;
    and gift-exchange, 342nn.62, 63;
    and law of distribution, 244–47; as
    primary cause of ecological destruc-
    tion, 210, 271–72; as running our
    systems, 244; and western market,
    263–67. *See also Nomos*
Efficient (or moving) cause: carpenter
    as, 281; father as, 157–59, 161–67;
    of a house, 141–42, 195; of a
    tree, 144
Eisler, Riane, 175, 309n.24, 327n.14
Elshtain, Jean Bethke, 17, 131,
    312n.16, 319n.7
Emotion. *See* Desire; Feeling; Heart
End. *See Telos*
Energy: consumption of, in West,
    333n.13; definition of, 234–35; as
    energeia and *dunamis,* 170, 235;
    electromagnetic, 233, 335n.23; in
    industrial revolution, 225; kinetic,
    230, 231, 233; mechanical rotational,
    230, 233; nature as, 169–70, 180,
    225–26; potential, 231, 233, 238;
    as power of Will to Power, 225,
    333–34n.14; as primary matter, 170,
    234; transforming of, 232–36. *See also*
    Nature, control of; Will to Power, the
Environment: destruction of, 190–91,
    210, 336n.8; environmental advertis-
    ing, 134; and ethic of place, 10,
    261–63, 287, 292–93; and setting

Environment *(continued)*
    aside and wilderness preserves, 268.
    See also Body; Earth; Ecofeminism;
    Ecology; Matter; Nature, control of;
    Phusis; World-earth-home
Epistemology. *See* Knowledge
Essence: definition of, 30; feminine as,
    307n.5. *See also* Essentialism
Essentialism: 7, 11, 12, 14–17, 24,
    29, 40, 134; definition of, 14; and
    motherhood, 16–17, 41
Ethics: of care, 16–17, 213, 278–80,
    299; critique of Kantian, 327n.3;
    environmental, of place, 10,
    261–63, 287, 292–93; *ethos* and,
    261, 272, 278, 280; Heidegger on,
    261; and home, 292. *See also* Caring;
    Compassion; Limits
Evernden, Neil, 279, 321–22n.32,
    334–35n.20, 341n.56
Existential-phenomenology: method of,
    7–8; use of, by feminists, 5–7. *See
    also* Heidegger, Martin; Husserl,
    Edmund; Merleau-Ponty, Maurice;
    Phenomenology; Sartre, Jean Paul

Factory farming, 334n.19; chickens in,
    247; and dehorning of calves, 232.
    See also Dairy cows
Farías, Victor, *Heidegger and Nazism,*
    6
Feeling: continuous with *logos* in Clas-
    sical Greece, 283–84; dominated
    by reason, 201, 281; and mood in
    Dasein, 295; and thinking, 115–20,
    203–7, 283–85, 288–89. *See also*
    Desire
Female experience, 4; of body, 15, 213;
    diversity of, 14–15. *See also* Breast-
    feeding; Mothering; Pregnancy
Female values, 12, 19–21
Feminine, the, 30–31; absencing of,
    31, 96–103, 160, 200, 266; Derrida
    on, 47, 99–101, 128; disruptive pos-

sibilities of, 96–103, 160; earth and
    nature associated with, 9, 45–46,
    82, 90, 138, 157; as essence, 307n.5;
    exile of, in metaphysics, 3, 4, 75;
    letting in of, 128, 171; life as, in
    Nietzsche, 87–88, 94, 225; in *Mlle
    Pogany,* 124; as multiple sexuality,
    101, 128; Neumann on, 323n.10,
    339n.38; Nietzsche on, 87–88,
    90–94, 99–101; as ontological prin-
    ciple, 11–12, 16, 125; as passive,
    97–98; philosophy of, 11–12; pres-
    encing of, 29–31; as resistant,
    91–92; sky as, 131. *See also*
    Ontology, feminist
Feminism: and feminist discourse, 46;
    goals of, in 1970s, 13; gynocentric,
    15, 20, 22, 41, 98–99, 103, 134–35;
    poststructuralist, 7, 14; representa-
    tion of women in, 24–25; spiritual,
    312–13n.18; use of existential-
    phenomenology in, 5–7; and women
    of color, 269, 307n.4. *See also* Eco-
    feminism; Gender; Ontology, femi-
    nist; Theory, feminist; Third World
Feminism from Pressure to Politics
    (Miles and Finn), 15
Final Cause: father as, 158–59; in mak-
    ing of a building, 141; in tree, 143.
    See also Telos
Finn, Geraldine, on Sartre, 305–6n.7
Flying Turtle (Brancusi), 122
Form: dominance of, 155–71; and
    eidos, 140–41, 216, 322n.4,
    334n.15; as gender-biased, 158–59;
    knowledge of, 216; in making, 194,
    211–12; naming of phusis as, 138,
    155–56, 159, 164–71, 229; overtak-
    ing of gathering by, 282; synthesis
    with matter as energy, 235. *See also*
    Formal cause
Formal cause: in coming-to-be of a
    baby, 157–59; dominance of,
    157–71; in growth of a tree, 143–44;

in making of a building, 140–41
Foucault, Michel, 6, 7, 23; Being in,
47; body in, 41, 42–43, 97, 313n.19;
and gender skepticism, 14; on law,
337n.18; power in, 47, 94, 95, 97,
98; on subjugated knowledge,
266–67, 297
Foundationalism, 24–33. *See also*
Ground; Origin
Four Zoas, The (Blake), 206
Fox, Warwick, 292–93, 327n.2,
329n.18
Free, etymology of, 329n.19
Freud, Sigmund, 40, 317n.16
Fuss, Diane, 15, 307n.11

Gadamer, Hans-Georg, 5; on Derrida,
308n.15, 309–10n.25
Gaia, 277; hypothesis, 232–33
Gatens, Moira, 329n.17
Gathering: breasts as, 184; and circle,
282–83, 297; compared with dissemination, 285; dominated by form, 282;
and early human gatherers, 338n.30;
gathering-round, 2, 282–83, 289;
Gestell as a, 146, 339n.34; in grape
harvest, 339n.33; lack of, in a fluid,
230; lack of, in a system, 245–47;
lack of, in storing, 242; *logos* as,
281–89; in *Mlle Pogany,* 105, 113;
place and, 290; *polis* and, 283; in *The
Seal,* 64; in the Snake Goddess, 180,
183, 184; social gatherings as, 276,
282–83; of a stream, 229; techne
and, 127, 281–82. *See also* Efficient
cause; Heidegger, Martin, the fourfold in
Gauthier, Xavière, 301
Gender: as ambiguous, 54–55, 57;
androgyny, 40–41, 131; and bisexuals, 1, 81; and body, 8, 12–22, 23,
24, 39–44, 57–58; denaturalization,
8–9; gay, 81; *genos* and, 43; heterosexual, 12, 39, 42, 54–55, 57–58,
81, 134; and lesbians, 15, 23, 81;
and Nietzsche's Overman, 93–94;
ontological significance of, 32; openness, 19; plurality, 12, 23, 26, 31,
41, 43, 58, 77; skepticism, 13–21.
See also Difference, sexual; Heterosexuality; Masculine/feminine
dichotomy
Gender Trouble (Butler), 23, 41
Generation of Animals, The (Aristotle),
156, 161–62, 165–66, 323–24n.20
Giacometti, Alberto, 64
Gifts, 270, 276, 289, 296; and gift-
exchange economy, 342nn.62, 63;
presencing as, 297–98; story as,
285–87, 299. *See also* Giving
Gilligan, Carol, 17, 279
Gimbutas, Marija, 161, 168, 174, 177,
309n.24, 323n.10
Giving: Being as, 29, 176, 284,
297–98; birth as, 59–60, 214–15,
219; of breasts, 62, 186; bringing-
forth as, 226; of Cycladic sculptures,
251; of Minoan art, 161; Nietzsche
on, 86–88; as not self-sacrifice,
298–99; power and, 297–303; techne
as, 187; telling of stories as, 299. *See
also* Gifts; Limits; Swaying
Goddess, the, 174, 295; association
of, with infancy of civilization, 176;
as Being, 161, 168–70, 171,
312–13n.18; Moon, 115–16;
as Phusis, 165, 168–71; Snake,
173–87; term as problematic, 251.
See also Demeter; *Dike;* Goddess,
religions; Hestia; Themis
Goddess, religions, 274; demise of,
168–70; Greek state control of, 275
Gorgias (Plato), 338n.23
Graybeal, Jean, 318n.30, 328–29n.9,
338n.27, 340n.43
Griffin, Susan, 133, 265
Ground, 25–38; as abyss of Being,
28–29, 32, 33; Being in metaphysics

Ground *(continued)*
as, 297–98; body as, 22, 42–43, 55;
earth as, 33, 47–48, 67, 202–3; need
for new conceptualization of, 26–27;
subject as, 22, 27–28
Guittari, Felix, 293

Harrison, Jane, 276–77, 278
Hartsock, Nancy, 10, 131, 133, 171,
307n.3, 312n.17, 320n.17; on power
centers, 98
Health: care, 211, 217, 221–23; and
mortality, 121; and techne in Aristotle, 150–51
Heart, and link to thinking in Classical
Greece, 284, 339–40n.39. *See also*
Feeling
Hearth, 276, 283
Hegel, G.W.F., 78, 85; *Aesthetics,*
288–89; on dialectic, 93, 94, 119;
on essence, 309n.21; home in, 131,
293–94; and representation of Being,
27; on sexual difference, 204–5; on
wonder, 288–89
Heidegger, Martin, 5, 8, 14, 22; agreement of, with Derrida, 3, 26, 285;
aletheia in, 27, 36–37, 79–80, 82,
101, 137–38, 194; on Anaximander,
297–98; on *arche,* 320n.19; on
Aristotle, 139–45, 150–51, 156,
320n.20; art in, 60, 65, 295; on
Being, 35–38, 77–80, 297–98, 300,
309n.23; on being-in-the-world, 18;
on building, 207–10; the clearing in,
302–3; on creativity, 295; criticism
of, 18, 27, 75, 156, 209, 330n.25;
and deep ecology, 321–22n.32;
Derrida on, 38, 309–10n.25; on
difference, 35–38, 65; *dunamis* and
energeia in, 170, 332–33n.9; on
dwelling, 208–9; *Ereignis,* 27, 28,
35, 36, 297, 300; *Es gibt,* 297; on
ethos, 261, 278; the fourfold in, 36,
111, 123, 315–16nn.3, 4, 325n.34,
330n.20, 335n.26; *Gestell,* 94–96,
145–51, 224–48; on heart, 284,
339–40n.39; on Heraclitus, 79–80,
282–83, 320n.18; on hints, 190; on
home, 204, 295; on human facticity,
217–18; on identity, 35; *logos* in,
281–82, 309–10n.25; on metaphysics, 27–29, 33, 289, 297–98; and
Nazism, 6; nearness and remoteness
in, 198–200, 309n.23; on need, 265;
Nietzsche in, 82–84, 94–96; and the
Open, 28, 35–36; origins in, 34–38;
on Parmenides, 203, 310n.26,
320n.18; philosophy of history, 75,
78–79, 82–84, 136–38, 297–98;
phusis in, 79–80, 137–39, 150–51,
338n.31; physics in, 333n.11; *poiesis*
in, 126, 138, 145–46, 149, 225,
226; presencing, 29–38; on releasement, 329n.12; and return to Greeks,
4, 37–38; on standing-reserve,
148, 157, 169, 235, 312n.10,
334–35n.20; on techne and phusis,
137–39, 150–51, 194; technology in,
95–96, 146–51, 224–25; on thinking, 28–29, 204, 331n.29; the turn,
67–69; unworld in, 246. *Works:*
Being and Time, 295, 330n.25;
"Building, Dwelling, Thinking,"
207; "Conversations on a Country
Path," 36; *Identity and Difference,*
35; *Introduction to Metaphysics,*
295; "The Origin of a Work of Art,"
35, 65, 295; "The Question Concerning Technology," 146. *See also*
Concealment; Dwelling; Gathering;
Thinking
Heidegger and Nazism (Farías), 6
Heidel, William, 315–16n.4
Heisenberg, Werner, 332n.8, 333n.10
Hera, 174
Heraclitus, 320n.18; on fire, 283; on
phusis, 79–80; on phusis and *logos,*
282
Hesiod, 277, 337n.19
Hestia, 132, 283

Heterosexuality, subversion of, 23–24
Holler, Linda, 285
Home: and culture/nature dichotomy,
    130–36, 151, 208, 294; definition of,
    291–92, 296–97; devaluation of,
    135–36; environmental, 296; as the
    familiar, 292–93, 295; in Hegel,
    131, 293–94; in Heidegger, 204,
    295; and homelessness, 204, 247,
    265, 295; in Husserl, 294–95;
    nomadic, 296; from *oikos* (eco) 10,
    289–90; and openness to others,
    296–97; place as, 291–92; and
    public/private dichotomy, 130–36,
    170–71; and subjectivity, 292–93; as
    wilderness, 130, 136; women con-
    fined to, in early Greece, 132–33,
    170–71; and wonder, 289. *See also*
    Building; Dwelling; Place
Homer, 276; *The Illiad*, 131
Human being: androcentrism of,
    192–93; attempt to redefine, 56–57,
    186, 191–223; building and making
    as central to, 156, 170–71, 193–94,
    207–23; as caring, 10, 171, 206,
    263; creating limits for, 278–80;
    dwelling as basic character, 207–8;
    as efficient cause, 141–43; feeling
    and, 203–7; as gender-biased,
    158–59; as meaning of the earth,
    86–88; need for redefinition of, 45,
    128, 153, 171, 190–91, 201; need
    for touch in, 72–73; and openness to
    Being, 21–22; and participation in
    Being, 32, 171, 217, 278, 300;
    reason as central characteristic of,
    191–93, 204–7; and techne and
    phusis, 139; and technology, 28. *See
    also* Body; Building; Dwelling; Feel-
    ing; Mortality; Nature, control of;
    Technology
Husserl, Edmund, 5; on body, 49;
    on home, 294–95; on intention-
    ality, 313–14n.22; on life-world,
    313–14n.22; on relation between

theoretical and lived world, 294–95,
    333n.12; on thinking, 205, 216
Hydroelectric reservoirs: in northern
    Manitoba, 238; in northern Quebec,
    240, 241

Identity and Difference (Heidegger), 35
"Immaculate Perception, The" (Nietz-
    sche), 85
Immortality: and Greek deities,
    110–11, 113–14, 277; search for,
    in metaphysics, 135–36, 191
Indigenous people: circle for Sioux,
    283; concept of nature in, 226; and
    environmental activists, 269; Euro-
    pean attempt to liquidate, 269. *See
    also* Difference, opening spaces for;
    Third World
Introduction to Metaphysics (Heideg-
    ger), 295
Inside/outside dichotomy: and body,
    56–57; in *Mlle Pogany,* 119–20,
    123; and techne and phusis, 140,
    141, 145, 164–65, 211–21; under-
    mined by cultivating-building, 212,
    213–15
Irigaray, Luce, 16, 77, 133; on being
    women, 202; use of Derrida, 7, 281;
    on desire, 92, 101; on metaphysical
    desire for the self-same, 289; on
    miming the feminine, 99, 125, 198,
    329n.17; use of physics, 329n.13;
    and Plato's myth of the cave, 80–81;
    on women as unrepresentable, 101,
    102, 309n.22; on women's multiple
    sexuality, 101, 309n.22, 312n.18

Jarret, Susan: on Cixous and Clément,
    342n.60; on *nomos* and *logos,*
    338n.22
Jouissance: definition of, 319n.15; and
    wonder, 289

Kant, Immanuel, 27, 78, 327n.3
Kheel, Marti, 285, 327n.2

King, Ynestra, 133, 296, 312n.9
Kinship, system, overtaking of,
    274–75, 276
Kiss, The (Brancusi), 110, 112
Knowledge: alternatives to western,
    299–300; bioregional, 287–88,
    299–300; bodily, 215–16; in
    cultivating-building, 215–16;
    and power, 298–300; subjugated,
    266–67, 297; techne as, 138, 159,
    215–16, 229; universal, 216–17
Kristeva, Julia, 7, 16, 309n.24,
    318n.30; Butler on, 311n.5; and
    prediscursive maternal, 312n.18;
    on pregnancy, 214

Lacan, Jacques, 7
Lame Deer, 283
Lampert, Laurence, 93, 317–18n.25
Law: bioregional, 275–76; and effect of
    establishment of Athenian democ-
    racy on women, 274; Foucault on,
    337n.18. *See also Dike; Nomos;*
    Themis; *Thesmos*
Lefort, Claude, 6
Leibniz, Gottfried Wilhelm, 27, 28, 78,
    192
Levin, David, 270, 308n.13
Limits, 275–76; establishing of human,
    278–80; place and, 290–92. *See also*
    Gifts; *Telos*
Little Bird (Brancusi), 70
Logos, 83; as Being, 297; of body, 52;
    and discordance with nature, 83,
    192, 281, 341n.55; and feeling, 204,
    283–84; as a gathering laying-out,
    286–89; and harmony with nature,
    282; history of, 192; and logocen-
    trism, 281; male as, 157; in a remote
    village, 285–87; rooted in *legein,*
    281; and sexual difference, 157;
    and the white Word, 271. *See also*
    Reason; Thinking
Lyotard, Jean-François, 7

Making, 209; in techne and phusis,
    194, 211–12
Mallin, Samuel, 306n.10
Marcuse, Herbert, 6
Martin, Biddy, and Chandra Talpade
    Mohanty, 102, 293, 297
Marx, Karl, 193; and Marxian analysis
    of reproductive labor, 219–20
Masculine/feminine dichotomy, 4, 19,
    76–77, 90–94, 96–103, 125–27,
    307n.6. *See also* Feminine, the; Gen-
    der, heterosexual; Heterosexuality
Material cause: father as, 161–67; in
    the growth of a tree, 142–43; in the
    making of a building, 140–41;
    mother as, 157–58, 161–62; and
    potential matter, 162. *See also*
    Matter; Primary matter
Matriarchy, 174–75
Matter, 162–67; definition of, 143;
    potential, 142–43, 162. *See also*
    Material cause; Matter/form dichot-
    omy; Primary matter
Matter/form dichotomy, 107, 191; in
    Aristotle, 157–58, 196
Merleau-Ponty, Maurice, 5, 6, 8, 14,
    330n.25; on Being, 73, 280; Butler
    on, 314n.24; on concealment,
    54–55; on the lived body, 49–58,
    60, 216, 285, 291; on thinking, 216
Metaphysics, The (Aristotle), 117, 155,
    159, 163, 164, 216, 324n.26
Metaphysics, western, 118; definition
    of, 3, 322n.2; denial of body and
    nature in, 32, 45–46, 48, 82, 191,
    198; Derrida on, 22, 24–27, 34, 289,
    300; the feminine in, 3–4, 31, 46,
    75, 90, 96–103, 160, 200, 206;
    foundationalism of, 25–31; as logo-
    centric, 281; gender bias of, 3,
    75–81; Heidegger on, 27–29, 33,
    289, 297–98; nature in, 48, 30,
    82–84, 169–71; need for security in,
    191, 270; Nietzsche and, 89–90;

principle of identity in, 35; representation of Being in, 9, 27–29, 77–81, 82–83, 297, 300. *See also* Being; Phallocentrism; Thinking

Method: of existential-phenomenology, 7–8; feminist, 7–8; need for new, 197, 198; of thinking through art, 7–8

Michelangelo, 107

Midgley, Mary, 296

Milk: cups for, on Minoan vessels, 326n.6; as life-giving, 184; and milking of bulls, 227; production of, in dairy cows, 226, 230, 231, 232

Miller, Meg, 132

Mills, Patricia, on Hegel, 317n.22, 24; 319n.9, 340n.52

Min, Yang-Soon, 268

Minh-ha, Trinh T., 10; on difference, 270; on different oppressions as interrelated, 264, 336n.10; on knowledge and power, 299; on leaking of categories, 268–69; on telling stories, 285–86

Minoan culture: arching of back in, 177; architecture of, 177–78; bull-leaping in, 177. *See also* Goddess, the, Snake

Mlle Pogany I (Brancusi), 105–23; caring in, 110–14; compassion in, 110–14, 118, 120–23; and gathering in, 105, 113; inside/outside dichotomy deconstructed in, 118–19, 123; openness to others in, 117–18; passivity in, 116, 119; sheltering in, 110–14, 116, 123

Mlle Pogany II (Brancusi), 120

Mlle Pogany III (Brancusi), 107, 120–24; the feminine in, 124

Monoculturalism, 269

Mortality, 120–21, 217–18; acceptance of, 73–74, 260, 277; in birth, 219; in Giacometti and Brancusi, 64–65; repression of, 135–36, 191, 201, 220, 222, 242, 277

Mother: nature as, 161, 171; historical change in concept of, 152. *See also* Aristotle, generation in; Mothering

Mothering, 102; body, 58–60, 130, 133–34, 170–71, 184, 212–16, 218–20; cultural devaluation of, 20, 152–53; cultural formation of, 19–21; essentialism and, 16–17; 41; and labor, 59; romanticization of, 19. *See also* Breastfeeding; Caring; Coming-to-be, of a baby; Female experience; O'Brien, Mary; Pregnancy; Reproduction; Rich, Adrienne; Ruddick, Sara

Movement: Aristotle's definition of, 224, 233; of Being, 29, 77–81, 125–27, 145–51, 165, 297, 300; being-moved, 64, 252; body as, 57; in Cycladic figurine, 249–50, 253–54, 256–61; description of, 125–26; of father in generation, 162–68; female as lacking, 164–65; in Minoan Snake Goddess, 176–81, 183–88; in *Mlle Pogany*, 105–24; need for new paradigms of, 192, 270; Newtonian laws of, 229; of phusis, 79–81, 144, 145; in *The Seal*, 61–74; of speech, 280; of techne, 145, 196; of Will to Power (and *Gestell*), 71–73, 75, 91–92, 143–51, 186, 224–48. *See also* Building; Change; Coming-to-be; Efficient cause; Energy; Gathering; Movement, backward; Movement, forward; *Poiesis;* Sheltering; Swaying; Touch; Will to Power, the

Movement, backward: concealment as, 78–81; drawing as, 196–97; as earthward pull, 62, 65, 120–21, 190, 217, 219; and ecofeminists, 207; and feeling, 205–7; as feminine, 76–77; 79–82, 200, 257; gravity as, 188, 231; and health, 217; and irreversible damage to environment, 206;

Movement, backward *(continued)*
need for, 217, 300–301; ontological
exile of, 88, 197–98; of phusis, 88,
127, 297–98; as regressive, 98–99,
123–24, 257, 300; as return to past
and prehistory, 4, 37–38, 195,
262–63, 300; rhythm as, 197; of a
stream, 228, 229; as transformation
to passive resistant, 231; in writing,
9, 195. *See also* Concealment;
Mortality; Resistant
Movement, forward: as challenging-
forth, 69, 145–51, 224; of economic
growth, 272; and functionality, 282;
human consciousness as, 207, 297;
as masculine, 76–77, 106; as phallic,
164–65, 196; of thinking, 205–7;
time as, 287–88; unconcealment as,
78–81; of the West, 265–66; of
western Being, 126, 297–98; as will
to live, 71–72; Will to Power as,
71–73, 75, 81–82, 91–92, 186,
224–48; and writing, 300–301
Multiculturalism, as a western solution,
269–70
Musing, 118–19, 123; in *The Thinking
Muse* (Allen and Finn), 305n.5,
306n.8

Naess, Arne, 39, 293, 312n.11
Nature: and art, 109; associated with
the feminine, 9, 45–46, 82, 90, 138,
157; bodily openness to, 14, 43–49,
50–57, 202–3; as concealment, 37,
79–81; control of, 18, 11–32, 60,
94–96, 109, 193–94, 295; as cultural
fiction, 12, 23, 24; demise of, 151,
161–71, 210, 211; domination of,
146–51; as fixed, 47–48, 202–3; as
fluid, 202–3; as form in Aristotle,
138, 155–71, 229; and gender,
39–40, 41, 43–44; as ground,
32–33, 67; history of, in metaphysics, 30, 48, 82–84, 169–71; human
alienation from, 8, 189–96, 201;
Marxian approach to, 193; merging
with, 199–200; as in need of human
intervention, 280; in Nietzsche, 3,
82, 84–88, 90, 94–95, 225; as
standing-reserve, 148, 157, 169,
235, 312n.10, 334–35n.20. *See also*
Concealment; Culture/nature dichotomy; Earth; Environment; Matter;
Phusis; Techne; Wild, the
Nearness: of Being, 309n.23; etymology of, 198; lack of, 263; and neighbor, 198–200, 208, 265–71
Necessity. *See Dike*
Need: *alegein* as place of, 283–84;
definition of, 73; Heidegger on, 265;
and needlessness, 265, 295
Neighborhood, 290, 292; etymology of, 198, 208; nearness and,
198–200, 208, 265–71; wonder
and, 289. *See also* Community;
Home; Place
Niagara Falls: and falls water as waste,
239; technological control of, 240
Nietzsche, Friedrich, 5, 9, 116; affirmation of play in, 26; artistic desire
(creativity) in, 85–88, 91–92, 94,
100, 317n.20; Being as Will to
Power in, 27, 75, 89–96, 196; on
the body, 218; and Derrida, 26–27,
99–101; on eternal recurrence, 218;
figure of Life in, 87–88, 94, 225; and
Foucault, 47; on the gulf between the
sexes, 92–94, 322n.9; Heidegger on,
82–84, 94–96; the herd as feminine,
90–94; the higher men as masculine,
92–93; love as a commanding in,
85–88, 179–80; nature in, 3, 82,
84–88, 90, 94–95, 225; on the Overman, 87, 89, 93–94, 218; on passing
away, 218, 341–42n.59; on power,
86–88, 89–96; the sex act in, 91; on
the will, 218, 246, 278; on women,
90–94, 99–101; and Zarathustra, 82,
84–88, 317–18n.25. *Works:* "The
Immaculate Perception," 85; *Thus*

Spoke Zarathustra, 82, 85, 86, 87, 94, 118, 180, 225; *Twilight of the Idols,* 317n.20; *The Will to Power;* 82, 316n.11. *See also* Will to Power, the
Nihilism, 26, 266, 270, 296
Noddings, Nel, 279
Nomos (custom, law): androcentrism of, 262; difference from *thesmos,* 277–78; and ethics, 278–79; etymology of, 272–75; first recorded meanings of, 275, 337n.19; Levin on, 337n.13; and *logos,* 338n.22; and *phusis,* 277; and *polis,* 338n.28; replacement of *thesmos* with, 273–77; as specifically written law, 274–75
Nurturance, 21, 210
Nye, Andrea, 190, 305–6nn.7, 8, 327–28n.4

O'Brien, Mary, 16, 133, 309n.24, 320n.17; on Hegel, 317n.22; on mothering, 152, 213; on philosophy of birth, 330n.25
Oldenberg, Claes, 206
Olympic Games, 326–27n.11
Ontology: feminist, 11, 18, 21, 75–82, 96–103, 125–28, 189, 305n.3; non-ontology, 76, 300–301
Origin, 24, 34–38, 64–65, 155; and *différance,* 34; as difference, 35–36; distinguished from cause, 34; as creative strife between world and earth, 35, 295. *See also* Birth; Coming-to-be, of a baby
"Origin of a Work of Art, The" (Heidegger), 35, 65, 295
Ostwald, Martin, 273, 275
Other, the, 117–18; in metaphysics, 94–95; opening to, 81. *See also* Difference; Otherness
Otherness, 160, 188–89; entities open to, 88, 194; and gender, 81; nature as, 84; Nietzsche on, 218; openness

to, of Minoans, 177–79; openness to, of *Mlle Pogany,* 117–18. *See also* Difference; Pregnancy, undermining of dichotomies in
Owen, Joseph, 320nn.18, 21, 321n.28, 323n.12

Padel, Ruth, 132, 133
Pandora, 160
Parmenides, 203, 310n.26, 320n.18
Passivity: Cixous and Clément on, 329n.12; and the feminine, 97–98, 143; seeming, of a stream's interrelations with the sky, 228; shown up positively in *Mlle Pogany,* 116, 120; sperm as, in Australian aboriginals, 127
Petersen, Eugen, 328n.7
Phallocentrism: of Being (as Will to Power), 4, 9, 18, 82; of concepts, 4; definition of, 2; gender as effect of, 23; of metaphysics, 3, 9, 19, 281
Phenomenology, 49; dialectic of, 306n.2; method of, 7–8. *See also* Existential-phenomenology; Husserl, Edmund; Merleau-Ponty, Maurice
Philip, Marlene Nourbese, 271
Philosophy: disrespect for earth in, 5, 201; as love of wisdom, 204, 217. *See also* Metaphysics; Ontology
Phusis, 78, 79–83, 109, 134; in Aristotle, 139–45, 154–55, 160; as Being, 145, 146–56, 168–71, 339–40n.39; decline of, 168–71, 211; definition of, 79–80, 194; in generation, 160; as Goddess, 165, 168–71; in Heraclitus, 79–80, 282; and *logos,* 281–83, 341n.55; movement of, 79–81, 88, 127, 144–45, 297–98; named as form rather than matter in Aristotle, 138, 155–56, 159, 164–71, 229; respect for, 221–22. *See also* Earth; Environment; Matter; Nature; Techne and phusis

Physics: and nature, 234–35; use of, by
　Irigaray, 329n.13
Physics, The (Aristotle), 195
Place: as Greek *chora,* 290–91; as
　Greek *topos,* 65, 171, 290; and
　placelessness, 295. *See also* Commu-
　nity; Dwelling; Ethics, environmen-
　tal, of place; Home; Neighborhood;
　Subjectivity
Plant, Judith, 284–85, 296
Plato, 83, 85, 114; body in, 46; and
　eidos, 83, 140–41, 322n.4, 330n.25;
　Gorgias, 338n.23; Irigaray on,
　80–81; on *logos,* 192
Play, 4, 9, 26, 126, 300
Plumwood, Val, 191, 296, 327n.3,
　329nn.10, 11
Poiesis (bringing-forth), 126, 138, 149,
　219, 225, 226; compared with
　challenging-out, 145–46
Politics, The (Aristotle), 131
Poseidon (460 B.C.), 326n.7
Poststructuralism: body in, 12, 44,
　308n.16, 311n.6; criticisms of, 7,
　12, 31–32, 39, 44, 46–48, 55,
　311n.3; and critique of foundation-
　alism, 24–27, 39, 41, 46; culture
　and nature in, 31, 39–40, 42–43,
　46–48, 202–3; feminist use of,
　7, 202–3. *See also* Butler, Judith;
　Cixous, Hélène; Deconstruction;
　Derrida, Jacques; Foucault, Michel;
　Irigaray, Luce
Power, 97–98; in Cixous, 91–92, 297,
　298–99; compared with gathering,
　184–86, 282–83; as *dunamis,* 170,
　235, 332n.9; etymology of, 277; in
　Foucault, 17, 47, 75, 92, 94, 95, 98;
　and giving, 297–302; and knowl-
　edge, 298–300; in Nietzsche,
　86–88, 89–96; redefining of, 99;
　securing of, 282, 287; undermining
　of, 135, 213. *See also* Energy; Sys-
　tem; Will to Power, the
Pratt, Minnie Bruce, 297

Precognitive experience, 49–53
Pregnancy, 152–53, 156; description
　of, 13, 16, 20, 39, 48–49; response
　to phusis in, 58–59; undermining of
　dichotomies in, 212–16, 218–20.
　See also Mothering; Reproduction
Price, Sally, 263
Primary matter: definition of, 143;
　energy as, 170, 234; female as,
　162–63
Primitive, 209, 251; western search for,
　268, 294–95
Primitive Art in Civilized Places
　(Price), 263
Princess X (Brancusi), 106
Psychiatry, 211, 331n.31
Public/private dichotomy, 19, 20,
　130–36, 293, 319n.6; and building,
　208; in Greek society, 130–33,
　170–71; and dark/light, inner/outer
　dichotomies, 131–33

"Question Concerning Technology,
　The" (Heidegger), 146

Radical Hermeneutics (Caputo), 26
Reason, 83, 114; Apollo as god of,
　181–83; as essential characteristic of
　being human, 114, 191–93, 204–7;
　and feeling, 114–19, 201, 203–7,
　283–85, 288–89; history of, 192;
　institutionalized, 206; as *logos,* 83,
　281; as male 46, 183, 192–93. *See*
　also Logos; Thinking
Reproduction, 40, 220, 313n.21,
　331n.30; and production, 219–20;
　social construction of, 19–20. *See*
　also Aristotle, generation in; Mother-
　ing; Pregnancy
Reproductive technology, 58, 312n.8,
　331n.30
Resistant: concealment serving as, 227;
　fluid serving as, 227; subjugated
　knowledge as, 266–67, 297; women
　serving as, 91–92, 230

Rhythm: bending to, 257; in caring labor, 212, 217; in childbirth, 59–60; control of, in nature, 193–94, 199, 210; etymology of, 196–97; knowledge of, 215–16; need for, in theory, 300; social, 285–87; of speech, 280; of water-wheel's turning, 228. *See also* Swaying

Rich, Adrienne, 16, 218, 317n.18

Rolston, Holmes III, 261

Rosaldo, Michelle, 17

Ruddick, Sara, 10, 133; on caring labor, 171, 210, 213; on maternal thinking, 17, 284, 340n.45; on pregnancy and birth, 214, 219

St. Matthew (Michelangelo), 107

Saliou, Monique, 169, 175, 274

Salleh, Ariel, 16, 327n.2

Sartre, Jean Paul, 5, 6

Schopenhauer, Arthur, 78

Seal, The (Brancusi), 61–74, 106; carving and, 63–64; despair and, 72–73; face of, 70–71; gathering in, 64; openness to touch in, 62–63; sheltering in, 62–63

Second Sex, The (de Beauvoir), 305n.6

Self. *See* Self/other dichotomy; Subject; Subjectivism; Subjectivity; Subject/object dichotomy

Self/other dichotomy, 59, 191, 193, 199–200; undermined in pregnancy, 214–15

Sewing, 188; and relation to neighbor etymologically, 198

Sheltering: and building, 209; in grape harvest, 339n.33; lack of, in modern technology, 226–27, 238; in *Mlle Pogany,* 110–14, 116, 123; in movements back, 298; in pregnancy, 219; in *The Seal,* 62–63. *See also* Concealment

Shipp, George Pelham, 273, 275

Shiva, Vandana, 264

Snake: history of, as a symbol, 178; Nietzsche on, 326n.8; and Snake Goddess, 179–81, 183–87

Snake Goddess (Minoan, 1600 B.C.), 179–81, 183–87; and gathering in, 180, 183, 184; and holding in, 180–81, 184–86

Sophocles, *Antigone,* 274

Spelman, V. Elizabeth, 21

Spivak, Gayatri Chakravorty, 10, 301; on need for self-criticality, 267–68; on "subjectivist normativity," 267; on thinking, 9

Spretnak, Charlene, 272, 285

Starhawk, 16, 171

Stone, Merlin, 161, 168, 309n.24, 323n.10

Storing: compared with gathering, 282; as cultivating, 236–38; and hydro-electric pumped storage, 334n.17; and overcoming of nature, 237; as a securing, 237, 242; and stocking of lakes, 334n.18; and storage reservoirs in hydroelectric plant, 236–43

Story telling, 270, 285–88, 299, 301–3, 312n.15; and bioregional narratives, 292–93, 301–3

Subject: and ground, 22, 27–28; as multiple, 12, 27–29, 31; as presencing, 29–31. *See also* Self/other dichotomy; Subjectivism; Subjectivity; Subject/object dichotomy

Subjectivism, 31–32

Subjectivity, 4, 7, 292–93, 297; and subjective gift, 298

Subject/object dichotomy, 11, 14, 27–28, 59, 84, 148, 191; undermined in pregnancy, 214–15

Swaying, 113, 190, 197, 200. *See also* Rhythm

System: etymology of, 66, 246; hydro-electric power-line, 243–47; river, 241–42; and self-regulation, 247; undermining authority of, 270–71

Techne: in Aristotle, 139–45, 164–71, 216, 323nn.17, 18; as building, 210; as challenging-out, 145–51; and *eidos,* 140–41, 334n.15; and gathering in, 127, 138; and human being, 28, 195, 256; as knowledge, 138, 159, 215–16, 229; as a mode of phusis, 139, 313n.20; as *poiesis,* 138, 149, 219, 226. *See also* Building; Dwelling; Techne and phusis; Technology

Techne and phusis, 129, 189; collapsing of distinction between, 149–51, 163–71; and culture/nature dichotomy, 108–9, 153–71, 195–96; difference between, 9, 139–45; as ways of bringing forth, 127, 137–39, 194, 196. *See also* Phusis; Swaying; Techne; Technology

Technology, 32; danger of, 148–49, 210; essence of, as *Gestell,* 94–96, 145–51, 224–25; and nature, 60, 187, 193, 194; need for small-scale, 265; and shrinking world, 263. *See also* Energy; Nature, control of; Physics; Waterwheel

Telos: domination of process and, 212; and final cause, 141; and immortals, 335n.26; lack of, in hydroelectric system, 245; meaning of, 141, 246, 335n.25; of techne and phusis, 328n.5

Themis (goddess), 276–78

Theory: Aristotle on, 294; etymology of, 217; feminist, 15–16; in Husserl, 294–95; and practice, 216–17, 288–89, 294; western, 270. *See also* Thinking

Thesmos (custom, justice, law): compared with *nomos,* 277–78; and linkage to Demeter, 275–76; meaning of, 273, 278; replacement by *nomos,* 273–77. *See also* Law, *Nomos,* Themis

Thinking: on absencing of the feminine, 96–103; and feeling, 114–19, 203–7, 283–85, 288–89; freewheeling, 9, 197, 206; Husserl on, 205; maternal, 17, 284, 340n.45; meditative, 28–29, 83, 204, 340n.43; metaphysical (representational), 27–29, 32, 33, 83, 204, 252, 284, 300; musing, 118–19, 123, 305n.5; and paternity, 207; softening of, 204, 206; tangible, 2, 7–8; through art, 2, 7–8

Thinking Muse, The (Allen and Young), 305n.5, 306n.8

Third World, 192–93, 263–65, 327n.1. *See also* Difference, opening spaces for; Indigenous people; Monoculturalism; Multiculturalism; West, the

Thus Spoke Zarathustra (Nietzsche), 82, 85, 86, 87, 94, 117, 180, 225

Time, and temporality of western Being, 297–98

Tools: and Cycladic sculptures, 256; first, 338n.30; Heidegger on, 238–39; master's, 188; metaphors of, 129–30, 188–90; storage reservoir as, 240; and weapons, 182, 183

Touch: carving as, 63–64, 108, 256; of face with world, 70–71; and mortality, 111–15; openness to, 62–63; pulled out of despair through, 72–73

Truth, 24; as Being, 82–83; as correspondence, 29; distinguished from appearance, 83; identified with the feminine, 99–101; as transcendent, 33. *See also* Heidegger, *aletheia* in

Twilight of the Idols (Nietzsche), 317n.20

Unlocking: as primary way of technological revealing, 224–25; and unconcealment of nature as energy, 225–32

Von Mirbach, Martin, 280

Wallace, Michele, 268–70
Warren, Karen, 286, 327n.2, 336n.5;
    on transformative feminism, 191
Water: being of, 10, 224–47; change
    of, to fire, 243; as life-giving, 174,
    201–2; as potential energy, 239; in
    rivers and streams, 227–29, 241–42;
    scientific definition of, as fluid, 230;
    in storage reservoir, 238–41; and
    sweating, 203; in turbine, 229–32.
    See also Crying
Waterwheel: being of water and,
    227–29; compared with turbine, 227,
    229, 232; singing of, 229
Weaving, 294; and Clotho, Lachesis,
    and Atropos, 335n.24; metaphor of,
    129, 189–90, 195, 198; of Moira,
    246
West, the: concept of nature in, 226;
    cracking identity of, 4, 220, 269;
    and exploitation of Third World,
    262, 263–71
Whitbeck, Caroline, 154, 213, 305n.3,
    306n.1
Whitford, Margaret, 8, 12
Wild, the: contact with, 184, 198–200;
    decline of, 190, 194; home as, 130;
    porcupine as, 198–99; snakes as,
    179, 183; western search for, 268;
    wilderness preserves of, 268
Willing: limitless, 246–47; in *The
    Seal*, 69–74; in the Snake Goddess,
    185–87. *See also,* Nietzsche,
    Friedrich, on the will; Will to
    Power, the
Will to Power, the: artistic desire
    (creativity) as, for Nietzsche, 27,
    75, 86–88, 91–92, 94, 100, 196,
    317n.20; dynamic of market econ-
    omy as, 147, 264, 317n.19; energy
    as power of, 225, 333–34n.14;
    movement of, 71–73, 75, 81–82,

91–92, 143–51, 186, 224–47;
    releasement from, 97–99, 199, 213,
    270, 297; sexual desire as, 90–92;
    and use of dissident forces, 266;
    western Being as, 94–96, 145–51,
    264; women as stimulus for, 91–92,
    318n.1. *See also* Resistant; West, the
Will to Power, The (Nietzsche), 82,
    316n.11
Wilson, Alexander, 336n.11
Winged Victories, 326nn.9, 10
Wittig, Monique, 7, 22, 41
Woman: association of, with darkness
    and pollution, 132–33; association
    of, with nature, 46, 102, 130–36,
    153–71, 211, 213; concept of, 21;
    cultural construction of, 22; depicted
    in temple of Zeus at Olympia,
    181–83; as multiple sexuality, 101,
    309n.22, 312–13n.18; as ''natural
    abnormality'' in Aristotle, 159–60;
    presencing of, 29–31; as stable sub-
    ject, 24–25; and techne and phusis,
    139; and truth, 99–101; as unrepre-
    sentable, 75–76, 88, 96, 101, 102,
    309n.22. *See also* Female experi-
    ence; Feminine, the; Gender; Home
Wonder: of being, 3, 60; in face of dif-
    ference, 270, 288–89, 296–97; and
    scientific analysis, 285; turning of,
    to fear, 270
World-earth-home, 49, 51, 54–55;
    definition of, 30, 51, 56

Young, Iris Marion, 5, 192–93; on
    body, 314n.23; on pregnancy, 214,
    219, 315nn.29, 30

Zeus, 277, 337n.19; temple of, at
    Olympia, 181–83, 326n.7
Zimmerman, Michael E., 278,
    321–22n.32, 327n.2; on logos
    and phusis, 341n.55; on wonder,
    340n.46